H. L. D Potter

Manual of Reading, in Four Parts

Orthophony, Class Methods, Gesture and Elocution - designed for teachers and students

H. L. D Potter

Manual of Reading, in Four Parts
Orthophony, Class Methods, Gesture and Elocution - designed for teachers and students

ISBN/EAN: 9783337178765

Printed in Europe, USA, Canada, Australia, Japan

Cover: Foto ©Paul-Georg Meister /pixelio.de

More available books at **www.hansebooks.com**

MANUAL OF READING,

IN FOUR PARTS:

ORTHOPHONY, CLASS METHODS, GESTURE, AND ELOCUTION.

DESIGNED FOR TEACHERS AND STUDENTS.

By H. L. D. POTTER.

NEW YORK:
HARPER & BROTHERS, PUBLISHERS,
FRANKLIN SQUARE.
1877.

EDUCATION DEPT.

Entered according to Act of Congress, in the year 1871, by
HARPER & BROTHERS,
In the Office of the Librarian of Congress, at Washington.

PREFACE.

This work is prepared with three objects in view: *completeness*, that nothing be wanting to assist the teacher or student of reading; *correctness*, that nothing erroneous be learned; and *brevity*, that its price be within the means of every person desiring it.

To teach reading properly, we must possess the knowledge or avail ourselves of the assistance of the following works, viz.: a work on *Calisthenics*, or chest development; *Orthophony*, or voice-training; *Elocution*, as a science; *Gesture*, or action; and *Rhetoric*, in order to review the selections which are read in class from time to time.

This Manual is intended to combine all the essential qualities of these books.

Part First contains Orthophony, or Voice-training, including Calisthenics; Part Second, the most popular and practical Class Methods, both primary and advanced; Part Third, Gesture; and Part Fourth, Elocution, including a chapter on Rhetoric.

The following works have been consulted during its preparation: Dr. Rush on the Voice, "Bell's Anatomy of Expression," Webster's and Worcester's Dictionaries, Vandenhoff's "Art of Elocution," and Murdoch's and Russell's "Vocal Culture."

Thanking William A. Wheeler, of Boston, and Miss Emily A. Rice, formerly of the Normal and Training School in Oswego, N. Y., now principal of a ladies' school in Darien, Conn., for valuable suggestions, this little work is respectfully submitted to the public.

HOW TO USE THIS MANUAL WITHOUT A TEACHER.

THE following series of graded lessons may serve as a guide to another plan more or less difficult, as may be required. If the lessons are too long as you proceed, alternate some of the exercises day by day, or omit a few of the easier ones. Thirty minutes' continuous vocal exercise should be succeeded by at least thirty minutes' rest.

First Week. Daily Exercises.

1. Rub the chest with the hand or brush every morning.
2. Percussion (page 25).
3. Sustain one note of the scale (page 20).
4. Count as many as possible (page 21).
5. Repeat a line or couplet (page 21).
6. Learn the definitions (one or two each day) on page 115.
7. Memorize one stanza each day of some favorite poem (see page 86).

Second Week. Daily Exercises.

1. Chafe the chest, and percuss, as in the first week (page 25).
2. Take the single thrust exercise (page 25).
3. Sustain the three first notes of the scale (page 58).
4. Read the examples for monotone upon each of the three notes (page 59).
5. Count (page 21), and repeat a line or couplet (page 21).
6. Practice Fig. 1 of Table 11 (page 13), and dissyllables (page 16).
7. Learn facts on page 117, and practice five of the examples on page 55.
8. Memorize one or more stanzas each day (page 86).

Third Week. Daily Exercises.

1. Chafe, percuss, and add the *double* to the former thrust exercise (page 26).
2. Sustain *five* notes of the scale, and read upon each key in monotone (p. 59).
3. Count and repeat a couplet, aloud and in a whisper (page 21).
4. Practice Fig. 1 and Fig. 2 (page 13), and dissyllables, and trisyllables (p. 16).
5. Learn facts on page 118, in connection with the table (page 116).
6. Memorize as usual, and practice ten examples (page 55).

Fourth Week. Daily Exercises.

1. Chafe, percuss, and take 2, 3, 4 chest exercises (pages 25 and 26).
2. Sustain five notes of the scale, and read upon each of them.
3. Count, and repeat stanzas aloud, and in an intense whisper.
4. Practice Figs. 1, 2, 3, Table 11 (p. 13), Figs. 1, 2, Table 10 (p. 12), and page 16.
5. Practice 15 examples (page 55), and drifting exercises (page 59).
6. Memorize prose or poetry.

Note.—Continue in this way until you have mastered every table and every exercise, also the entire scientific portion of the Manual.

CONTENTS.

TABLES.

	Page
No. 1. Orthophony, or Voice-culture	1
No. 2. Vowel Elements of the English Language	2
No. 3. Consonant Elements of the English Language	4
No. 4. {Vowel Combinations, Diphthongs, etc.	6
{Dissyllabic Vowel Combinations	6
No. 5. Vowel Digraphs	7
No. 6. Units of Speech	8
No. 7. Classification of the Subtonics and Atonics	9
No. 8. Consonant Combinations	10
No. 9. Consonant Combinations continued	11
No. 10. Vocal Gymnastics—Force and Pitch	12
No. 11. Vocal Gymnastics—Stress	13
No. 12. Vocal Gymnastics—Pitch, or Inflection	14
No. 13. Vocal Gymnastics—Pitch and Force combined	15
No. 14. Accent	16
No. 15. Words for Practice by contrast	35
No. 16. List in Substitution of Vowel Sounds	37
No. 17. List in Omission of Consonant Sounds	39
No. 18. List in Addition of Sounds	40
No. 19. Words to practice—Contrasts No. 1 and No. 2	41
No. 20. Words to practice—Contrasts No. 3 and No. 4	42
No. 21. Words to practice—Contrasts No. 5, No. 6, and No. 7	43
No. 22. Pronunciation—Rules and Examples	44
No. 23. Terminations—el and en	45
No. 24. Reading-class Formula	73
No. 25. Composition	88
No. 26. Gesture	100
No. 27. Vocal Gymnastics—Orthoëpy, Pitch, Force, and Time	114
No. 28. Orthoëpy	116
No. 29. Elements of Language	130
No. 30. Pitch	138
No. 31. Force	154
No. 32. Time	164
Examples for Declamatory Gesture	112, 113

PART I.—ORTHOPHONY.

HYGIENIC SUGGESTIONS: Page
  Food... 17
  Clothing... 18
  Exercise... 18
  Sleep... 19

GENERAL EXERCISES:
  I. Respiration.
    1. Inspiring... 19
    2. Expiring... 20
    3. Sighing... 20
    4. Gasping... 20
    5. Panting... 20
    6. Sobbing... 20
  II. Intonation.
    1. Sustaining... 20
    2. Counting... 21
    3. Repeating... 21
    4. Repeating in a Whisper... 21
    5. Laughing... 21
    6. Intoning with Changes of Force... 21
    7. Intoning with Changes of Force and Pitch... 21

CALISTHENICS:
  I. Positions for Hygienic Exercise... 23
    1. Chest Series... 25
    2. Shoulder Series... 26
    3. Elbow Series... 28
    4. Arm Series... 29
    5. Hand Series... 30
    6. Head and Neck Series... 31
    7. Trunk Series... 31
  II. Direction of Movement... 32
  III. Order of Movement... 32
  IV. Manner of Movement... 33
  V. Time of Movement... 33

ARTICULATION:
  Defects, Causes, and Remedies:
    1. Weak Utterance... 34
    2. Thick Utterance... 34
    3. Lisping... 34
    4. Stammering... 36

ENUNCIATION:
  1. Substitution of Sounds in Syllables... 37
  2. Omission of Sounds in Syllables... 39
  3. Addition of Sounds in Syllables... 40

PRONUNCIATION: Page
    Tables for Practice... 44
    Rules for Pronunciation....................................46, 47
    Reading Exercises... 55

PART II.—CLASS METHODS.

PRIMARY CLASS METHODS.. 65
    Analytical or Objective Methods............................. 66
    Synthetical Methods... 68
    Phonic Method... 70
ADVANCED CLASS METHODS... 73
    I. Reading-class Formula..................................... 73
    II. Explanation of the Formula.............................. 74
        1. Pronouncing Words.................................... 74
        2. Analyzing Words...................................... 74
        3. Phonic Spelling...................................... 75
        4. Elocution—Facts and Drill............................ 76
        5. Calisthenics, or Gesture............................. 76
        6. Selections... 78
        7. Reviews.. 80
        8. Memorizing Literature................................ 86
        9. Examination of the Advance Lesson.................... 87
    III. Standard Methods.. 78
    IV. Occasional Methods....................................... 81
LITERARY COMPOSITION—a Chapter of Rhetoric...................... 89

PART III.—GESTURE.

Feet.. 101
Head.. 102
Arms.. 102
Hands... 102
How to explain Direction... 104
How to teach Declamatory Gesture................................. 105
Facial Expression.. 108
Twenty-six general Rules and Suggestions........................ 109
Examples for Practice of Declamatory Gesture.................... 112

PART IV.—ELOCUTION.

	Page
ELOCUTION—Vocal Gymnastics	115
ORTHOËPY	117

   I. Articulation of Sounds.
      1. Organs of the Chest... 118
          Muscles, Diaphragm, Thorax, Pleura, etc.
      2. Organs of the Throat... 119
          Larynx, Cartilages, Vocal Chords, etc.
      3. Organs of the Mouth... 122
          Eustachian Tubes, Nasal Passages, etc.
   II. Voice... 125
      Compass, Volume, Rate.. 125
      Qualities—Aspirate, Pure, Orotund, etc.................. 126
   III. Elements of Language... 131
      Table of Vowel Sounds.. 134
      Labials... 135
      Linguals... 136
      Palatals.. 137

PITCH:
   Scale, Key.. 139
   Melody... 141
   Inflection... 142
   Degrees or Intervals of Inflection............................ 144
   Rules for Inflection... 146
   Series.. 148
   Sentential Inflections or Cadences.......................... 151
   Transition or Modulation...................................... 152

DYNAMICS OR FORCE:
   Degrees.. 155
   Stress—Radical, Final, Median, etc......................... 158
   Accent—Primary, Secondary.................................. 162
   Emphasis... 162

TIME:
   Quantity... 165
   Rests or Pauses... 166
   Sentential and Emotional Pauses............................ 166
   Rhythmical Pauses.. 168
   Grammatical Pauses, or Punctuation....................... 169

SELECTIONS FOR THE LITTLE FOLKS.

	Page
Johnny's First Snow-storm	174
The Snow Man	175
Jingle, jingle!	175
Learning to fly	176
Mind your Steps	176
Hang up the Baby's Stocking	177
Fretting Jennie	178
Old Hero	179
The First Snow	180
The Mother-bird	180
What the Flowers wished	181
Who killed Tom Roper?	182
Playing School	183
Little Boy's Pocket	185
Aunt Mary's Bullfinch	186
Little Mary's Bouquet	187
Choice of Trades	189
Mysteries	192
Water	192
Tommy's Week	193
Heedlessness	214

SELECTIONS FOR THE YOUNG FOLKS.

Columbia's Union Party		215
The Tea-kettle's Party		221
The White Giant		223
In School-days	*J. G. Whittier*	228
New Gowns		229
Lecture on Heat	*Louise E. Chollet*	234
Birds and their Ways		240
Handy Andy	*Samuel Lover*	243
School		249
Second Lecture on Heat	*Louise E. Chollet*	250
Life	*B. F. Taylor*	254
The Guard on the Rhine		256
A Singing Lesson	*Jean Ingelow*	257
The Soldier's Reprieve		258
The Smack in School	*J. W. Palmer*	263
The Bridal Wine-cup		264
The Christmas Tree		267
Barbara Frietchie	*J. G. Whittier*	268
Death of Little Nell	*Charles Dickens*	269

1*

	Page
Katie Lee and Willie Gray	271
Sheridan's Ride.................T. B. Read	273
The Bottle Imp..................Julia M. Thayer	275
Rules for Life	282
German Quotations and Proverbs	282

MISCELLANEOUS SELECTIONS.
POETRY.

Full of Snow	Rev. Joseph Cook	283
Labor	Mrs. Frances S. Osgood	284
Gethsemane	Mrs. E. Clementine Howarth	285
A Ballad of Sir John Franklin	George H. Boker	286
The King of Denmark's Ride	Mrs. Caroline Norton	289
Over the River	Miss Priest	290
Young Lochinvar	Sir Walter Scott	292
The Inquiry	Charles Mackay	293
Wounded	J. W. Watson	294
We Meet and we Part		296
Baby Bunn	Josie H.	296
Drifting	T. B. Read	298
To a Mouse	Robert Burns	300
The Miser's Death	Osborne	301
Little Bennie		303
Ivry	T. B. Macaulay	305
Auction extraordinary	Lucretia Davidson	306
The Gain of Loss	Horatius Bonar	307
The Fireman	R. T. Conrad	309
The Picket-guard		310
Jesus' Seat	Miss F. Eastwood	311
Abou Ben Adhem	Leigh Hunt	313
Dora	Alfred Tennyson	313
The Bugle Song	Alfred Tennyson	317
Little Gretchen	From the German	317
There's but one Pair of Stockings to mend to-night		319
The Starless Crown	American Tract Society	321
Only waiting		322
I'm mustered out		323
Where does the Water Spring?		324
High Tide on the Coast of Lincolnshire	Jean Ingelow	325
The everlasting Memorial	Horatius Bonar	329
The World would be the better for it	M. H. Cobb	330
Thank God there's still a Vanguard	Mrs. H. E. G. Arey	331
Creeds of the Bells	G. W. Bungay	332
Building of the Ship	H. W. Longfellow	333
Evening at the Farm	J. T. Trowbridge	335

CONTENTS. xi

		Page
The News of a Day	*Mrs. S. T. Bolton*	336
Borroboola Ghä		338
The Christian Mariner	*Mrs. Southey*	340
No Sect in Heaven	*Mrs. Cleveland*	341
John Burns of Gettysburg	*Bret Harte*	343
Annie and Willie's Prayer	*Mrs. S. P. Snow*	346
The Soul-dirge	*A. Cleveland Coxe*	349
The Triad	*A. B. Street*	350
The Bobolink	*G. H. Barnes*	352
The Ride from Ghent to Aix	*Robert Browning*	354
The Passions	*William Collins*	355
The Child and the Sunshine		358

PROSE.

Toleration	*Jeremy Taylor*	359
From the Dodge Club in Italy	*James De Mille*	359
Sam Weller's Valentine	*Charles Dickens*	361
Putting up Stoves		371
The Power of Habit	*J. B. Gough*	373
Chrysostom's Eloquence		374
The Twenty-fourth Psalm		375
Dante and Milton	*Macaulay*	375
Gabriel Grub	*Charles Dickens*	376
Patrick O'Rourke and the Frogs	*G. W. Bungay*	386
A Camp-meeting in Texas		388
An Irish Letter		391
Scene from "Richard III."	*Shakspeare*	392
Scene from "The Siege of Valencia"	*Mrs. Hemans*	393
Scene from "The Merchant of Venice"	*Shakspeare*	397
Scene from "The Rivals"	*Richard Brinsley Sheridan*	401
Quarrel Scene between Brutus and Cassius	*Shakspeare*	404
From "School for Scandal"	*Richard Brinsley Sheridan*	407
Courtship under Difficulties		413

TABLE NO. I. ORTHOPHONY, OR VOICE-CULTURE.

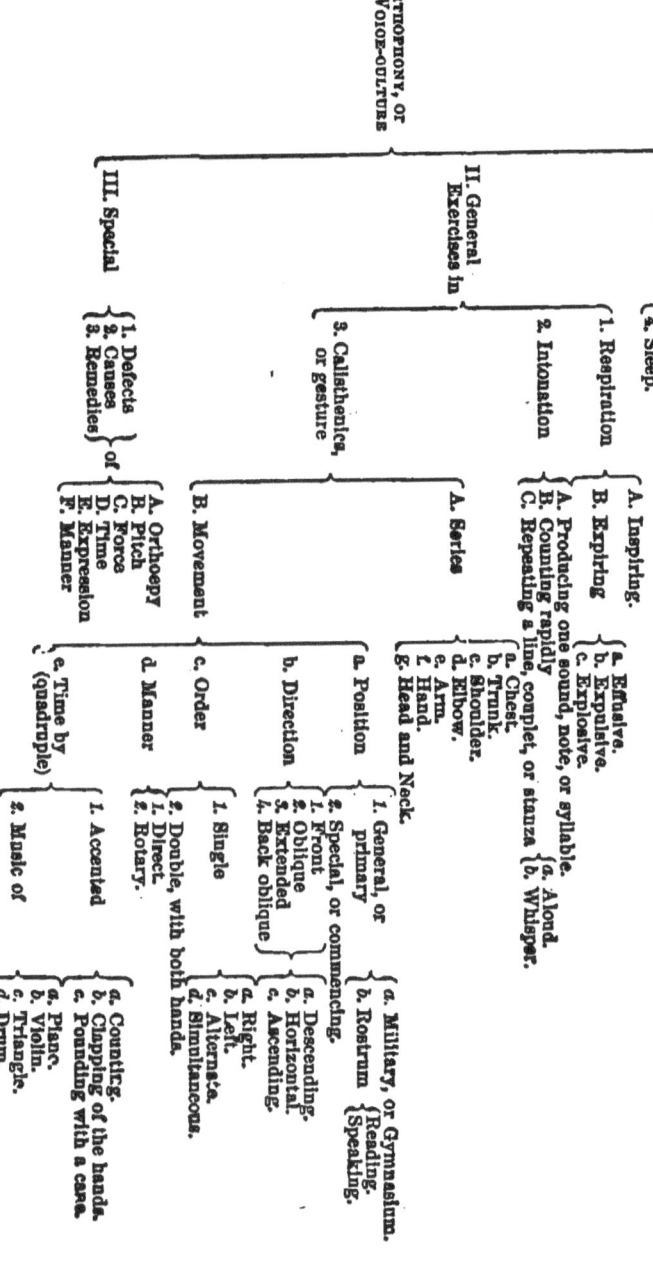

A

TABLE NO. 2. VOWEL ELEMENTS OF THE ENGLISH LANGUAGE.

Names	Type Signs			Sounds Represented					Formation and Common Names		Equivalents
	Ro-man.	Italic.	German Text.	No.	Dictionary Notation			Examples	Oral-la-ryngeals Modified		Diphthongs, Triphthongs, etc.
					Webster			Worcester			
					Pure	Diphth. and Com-mon.	Compo-nents, or Ori-gin.				
A	A, a	*A, a*	𝔄, 𝔞	1.	ā		...	as in āle	lingual	long	14. Laigh, gauging, gauge, bael-fire, their, they, tete, reign, weigh, fade, pain, campaign, goal, pray.
				2.	ă		...	" ăt	.....	short	2. Isaac, plaid.
				3.	ä		...	" ärm	lingual	Italian	5. baa, ah, heart, guard, Haerlem.
				4.	ạ		...	" ạll	labial	broad	8. land, awl, awe, aught, George, form, broad, bought.
E	E, e	*E, e*	𝔈, 𝔢	5.	ē	â† ă ǎ	(ē)	cāre, anyt fāst, whạt, ēve	lingual	long	12. bee, eat, ægis, impregn, conceit, key, grief, people, receipt, quay, marine, mosquito.
				6.	ĕ		...	" ĕnd	lingual	short	7. any, said, says, heifer, guess, leopard, friend.
				(7.)		ĕ ê ẽ ọ ī	(ŭ) (â) (ī) (ā) (ūē)	" hẽr, whêre, prĕtty, prọy. Īce	.....	obtuse	
I	I, i	*I, i*	𝔍, 𝔦	8.	ī		...	" ĭt	lingual	long	13. aisle, eider, height, eying, eye, indict, pie, fine, high, island, buy, by, rye.
						ī ī ī	(ē) (ŭ) (y)	" marĭne, sĭr, ūnion	lingual	short	11. duties, carriage, guinea, been, busy, hymn, women, Burleigh, forfeit, barley, build.
									.....	French.	
									.....	obtuse.	(Equals the consonant y.)

ORTHOPHONY.

				as in		labial	long	
O	O, o	9.	ō	:	as in ōld	:	long	14. sew, yeomen, beau, hautboy, four, though, snow, owe, oar, ore, oh, floor, dépôt, foe.
		10.	ŏ	:	" rŏmp, ŏn	....	short	
	O, o	11.	ọ	ọ	" dọ	labial	{ long close	3. what, knowledge, honor.
							broad.	7. { shoe, food, soup, sous, through, billet-doux.
				(a)	" fôrm†			
				(a)	" sŏn.			
				(ĭ)	" women.			
				(wŭ)	" one.‡			
				(u)	" wolf.			
				(ēoo)	" lūte	lingual	long	1. view.
				:	" ŭp.		short	12. transfer, fir, son, does, love, flood, tough, subtle, liquor, cupboard, myrtle, earth.
U	U, u		ŭ	:	" full.	labial	obtuse	4. wolf, foot, could, now.
	U, u	(12) 13.	ū	(o)	" rūle.		{ long close	
		14.	u	(ĕ)	" bury.			
				(ĭ)	" business.			
				(yū)	" use.‡			
				(ĭ)	" ȧnge.†			
Y	Y, y			(ĭ)	" bȳ		long	
				(ĭ)	" sylph		short	
	Y, y			(ŭ)	" myrrh		....	(See subtonic y.)
				ȯu	" now		....	
				oi	" ôil		....	(See subtonic w.) 5. now, doubt, bough, hour, compt. 1. boy.
Double-you	W, w			(ọ)	" tōōl, fōōd		long.	
	W, w			(ụ)	" good, foot		short.	
				(ō)	" flōod.		....	
				(ô)	" dōor		long.	

*The column headed *pure* includes all the vowel units of sound in the English language, all others being duplicates or combinations (more or less close) of these. The columns of duplicates are called *common*, because these sounds are common to several signs or letters; the corresponding *sound-units* in the column called *components* show whence these sounds are derived. The diphthongs are i, u, oi, ou.
† Modified by r, according to Webster.   ‡ Consonant-vowel diphthong.

MANUAL OF READING.

TABLE NO. 2.* CONSONANT ELEMENTS OF THE ENGLISH LANGUAGE.

Names.	Type Signs.				Sounds Represented.					By Formation.	Common Name.	Equivalents.
	Sufforics.					Dictionary Notation.			Worcester.			
	Romaic.	Italic.	German Text.	No.	Webster.							
					Pure Sounds.	Diphth. and Common.	Compounds.		Examples.			
Be	B, b	*B, b*	𝔅, 𝔟	1.	b	...	...	as in bulb		labial	...	1. ebb.
Ce	C, c	*C, c*	ℭ, 𝔠	2.	c	...	...	" ocean		palatal	...	5. etch or chaise, sure, Schiller, assertion, assure.
				3.	...	c	(s)	" cent		...	soft.	
					...	¢	(k)	" cat		...	hard.	
					...	c	(z)	" suffice.				
De	D, d	*D, d*	𝔇, 𝔡	3.	d	...	...	" did		lingual	...	3. bdellium, add, signed.
Ef	F, f	*F, f*	𝔉, 𝔣	4.	...	d	(t)	" mixed.		labial	...	
					f	...	...	" fife				
					...	f	(v)	" of.				
Ge	G, g	*G, g*	𝔊, 𝔤	5.	g̃	...	...	" gig		palatal	hard	6. off, cough, calf, phonic, Sappho.
				6.	...	g	(j)	" gem		palatal	soft.	3. Hogg, ghost, rogue.
Aitch	H, h	*H, h*	𝔥, 𝔥	:	h	...	...	" home		...	soft	1. who.
Jay	J, j	*J, j*	𝔍, 𝔧	7.	...	...	(dzh)	" joy				5. ledger, ledge, adjective, gem, age.
					...	j	(y)	" hallelujah.				
Kay	K, k	*K, k*	𝔎, 𝔨	8.	k	...	...	" kick		palatal	hard	6. can, chord, lack, lough, pique, queen.
El	L, l	*L, l*	𝔏, 𝔩		l	...	...	" lull		lingual	hard	5. ill, kiln, bagatelle, whistle, belles-lettres.
Em	M, m	*M, m*	𝔐, 𝔪	9.	m	...	...	" man		labial	...	3. dumb, crammed, condemn.
En	N, n	*N, n*	𝔑, 𝔫	10.	n	...	...	" noon		lingual	...	6. gnaw, know, mnemonic, compt, sinned, pneumatics.
				11.	ng, n	...	...	" sing, ink				1. tongue.
Pe	P, p	*P, p*	𝔓, 𝔭	12.	p	...	...	" pipe		labial	...	2. hiccough, stopped.
Qu	Q, q	*Q, q*	𝔔, 𝔮	:	...	q(u)	(kw)	" queen.		palatal	...	
					...	q(u)	(k)	" coquette.		labial		

ORTHOPHONY.

Ar	R, r	R, r	R, r	13.	r		as in war	lingual	soft	4. myrrh, mortgage, burr, corps.
Ees	S, s	S, s	S, s, ß	14.	s	(sh) (zsh) (z)	" sense " mission. " measure. " Sion, his. " tent	lingual	soft.	7. Ctesiphon, hoped, phthisic, Thomas, Pitt, gazette, ptyalism.
Te	T, t	T, t	T, t	15.	t	(sh)	" patient.	lingual		
				16. 17.	th th		" this, with " thin, pith	lingual lingual	soft sharp	1. wreathe. 4. eighth, withe, Matthew, apophthegm. 3. of, Stephen, have.
Ve	V, v	V, v	V, v	18.	v		" valve	labial		
Double-you	W, w	W, w*	W, w	19.	w	(z) (gz) (ks) (ksh)	" wing " Xerxes " exalt. " box. " anxious.	labial	hard soft.	2. one, quire.
Eks	X, x	X, x	X, x					palatal lingual palatal	hard	3. union, use, hallelujah. 3. suffice, his, Xerxes. 4. ledge, jet-d'eau, vision, scission.
Wy	Y, y	Y, y	Y, y	20.	y	(hw) (tsh) (k) (sh) (f)	" yet " zinc " azure " when. " church " character " chaise " phantom.			
Ze	Z, z	Z, z	Z, z	21. 22.	z z				hard soft	1. etch.
					wh ch th ch ph					

* This table is designed to show every sound ever given to the consonants of our language. Practice across this table, thus, "Be (giving the name), b (making the sound of b), as in bulb, is a labial, because modified principally by the lips, and has one equivalent, bb, as in ebb." Practice down the columns, giving the name, and then producing the sound of each letter representing a pure sound.

TABLE NO. 4. VOWEL COMBINATIONS.* DIPHTHONGS,† ETC.

No.	Signs.	Radical.	Vanish.	Examples.	No.	Signs.	Radical.	Vanish.	Examples.
		(*Acc.*)					(*Acc.*)		
1.	ā (ay)	ā———ĭ	as in	ale, pay.	9.	ṳă	ṳ———ă	as in	suav′ity.
2.	ī	ä———ĕ	"	ice.	10.	ṳä	ṳ———ä	"	gua′no.
3.	ō	ō———ǫ	"	old.	11.	ṳĕ	ṳ———ĕ	"	ques′tion.
4.	ǫ	ǫ———ū	"	do.	12.	ṳī	ṳ———ē	"	suite.
5.	ū	ū———ǫ	"	lute.	13.	ṳĭ	ṳ———ĭ	"	lan′guid.
6.	ŏĭ(oy)	ŏ———ĭ	"	oil, toy.	14.	ṳō	ṳ———ō	"	quote.
7.	ŏṳ	ŏ———ṳ	"	our.	15.	äÿ	ä———ĭ	"	ay!
		(*Acc.*)					(*Acc.*)		
8.	ṳă	ṳ———ă	"	assuage′.	16.	ṳǫÿ	ǫ—ă—ĭ	"	buoy.‡

DISSYLLABIC VOWEL COMBINATIONS.

No.	Signs.	Radical.	Vanish.	Examples.	No.	Signs.	Radical.	Vanish.	Examples.
		(*Acc.*)					(*Acc.*)		
1.	ăă	ā———ă	as in	Bā′al.	1.	ăą	ă———ą	as in	äŏr′ta.
2.	āŏ	ā———ŏ	"	ā′orist.	2.	ăŏ	ă———ŏ	"	Aŏ′nian.
3.	āyeÿ	ā———ĭ	"	clāy′eÿ.	3.	ĕă	ĕ———ă	"	Borĕă′lia.
4.	āǫu	ā———ǫ	"	dā′ǫurĕte.	4.	ĕă	ĕ———ă	"	reăl′ity.
5.	āŏ	ā———ū	"	ā′ĕronaut.	5.	ĕă	ĕ———ă	"	fĭă′cre.
6.	āÿe	ā———ĭ	"	āÿe.	6.	ĕŏ	ĕ———ŏ	"	ĕŏ′lian.
7.	ąwī	ą———ī	"	sąw′ing.	7.	ĕŏ	ĕ———ŏ	"	ĕŏl′ic.
8.	ĕă	ĕ———ă	"	rĕ′al.	8.	ĭō	ĭ———ō	"	Iō′na.
9.	ĕă	ĕ———ă	"	idĕ′ă.	9.	ĭă	ĭ———ă	"	explĭă′tion.
10.	ĕĭ	ĕ———ĭ	"	dĕ′ity.	10.	ĭă	ĭ———ă	"	gallĭăm′bic.
11.	ĕō	ĕ———ō	"	Lĕ′ŏn.	11.	ĭă	ĭ———ă	"	patrĭärch′al.
12.	ĕū	ĕ———ū	"	dĕ′um.	12.	ĭō	ĭ———ō	"	furĭō′so.
13.	īă	ī———ă	"	fī′at.	13.	ŏă	ŏ———ă	"	Jŏăn′na.
14.	īă	ī———ă	"	Messī-äh.	14.	ŏă	ŏ———ă	"	Geu′ŏă.
15.	īō	ī———ō	"	pī′ety.	15.	ŏŏ	ŏ———ŏ	"	Genŏĕse′.
16.	ÿī	ī———ī	"	fīÿ′ing.	16.	ǫuī	ǫ———ē	"	Lǫuīse.
17.	eÿō	ī———ō	"	eÿ′ŏt.	17.	ūă	ū———ă	"	fluctūā′tion.
18.	īǫ	ī———ǫ	"	I′ǫwa.	18.	ūŏ	ū———ŏ	"	Fīdĕl′en.
19.	īō	ī———ō	"	Orī′ŏn.	19.	ūī	ū———ī	"	frūī′tion.
20.	ōă	ō———ă	"	Nō′äh.	20.	ǫīă	ǫī———ă	"	guaĭā′cum.
21.	ōĕ	ō———ĕ	"	pō′ĕt.	21.	ūŏ	ū———ŏ	"	impetūŏs′ity.
22.	ōī	ō———ī	"	stō′ic.	22.	ūū	ū———ū	"	dūum′vir.
23.	ewĕ	ō———ū	"	sew′ĕr.			(*Acc.*)		
24.	ṳă	ǫ———ă	"	trṳ′ant.	23.	ĕă	ĕ———ă	"	crĕ′ăsōte.
25.	ǫuī	ǫ———ī	"	Lǫuīs.	24.	ĕō	ĕ———ō	"	crĕ′ōle.
26.	ewĕ	ǫ———ū	"	sew′er.	25.	īō	ī———ō	"	Ohī′ō.
27.	ūă	ū———ă	"	dū′al.	26.	ŏă	ŏ———ă	"	ō′ăses.
28.	ūĕ	ū———ĕ	"	dū′ĕl.	27.	ūă	ū———ă	"	fiū′ăte.
29.	ewÿ	ū———ī	"	dew′ÿ.	28.	ūŏ	ū———ŏ	"	dū′ō.
30.	ewŭ	ū———ŭ	"	sew′ĕr.	29.	ĭă	ĭ———ă	"	că′ic (kă′ĕk).
					30.	ǫă	ǫ———ă	"	rǫu′et.

* A union or coalition of vowel or tonic sounds, uttered in one syllable, or by a single impulse of voice.

† A union of two sounds in one syllable, closely blended, seven of which are accented on the radical.

‡ A triphthong is a union of three vowel sounds in one syllable. Uoy is a triphthong accented on the middle sound.

ORTHOPHONY. 7

TABLE NO. 5. VOWEL DIGRAPHS.*

No.	Sign	Equivalents and Examples.
1.	aa	ā, ä, as in I'sāac, bäa.
2.	ae	ā, ä, ē, ĕ, as in Bāel'-fire, Häer'lem, paë'an, faër'y.
3.	ai	ā, ä, ĕ, ī, ĭ, as in pāil, plăid, said, aĭsle, cur'taĭn.
4.	ao	ā, ạ, as in gāol, extraôr'dinary.
5.	au	ā, ä, ạ, ŏ, as in gāuge, äunt, hạul, haut'-boy (hŏ-boy).
6.	aw	ạ, as in bạwl.
7.	awe	ạ, as in ạwe.
8.	ay	ā, ĕ, ĭ, as in pāy, says, Friday̆.
9.	ea	ē, ä, ē, ĕ, ī, ŭ, as in breāk, heärt, rēap, hĕad, guĭn'ea, earth.
10.	eau	ō, ū, as in beau, beaū'ty.
11.	ee	ē, ĕ, ĭ, as in sēen, ĕ'er, been.
12.	ei	ā, ē, ĕ, ī, ĭ, as in eight, cēil, hĕlfer, heĭght, for'feĭt.
13.	eo	ạ, ē, ĕ, ō, ū, ŭ, as in George, pēo'ple, lĕop'ard, yeō'man, feod, surgeŏn.
14.	eu	ū, (y)ū, ọ, as in feūd, Eū'nice, feụ-de-joie' (zhwä).
15.	eui	ụ, as in feụill-e-märte.
16.	ew	ō, ū, ọ, as in sew, few, sewer.
17.	ewe	ū, as in ewes.
18.	ey	ā, ē, ī, ĭ, ŏ, as in bey, kĕy, valleȳ, eȳ'ing, ŏy'rȳ.†
19.	eye	ī, as in eȳe'let.
20.	ia	ĭ, as in car'riage.‡
21.	ie	ē, ĕ, ī, ĭ, as in chiĕf, friĕnd, dīe, sĭeve.
22.	io	ŭ, as in re'giŏn.
23.	ieu	ū, as in lieū.
24.	iew	ū, as in view.
25.	oa	ạ, ō, as in broạd, bōat.
26.	oe	ē, ĕ, ō, ọ, ū, as in Phoēbe, assafoĕ'tida, fōe, shọe, dóes.
27.	oeu	ọ, as in mangeu'vre.
28.	oi	ī, ū, ĭ, as in boịl, avoịrdupois, chamoĭs.
29.	oo	ō, ọ, ŭ, ū, as in flōor, mọon, flŏod, fọot.
30.	ou	ạ, ō, ŏ, ọ, ŭ, ụ, as in boūght, cōurt, hōugh, groụp, coŭp'le, coụld.
31.	ow	ō, ŏ, as in grōw, knŏwl'edge.
32.	owe	ō, as in Stōwe.
33.	ua	ā, ä, ŏ, as in guär'anty, guărd, guár'ish.
34.	uay	ā, as in quay (kē).
35.	ue	ĕ, ọ, ū, ŭ, as in guĕst, trụe, dūe, guĕrdon.
36.	ui	ē, ī, ĭ, ọ, ū, as in mosquī'to, guīde, buĭld, frụit, jūice.
37.	uo	ŭ, as in liq'uor.
38.	uy	ī, as in buȳ.
39.	ye	ī, as in rȳe.

* A digraph is a union of signs or letters, but not of sounds.
† Ey, in ey-ry, is, according to Worcester, ĕ, ā, ī, or ĕ, properly ā.
‡ See (equivalents) Table 2, Vowel Elements.

Note.—Practice all the sounds and examples successively. Example: "Double a is pronounced ā, as in Isaac; ä as in bäa; *a-e* is pronounced ā, as in Bäel-fire; ä as in Häer'lem; ē as in paē'an, and ĕ as in faĕr'y," etc.

TABLE NO. 6. UNITS OF SPEECH.*

No.	Long Tonics.				No.	Short Tonics.
1.	ē	as in	eve	oral-lingual.	7.	ĭ as in it.
2.	ā	"	ale	" "	8.	ĕ " ell.
3.	ä	"	arm	" "	9.	ă " at.
4.	ạ	"	all	oral-labial.	10.	ŏ " not.
5.	ō	"	old	" "	11.	ŭ " up.
6.	ǫ	"	do	" "	12.	u " full.

	Single Sign Diphthongs.†				Double Sign Diphthongs.
1.	ɪ (ŭē) as in ice (1)	oral-lingual.	4.	ȏɪ, ȏў, as in oil, boy (2)
2.	ū (ēǫ) " lute.		5.	ȏû " our.
3.	j (dzh) " joy.		6.	ch (tsh) " church.
			7.	wh (hw) " when.

	Subtonics.					Atonics.
1.	b	as in	bulb	labial.	1.	p as in pipe.
2.	d	"	did	lingual.	2.	t " tent.
3.	g	"	go, gig	palatal.	3.	k " kick.
4.	v	"	valve	labial.	4.	f " fife.
5.	z	"	zinc	lingual.	5.	s " sense.
6.	z, zh	"	azure	palatal.	6.	c, sh " ocean, shall.
7.	th	"	this	lingual.	7.	th " thin, kith.
8.	y	"	yet	palatal.	8.	h " home (3).
9.	w	"	wing	labial.		
10.	l	"	lull	lingual.		
11.	m	"	man	labial.		
12.	n	"	noon	lingual.		
13.	ṇ, ng	"	ink, song	palatal.		
14.	r	"	war	lingual.		

*There are twelve tonic elements or units of speech—six long and six short, fourteen subtonics, and eight atonics. All other sounds whatsoever are more or less closely united combinations of these sounds or elements.

† There are seven close diphthongs, three having single signs, and four more worthy of single signs. (See Table No. 4, Vowel Combinations.)
 (1) According to Walker and Webster, ąī Russel and Murdoch, áĭ, and Smart and Vandenhoff, ŭĕ. The latter seems decidedly the best.
 (2) According to Worcester and Webster, ǭī, and Murdoch and Russel, ȏī.
 (3) The sound of h can be classed as a lingual, labial, or palatal, since it is simply an emission of breath.

Note.—Practice this table horizontally, as follows: "ē, ĭ, ā, ĕ, etc.," by sound, and not by name; practice perpendicularly by sound, as "ē, ā, ä, ạ, ō, ǫ, etc.;" practice by pronouncing the words, naming the signs, and producing the sounds, as "ēve, ē; āle, ā," etc.

TABLE NO. 7. CLASSIFICATION OF THE SUBTONICS AND ATONICS.

BY THEIR ORGANIC FORMATION—

1. Labials: *m*-an, *b*-abe, *p*-ipe, *v*-ine, *f*-ine, *w*-ine.
2. Linguals: *n*-oon, *d*-id, *t*-ent, *th*-is, *th*-in, *s*-in, *z*-inc, *r*-ill, *l*-ull.
3. Palatals: ri-*ng*, *g*-o, *k*-ing, *sh*-all, a-*z*-ure, *h*-ome, *y*-et.

BY THEIR EMISSION AND FORCE—

I. Abrupts (1)
 { 1. (Sonant) subtonics, b, d, g.
 { 2. (Surd) atonics, p, t, k.

II. Continuants (2)
 { 1. (Sonant) subtonics { Liquids (3), r, l.
 {   { Nasals (4), m, n, ng.
 {   { Semi-vowels (5), w, y.
 { 2. (Surd) atonics   { Aspirate (6), h.
 {   { Semi-vowel (5), wh.

(1) Named "abrupts" because of their explosive emission.
(2) Named "continuants" because they can be prolonged.
(3) Called "liquids" because they readily and smoothly unite with other consonants.
(4) Called "nasals" because the sound is emitted through the nose.
(5) Called "semi-vowels" because they possess nearly perfect vocality like the vowels.
(6) Called "aspirate" because it is a breath-sound.

A 2

TABLE NO. 8. CONSONANT COMBINATIONS.

bd	rob'd.	jd	goug'd.	lsk	Tobolsk.
bdst	prob'dst.	kl	uncle.	lst	call'st.
bl	bland.	kld	trickl'd.	lsh	walsh.
bld	humbl'd.	kldst	truckl'dst.	lt	melt.
bldst	troubl'dst.	klst	chuckl'st.	lth	health.
blst	troubl'st.	klz	wrinkles.	lths	stealths.
blz	crumbles.	kn	blacken.	lts	colts.
br	brand.	knd	reck'n'd.	ltst	wilt'st.
bz	ribs.	knst	black'n'st.	lv	delve.
ch	church.	knz	reck'ns.	lvd	shelv'd.
cht	fetch'd.	ks	checks.	lvdst	delv'dst.
dj	edge.	kt	act.	lvz	elves.
djd	hedg'd.	kts	facts.	lz	halls.
dl	bridle.	ktst	conduct'st.	md	doom'd.
dld	riddl'd.	kr	crank.	mdst	roam'dst.
dlst	handl'st.	lb	bulb.	mf	triumph.
dlz	bundles.	lbd	bulb'd.	mp	hemp.
dn	hard'n.	lbs	bulbs.	mps	mumps.
dr	drove.	lch	filch.	mpst	pump'st.
dth	width.	lcht	filch'd.	mpt	tempt.
dths	breadths.	ld	hold.	mpts	attempts.
dz	odds.	ldst	fold'st.	mst	entomb'st.
fl	flame.	ldz	holds	mz	tombs.
fld	rifl'd.	lf	self.	nch	bunch.
flst	stifl'st.	lfs	gulfs.	ncht	pinch'd.
flz	rifles.	lft	engulf'd.	nd	and.
fr	from.	lfth	twelfth.	ndst	end'st.
fs	quaffs, laughs.	lfths	twelfths.	ndz	ends.
fst	quaff'st, laugh'st.	lj	bulge.	ng	sung.
ft	raft.	ljd	bilg'd.	ngd	bang'd.
fth	fifth.	lk	elk.	ngdst	long'dst.
fts	wafts.	lks	silks.	ngk	ink.
ftst	graft'st.	lkt	milk'd.	ngks	banks.
gd	begg'd.	lkts	mulcts.	ngkst	think'st.
gdst	bragg'dst.	lm	elm.	ngkt	thank'd.
gl	glide.	lmd	whelm'd.	ngth	length.
gld	struggl'd.	lmz	helms.	ngz	songs.
gldst	haggl'dst.	ln	fall'n.	nj	range.
glst	strangl'st.	lp	help.	njd	rang'd.
glz	mingles.	lpt	gulp'd.	nk	sink.
gr	grove.	lps	scalps.	nks	ranks.
gst	begg'st.	lpst	help'st.	nkst	thank'st.
gz	figs.	ls	false.	ns	dense.

* This table should be practiced until every combination can be distinctly pronounced or articulated by itself, independent of words. Ex. 1. Pronounce the word, and then the combination, as rob'd, bd; prob'dst, bdst, etc. Ex. 2. Spell the combination, and then pronounce it, as b, d, bd; b, d, s, t, bdst. Ex. 3. Analyze the words, as bulb, ulb, lb, b; troubl'dst, roubl'dst, oubl'dst, bl'dst, l'dst, 'dst, st, t, etc.

ORTHOPHONY. 11

TABLE NO. 9. CONSONANT COMBINATIONS.

nst	canst, winc'd.	rlz	hurls.	spt	clasp'd.
nt	sent.	rm	arm.	st	start.
nth	tenth.	rmd	arm'd.	str	strike.
nths	tenths.	rmdst	harm'dst.	sts	rests.
nts	rents.	rmst	armst.	sw	swing.
ntst	went'st.	rmz	charms.	th	thine.
nz	runs.	rn	urn.	thd	breath'd.
nzd	bronz'd.	rnd	turn'd.	thdst	breath'dst.
pl	plume.	rndst	earn'dst.	thm	rhythm.
pld	rippl'd.	rnst	learn'st.	thr	three.
plst	rippl'st.	rnt	burnt.	ths	Ruth's.
plz	apples.	rnz	urns.	thst	breath'st.
pr	prince.	rp	carp.	tht	scath'd.
ps	sips.	rps	harps.	thw	thwack.
pst	rapp'st.	rpst	usurp'st.	thz	writhes, paths.
pt	ripp'd, rapt.	rpt	warp'd.	tl	title.
pts	Copts.	rptst	usurp'dst.	tld	settl'd.
ptst	shap'dst.	rs	verse.	tldst	settl'dst.
rb	herb.	rsh	harsh.	tlst	settl'st.
rch	search.	rst	first.	tlz	nettles.
rcht	church'd.	rsts	bursts.	tr	trunk.
rchtst	lurch'd'st.	rt	dart.	ts	fits.
rchdst	perch'dst.	rth	carth.	tst	waftst.
rbd	orb'd.	rtht	earth'd.	tw	twirl.
rbdst	barb'dst.	rths	births.	vd	curv'd.
rbz	orbs	rts	marts.	vdst	liv'dst.
rd	hard.	rtst	dart'st.	vl	driv'l.
rdst	heard'st.	rv	curve.	vld	grov'l'd.
rdz	words.	rvd	nerv'd.	vldst	grov'l'dst.
rf	turf.	rvdst	curv'dst.	vlst	driv'l'st.
rfs	turfs.	rvst	swerv'st.	vn	driv'n.
rft	scarf'd.	rvz	nerves.	vst	liv'st.
rg	burg.	rz	furs.	vz	lives.
rgst	urg'st.	rzd	furz'd.	wh	when.
rgz	burgs.	sh	hush.	zd	mus'd.
rj	dirge.	sht	hush'd.	zl	dazzle.
rjd	urg'd.	sk	skip, scan.	zld	muzzl'd.
rjdst	urg'dst.	sks	basks.	zldst	dazzl'dst.
rk	ark.	skst	ask'st.	zlst	dazzl'st.
rks	arks.	skt	risk'd.	zlz	muzzles.
rkst	work'st.	sl	slow.	zm	spasm
rkt	dirk'd.	sld	nestl'd.	zmz	chasms.
rktst	embark'dst.	slz	wrestles.	zn	ris'n.
rl	girl.	sm	smile.	znd	reas'n'd.
rld	world.	sn	snag.	znz	pris'ns.
rldst	hurl'dst.	sp	sport.	zndst	impris'n'dst.
rlst	whirl'st.	sps	lisps.		

TABLE NO. 10. VOCAL GYMNASTICS. FORCE AND PITCH.

Fig. 1. *Variations in Force.*

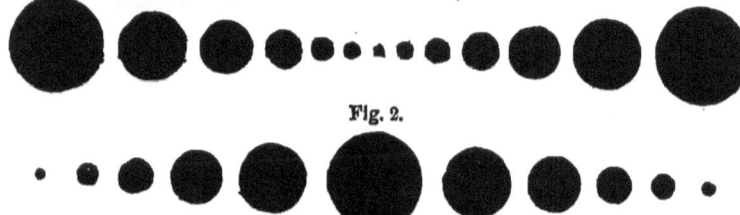

Fig. 3. *Variations in Pitch and Force.*

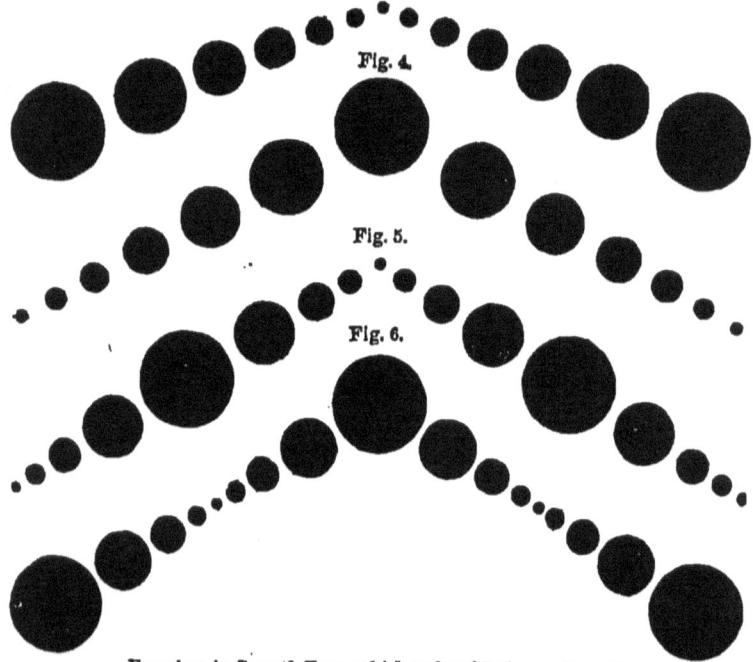

Exercises in Smooth Tone, which end suddenly, or die out.

1. Fill the lungs and intone slowly from a heavy voice to a whisper, or "diminuendo" (½ of Fig. 1).
2. Fill the lungs and intone reversely, or "crescendo"—from light to heavy (last ½ of Fig. 1).
3. Fill the lungs and intone "diminuendo" and "crescendo" (through the entire 1st Fig.).
4. Fill the lungs and intone "crescendo" and "diminnendo," or "swell" (through the 2d Fig.).
5. Fill the lungs and intone, decreasing in force while ascending the scale (½ of Fig. 3).
6. Fill the lungs and intone, increasing in force while descending the scale (last ½ of Fig. 3).
7. Fill the lungs and intone, continuing from the decrease to the increase downward (Fig. 3 entire).
8. Fill the lungs and intone, increasing in force while ascending the scale (½ of Fig. 4).
9. Fill the lungs and intone, decreasing in force while descending the scale (Fig. 4, last half).
10. Fill the lungs and intone, continuing from the increase to the decrease (Fig. 4 entire).
11 and 12. Fill the lungs and intone, making a swell midway in ascent and descent (Fig. 5 entire).
13. Fill the lungs and intone slowly, decreasing in force to the middle, and increasing in force to the last while ascending the scale (½ of Fig. 6).
14. Decrease in force to the middle, and increase to the last in descending the scale (last ½ of Fig. 6).
15. Change by taking each of the pure *vowel sounds* and *consonant continuants*, and by assuming some of the *qualities* of voice.
16. Apply sentences to the figures. Example:
 "Then fear not, doubt not, which thou wilt;
 We'll try this quarrel hilt to hilt."

TABLE NO. 11. VOCAL GYMNASTICS. STRESS.

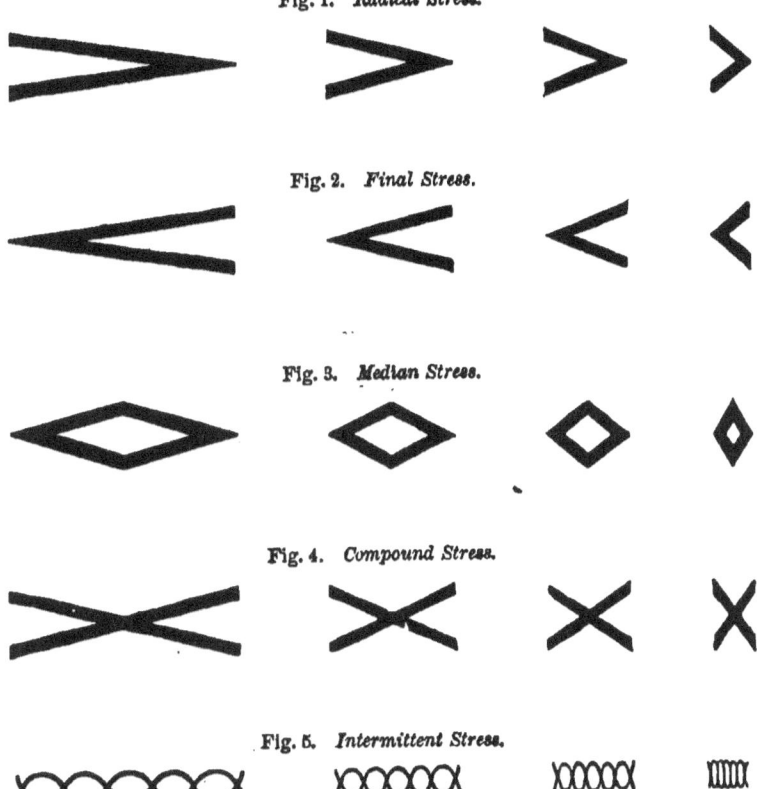

Fig. 1. *Radical Stress.*

Fig. 2. *Final Stress.*

Fig. 3. *Median Stress.*

Fig. 4. *Compound Stress.*

Fig. 5. *Intermittent Stress.*

This table is devoted exclusively to stress.

To practice Fig. 1. Begin heavily, and end lightly upon one note. A smooth diminuendo.

Fig. 2. Begin in a whisper and end heavily. A smooth crescendo.

Fig. 3. Begin and end lightly, with a full, heavy sound in the middle of the note. A smooth swell.

Fig. 4. Begin and end heavily, diminishing to a whisper in the middle of the note.

Fig. 5. Produce a note in a tremulous tone, such as represents sorrow, age, etc.

No. 6. Thorough or Staccato Stress is not represented, but should be practiced by repeating each sound abruptly four times.

Take successive vowel sounds for this practice, and be careful not to vary the pitch.

TABLE NO. 12. VOCAL GYMNASTICS. PITCH, OR INFLECTION.
NOTES REPRESENTED BY LINES.

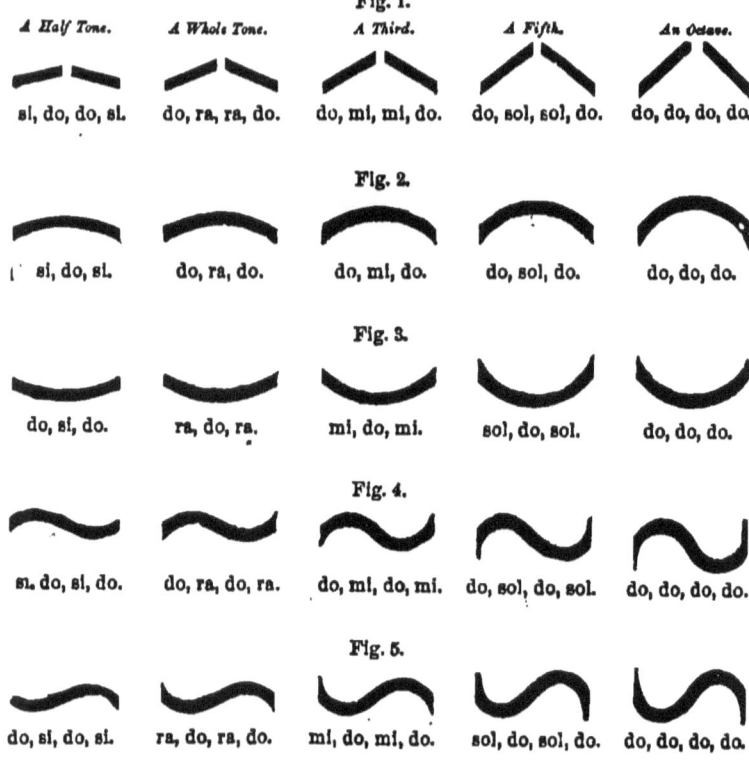

This table is devoted exclusively to pitch, and is designed to educate the ear to distinguish kinds and degrees of inflection.

To practice Fig. 1. First produce the given notes of the scale with syllables, si, do, do, si, etc. When this can be done, substitute a vowel sound for the syllables, and produce a smooth, even rise and fall of the voice, to correspond in degree with the notes or characters in the figure. Do not increase nor decrease in volume, and avoid dragging the sound from one character to another.

Practice the remaining figures in the same way, observing to continue the sound to the end of each character in the figures, and no farther. In Fig. 1, two notes are united in each character; in Figs. 2 and 3, three notes; in Figs. 4 and 5, four notes are smoothly connected.

ORTHOPHONY. 15

TABLE NO. 13. VOCAL GYMNASTICS. PITCH AND FORCE COMBINED.

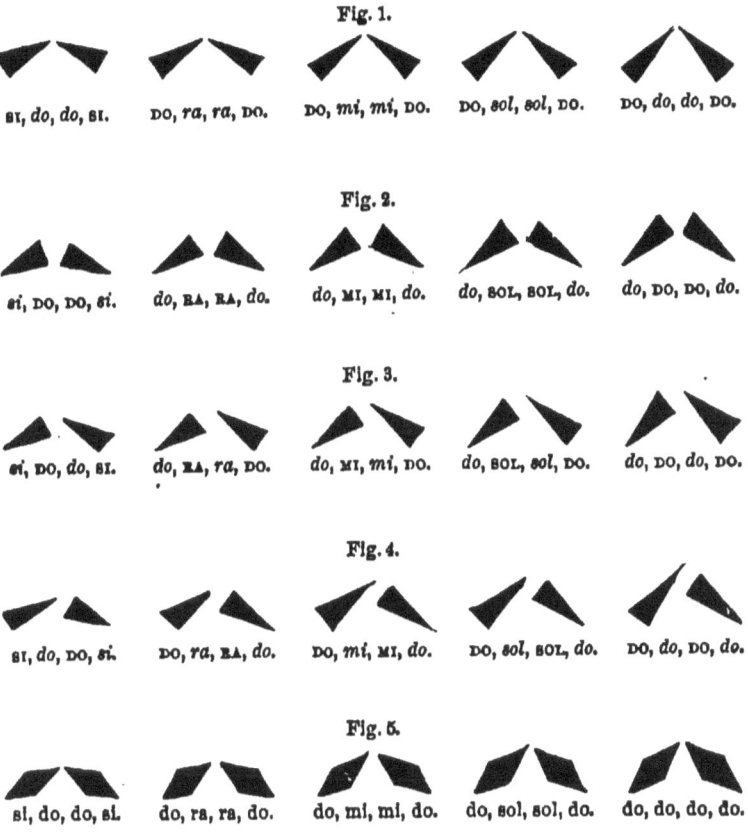

This table combines stress and inflection for practice.
To practice Fig. 1. Sound the syllables, accenting the first and last in each group, as indicated by the capitals and small letters. When this can be readily done, use a single vowel sound instead of the syllables.
Practice the remaining figures in the same manner, applying various vowel sounds to keep up an interest in the exercise.
Fig. 5 can be rendered more easily by using a single sound at the outset.

TABLE NO. 14. ACCENT.

To learn accent, practice the following Table of Accented and Unaccented Sounds. The table may be written on the blackboard, and the class exercised in concert, the leader pointing to the groups of sound in the order and time required.

DISSYLLABLES.   TRISYLLABLES.

(tables of accented and unaccented vowel symbols in dissyllable, trisyllable, and polysyllable groupings)

POLYSYLLABLES.

MANUAL OF READING.

PART I.
ORTHOPHONY.

ORTHOPHONY is systematic voice-training.

I. HYGIENIC SUGGESTIONS.

To attain the highest voice capacity requires health and practice. To insure or perpetuate health, we must have—
1st. Plain food, regularly taken.
2d. Comfortable clothing, warm, light, and loose.
3d. Exercise and pure air.
4th. Plenty of sleep.

FOOD.

The most wholesome diet for pupils in voice-training, amateur and professional voice artists, excludes all *greasy* food, soups, pork in any form, nuts, rich food, as suet or plum puddings, fruit-cake, mince pie, pickles, lobster, hot breads, candy, and all other food that causes indigestion and feverishness, together with all stimulating drinks, including strong tea and coffee.

To guard against the imputation of having excluded every thing palatable, a list of dishes, both pleasant and harmless, is added. Fish, fowl, rare-boiled or poached eggs, tripe, rare-roasted or broiled beef, cold breads, toast, crackers, wheat grits, oatmeal mush and cakes, plain puddings and pies, fruit, cold water, milk or weak tea. No food should be taken between meals or late at night. Persons using the voice professionally take no food for at least one hour before using the voice, and oftener two or three hours intervene between dinner and the concert or lecture. But one exception has been given among distinguished singers, and that is Adelaide Patti, who is said to dine between the acts of the opera. Parepa, whose voice is not only wonderful for its power, but for its clearness, dines four hours before concert, taking a light lunch, if needful, just before singing, but nothing afterward, and avoids all voice-smoothers, such as lozenges, lemon, sugar, etc. To avoid a sensation of hunger or faintness, a little toast and weak tea, or, what is better, a raw egg, may be taken just before using the voice.

CLOTHING.

The clothing should be at all times sufficiently *warm* for the climate and season. *Light*, so as to give ease and warmth without weight, and *loose* in those much-abused parts of the body, viz., the throat, waist, and feet. One thickness of flannel should cover the chest, to avoid the chill of damp cotton or linen garments after exercise. The weight of clothing should rest, as much as possible, upon the shoulders, by means of bands or suspenders, and the feet should be kept at all times dry and warm.

EXERCISE AND PURE AIR.

Fresh air should be plentiful at all times by means of ventilators, windows, and doors; and this should be not only in halls and churches, but in all business places, school-rooms, and sleeping apartments. This note may seem unnecessary in a teacher's manual; but so little thought is given the subject elsewhere, we would have the children thoroughly taught the necessity as well as comfort of pure air. When about to practice calisthenics or gesture, it is safe to have windows and doors open; but when warm and resting, they should be closed, and all drafts avoided. Upon going into cold or damp air after using the voice, as in reading, lecturing, or singing, the lungs and mouth should be carefully protected, the process of breathing carried on through the nostrils or a thickness of flannel.

SLEEP.

Let no one think sleep unworthy of consideration, for it is a cosmetic, a tonic, and an indispensable voice-agent. No stimulants, lotions, or cordials can give that vigor to the vocal organs; no cosmetics can give that freshness of feeling and appearance that perfect rest and sleep give. Children will waken when fully rested, and it is nothing less than cruelty to waken and force them to rise. They should be sent to bed earlier, that they may have the needed amount of rest.

Besides *health*, voice-culture requires continued systematic *exercise* or *practice* in *respiration, intonation,* and *calisthenics,* or *gesture.* These exercises bring into action all of the muscles of the chest and throat, head and mouth. Exercises in breathing, by noting the number of seconds required to fill the lungs by slow inhalation, and the seconds required to empty them by slow exhalation, together with exercises in intoning, noting the number of seconds that a full smooth tone can be produced, and how many syllables can be uttered without a fresh supply of breath, have been found very beneficial to the respiratory and vocal organs. These exercises give the power and ability to produce many words with a small supply of breath or voice-material, thus enabling a speaker to render long passages of composition smoothly and effectively — passages that would lose half their force by an interruption for breath. The general or primary position for exercises in breathing and intoning is the *military* or *gymnasium* position (see page 24), and the special position No. 1, page 25, i. e., the hands upon the sides, so that the finger-tips may touch in the back, thumbs point front, elbows back, and chin curbed.

II. GENERAL EXERCISES.

RESPIRATION.

1. INSPIRING. The lungs must first be emptied in order to ascertain how long it takes to fill them; hence, begin this exercise by expelling the air from the lungs, making a continuous hissing sound; when the sound ceases the air in

the lungs is sufficiently exhausted. Now *inspire* very slowly, making a slight noise, until the lungs are filled, noting the time in seconds.

2. EXPIRING. Assume the required military and special position. Place the upper teeth upon the lower lip, as if to say *v;* inspire slowly until no more air can be inhaled; then, with the tongue near the teeth, as if to give the sound of *s*, emit the breath as slowly as possible, making an even and continuous hissing sound, so that there can be no mistake whether the breath is constantly escaping or being held at intervals.

 a. Effusive. Inspire and emit the breath freely, as in the prolonged sound of the aspirate *h*.

 b. Expulsive. Inspire and emit the breath more quickly and forcibly than in the effusive, with the sound of the aspirate *h*.

 c. Explosive. Inspire and expel the breath suddenly and violently, making the sound of *h* like a whispered cough. (Combine this exercise with the thrust movements in calisthenics.)

3. SIGHING. Combined *inspiration* and *expiration* emotionally.

 a. Inspire and expire suddenly.
 b. Inspire and expire moderately.
 c. Inspire moderately and expire suddenly.
 d. Inspire suddenly and expire moderately.

4. GASPING. Convulsive inspiration and gradual expiration.

5. PANTING. Rapid and forcible inspiration and expiration several times in succession.

6. SOBBING is sighing or gasping made slightly vocal.

INTONATION.

Intoning Exercises without change of Force or Pitch.

1. PROLONGING A NOTE OR SOUND. Fill the lungs, and note the number of seconds that one sound can be smoothly prolonged. The sound may be one of the vowels or consonant continuants.*

* See Table of Sounds, No. 2. The sound may be concrete or smoothly

2. COUNTING. Inspire as before, and note the number that can be counted at one expiration.

3. REPEATING ALOUD A LINE, COUPLET, OR STANZA. Inspire and note the number of times that one line, couplet, or stanza can be repeated at one expiration. The selection for this exercise should consist mostly of monosyllables.

4. REPEATING IN A WHISPER A LINE, COUPLET, OR STANZA. This exercise is more difficult than No. 3, in that the repetition is made in a whisper, but it is considered *very* beneficial in strengthening the lungs.

5. LAUGHING. Fill the lungs, and laugh in a forcible expulsive manner. This exercise strengthens the abdominal muscles more than any other. A great variety of laughing exercises can be produced by placing *h* before the different vowel sounds. Hā, hā, hā; hă, hă, hă; hä, hä, hä; hâ, hâ, hâ; hē, hē, hē; hŭ, hŭ, hŭ; hī, hī, hī; hĭ, hĭ, hĭ; hō, hō, hō; hŏ, hŏ, hŏ; hô, hô, hô; hū, hū, hū; hŭ, hŭ, hŭ.

Intoning Exercises with changes of Force.

6. Prolong a note or sound, or repeat a sentence.
   a. Increasing in force to the end.
   b. Decreasing in force to the end.
   c. Increasing to the middle, and *decreasing* to the end.
   d. Decreasing to the middle, and *increasing* to the end.

Intoning Exercises with changes of Force and Pitch.

7. Prolong a note or sound, or repeat a sentence.
   a. Increasing in force while *ascending* the scale.
   b. Increasing in force while *descending* the scale.
   c. Decreasing in force while *ascending* the scale.
   d. Decreasing in force while *descending* the scale.
   e. Increasing in force to the *middle*, and *decreasing* to the *last* while *ascending* the scale.
   f. Decreasing in force to the *middle*, and *increasing* to the *last* while *ascending* the scale.

connected, as ō continued; discrete or disconnected, as fa, fa, fa, etc. Another change may be produced by making the sound intermittent or in tremor; and again, by assuming different qualities of voice.

g. Increasing in force to the *middle,* and *decreasing* to the *last* while *descending* the scale.

h. Decreasing in force to the *middle,* and *increasing* to the *last* while *descending* the scale.

These exercises may be varied by changes in *quality* of *voice,* and by tremor, or tremulous voice.

At this time the vowel and consonant sounds should be thoroughly learned, and their combinations practiced, until a word or succession of words can be pronounced without difficulty. The tables for this drill are Nos. 2, 3, 4, 5, 6, 7, 8, 9, 10, and 11, and the tables in Orthophony called "Contrast Exercises" for imperfect pronunciation.

To overcome the habit of speaking and reading with the teeth closed, or nearly closed, practice the vowel sounds with a stick or finger between the teeth. Increase the thickness of the stick until the distance between the teeth is satisfactory.

Again, repeat a sentence, and insert two fingers between the teeth at every syllable.

CALISTHENICS.

CALISTHENICS, from two Greek words, signifying *beautiful* and *strength*, is distinguished from gymnastics by quick, light movements, without apparatus or mechanical aid, producing grace and symmetry. Gymnastics may be graceful, brisk, and slight, but are generally understood to mean athletic strength in attitudinizing, lifting, swinging, climbing, requiring slow time and heavy work. Dio Lewis calls his later and improved exercises "*Light* or *Free Gymnastics*," to distinguish them from the older and partially discarded heavy gymnastics; wooden bells, wands, rings, and clubs taking the place of iron bells, weights, etc. But light gymnastics are not as easily adapted to the school-room as calisthenics, which require no apparatus, and can be abandoned and resumed at pleasure. Such exercises only as are best calculated to aid and improve the voice will be inserted in these pages. These will include a series of movements for the chest, shoulder, arm, hand, head, neck, and trunk.

The calisthenics in this volume are for those who have no system learned, and not to supersede those producing the same results.

MOVEMENT.*

Movement includes all the requirements of action from the beginning to the end of an exercise. 1st, Position; 2d, Direction; 3d, Order; 4th, Manner; 5th, Time.

I. POSITION FOR HYGIENIC EXERCISE.

There are two general or primary positions, termed *military* or *gymnasium*, and *rostrum*, and an indefinite number of SPECIAL positions, indicating the series of movements or exercises which are to follow.

---

* Much of the benefit arising from calisthenics is derived from the alternation of rigid and relaxed muscles. There should be an accent to the motion, and that accent should occur at the climax of the outward movement; hence the muscles should be firm in the outward movement, and relaxed in the return.

General Positions.

1. The military, or gymnasium position, is to place the heels together, toes out, and hands at the side; the ear, shoulder, hip, knee, and ankle appearing to be in a perpendicular line, and the weight equal on both feet.

Full Description of the Military Position.
a. Heels together, or an inch apart.
b. Feet at right angles.
c. Knees together.
d. Body and head upright.
e. Shoulders back.
f. Eyes front.
g. Arms at the side.
h. Palms in, and thumbs front.*
i. Mouth closed (except in vocal exercise).

2. The rostrum position is an easy, upright speaking position, with one foot advanced, and the weight of the body principally upon the foot in the rear.

Full Description of the Rostrum Position.
a. Body erect and easy.
b. One foot three or four inches in advance of the other.
c. Toes turned out in an angle of about 45 degrees.
d. Arms at rest at the side.
e. Heel of the foot in advance, in a line with the heel of the other.
f. Hands relaxed and natural (as they would hang at the side).

3. The reading position is similar to the rostrum, save that the book should be held in the left hand, high enough to keep

* This position is sometimes given with the palms front and thumbs out. (See Figure.)

the head from drooping, yet not so high as to hide the face of the reader from the audience.

Special Positions and Movements. (See Table No. 1.) The special positions are always taken *at the commencement* and *between* the movements of a series. The *military* always precedes the *special* position, unless otherwise stated.

I. CHEST SERIES.

1. *Percussing.**—Position: hands upon sides, so that the fingers may touch in the back; thumbs pointing front, with the elbows pressed back, and the chin curbed; action: fill the lungs, and, with open hands, pat the chest rapidly and gently from the neck to the girdle; increase the intensity of action when no inconvenience is felt therefrom, *but never bruise the flesh.*

2. *Single Thrusting from the Arm-pit.†*—Position: fists upon the chest, near the arm-pit, in front; elbows elevated and pressed back; wrists bent inward; direction, the twelve points: three front, three oblique, three extended, and three backward; order, single; manner, direct. (See Table No. 1.)

---
* Percussing distributes the air to the remote portions of the lungs that are less often inflated, and strengthens them.

† All the thrust exercises widen the chest in front, and make the back straight and narrow.

B

3. *Double Thrusting from the Arm-pit.**—Position as in No. 2; direction, contrasting, up and down, or right and left; order, double; manner, direct; action: 1st, descending and ascending front, alternating four times with both fists; 2d, descending extended to the right, and the same to the left, four times alternately; 3d, horizontal extended to the right twice, the same to the left, and four times alternately; 4th, ascending extended to the right twice, and the same to the left, and four times alternately.

4. *Thrusting from the Chest centre.*—Position: fists on the chest, backs front, knuckles touching; elbows horizontal with the shoulders; direction, the twelve points; order, single; manner, direct.

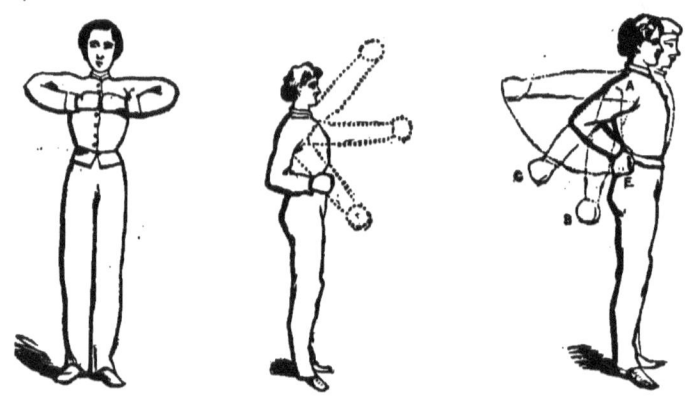

5. *Thrusting from the Sides.**—Position: elbows back; fore-arm and fists parallel upon the sides, and horizontal; direction, three points front; order, single; manner, direct.

6. *Thrusting from the Hips.*—Position: fists upon the back of the hips, near the girdle, palms in, thumbs closed, and elbows pressed backward; direction, backward; order, single; manner, direct.

II. SHOULDER SERIES.

1. *Extending the Arms from the Arm-pit.*—Position: elbows horizontal with the shoulders, thumbs and fingers joined, and drawn up under the arms; direction, extended

---
* Inspire at the return, and expire at the outward movements.

(descending and horizontal); order, single; manner, direct; action: 1st, bring the arms from the special position directly down in the single order, i. e. right hand twice, left hand twice, alternately twice, and simultaneously twice; 2d, bring the arms from the special position to the horizontal extended in single order.

2. *Extending the Arms from the Shoulder top.*—Position: fingers rest upon the top of the shoulder near the joint, thumbs back, elbows extended horizontally from the shoulders; direction, extended (three points); order, single; manner, direct; action: bring the arms from the special position, 1st, to the descending extended; 2d, to the horizontal; 3d, to the ascending extended in the usual single order. (See No. 1 of this series.)

3. *Shoulder Lifting.*—Position, military; arms relaxed; direction, upward; order, single; manner, direct; action: raise the right shoulder twice, the left twice, alternate twice, and twice simultaneously.

4. *Rotary Movement.**—Position and order as in No. 3; manner, rotary; action: bring the right shoulder forward, upward, backward, downward twice, twice with the left,

---

* To teach quickly, let the pupils count four; at one, bring shoulder forward; two, upward; three, backward; four, downward. It is a good exercise for removing a stoop or round of the shoulders, as indeed are all the chest and shoulder exercises, with No. 4 of the Elbow Series, and No. 7 of the Arm Series.

etc. Let the arms be loose, and swing as they may, during this exercise.

5. *Swinging the Arms horizontally backward.*—Position: the palms together, horizontal front; direction, backward; order, double; manner, direct; action: swing the arms backward and forward eight or sixteen times.

III. ELBOW SERIES.

1. *Hands clasped and upon the Head.*—Position: hands clasped and placed upon the head, palms down, and elbows extended at the side; direction, upward, etc.; order, double;

manner, direct; action: 1st, raise the hands above the head without unclasping four times; 2d, upon the back of the neck, and back to the top of the head four times; 3d, upon the chest in front and back four times; 4th, alternate from the back to the crown, and from the front to the crown four times, and finally from front to back four times without stopping at the top of the head.

2. *Throwing back the Elbows.**—Position: hands upon the hips, thumbs back; action: press the elbows as far back as possible, returning each time to the extended. Repeat this exercise four or eight times.

IV. ARM SERIES.

1. *Swinging the Arms backward.**—Position: palms together, horizontal front; action: swing the hands down to the side, and back as far as possible.

2. *Swinging the Arms upward.*†—Position like No. 1; action: swing the arms from the horizontal front up to the perpendicular and back four or eight times.

3. *Swinging the Arms outward and upward.*†—Position, military; action: swing the arms through the line called extended to the perpendicular.

4. *Twisting the Arms.*—Position, arms horizontal front;

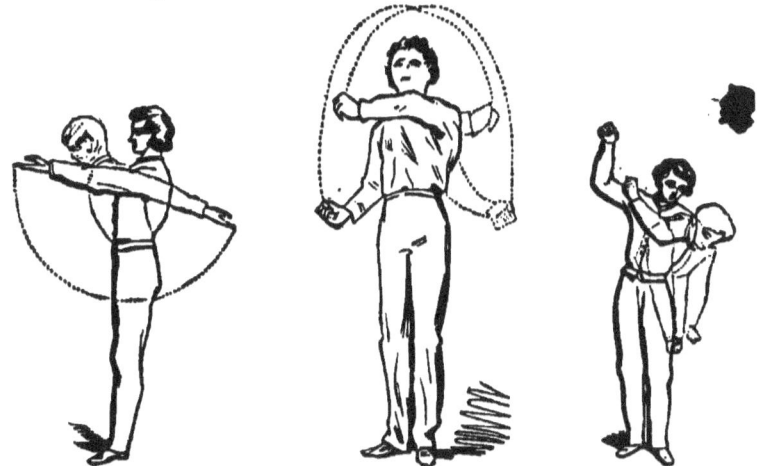

* Take full breath at the relaxation of muscle, and breathe out suddenly at the backward movement.

† Let these exercises be done in regular order; right arm twice, left twice, alternate twice, and simultaneous twice.

order, double; action: twist the arms by turning the hands over and back eight times; change position to perpendicular, and repeat; change to the horizontal, and repeat.

5. *Chopping.*—Position, hands raised above the head to the right; direction, descending to the left in front; order, double; action, like chopping, eight times; reverse, and chop upward to the left.

6. *Mowing.*—Position, arms to the right (see Figure); direction, horizontal to the left; order, double; manner, direct; action as if mowing on level ground; reverse, and move as if mowing up hill.

7. *Sawing.**—Position: body bent to the right, elbow above the line of the shoulders, and hands closed; direction, downward; order, double; manner, direct; action, moving both hands up and down as if sawing.

V. HAND SERIES.

Opening and shutting the Hands. Position: arms at the side, hands closed; action: open and close the hands four times; arms to horizontal extended; open and close the hands four times; perpendicular and repeat; to the horizontal front and repeat.

* The sawing exercise is excellent for enlarging the chest and increasing the strength of the muscles.

VI. HEAD AND NECK SERIES.

1. *Turning the Head.*—Position, military; action: turn the head horizontally to the right, so that the face will be over the right shoulder, and back to the front twice, to the left twice, alternate right and left twice, stopping in front each time.

2. *Bowing.*—Position, military; direction, up and down; action: 1. look down to the point descending front, and then horizontal front four times; 2. look up to the point ascending front, then horizontal four times; 3. look alternately down and front, up and front four times; 4. look down and up four times without stopping in front. (This may be repeated, letting the head fall to the right and left instead of front.)

3. *Looking up to right and left.*—Position, military; direction, ascending oblique and descending front; action: 1. look up to the point ascending oblique, and down in front four times; 2. the same to the left; 3. alternate right and left four times, stopping each time to look down.

4. *Rotary or Rolling Movement.*—Position, military; manner, rotary; action: bow the head front, and, letting it helplessly fall, move it horizontally in a circle upon the shoulders. Repeat the circle four times.

VII. TRUNK SERIES.

1. *Bending the Body forward and backward.*—Position, military; action: 1. bend the body horizontally front, and resume the perpendicular four times; 2. bend backward, and resume the perpendicular four times; 3. alternate forward and backward, stopping each time at the perpendicular four times; 4. bend forward, then backward four times without stopping at the perpendicular.

2. *Bending the Body to the right and left.*—This is like No. 1, except in direction, which is right and left instead of forward and back.

3. *Rotary, or Body rolling.*—Position, military; action: bend the body horizontally front, and, relaxing the muscles, move it to the right, back, left, and around to the front again in a kind of circle; repeat four times.

II. DIRECTION OF MOVEMENT.

Direction is the line or course in which any thing moves. In calisthenics or gesture, *direction* is the course which the arm, hand, etc., takes with regard to the body, and is named both from the side of the person where it ends, and from the degree of elevation which this ending or climax attains.

All gestures made before one are called "*front;*" those made directly to the *right* or *left* are called "*extended;*" those made between the "*front*" and "*extended*" are called "*oblique;*" and, lastly, those made back of the *extended* are called "*back-oblique,*" or "*backward.*" With regard to the *elevation*, all gestures or motions whose climax or ending is on a horizontal line with the shoulders, are called *horizontal;* all that have their climax or ending below the horizontal are called *descending;* and all above the horizontal are called *ascending.*

Hence we have twelve different points of direction:

I. 1. Descending front.   III. 1. Descending extended.
   2. Horizontal front.   2. Horizontal extended.
   3. Ascending front.   3. Ascending extended.
II. 1. Descending oblique.   IV. 1. Descending backward.
   2. Horizontal oblique.   2. Horizontal backward.
   3. Ascending oblique.   3. Ascending backward.

III. ORDER OF MOVEMENT.

By *order* of movement is meant the successive order in which the right or left hand, arm, etc., are used in action. For convenience, *Order* has been given as No. 1 *Single*, and No. 2 *Double*.

Single order is when the motions are made first with the right arm or hand; then with the left, each a certain number of times; second, alternate with the right and left a corresponding number of times; and third, a simultaneous action of the right and left the same number of times. Example: thrusting with the right hand twice, with the left twice, alternate twice, and simultaneous twice.

Double order is made with the hands simultaneously, changing only the directions during the exercises; i. e., make a certain number of motions in some one direction with both hands, then in another direction with both hands, thus continuing until the exercise is completed. Example: thrust both hands down front twice, up front twice, alternate up and down twice; then twice to the right, twice to the left; then alternate right and left twice.

IV. MANNER OF MOVEMENT.

The *manner* of movement in calisthenics or gesture may be *direct* or *rotary: direct*, when the point of direction in the climax is attained in a straight or direct line, and *rotary* when by a roundabout or rotary motion.

V. TIME OF MOVEMENT.

In these exercises there should be a regularly recurring *accent* of motion or rhythm. The *outward* motion in many exercises will most naturally receive the accent, and can be timed in various ways: by *counting* in quadruple time, by *tapping* with pointer or cane, or by *music* itself in quadruple time. If *counting* is preferred, and a class is to practice, let *all* count, accenting the *odd* numbers to eight, or, substituting *and* for the unaccented part, count four; thus, ONE *and*, TWO *and*, THREE *and*, FOUR *and;* again, ONE *and*, etc., over and over again until the exercise is finished.

ARTICULATION.

The principal *defects of articulation* consist of a uniformly weak or *thick* utterance, *lisping* and *stammering*.

1. A *weak* manner of speech may arise from ill health or lassitude, from diffidence or embarrassment, from indolence or affectation. In cases of weakness, *health* must be improved before any great change can be made in the voice power. Such exercise in respiration, intonation, and calisthenics as can be borne from day to day, will greatly aid in regaining strength if the weakness is chiefly in the lungs. Indeed, tendencies toward consumption have, in many instances, been overcome by judicious vocal training.

If weakness of utterance arises from diffidence, let no opportunity pass that will overcome want of confidence. Conversation, recitation, declamation, singing, and dialogues should be engaged in, however irksome the task, and whatever failures accrue. If it arises from embarrassment, keep the lungs well filled or inflated, and there will follow comparative self-possession. When the defect arises from indolence or affectation, there is little hope of remedy.

2. A *thick* manner of utterance is sometimes the result of malformation, or accidental injury of the vocal organs. In such cases permanent cures are rare. Surgical operations will remove any superfluous growth, but for an absence of parts there is no chance of remedy. A thick manner of speech is often the result of *intemperance* in the use of liquors, tobacco, snuff, or other drugs, and can only be cured by abstemiousness, exercise, and cleanliness of the head-cavities, chest, and throat. The mucous linings of the head-cavities may become thickened by catarrhal difficulties, and produce thickness of speech.

3. *Lisping* is the habit of substituting *th* soft for *s* and *z*. It can be cured if the lisper has sufficient will-power and patience. Practice faithfully, two or three times a day, a list of words containing *s* and *z*, and *th*. Care should be taken

that the tip of the tongue be pressed lightly against the edges of the upper incisor teeth to produce *th*, and against the gums of the same upper teeth to produce the sound of *s*. Besides the practice, every lisp in reading, speaking, or conversing should be corrected when made.*

TABLE NO. 15.

Words for Practice by Contrast.

thale	for sale.	hathte	for haste.
thake	" sake.	patht	" past.
that	" sat.	carth	" cars.
thalt	" salt.	thtarth	" stars.
thee	" see.	callth	" calls.
thend	" send.	pleathe	" please.
thigths	" sighs.	betht	" best.
thick	" sick.	thkeith	" skies.
thold	" sold.	kith'd	" kissed.
thoon	" soon.	ro-thy	" rosy.
thot	" sot.	loth-ing	" losing.
thuit	" suit.	jŏth-ling	" jostling.
thuch	" such.	mu-thic	" music.
thouth	" south.	duth-ter	" duster.
thour	" sour.	tru-ithm	" truism.
thong	" song.	con-the-quenthe	" consequence.
thilly	" silly.	con-thtan-thy	" constancy.
thwingths	" swings.	cauth-eth	" causes.
thlow	" slow.	murmurth	" murmurs.
thmile	" smile.	whith-le	" whistle.
thnatch	" snatch.	bleth-ed	" blessed.
thpade	" spade.	rith-eth	" rises.
thrau	" straw.	roth-eth	" roses.
thky	" sky.	raith-eth	" raises.
thtout	" stout.	wish-eth	" wishes.
thenths	" cents.	thooth-ing	" soothing.
thel-lar	" cellar.	thlum-berth	" slumbers.
thi-der	" cider.	dith-mith	" dismiss.
Tha-rah	" Sarah.	exer-thith-eth	" exercises.

* Lisping really belongs under "*defects* by substitution," but has been considered worthy of special study.

4. *Stammering* is caused by diffidence, embarrassment, or an attempt at speech without proper control of the vocal organs. To overcome this defect is more difficult than that of lisping. The stammerer should keep the lungs well inflated while speaking, and try to be hopeful, cheerful, and self-confident. First, the stammerer must believe that he *can* be cured, not despairing with any number of failures, but energetically persevering in the exercises as directed. There should be systematic training in all the tables belonging to Orthophony, particularly on those in respiration, intonation, and calisthenics, in order to obtain control of the voluntary muscles.

Note.—Some people's thoughts outrun their power of utterance, and they stammer because all the words can not come forth at once. It is a fact worthy of attention that stammerers seldom stammer when singing. Is it not because the words are arranged in proper order and time without their assistance, thus relieving them of all responsibility? It is the same with poetry. Cures have been performed by repeating lines of poetry, giving the rhythmical accent, and keeping time with the finger. At every repetition increase the speed. Try this three times a day, sleep enough, live temperately in all things, do nothing to prostrate the nervous system, and the chances are you will recover.

Example. "'Come back! come back!' he cried in grief,
 Across the stormy water,
'And I'll forgive your highland chief,
 My daughter—oh my daughter!'"

ENUNCIATION.

The most common defects or errors of enunciation are found in the *substitution, omission,* and *addition* of sounds in syllables, and the *overlapping* of words in sentences. When there is no organic defect, these faults result from carelessness or ignorance, and can be remedied by constant attention to, and correction of every error of the kind. Fixed habits of articulation or enunciation contracted by uncultivated associations and incompetent teachers are exceedingly difficult to correct. To correct an error the moment it is noticed, either in reading or speaking, may be humiliating, but will prove a sure remedy. In the following list the right-hand column is the corrected one, for practice in substitution, omission, and addition.

TABLE NO. 16.
List in Substitution.*
Vowels.

bĭ or bŭ		for bȳ.	fărm	}	for färm.
lĭk or lŭk		" līke.	fawrm		
sĕt		" sĭt.	fäther	}	" fäther.
shĕt		" shŭt.	fäther		
sĕnce		" sĭnce.	dĕnce	}	" dănce.
gĭt		" gĕt.	darnce		
sāid	(said)	" sĕd.	heerd		" hĕard.
dooz	(does)	" dŭz.	fŭst		" fĭrst.
ketch		" cătch.	ceetee		" cĭty.
hŏm		" hōme.	maysure		" mĕasure.
agāin	(again)	" agĕn.	stiddy		" stĕady.
cärse		" course.	bŭnnit		" bŏnnet.
īle		" oil.	suller		" cĕllar.
sīle		" soil.	mellër		" mĕllōw.
pīnt		" point.	pĭllër		" pĭllōw.
bĕn	(been)	" bĭn.	childurn		" childrĕn.

* Make a sentence for each word, and pronounce it properly.

shŭll   for shăll.   forgĭt   for forgĕt.
wāre   " wēre.   modĭst   " modĕst.
lăss   " lŏss.   mŭnt   " mĕnt.
năr   " nŏr.   Gawd   " Gŏd.
cawurd   " cörd.   nawt   " nŏt.
dreen   " drāin.   rĕnch   " rĭnse.
lärn   " learn.   gwīne   " going.
idee   " idēă.   atter   " after.

Consonants.

    t for *d*, as worts for words.
             lats   " lads, etc.
    th soft for *th* hard, as baths   for baths.
                  beneath " beneath.
    z for *s* soft, as rize   for rise.
               deceazed " deceased.
    w for *v*, as wine   for vine.
             winegar " vinegar.
    v for *w*, as vill   for will.
             valking " walking.

The errors with *w* and *v* are peculiar to foreigners; there are also those peculiar to children, viz. :*

    t for *ch*, as tarles for Charles.
             ticken " chicken.
    t for *c* hard, as take for cake.
             tart " cart.
    d for *g*, as dood for good.
             dirl " girl.
    d for *j*, as doe for Joe.
             don " John.

* Dr. Comstock says: "*First* I try to show the children the difference of the position of the organs of speech in producing *k* and *g*, *t* and *d*, etc. If this fails, I open my mouth as widely as possible, so that the tip of the tongue can not touch the gums of the upper teeth, and request the child to open his in like manner. I then direct him to pronounce after me the following syllables: gä, gü, gâ, gă, gī, gĭ, gō, gọ, gŏ, gū, gu, gṳ, kä, kä, kâ, kă, etc." When this scheme fails he advises the teacher and pupil to press back and down the tongue with the index finger, and pronounce the syllables given in the preceding exercise.

ORTHOPHONY.

TABLE NO. 17.
List in Omission.

Omission of r.

gä'den	for gärden.
kä'd	" cärd.
wo'd	" word.
lo'd	" lord.
regä'd	" regard.
wä'mer	" warmer.
gove'n	" góvĕrn.
Feb'uary	" Fĕbruäry.
heä'ken	" heärken.
scä'	" scär.
fä'	" fär.
mä'k	" märk.
fä'thü	" färther.

Omission of g.

readin'	for reading.
feelin'	" feeling.
writin'	" writing.
bein'	" being.
seein'	" seeing.
buyin'	" buying.
singin'	" singing.

Omission of t by prolonging s.

consis'	for consists.
enlis'	" enlists.
protes'	" protests.
wris'	" wrists.
fac's	" facts.
sof'ly	" softly.
swif'ly	" swiftly.
las'	" last.

Omission of d.

wīl's	for wilds.
fiēl's	" fields.
friĕn's	" friends.
ăn'	" and.
lăn'	" land.
săn'	" sand.
kīn'ness	" kīndnĕss.

Omission of h.*

wīle	for while.
wĕn	" when.
wȳ	" why.
wistle	" whistle.
wĭp	" whip.
wät	" what.
s'roud	" shroud.
'urt	" hurt.
'andful	" handful.
'arvest	" harvest.
s'rink	" shrink.
'ermit	" hermit.

Omissions Miscellaneous.

reg'lar	for rĕgūlar.
sev'ral	" sĕvĕral.
rhet'ric	" rhĕtoric.
jub'lee	" jubĭlee.
trav'ler	" travĕler.
fam'ly	" famĭly.
hist'ry	" hĭstŏry.
des'late	" dĕsolate.
prob'ble	" prŏbāble.

* In the following words *wh* has the sound of *h*:
whoot.   whole.   wholly.   whose.
whoop.   who.   wholesome.   whom.

TABLE NO. 18.
List in Addition.

Addition of ŭ.
elum   for elm.
helum   " helm.
overwhelum " overwhelm.
realum   " realm.
āŭr   " air (ĕr).
nōŭr   " nör.

Addition of ē.
kēow   for cow.
teown   " town.
feound   " found.

aēl   for ale.
kēärd   " card.

Addition of h.
hour   for our.
hink   " ĭnk.
härm   " arm.
hown   " own, etc.

Addition of n.
mīnt   for might.

The addition of ă or ä is so common, examples are not necessary. Heä wentä toä schoolä.

Overlapping.

There is an error of enunciation which deserves especial attention, and that is, the overlapping of successive words, a blending of the last sounds of one word with the first sounds of the succeeding word.*

His small eyes   instead of His small lies.
His hour is up   " " His sour is sup.
Let all men praise him   " " Let tall men pray sim.
Water air and earth   " " Water rare and dearth.

The man had oars to row her over.
The man had doors to row her rover.

Can there be an aim more lofty?
Can there be a name more lofty?

He was awed at the works of labor and art before him.
He was sawed at the works sof labor an dart before rim.

Oh for a lodge in some vast wilderness.
Oh for a lodge in some vas' swilderness.

* The examples here given are from the Introduction to "Sanders's Readers."

Words to Practice in Contrast.

These tables, arranged so as to place words of similar termination in contrast, are of importance to students who desire to speak perfect English. Contrasted words should be practiced alike with the rising or falling inflection, as continent', consonant'; or, continent`, consonant`; or, double thus, continent', continent`, consonant', consonant`.

TABLE NO. 19.

Contrast No. 1. *ĭble* and *ăble* (often given *ŭble*).*

fēas'ĭ-ble.	lâud'ă-ble.
rĭs'ĭ-ble.	ĕn'vĭ-ă-ble.
ter'rĭ-ble.	prĕf'er-ă-ble.
plâus'ĭ-ble.	crēd'ĭt-ă-ble.
ĕl'ĭ-gĭ-ble.	rĕv'ō-că-ble.
crĕd'ĭ-ble.	vŏn'ĕr-ă-ble.
lĕg'ĭ-ble.	sўl'lă-ble.
vĭs'ĭ-ble.	mĭs'ĕr-ă-ble.
âud'ĭ-ble.	mĕm'o-ră-ble.
ĭn-vĭn'cĭ-ble.	rea'son-ă-ble.
rē-spŏn'sĭ-ble.	ad-vīs'ă-ble.
dē-dū'cĭ-ble.	cŏn-sĭd'ĕr-ă-ble.
dĭ-vĭs'ĭ-ble.	com-mĕnd'a-ble.
ĭn-cŏm-păt'ĭ-ble.	as-sīgn'ă-ble.
ĭn-tel'lĭ-gĭ-ble.	rē-lī'ă-ble.

Contrast No. 2. *ĕss* and *oŭs* (often given *ĭss*).

count'lĕss.	grā'ciŏŭs.
good'nĕss.	pre'ciŏŭs.
blĕss'ed-nĕss.	val'or-oŭs.
cost'li-nĕss.	măg-năn'ĭ-moŭs.
bus'i-nĕss.	vo-lū'min-oŭs.
la'zi-nĕss.	su-per'flu-oŭs.
daunt'lĕss.	mul-ti-tu'din-oŭs.
list'less-nĕss.	in-con'gru-oŭs.

* Repeat these endings alternately several times in quick succession.

TABLE NO. 20.

Contrast No. 3. ĭty and ĕty.

i and y short.   *e and y short.*

u-tĭl'ĭ-tў.   so-brī'ĕ-tў.
nō-bĭl'ĭ-tў.   sa-tī'ĕ-tў.
de-bĭl'ĭ-tў.   anx-ī'ĕ-tў.
a-bĭl'ĭ-tў.   pī'ĕ-tў.
fĕr-tĭl'ĭ-tў.   sō-cī'ĕ-tў.
u-tĭl'ĭ-tў.   prō-prī'ĕ-tў.
fā-cĭl'ĭ-tў.   va-rī'ĕ-tў.
ăc-tĭv'ĭ-tў.   ē-brī'ĕ-tў.
ac-clĭv'ĭ-tў.   gāy'ĕ-tў.
ăf-fĭn'ĭ-tў.   cŏn-trā-rī'ĕ-tў.
dū-plĭc'ĭ-tў.   nō-tō-rī'ĕ-tў.
pos-sĭ-bil'ĭ-tў.

Contrast No. 4. ĕnt and ănt.

con'ti-nent.   cŏn'so-nant.
el'e-ment.   el'e-gant.
gov'ern-ment.   cor'mo-rant.
em'i-nent.   ĕl'e-phant.
som'no-lent.   ăr'ro-gant.
judg'ment.   rĕc're-ant.
con-sist'ent.   mĕn'di-cant.
nu'tri-ment.   rĕs'o-nant.
al-lure'ment.   at-tĕnd'ant.
sen'ti-ment.   ĭn-cĕs'sant.
com'pli-ment.   ŏb-sĕrv'ant.
rep-re-sent'.   mil'i-tant.
tran-scend'ent.   mĭs'cre-ant.
tur'bu-lent.   ma-lig'nant.
firm'a-ment.   syc'o-phant.
de-lin'quent.   prot'est-ant.
com-po'nent.   dom'i-nant.
ru'di-ment.   con-vers'ant.
in'stru-ment.   in-con'stant.
im-per'ti-nent.   pur-su'ant.

ORTHOPHONY.

TABLE NO. 21.

Contrast No. 5. ŏr and ăr (given as ŭr.)

coun'sel-or.	cir'cu-lar.
góv'ern-or.	con'su-lar.
mē'dĭ-ā'tor.	sim'i-lar.
sĕn'a-tor.	mus'cu-lar.
ŭn-tē'rĭ-or.	jug'u-lar.
ĕx-tē'rĭ-or.	pop'u-lar.
ĭn-tē'rĭ-or.	in'su-lar.
sū-pē'rĭ-or.	gran'u-lar.
cŏm-pĕt'ĭ-tor.	sec'u-lar.
ĕx-ĕc'ū-tor.	par-tic'u-lar.
prĕd-ē-cĕs'sor.	ver-nac'u-lar.
ĭn-tĕr-cĕs'sor.	au-ric'u-lar.
lĕg-ĭs-lā'tor.	per-pen-dic'u-lar.

Contrast No. 6. ĭtĭve and ătĭve (given ātive).

pos'ĭ-tĭve.	cŏm-păr'ă-tĭve.
prĭm'ĭ-tĭve.	sū-për'lă-tĭve.
ĭn-fĭn'ĭ-tĭve.	ĭn-dĭc'ă-tĭve.
sens'ĭ-tĭve.	năr'ră-tĭve.
ĭn-quĭs'ĭ-tĭve.	dē-clăr'ă-tĭve.
len'ĭ-tĭve.	im-per'ă-tĭve.
de-fĭn'ĭ-tĭve.	de-riv'ă-tĭve.
in-tu'ĭ-tĭve.	re-stor'ă-tĭve.
in-trans'ĭ-tĭve.	pre-rŏg'ă-tĭve.

Contrast No. 7. ĕt and āte, etc.

vi'o-lĕt.	vi'o-lāte.
min'u-ĕt.	vin'di-cāte.
cab'ĭn-ĕt.	prĕl'āte.
vi'o-leñt.	vi'o-lāte.
sē'rĭ-ēs.	sē-rĭ-oŭs.
spē'cĭ-ēs.	spē'cĭ-oŭs.

PRONUNCIATION.

TABLE NO. 22.

Words in which *u* has the sound of *o* in *do* (see Rule for *U*, page 48):

true.	fruit.	intrude.	prune.
truly.	fruitful.	intrusion.	pruning.
imbrue.	fruitfulness.	truce.	sure.
construe.	rude.	spruce.	surety.
truth.	rudely.	ruse.	surely.
truthfully.	rudeness.	sprucely.	assurance.
truthfulness.	protrude.	abstruse.	insurance.
truism.	protrusion.		

Words in which *u* has the sound of *iew* in *view*:

due.	nudely.	induce.	presume.
duly.	purely.	conduce.	consume.
sue.	exude.	June.	tune.
suit.	interlude.	use.	tuning.
suited.	prelude.	useful.	pure.
suiting.	preclude.	usefully.	dual.
nude.	deduce.	illume.	lunar.

In preterits of verbs and participles, the *e* in *ed* is suppressed.

feared.	suppressed.	blessed.	picked.
praised.	stopped.	cursed.	winged.
admired.	soused.	learned.	toused.
tossed.	beloved.		

In adjectives not participial, the *e* in *ed* is sounded.

naked.	wretched.	learned.	soused.
ragged.	beloved.	winged.	confounded.
striped.	blessed.	toused.	abused.
wicked.	cursed.		

TABLE NO. 23.
Terminations *el* and *en*.

In the following words the last *e* should be suppressed:

hazel.	sunken.	burden.	shorten.
navel.	leaven.	garden.	seven.
ravel.	driven.	riven.	fallen.
shekel.	quicken.	even.	deepen.
shrivel.	thicken.	woven.	threaten.
swivel.	smitten.	tighten.	shaken.
weasel.	listen.	sicken.	open.
Lovel.	roughen.	silken.	weaken.
drivel.	spoken.	wooden.	taken.
grovel.	soften.	broken.	token.
mantel.	often.	swollen.	
ousel.	fasten.	leaden.	laden.
rivel.	deafen.	earthen.	harden.
shovel.	hasten.	glisten.	graven.
snivel.	raven.	kitten.	oven.
casel.	heaven.	stiffen.	given.
golden.	happen.	vixen.	frighten.
waxen.	waken.	dozen.	whiten.
frozen.	drunken.	sloven.	lighten.
molten.	gladden.		

In the following words the last *e* should be sounded:

vessel.	aspen.	gravel.	bitumen.
travel.	catechumen.	tinsel.	cerumen.
flannel.	chicken.	sorrel.	hymen.
chisel.	flāmen.	gospel.	hyphen.
kernel.	kitchen.	hovel.	latten.
revel.	legumen.	model.	linen.
level.	marten.	fuel.	mitten.
bevel.	mynchen.	chapel.	omen.
morsel.	hatter.	pommel.	platen.
laurel.	pollen.	towel.	regimen.
parcel.	siren.	trowel.	sloven.
marvel.	specimen.	rowel.	sudden.
tassel.	ticken.	vowel.	woolen.

Adjectives changed into adverbs by the addition of *ly*, the *ed* is often full, as confess'd, *confessedly*, design'd, *designedly*.

My is pronounced *mȳ* when emphatic, otherwise *mў* (not *mē*, as many seem to think), and *mine* is pronounced *mĭne* in common language, drama, etc., where sublimity does not require the full long sound of *i*, and when not emphatic.

The article or adjective *the* is pronounced *thē* (*thēe*) before a vowel or *h* mute, and *thu* (*thŭ*) before a consonant or *h* aspirate.

The article or adjective *a* has a short sound nearly like *a* in *at*.

So powerful is the influence of habit, that after systematic training pupils will frequently commit errors in articulation and enunciation when reading successive paragraphs. To remedy this, the teacher must return to the analyzing process, beginning by pronouncing every word of a sentence separately, then each syllable of the words, followed by the sounds in the syllables. (Class Methods, page 66.) William Russel gives a very excellent and similar mode of correction, viz., "Begin at the end of a line, sentence, or paragraph, so as to prevent the possibility of reading negligently; then, 1st, articulate every *element* in every word separately and very distinctly throughout the line or sentence; 2d, enunciate every *syllable* of each word throughout the line or sentence clearly and exactly; 3d, pronounce every *word* in the same style; 4th, read the *line* or *sentence* from the beginning forward, with strict attention to the manner of pronouncing every word; 5th, read the whole line or sentence with an easy, *fluent enunciation*, paying strict attention to the expression of *the meaning*, but without losing correctness in the style of pronunciation."

Pronunciation depends upon the law of prevailing good custom, hence is subject to changes from time to time. Notwithstanding this bar to a fixed standard of pronunciation, a few rules will be inserted to meet the demands of the pupils of this period. These rules are based upon the "Principles of Pronunciation" found in *Worcester's Unabridged Dictionary*, and will not conflict with those of Webster.

Rules for Pronunciation. Single Vowel Sounds.
1. A *final vowel* in an accented syllable has the *long* sound, as in bā-sis, lē-gal, trī-al, sonō'-rous, cū'-bic, tȳ-rant.
2. In *monosyllables* ending with *silent e*, preceded by a single consonant, vowels have usually the *long* sound, as in fāte, mete, pine, note, tube, type. Exceptions: hăve, ärc, and băde, the preterit of bid.
3. In *monosyllables* not ending with silent *e*, vowels generally take their *short* sound, as in făt, mĕt, pĭn, nŏt, tŭb.
4. In accented *syllables* ending with *consonants*, vowels usually take their short sounds, as in abăn'don, atten'tive, exhĭb'it, lacŏn'ic, relŭc'tant, lȳrical.

A.

5. *A, unaccented,* and ending a word, or constituting an unaccented syllable at the beginning of a word, has the sound of *a* in fäther, as Amer'icä, idéä. And *ah* final has still more of the Italian sound, as in Jehoväh, Messiäh. Exceptions: ā-ôr'-ta, ā-ē'rial, because followed by a vowel.
6. *A,* followed by *f, s,* or *n* in the same syllable, should receive an intermediate sound between short *a,* as in man, and the Italian *a,* as in fär. It is a sound shorter than ä, as gráss, gráft, commánd, pást.
7. *A, e, ai,* and sometimes *ea,* when followed by *r,* take the sound of short *e,* as in fare, whĕre, pair, bear. The sound is called by some an intermediate sound between short *a,* as in făt, and long *a,* as in āle, but is really long *a* modified by the succeeding *r,* and equal to short *e.*
8. *A,* preceded by *qu, w,* or *wh,* takes the sound of short *o* in nŏt, as in quality, swallow, wad, what.

E.

E, followed by *l* or *n* in an unaccented final syllable, has in some words an indistinct short sound, and in some it is entirely suppressed. (See page 45, List for Practice.) In most words ending in *el* the sound of *e* is given, as in flannel. And in most of those ending in *en* the sound of *e* is suppressed, as in oft-en.

The sound of the letter *e* is generally suppressed in the *preterits of verbs*, and in participles ending in *ed*, when the *e* is not preceded by *d* or *t*, as fearéd, praiséd.

Adjectives ending in *ed*, unless they are participles as well as adjectives, commonly preserve the sound of *e* before *d*, as in rag-ged, na-ked. See Table, page 44.

I.

That class of words, mostly derived from the French and Italian, which contain *i*, retain the sound of long *e*, as in antīque.

In words which terminate in *ile* or *ine*, with the accent on the penultimate syllable, the *i* in the final syllable is generally short, as in fertile, adamantine, etc. Exceptions: exile, Gentile, pentile, feline, confine, and a few others. Also, when the accent is on the *antepenult*, words ending in *ile* generally have the *i* short, as juvenile, puerile. Exceptions: chamomīle, reconcīle, eo'lipīle.

Words ending in *ity* usually require the final *i* and *y* short, as abĭlĭtў. Also the short sound of *e* and *y* in the termination *ety*, as variety. When *i* ends an initial syllable without accent, and the succeeding syllable begins with a consonant, the *i* is generally short, as in cĭvĭlĭty, dīvīne, fīnance. Exceptions: bīography, lībrarian, etc. See List, page 42.

O.

O, in monosyllables ending in *f*, *ft*, *ss*, *st*, and *th*, takes its short sound somewhat prolonged, as in off, often, cross, cost, broth.

In many words ending in *on* the sound of *o* is suppressed, as in bacon, pardon, reason.

U.

U at the beginning of words, when long, has the sound of *yu*, as in use.

U, preceded by *r* (also *ure* by *s*), has the sound of *o* in *do*, as in true, sure.

Vandenhoff, in "Art of Elocution," gives a more definite rule, as follows: *U* has the sound of *iew* in view in the syllables and terminations *ue, uit, ude, ucc, use, uke, ume, une, ure* (accen̈ted), *ual, ular, unar,* and *uble.* When any of the above combinations are compounded with *r,* or *s* with *ure, u* has the sound of *o* in *do.* See List, page 44.

Y.

Y at the end of a word, preceded by a consonant, has the sound of short *i,* as in pĭtў. The exceptions are monosyllables, as by, cry, etc.

Rules for Pronunciation. Improper Diphthongs.

Æ is a Latin diphthong, and is always pronounced like *e* in Latin. In English it is used only in words of Latin origin or formation, as aqua-vitæ, minutiæ, æsthetics, and commonly has the long sound, as in paëan, but is sometimes short, as in Daĕdalus.

Ai has usually the sound of long *a,* as in pail, pain, but has the sound of short *e* in said, saith, again, and against; that of short *a* in plăid and răillery; that of long *i* in aisle; and, in final unaccented syllables, it has the sound of indistinct short *i,* as in mountain, curtain, etc.

Ao occurs only in the word gaol, pronounced, as it is now more frequently written, jail.

Aw has the sound of broad *a;* bâwl and ball being pronounced exactly alike.

Ay has the sound of long *a,* as in pay, jay, hay, etc.; except in quay, which is pronounced *kē.* It has the short sound of *e* in says, and that of short *i* in Sunday, Monday.

Ea has the sound of long *e,* as in beat, hear; of short *e,* as in hĕad, lead; of short and obtuse *e,* as in ëarn, hëard, pëarl; of long *a,* as in break; of broad *a,* as in heärt, heärth; and, when unaccented, it has an obscure sound, as in vengeance.

Eau is only used in words derived from the French, and its regular sound is that of long *o,* as in beau and bureau. It has the sound of long *u* in beauty.

Ee has almost invariably the sound of long *e;* the principal exceptions are *been* and *breeches,* having the short sound of *i.* The poetical contractions e'er and ne'er, for ever

C

and never, are pronounced with the short sound of *e*, as ĕr, nĕr.

Ei. This diphthong has usually the sound of long *a* or *e*, as in neighbor, ceiling, etc. (See page 7.) It has the sound of long *i*, as in heighten; of short *e*, as in hĕifer; and in an unaccented syllable, the indistinct sound of *i*, as in foreign.

Eo has the sound of long *o*, as in yeŏman; like long *e*, as in pēople; like short *e*, as in jĕopardy; like broad *o* (as in nör), as in Geörgic; like long *u*, as in feod (now written feud); and when unaccented, it has the indistinct sound of *i* or *o*, as in pigeon.

Eu has the sound of long *u*, as in feud, deuce.

Ew has the sound of long *u*, as in few, new; but if *r* precedes it, it takes the sound of *o* (as in dô), as in brew, drew; and the sound of long *o*, as in sew, shew, strew. See *U,* page 48.

Ey has the sound of long *a* in bey, grey; of long *e* in key, ley; and when unaccented and final, it has the sound of short *i*, as in valley.

Ia, in the terminations *ial, ian, iard*, often forms but one syllable, the *i* being sounded like the consonant *y*, as in filial, Christian, poniard; pronounced as if written filyal, Christyan, etc. In some words it has the obscure sound of indistinct short *i*, as in carriage, marriage.

Ie, io, ieu, iew. The regular sound of *ie* is that of long *e*, as in chief. It has the sound of long *i* in die, lie; and the sound of short *e* in friend. When *i*, in the termination ion, is preceded by a liquid, it has the sound of yun, as in million and minion. The terminations *sion* and *tion* are pronounced shun, as in version, nation. But when the *t* is preceded by *s* or *x*, *ion* is pronounced yun, as in question and mixtion. The triphthong *ieu* is found only in a few words, which are derived from the French, as adieu, lieu; and it has the sound of long *u*. The triphthong *iew* occurs only in view and interview.

Oa. The regular sound of this diphthong is that of long *o*, as in bōat, lōaf; and the sound of broad *a* in broad and abroad.

Oe is derived from the Latin, and it is retained in but very few words used in English. It has the sound of short *e*, as in assafoĕt'ĭda; and that of long *e* in oēdinia, oēsoph'agus.

Oeu. This triphthong is found only in the word manôeuvre, where it has the sound of *o* in dô.

Oi and *oy* have one and the same sound, which is the combined sound of broad *a* and short *i* or *y*, as in böïl, töy̆.

Oo has the sound of *o* in do, as in moon, stoop; and also a shorter sound, like *u* in full, or *o* in wolf, as in good, book, wood, and foot; and the sound of long *o* in door, floor, and that of short *u* in blood and flood.

Ou is the most irregular diphthong in the language. Its most common or regular sound is that in which both letters are heard, as in bound, sound, cloud, south, etc. It has the sound of short *u* in country, cousin, couple, rough, and young. It has the sound of *o* in dô, as in accoutre, group, tour, surtout, uncouth, and other words derived from the French. It has the sound of long *o* in court, accourt, and the sound of broad *a*, as in bâll, or the sound of *o* in nör, in bought, brought, wrought; the sound of *u* in full, as in could, would, should; the sound of short *o* in hough.

Ow. The regular sound of this diphthong is the same as the regular sound of *ou*, as in how, bow, now, and tower. It has the sound of long *o* in below, blow, glow, owe, and show, besides the following words in some of their senses: bōw, lōw, mōw, mōwer, and sōw. It has the slight sound of *o* when it forms an unaccented syllable. ·

Ua. When both letters of this diphthong are sounded they have the power of *wa*, as in equal, language, persuade, and suavity. In some words the *u* is silent, as in guard, guardian, guarantee, piquant; and in victuals and victualing both letters are silent.

Ue. When these letters are united in a diphthong, and are both sounded, they have the power of *we*, as in conquest, consuetude, and desuetude. In some words the *u* is silent, as in guerdon, guess, and guest. When this diphthong is final, the *e* in many words is silent, as in due, hue, pursue; and in some words *both* letters are silent, as in league, fatigue, antique, opaque, and oblique. In the termination *ogue,* the *o* is short when preceded by *g* or *l*, as in demagŏgue, dialŏgue, except collōgue; but when any other consonant precedes *o* it is long, as in brōgue, rōgue, and vōgue.

Ui. These letters, when united in a diphthong, and both are sounded, have the power of *wi*, as in anguish, languid, and vanquish. In some words the *u* is silent, as in guide, guile, build, and guinea; and in others *i* is silent, as in juice, pursuit, and fruit.

Rules for Pronunciation. Consonants.

B, preceded by *m* in the same syllable, is generally silent, as in lamb, limb, comb, and dumb; exception, succumb. *B* is also silent before *t* in the same syllable, as in debt and doubt.

C is hard, and sounds like *k* before *a*, *o*, and *u*; and it is soft, and sounds like *s* before *e*, *i*, and *y*, except in sceptre and scirrhus, with their derivatives, in which *c* sounds like *k*. In the word indict and its derivatives *c* is silent. When *c* comes after the accent, and is followed by *ea*, *ia*, *io*, or *eous*, it takes, like *s* and *t* under the same circumstances, the sound of *sh*, as in social, ocean, tenacious, and cetaceous. In the words discern, sacrifice, and suffice, and in several words derived from them, also in the word sice, *c* has the sound of *z*.

D takes the sound of *t* in some words ending in *ed*, as in distressed, mixed, fixed, etc., pronounced distrest, mixt, and fixt.

F has always the same sound, except in the preposition of, in which it has the sound of *v*.

G is hard before *a*, *o*, and *u*. The only exception is *goal*, which is commonly written jail. When *g* is followed by *n* at the beginning of a word it is silent, as in gnarl, gnash, gnomon. It is also silent when followed by *n* at the end of a word: arraign, assign. *G* is sometimes hard and sometimes soft before *e*, *i*, and *y*. It is hard before *e*, as in geese, get, dagger; before *i* in gibber, gift, girl, gimp; before *y* in baggy, cloggy.

H is always silent after *r*, as in rheum, rhetoric, rhapsody.

K is always silent before *n*, as in knee, know.

M is never silent except in accompt, comptroller, pronounced, and also more commonly written, account, controller.

N has the sound of *ng* before *k*, *c*, *g* hard, *qu*, or *x*, as in thank, zinc, anger, banquet, and anxious. It is mute when it ends a syllable and is preceded by *l* or *m*, as in kiln, hymn, column, and autumn.

P is silent before *s* and *t* at the beginning of words, as in psalter, psalm.

Q is always followed by *u*, and *qu* has the sound of *kw*, as in queen, quill. In many words derived from the French it has the sound of *k*, as in etiquette, mosque, liquor.

S has always its sharp or hissing sound at the beginning of words, as in son, safe; also at the end of words when they terminate in *as*, except the words as, has, was, whereas, and the plural of nouns ending in *ea*, as seas, pleas. It is soft in all words ending in *ss*, as less, express; in words ending in *is*, except the monosyllables is and his; in all words ending in *us* and *ous*, as genius, famous; in all words when *s* is preceded by either of the mutes *k*, *p*, *t*, or by *f*, as locks, caps, hats, muffs. *S* final has the sound of *z* when it immediately follows any consonant except the mutes *k*, *p*, *t*, the semivowel *f* and *th* aspirated, as in ribs, heads; also when it forms an additional syllable with *e* before it; in the plural of nouns, and the third person singular of verbs ending in *se*, to distinguish them from nouns and adjectives of the same form, as use, abuse, close, diffuse. *S* takes the sound of *sh* in words ending in *sion* preceded by a consonant, as in diversion; also in a few other words: sugar, sumach, fissure, censure, seisure, sure, insure, pressure, sensual, nauseate, and tissue. *S* has the sound of *zh* in the termination *sion* preceded by a vowel, as in cohesion, evasion, and explosion.

T, like *s* and *c*, is aspirated when it comes immediately after an accent, and is followed by the vowels *ai*, *ie*, or *io*, taking the sound, in these cases, of *sh*, as in partial, patient, nation, militia, and negotiate.

W is always silent before *r*, as in write, wren, and wrist.

X has the sound of *ks* usually, as in excellent, expect, tax; also the sound of *gz* when the next syllable following begins with an accented vowel, as in exalt, exert. At the beginning of words it has the sound of z, as in Xenophon, Xerxes. *X* also takes the sound of *ksh* in some words when the accent immediately precedes it, as in fluxion, anxious, luxury, complexion.

Ch, preceded by *l* or *n*, has the sound of *sh* (some authors say *ch*, as in rich), as belch, filch. *Ch* has the sound of *k* in words derived from the ancient language, as in alchemy, anarchy, and anchor. Exceptions are charity, chart, charter. *Ch* is hard in all words in which it is followed by *l* or *r*, as Christian, chlorosis. When *arch*, signifying *chief*, begins a word from the Greek language, and is followed by a vowel, it is pronounced ark, as in archangel, architect; but when arch is prefixed to an English word, it is pronounced to rhyme with march. *Ch* is silent in drachm, schism, and yacht.

Gh. At the beginning of a word *h* is silent, as in ghost, ghastly, gherkin. In bough, *h* is silent at the end of a word. *Gh* is commonly silent at the end of words, as in high, sigh, and weigh. In some words it has the sound of *f*, as in tough, laugh; and in some the sound of *k*, as in hough, shough. In clough and slough it is sometimes silent, and sometimes has the sound of *f*. The combination of letters *ough* has no less than seven different sounds, which are exhibited in the following lines:

> " 'Tis not an easy task to show
> How *ough* sound: since, though
> An Irish lough and English slough,
> And cough and hiccough, all allow,
> Differ as much as bough and through,
> There seems no reason why they do."

Ght. In this termination the letters *gh* are always silent, as in fight, height; except in *draught*, which is pronounced, and in some of its senses written, *draft*.

Ph has generally the sound of *f*, as in philosophy. In nephew (according to the principal English orthoepists) and in Stephen it has the sound of *v*, and in the triphthong naphtha, etc., the *h* is silent (năp'tha or năf'tha).

Th at the beginning of words is generally sharp, as

ORTHOPHONY. 55

in thin, think (see page 35, List for Lispers), and also at the end of words, as in death, breath. In some nouns it is sharp in the singular and flat in the plural, as in bath, baths, lath, laths. In some words the *h* is silent, as in Thomas, thyme.

Wh. In some words the *w* is silent, as in who, whole.

READING EXERCISES.
ARTICULATION AND PRONUNCIATION.

1. It was indū'bĭtably an abom'inable eccentric'ity.
2. Up a high hill he heaved a huge round stone.
3. The glassy glă'cĭers gleamed in glowing light.
4. The invin'cĭble duplĭc'ĭty of inquĭs'ĭtĭve men.
5. The list'lĕssnĕss and la'zinĕss of the friv'olŏŭs.
6. Ev'ery gov'ernment has its his'tōry.
7. The el'emĕnts of our language inclūde con'sonănts.
8. Coun'selŏrs should be partic'ulărly sūpe'riŏr.
9. Round and round the rugged rocks the ragged rascal ran.
10. The stripling stranger strayed straight toward the struggling stream.
11. The incomprehensĭbĭl'ĭty of the ar'ticle, etymolog'ically considered, is ev'ĭdĕnt.
12. It was a famĭly ōpĭn'ĭon majes'tĭcally expressed.
13. The manifesta'tions of force are vĭs'ĭble, relī'ăble, and rea'sonăble.
14. A big black bug bit a big black bear.
15. Socks and shoes shock Susan. (*Repeat.*)
16. Truly rural, truly rural rationalist.
17. Feb'ruary and Jūne, Feb'ruary and June.
18. (*Quick.*) Peter Prangle, the prickly prangly pear-picker, picked three pecks of prickly prangly pears from the prangly pear-trees on the pleasant prairies.
19.   "Amidst the mists, with angry boasts,
   He thrusts his fists against the posts,
   And still insists he sees the ghosts."
20. The vile vag'abond ven'tured to vĭl'ĭfy the ven'erăble vet'eran.

21. (*Quick.*) Thĕŏph'ĭlŭs Thistle, the successful thistle-sifter, in sifting a sieve full of unsifted thistles, thrust three thousand thistles through the thick of his thumb. Now, if Theoph'ilus Thistle, the successful thistle-sifter, in sifting a sieve full of unsifted thistles, thrust three thousand thistles through the thick of *his* thumb, see that *thou*, in sifting a sieve full of unsifted thistles, thrust not three thousand thistles through the thick of *thy* thumb. Success to the successful thistle-sifter.

22. Masses of immense mag'nitude move majes'tĭcălly through the vast empire of the solar system.

23. She uttered a sharp, shrill shriek, and shrunk from the enshrouded shrine.

24. The mis'erăble accom'panĭmĕnt is unnĕc'ĕssary and intol'erăble.

QUALITIES OF VOICE.

1. Pure Tone.

"I love my country's pine-clad hills,
Her thousand bright and gushing rills,
Her sunshine and her storms;
Her rough and rugged rocks, that rear
Their hoary heads high in the air
In wild fantastic forms."

2. Orotund.

"'Drink,' said the demon, 'drink your fill;
Drink of these waters mellow;
They'll make your eyeballs sear and dull,
And turn your white skins yellow;
They'll fill your homes with care and grief,
And clothe your backs with tatters;
They'll fill your hearts with evil thoughts—
But, never mind, what matters?'"—MACKAY.

3. Pectoral.

"The skies they were ashen and sober,
The leaves they were crisped and sear,
The leaves they were withering and sear.
It was night in the lonesome October
(Of my most immemorial year),
It was hard by the dim lake of Auber,
In the misty mid-region of Wier—
It was down by the dank tarn of Auber,
In the ghoul-haunted woodland of Wier."—POE.

4. *Guttural.*

"Thou slave, wretch, coward."

"I'll strip you of your commission;
I'll lodge a five-and-threepence in the hands of trustees, and you shall live on the interest.
I'll disown you; I'll disinherit you; and hang me if ever I call you Jack again while I live."—SHERIDAN.

5. *Aspirate.*

" 'Twere better by far
To have matched our fair cousin with young Lochinvar."—SCOTT.

"Or whispering with white lips,
The foe—they come—they come!"—BYRON.

6. *Nasal.*

" 'The birds can fly,
An' why can't I?
Must we give in,'
Says he, with a grin,
'That the blue-bird an' phœbe
Are smarter 'n we be?
Jest fold our hands, an' see the swaller
An' blackbird an' catbird beat us holler?' "—TROWBRIDGE.

7. *Oral.*

"She 'perfectly scorned the best of his clan,
And reckoned the ninth of any man
An exceedingly vulgar fraction.'
He 'quite regretted the step, 'twas true—
The lady had pride enough for two;
But that alone would never do
To quiet the butcher and baker.' "—SAXE.

8. *Falsetto.*

"Do, good people, move on; such a rabble of boys!
I'll break every bone of 'em I come near;
Go home—you're spilling the porter—
Go home, Tommy Jones, go along with your beer.
This is the sorrowfulest day of my life,
Ever since my name was Betty Morgan."—HOOD.

Note.—To overcome a monotonous habit of delivery, read alternate lines of a poem in the pure tone, contrasted with another quality of voice, as the pure with the orotund, the pure with the aspirate or nasal. For personation, give each character in a dialogue or drama a particular quality of voice as his own.

PITCH.

Scale Exercise.

do. ◐ High worth is elevated place.
si. ◐ High worth is elevated place.
la. ◐ High worth is elevated place.
sol. ◐ High worth is elevated place.
fa. ◐ High worth is elevated place.
mi. ◐ High worth is elevated place.
re. ◐ High worth is elevated place.
do. ◐ High worth is elevated place.

Note.—Repeat each note of the scale four times, beginning with the lowest: Do, do, do, do, re, re, re, re, etc. When the octave has been completed, reverse the exercises, and repeat them, beginning with the *highest* note of the scale. Next repeat the sentence in each of the keys from the lowest to the highest, and from the highest to the lowest, remembering to keep the reading voice.

Reading upon the Scale in Lines.

"Like to the falling of a star,
Or as the flights of eagles are;
Or like the fresh Spring's gaudy hue,
Or silver drops of morning dew;
Or like a wind that chafes the flood,
Or bubbles which on water stood—
E'en such is man, whose borrowed light
Is straight called in and paid to-night:
The wind blows out, the bubble dies;
The Spring entombed in Autumn lies;
The dew dries up, the star is shot,
The flight is past, and man forgot."—KING.

Note.—Begin with the lowest note of the voice, and read each line one note higher than the one before, until you reach that point in your voice where it is said to "break" or change to the falsetto. You may not be able to reach an octave at first, but after a few weeks' steady, careful practice you will probably be able to read upon any key within the compass of an octave and a half.

Reverse this exercise, and read down from the highest to

the lowest note of the voice. Fifteen minutes' practice, without rest, is enough.

Reading upon the Scale in Syllables.
"Then fear not, doubt not, which thou wilt,
    We'll try this quarrel hilt to hilt."

Note.—Practice this, or any other couplet of monosyllables, raising the pitch *one note* on every syllable. Reverse, and read down the scale. See Table 10.

Monotone.
1. "O thou that rollest above, round as the shield of my fathers! whence are thy beams, O sun! thy everlasting light?"—OSSIAN.
2.   "High on a throne of royal state, which far
        Outshone the wealth of Ormus or of Ind,
        Or where the gorgeous East, with richest hand,
        Showers on her kings barbaric pearls and gold,'
        Satan exalted sat!"—MILTON.
3. Wisdom (*Job* xxviii., 12) is also a fine example of the monotone.

Drifting, full Rising and Falling Inflections.
"*He* never *dines* with *comfort*, | but WHERE he is SURE to create a FAMINE; | *he* never *robs* from the loose superfluity of standing *greatness;* | HE devours the FALLEN, the INDIGENT, the NECESSITOUS; | his *extortion* is not like the generous rapacity of the princely *eagle*, who snatches away the *living*, struggling *prey;* | HE is a VULTURE who feeds upon the PROSTRATE, the DYING, and the DEAD."

Note.—Read this example with a strong rising inflection on the words in italic, and a full falling inflection on the words in small capitals, as an exercise in sweeping inflections of a fifth or an octave.

Words in Antithesis take opposite Inflections.
1. "I said an *elder* soldier', not a *better'*."
2. "It is *sown* in *weakness';* it is *raised* in *power'*. It is *sown* a *natural* body'; it is *raised* a *spiritual* body'."

3. "I come to *bury*` Cæsar, not to *praise'* him."

4. "The *king*` was without *power'*, and the *nobles'* without *principle*`. They were *tyrants*` at *home'*, and *robbers' abroad*`."

5. "We live in *deeds*, not *years*—in *thoughts*, not *breath*—in *feelings*, not in *figures on a dial.* We should count time by *heart-throbs.* He *most lives* who THINKS THE MOST—FEELS THE NOBLEST—ACTS THE BEST."

6. "*You* have done the *mischief,* and *I* bear the *blame.*"

7. "The *wise man* is happy when he gains his *own* approbation; the *fool* when he gains that of *others.*"

Words in Apposition take the same Inflection.

1. "Oh *comrades*`! *warriors*`! *Thracians*`! if we must fight, let us fight for ourselves! If we must slaughter, let us slaughter our oppressors."

2. *Thomas Moore'*, the *poet'*, was born in Dublin in 1780.

Climax.

1. "If I were an American, while a foreign troop were landed in my country, I never would lay down my arms—NEVER, NEVER, *never!*"—EARL OF CHATHAM.

2. "In a clamorous appealing to the mercy of the fire,
In a mad expostulation with the deaf and frantic fire."—POE.

3. "Clarence has come! *false!* FLEETING! PERJURED *Clarence!*"

Irony.

"Oh excellent interpreter of the laws! master of antiquity! corrector and amender of our Constitution!"—CICERO.

Compound Inflection.

"I knew when seven justices could not make up a quarrel; but when the parties met themselves, one of them thought but of an *if;* as, 'If you said sŏ, then I said sô.' 'Oh ho! did you say sŏ?' So they shook hands and were sworn brothers."

"Must I budge; must I observe you;
Must I stand and crouch under your testy humor?"

FORCE.
Rhythmical Accent.
"Pause' not to dream' of the fu'ture before' us,
Pause' not to weep' the wild cares' that come o'er' us :
Hark' how Crea'tion's deep mu'sical cho'rus
Un'intermitting goes up' into heav'en!
Nev'er the o'cean-wave stops' in its flow'ing;
Nev'er the lit'tle seed stops' in its grow'ing;
More' and more rich'ly the rose'-heart keeps glow'ing
Till' from its nour'ishing stem' it is riv'en."—OSGOOD.

Absolute Emphasis.
1. "What *destiny* sends, bear."—HERDER.
2. "There is nothing more *fearful* than imagination without taste."—GOETHE.

Antithetic Emphasis.
1. "Be noble-minded! Our own *heart*, and not other men's *opinions* of us, forms our true honor."—SCHILLER.
2. "What makes old age so sad is not that our *joys*, but that our *hopes* cease."—RICHTER.

Emphasis of Emotion.
1.   "STAND! *the ground's your* OWN, my braves—
       Will ye give it up to *slaves?*
       Will ye look for *greener graves?*
       Hope ye mercy still?
       What's the mercy *despots* feel?
       Hear it in that *battle-peal*—
       Read it on yon *bristling steel*—
              Ask it—*ye who will!*"—PIERPONT.

2.   "UP, *comrades*, UP! in Rokeby's halls
       Ne'er be it said our courage falls!"

3.   "'HOLD!' tyranny cries; but their resolute breath
       Sends back the reply, 'INDEPENDENCE or DEATH!'"

Cumulative Emphasis.
1. "The Union—it MUST AND SHALL BE PRESERVED."
2. "Heaven for HARRY, ENGLAND, and ST. GEORGE!"
3. "CHARGE, Chester, CHARGE! ON, STANLEY, ON!"

STRESS.

1. Radical Stress.
"Hence, horrible shadow!
Unreal mockery, hence!"

2. Final Stress.
"Too much horrified to speak,
They can only shriek—shriek."
"What! you threaten us? Do your worst;
Blow your pipe, there, till you burst."

3. Median Stress.
"Roll on, thou deep and dark blue ocean, roll."

(⁄) "The loud wind dwindled to a whisper low,
And sighed for pity as it answered (>) 'No.'"

"The loud waves, rolling in perpetual flow,
Stopped for a while, and sighed for answer (*dim. in swells*) 'No!'

4. Thorough Stress.
"Flash'd all their sabres bare,
Flash'd as they turned in air,
Sabring the gunners there,
Charging an army, while
All the world wonder'd:
Plunged in the battery-smoke,
Right through the line they broke;
Cossack and Russian
Reeled from the sabre-stroke
Shattered and sundered.
Then they rode back, but not,
Not the six hundred."

5. Compound Stress.
"Gone to be married! gone to swear a peace!
False blood to false blood joined! gone to be friends!
Shall Louis have Blanche, and Blanche these provinces?"

6. Tremor.
"If they should fire on Pickens, let the colonel in command
Place me upon the ramparts, with the flag-staff in my hand.
No odds how hot the cannon-smoke, or how the shells may fly,
I'll hold the stars and stripes aloft, and hold them till I die.
I'm ready, general, so you let a post to me be given
Where Washington can see me as he looks from highest heaven,
And say to Putnam at his side, or may be General Wayne,
'There stands old Billy Johnson, that fought at Lundy's Lane.'"

TIME, OR SPEED.

1. *Fast.*
"Away! away! our fires stream bright
Along the frozen river,
And their arrowy sparkles of brilliant light
On the forest branches quiver."

(*Rit.*) {"There was racing and chasing on Cannobie Lea,
But the lost bride of Netherby ne'er did we see."

2. *Moderate.*
"Oh, sweet and beautiful is night,
When the silver moon is high,
And countless stars like clustering gems
Hang sparkling in the skies;
While the balmy breath of the summer breeze
Comes whispering down the glen,
And one fond voice alone is heard—
Oh! night is lovely then."

3. *Slow.*
"He is gone on the mountain, he is lost to the forest,
Like a summer-dried fountain, when our need was the sorest;
The fount, reappearing, from the rain-drops shall borrow,
But to us comes no cheering, to Duncan no morrow.
The hand of the reaper takes the ears that are hoary,
But the voice of the weeper wails manhood in glory;
The autumn winds, rushing, waft the leaves that are serest,
But our flower was in flushing when blighting was nearest.
Like the dew on the mountain, like the foam on the river,
Like the bubble on the fountain, thou art gone, and forever."

Long Pause.

Pause a moment. (5) I heard a footstep. (6) Listen now. (10) I heard it again, (4) but it is going from us. (4) It sounds fainter, (8) still fainter, (2) it is gone.

Short Pause.

John, be quick. (1) Get some water. (1) Throw the powder overboard. (3) "It can not be reached." (1) Jump into the boat, then. (1) Shove off. (1) There goes the powder. (1) Thank heaven! we are safe.

Note.—The figures denote the number to count at each pause.

MODULATION.

Abbreviated Signs for marking Sentences.

Origin.	Sign.	Meaning.	Origin.	Sign.	Meaning.
Adagio,	ad., or v. sl.,	very slow.	Crescendo,	<	incr's'g force.*
Largo,	lar., or sl.,	slow.	Diminuendo,	>	dimin'g force.*
Andante,	adt.,	middle time.		l., or (o),	low.
Presto,	prs., or q.,	quick.		md., or (o),	middle.
Prestissimo,	prss., or v.q.,	very quick.		h., or (°),	high.
Accelerando,	acc.,	quickening.		tr., or ~~~,	tremulously.
Ritard,	rit.,	slackening.		pl.,	plaintively.
Pianissimo,	pp.,	very soft.		asp.,	aspirate.
Piano,	p.,	soft.	Affetuoso,	fts., or af.,	affectionately.
Mezzo,	mz.,	moderate.	Brillante,	brl., or br.,	brilliantly, gay.
Forte,	f.,	loud.	Furioso,	frs., or fr.,	fiercely, mad.
Fortissimo,	ff.,	very loud.	Spirituoso,	spt., or sp.,	spirited.

(*Slow.*)   "At length, o'er Columbus slow consciousness breaks—
(*Loud and*   { 'LAND! LAND!' (*Moderate*) cry the sailors; (*Loud*) 'LAND!
High.)   LAND!'—he awakes—
(*Fast.*)   He runs—yes! behold it! it blesseth his sight!
(*Spirited.*)   THE LAND! *Oh dear spectacle! transport! delight!*"

(*pp.*) { "Soft is the strain when zephyr gently blows,
       And the smooth stream in smoother numbers flows;
(*ff.*) { But when loud surges lash the sounding shore,
       The hoarse, rough verse should like the torrent roar."
(*Slow.*) { "When Ajax strives some rock's vast weight to throw,
       The line, too, labors, and the words move slow;
(*Fast.*) { Not so when swift Camilla scours the plain,
       Flies o'er the unbending corn, and skims along the main."
                                                                                                 POPE.

(*High and*   { "Go ring the bells and fire the guns,
Quick.)   And fling the starry banner out;
               Shout 'FREEDOM' till your lisping ones
               Give back the cradle shout."—WHITTIER.

(*Slow.*)   "Through glades and glooms the mingled measure stole,
(*Moderate.*)   Or o'er some haunted stream, with fond delay
(*Low and Soft.*)   (Round a holy calm diffusing,
(*Very Soft.*)   Love of peace and lonely musing),
(>)   In hollow murmurs died away."

         "He said, and on the rampart heights arrayed
         His trusty warriors, few, but undismayed;
(*Slow.*)   Firm-paced and slow, a horrid front they form,
(*Soft.*)   Still as the breeze, (*Loud*) but dreadful as the storm!
(*Low.*)   Low murmuring sounds along their banners fly,
(*Low & Loud.*)   'REVENGE, or DEATH!'—the watchword and reply;
(*High & Loud.*)   Then pealed the notes omnipotent to charm,
(*Moderate.*)   And the loud tocsin tolled their last alarm!"—CAMPBELL.

---

* These signs, when placed *before* a line, apply to the entire line.

PART II.
CLASS METHODS.

PRIMARY READING.

PRIMARY reading may be taught *analytically*, by beginning with words, and concluding with their component elements (sounds and letters), or *synthetically*, by beginning with the elements (sounds and letters), and concluding with words and sentences.

In these methods the teacher will need a blackboard, and a greater or less number of the following articles, viz., real-objects, picture-objects, word-objects, slates, cards, charts, and books, according to the method employed. The blackboard is indispensable in any method, and if used, each pupil in the class should have a slate, with a pencil and bit of sponge attached. In ungraded schools, the slates serve to occupy and amuse the small children while the teacher is engaged with older classes. They can, in the time thus occupied, learn to print, write, draw simple objects, or very profitably occupy their time in inventive drawing.

The *real object* employed must correspond with the picture and word objects selected for the lesson. The *picture-objects* will be found in primers, cards, and various books, and all should be fair representations of the objects whose corresponding words are to be learned. The *word-objects* should at first consist of two or three letters only, none of which should be silent, and should be such words as are capable of representation or demonstration, as bat, cat, hat, up, on, in. The teacher may print the word upon the blackboard for the class, or it may be shown from a primer, card, or chart. The primary methods should continue until the pupil can read and print from memory any simple sentence of monosyllables or dissyllables.

The following *rules*, derived from the principles of teaching as advanced by Pestalozzi, may serve as a guide to many young persons who desire to make teaching a profession.

1. Never tell a child what he can discover for himself.
2. One difficulty at a time to overcome, and but one.
3. The measure of information is not what the teacher can give, but what the child can receive.
4. Accustom the child to do. Educate the hand.
5. Develop an idea, and then give the term.
6. Proceed from the known to the unknown, from the particular to the general, from the concrete to the abstract, from the simple to the more difficult.

Note.—Require the pupils to express themselves in complete terms, leaving no part of a sentence to be understood; never accepting nods, yes or no, as replies.

ANALYTICAL OR OBJECTIVE METHODS.

The analytical or objective method takes the name "objective" from its dependence upon the use of objects to introduce the lessons, and "analytical" because a word is first learned as a whole, and then analyzed or reduced to its primary elements.

Each lesson of one word is arranged something like the following plan; then, when a sentence can be formed from the words that have been thus learned, it should be done. At first no letter should receive more than one sound. The vowels should take their short sounds, afterward their long sounds, the remaining ones last.

ORDER OF THE OBJECTIVE PLAN.

1st. Show a *real object*, or illustrate or demonstrate a word, and draw out its name, nature, qualities, parts, and uses. Be sure to allow each pupil the opportunity to tell all he or she connectedly can about the object, without prompting or questioning. If the class be large, divide the work, allowing *A* to give its name and nature, *B* its qualities, *C* its parts, and *D* its uses, in order to get through the work in the allotted time.

2d. Show the class a picture (object) representing the real object, and draw from the pupils the points of resemblance, difference, etc.

3d. Show the class a word (object) representing the real

and picture objects. Draw out a description of the word as to outline; then require the pupils to discover and point out duplicates of this word from the cards, charts, or books. Continue this exercise until the pupils can recognize the word readily at sight.

4th. Require each pupil to produce sentences containing the word of the lesson until the *use* of the word is perfectly understood.*

5th. Print the word upon the board, and explain its separate elements (letters or sounds) as to the formation of the word—how the sounds are produced, whether with the lips, tongue, teeth, or palate principally. Let each pupil copy the letters (from memory) upon the blackboard or upon the slate. Pronounce the word slowly, so that each element can be distinguished singly; then increase in rapidity of pronunciation. Reverse the time, and require the class to follow in the phonic spelling.

6th. Combine words that have been learned into sentences, and print them upon the board, requiring the class to make out the sentences alone.

7th. Allow the pupils to select word-cards, and to combine them so as to make sentences. If word-cards are not in use, the pupils may be detailed in groups to reproduce a whole sentence upon the board or upon their slates, and afterward correct them, as in Nos. 5 and 6, page 68.

Note.—Before class-hour the teacher should select the word or words which will constitute the lesson, and have ready the necessary illustrations. If the words can be illustrated by the real object, in or out of doors, arrangement should be made to do so. If it must be illustrated by other means, preparation should be made that nothing be omitted that will aid in giving a clear perception of the meaning and use of the word. The words in, out, under, over, more, less, etc., are words simple enough when developed by comparison, experiment, and reason.

---

* The teacher should not go too rapidly with these steps. Here is work enough for weeks and months. The work of the fifth step may be postponed until many words are learned as sight-words, both in print and as reproduced upon the slates and board.

Objects should be presented—
1st, to the senses, or perception.
2d, to the laws of memory.
3d, to the reflective or reasoning powers.

Ideas are developed—
1st, by appealing to the senses.
2d, by comparison.
3d, by experiment.
4th, by reason.

SYNTHETICAL METHODS.

There are three synthetical class methods: Memorizing letters in selections of two, three, etc., which will make one or more words; memorizing letters in alphabetic order; and the phonic or phonetic method.

MEMORIZING LETTERS IN GROUPS OR SELECTIONS.

1st. Short vowels and a few consonants.
2d. Long vowels and a few consonants.
3d. Other vowel sounds and consonants.

This is a very good method, and is employed by many excellent primary teachers. The lessons may be given in about the following order, varying, of course, to suit the material and apparatus at hand.

1st. Select two or three letters which, when joined, will produce a word or words.

2d. Print the first of these letters sufficiently large upon the blackboard to be seen by the entire class.

3d. Let the class give the sound of the letter; its form and resemblance to some familiar object.

4th. Detail the class in groups òr divisions suited to the size of the board, to reprint or copy the letter and give its sound.

5th. Obtain criticisms from the class by comparing each copy with the original printed letters, and have all errors corrected by the pupil who made them.

6th. Let the class reproduce the letter upon their slates. The teacher will examine the slates, and copy the mistakes upon the board for the class to correct. After correction, the pupils should examine their respective slates, and note how many errors are their own. The slate review should be entirely from memory.

7th. Detail several to find the same or duplicate letters among the letter-cards, upon the charts, or in books.

8th. When all the selected letters have been learned, put them together to form words.

9th. Write or print the word upon the board, to be criticised by class divisions as were the letters before.

10th. Let the word be reviewed upon the slate without a copy, and criticised as was the former slate exercise.

11th. Require each pupil to originate a sentence containing the word.

12th. If the letters can be arranged so as to form another simple word or words, it may be done at this point of the lesson, and each of the words thus formed be treated as the first word.

13th. The class should be trained upon the sounds of the letters in succession, as arranged in the tabular view.

14th. Require the pupils to point out or mark the silent letters in words.

15th. Sometimes the form can be impressed by uniting instruction and amusement. Make the capital letters upon the board; then give each pupil two cuts of straw or sticks, to make as many of these simple capitals as can be made with two lines. When they have made L, T, V, X, give each one more, and have A, E, F, H, I, K, N, Y, Z, and with another add M and W. The remaining letters with curved lines they will soon learn to make.

Card and Chart Lessons.

The following method of teaching selections of letters by means of cards and charts alone has been so successfully employed in teaching small classes, that it deserves a place among the best methods of teaching primary reading. Give each member of the class a letter-card, whispering its sound, charging them to remember, but not to reveal to any one else. When they have had time to memorize the shape, collect the cards, and call the class one by one to select from the cards on the table the letter which they held, or point out a similar one on the chart. When a child has learned two letters that will make a word, as ox, give the name of the word, then prefix *b* for box, *f* for fox, etc. In this way a great many words may be learned by changing the initial or terminal letter.

When a number of letters are known by the whole class, one may be sent to the chart to point out and name letters that will make words, as s, a, t, sat; h, a, t, hat; b, a, t, bat; c, a, t, cat; r, a, t, rat. Let the one at the chart spell in this manner (by sound) as many words as he can; the one, however, who first observes a mistake to supersede the one at the chart. Another instructive amusement is to allow the class to select letters from the cards or blocks that will build words found upon the word-chart.

Memorizing Letters in Alphabetical Order.

This method is now entirely abandoned, other and better methods having been adopted in its place.

PHONIC OR PHONETIC.

Phonetics, phonics, or phonology is the science of representing the elements of language.

A *phonograph* is a graphic or written sign, a distinct letter to represent a unit of speech, and always one and the same unit of speech or vocal sound.

Phonography is writing by phonographs, and is long or short.

"Phonetic long-hand, or long-hand phonography, is writing produced with a phonetic alphabet, consisting of most of the ordinary script letters, and additional ones of the same general character for the additional sounds."

Stenography, or short-hand phonography, is a term expressing extreme brevity of word-signs founded on the phonographic system of sounds and signs.

The phonic or phonetic method of teaching primary classes may be made analytical or synthetical, according to the desire of the teacher.

This method, although founded upon reason and common sense, has as yet but indifferently succeeded.

It is based upon the principle that every distinct unit of speech or elementary sound of a language should have a corresponding sign. The English language is composed of thirty-four or thirty-six sounds, and hence should have thirty-four or thirty-six signs or letters to represent those sounds. Then every word would be pronounced as it is spelled, and spelled without silent letters.

In the phonic or phonetic method, pupils who have learned these corresponding sounds and signs will have no trouble in pronouncing a word when seen in print, or spelling words properly pronounced.

Phonography would save much time and labor when contrasted with the present English orthography, in which pronunciation is learned orally or from the dictionary.

Some learned philologists object to the change, because, in their opinion, the language would lose its etymology, which is chiefly known from the spelling. But we could not lose the origin of the words if the present orthography were placed immediately after the words in the dictionaries; and this would add but one link more to the chain of etymological study, while it would save time and labor for the student.

The nearest approach to a strictly phonetic method in elementary instruction, consistent with accepted orthography and the printed characters in common use, is the following, which has been used and approved by some of our best primary teachers. The teacher, taking a single word, as *map*, brings out the *oral elements*, showing on the board how each one is represented by printed characters. Let the marks be those of some standard authority, using them with such letters as represent more than one sound.

When these characters are learned so as to be read and written, take another word with not more than *one new character*, as *n* in *man*. Proceed in this manner, requiring the pupil to write the characters for the sounds previously given. As soon as enough characters are given to make new familiar words, as with the above, we may make map and pan; let them be printed on the board, and copied by the children for the next lesson. Continue thus with the short sound of *a* in words of three letters; follow with the short sounds of the other vowels in monosyllables having no silent letters, then with the other sounds of the vowels, until all the characters and elementary sounds are learned. Silent letters may be marked with a line underneath.

Thus we have a complete phonetic system for learning to read words. As soon as possible, omit the marks, and let the letters and orthographic spelling be learned in connection with the phonetic. When words occur (like *they*) in which the sounds are not represented by any marks given, they may be spelled with the common letters, and the pronunciation given with phonetic characters in parenthesis (*thā*). To write sentences before the sounds can all be presented to the class, a few words may be printed on the board, and learned as *sight words*.

See Introduction to Selections.

TABLE NO. 24.
READING-CLASS FORMULA.*

I. PRELIMINARY EXERCISES.† (Time from one to five minutes.)
Vocal Gymnastics:
1. Pronouncing words.‡
2. Analyzing words.‡
3. Phonic spelling.‡
4. Learning some fact in elocution, or practicing the tables in Orthophony.

Calisthenics or Gesture. (See page 76.)

II. SELECTIONS OR LITERARY PRODUCTIONS.‡ (To be read according to any of the standard methods described on pages 78 to 81.)

III. REVIEWS.
Of the selections (page 89):
1. The form and manner‡ (prose or poetry, etc., page 86, 89).
2. The thought or subject‡ (pastoral, historical, etc., page 86, 89).
3. The objects (their names, natural or artificial, etc.).
4. The incidents.
5. The meaning of words (technical or received).
6. The moral or the personal application.

Of the errors of pupils in—
1. Reading position. (See page 24.)
2. Articulation. (See pages 34 to 44.)
3. Pronunciation. (See pages 44 to 54.)
4. Phonic spelling. (See page 75.)
5. Definition. (See note, page 75.)
6. Elocution (general or particular faults).

IV. PORTIONS OF COMPOSITION TO MEMORIZE.‡ (See page 86.)

V. EXAMINATION OF THE ADVANCE LESSON.‡ (See page. 87)

* This Formula can, by attention to the capacity of the pupils, be adapted to any class in reading that has mastered monosyllables. The younger classes should receive *drill* in elocution, but not facts or rules, and the review should be simplified.

† The preliminary exercises should not occupy more than five minutes in any class; and if the time for recitation be less than 20 minutes, then one or two minutes only should be used.

‡ This sign is placed after such exercises, etc., in the Formula as can not well be omitted.

D

EXPLANATION OF THE FORMULA.
I. PRELIMINARY EXERCISES.

The reading hour having arrived, the pupils should quietly put their desks in order, and repair to the recitation seats with all necessary articles for the hour, as readers, slates, etc.

The *preliminary* exercises should not exceed five minutes' duration in a primary or collegiate class, and if the exercises are carried on briskly, as they should be, little or no uneasiness will be manifested.

No. 1. *Pronouncing Words.*

A list of such words as are most frequently mispronounced or badly articulated in the class-room should be jotted down, and a few of them pronounced each class-time to begin the preliminary exercises. The class should repeat them in concert after the models produced by the teacher. Let this be done accurately and rapidly. These words may be placed upon the upper corner of a blackboard, and new ones added, until a column is obtained for practice. The hardest words in or over the lesson may be substituted for those upon the blackboard.

Again, for variety, the pupils may alternate in pronouncing words from the book or from the board, either in class-divisions or with the teacher.

(Ex. of repetition.) *Teach.* Amidst', amidst'. *Pupils.* Amidst', amidst'.

(Ex. of alternation.) *Class.* Carelĕss'. *Lazy Pupils.* Listlĕssnĕss'.

(Ex. of alternation.) *Teach.* Civĭlĭty'. *Class.* Piĕty'. (See Lists of Words, pages 41, 43.)

No. 2. *Analyzing Words.*

Words may be analyzed by syllable or by sound. To analyze by syllable, first pronounce the whole word, then repeat it, leaving off the first syllable; repeat again, leaving off the second syllable; so continue until the last syllable. To analyze by sound, pronounce the whole word, and repeat it, leaving off the first sound at each repetition, until one sound remains alone.

Examples.

By Syllables.

Cŏm-mū-nĭ-cā-bĭl′ĭ-ty.
-mu-nĭ-cā-bĭl′ĭ-ty.
-nĭ-cā-bĭl′ĭ-ty.
-cā-bĭl′ĭ-ty.
-bĭl′ĭ-ty.
-ĭ-ty.
-ty.

Gov-ern-ment.
-ern-ment.
-ment.

By Sounds.

Strangl'dst.
trangl'dst.
rangl'dst.
angl'dst.
ngl'dst.
gl'dst.
l'dst.
dst.
st.'
t.

band.
and.
nd.
d.
Coughing.*
oughing.
ghing.
ing.
ng.

No. 3. Phonic Spelling.

It is not thought advisable to require orthographical spelling in the reading hour,† but phonic spelling instead. The teacher should pronounce a word, and the pupils repeat it and spell it by sound in concert. In order to detect individual errors, the words may be spelled by the pupils successively. It is better, in phonic spelling, to mark the division of syllables by pauses instead of repetitions, as has been our custom. The syllabic divisions will thus be retained, and much valuable time saved. Of course the silent letters are omitted in phonic spelling, and, if the teacher finds it difficult to discover and produce the true sounds of

---

* If any silent letters occur in the word you wish to analyze, of course you will omit them, since you are spelling by sound, and silent letters have no sound. The pupils will do better to look at the teacher, while analyzing by sound, than at the words. The accent should be retained throughout each word, which is perhaps the most difficult part of the exercise. This exercise is very important in developing a distinct and beautiful articulation. You can not afford to omit it, though no more than two words can be analyzed at each lesson.

† Spelling by letter should be learned in spelling class, beginning soon after the child can read words at sight. The *meaning* of words come more properly in connection with reading. Definitions, however, should not be forced upon the memory of the young.

a word, it is best to seek the correct pronunciation of the word from the dictionary, then pronounce it very slowly, so that the sounds appear to the ear as m—a—n (pronounced slowly).

No. 4. *Elocution.*
GENERAL OR SPECIAL FACTS, FAULTS, AND DRILL.

It is proper at this point to give such instruction in the science of speech as the teacher believes the class able to comprehend and execute. There is drill suited to the smallest pupils, and matter sufficiently difficult for seniors in college. Drill upon orthoepy, pitch, force, and time, should be introduced at this point, giving one fact at a time, with copious illustrations.

Young pupils should be taught by actual example and practice rather than by rules and theories. If a pupil has a defect in, or peculiarity of speech, correct it if possible, and do not forget to drill upon the elementary sounds of our language.

No. 5. *Calisthenics, or Gesture, etc.*

A little exercise in calisthenics is next in order, and of considerable importance. It quickens the blood, brightens the eye, makes pliant and strong the muscles—in fact, gives life and elasticity to the whole system. See Table No. 1.

Avoid colds from drafts, and also violent exercise, like pounding the chest.

Note 1. There has been well-grounded complaint of injuries caused by physical training, and therefore the warning is repeated. If the outward motions of the arms be strong, and the return movements be made with *relaxed muscles,* no bruises can occur. It is severe and constant rigidity of muscle that causes injury, and at the same time the exercises lose in excellence and grace as they gain in severity.

Note 2. Sudden transitions from rest to violent exercise, and the reverse, should be avoided. Begin with light exercises, and let the most difficult ones come in the middle of the lesson.

The exercises contained in this volume are not expected

to supersede any good hygienic training, but for the benefit of those teachers who have no method of physical training at command, and for those students who desire special directions for self-culture.

Ventilation.

Begin all exercises in respiration, intonation, and calisthenics by giving free ingress to pure air.

The importance of ventilating school-rooms can not be too strongly impressed upon teacher and pupil.

There is little danger of contracting colds during exercise, even if windows and doors are partially opened in cold weather, provided care be taken to close them when resting, and to throw some extra clothing about the person if very warm.

The climate and condition of weather will of course govern the *manner* of ventilation, but a change of air you *must* have to insure vigor of mind and body.

It is the teacher's duty to see that pupils, when warm, are properly protected from air currents.

For exercises in calisthenics, see page 23; in intonation, page 20; in gesture, page 101.

Rhythm of Movement or Time.

The exercises in calisthenics should be rhythmical—that is, produced with regularly recurring accent; and to render it so requires an indication of quadruple time. This may be accomplished in various ways. The first and most simple means is counting. The accented or outward motion should correspond with the odd numbers, and the unaccented or inward motion with the even numbers. Thus: ONE, *two;* THREE, *four;* FIVE, *six;* SEVEN, *eight:* ONE, *two*, etc. Another method is that of calling the unaccented syllable "*and.*" Thus: ONE *and;* TWO *and;* THREE *and;* FOUR *and:* ONE *and;* TWO *and*, etc.

If the exercise be "*thrusting*," the hand should go out at "*one,*" and return to the body at "*and;*" go out again at "*two,*" and return at "*and;*" go out at "*three,*" and return at "*and,*" etc. The odd number, or "*and,*" represents the return movement. Some persons make accented raps with a stick, ruler, or cane to time the exercises, while those who find it convenient adapt the exercises to music of the violin, piano, or other instrument.

II. SELECTIONS.

The literary productions to be read after the preliminary exercises should not be confined to the Reader, but should be drawn from various sources—libraries, periodicals, and papers.*

In using a reader, do not feel obliged to follow the compiler's arrangement of selections, but select to suit the time and need. If the selections are from another source, they should be examined by the teacher before being used, to see that the matter is wholesome and instructive. (See Class Methods, pages 79 to 85.)

Usually the selection should be given out a day or two before it is to be read. Occasionally let the pupils select the reading matter, giving them ample time to do so. The selections should be short and interesting.

In this book are given ten standard and twenty-six occasional methods for conducting reading-classes. The former are called "standard" because better adapted to daily use and wear well, while the latter are named "occasional methods" because suited to give variety by occasional use. Let the occasional methods be used for rest, or holiday, or rewards of merit. In many schools the classes are too large to do justice to them. In such cases the preliminary exercises should be given as general exercises to the whole school, or be cut down to one or two minutes.

Standard Methods.

Those particular reading-class methods that can be used the longest without wearying, and have proven most efficacious in practice, are termed *Standard* Methods. Of these there are ten, viz.:

* At this time many teachers are using periodicals in reading-classes. *Our Young Folks* and *The Nursery* are admirably adapted to intermediate and primary instruction, as are other magazines for older classes.

I. Beginning back at each mistake.

Note.—Name a certain number of lines (perhaps three or four) which each pupil may read, requiring the reader to begin back at the beginning every time a mistake is made,* until there are no longer errors for special criticism. This method makes careful and accurate readers.

II. By competition, each reading the same stanza.

Note.—Allow each member of the class to read the same stanza or division of prose, to see who will make the fewest blunders in once reading. Impress the pupils with your desire for their success, and this method will prove a good one.

III. By alternation of class divisions.

Note.—Divide the class into two or more sections, and request the pupils of each section to read in concert the successive lines, couplets, or stanzas in the lesson. Section A reads two lines, Section B the two following, etc. This keeps all the class occupied and attentive.

IV. By couples.

Note.—Allow the pupils to read in couples (A and B together, C and D together, etc.) any division of composition, as a sentence or a stanza, until all the class have read. Each pupil can read in this manner twice as much as one could singly, without materially hindering the teacher from detecting individual errors.

V. Looking off as much as possible.

Note.—Let the class read in concert, by couples, or singly, looking off the book as much as possible, in order to train the eye to see ahead. Every person who is able to read new or strange composition *well* must be able to see more than the solitary word he is pronouncing. Choose simple verse at first, that can be easily seen and retained. Try to see the whole line at one glance.

This method adds materially to the grace of a reader by giving the hearers frequent and continued expressions of intelligence and emotion through eye and gesture. In this way a person of quick comprehension and close memory can render a written or printed discourse almost like extemporaneous matter or improvisation.

* See Errors of Speech, pages 34 and 37.

VI. Repeating after the teacher.

Note.—The teacher reads a line or sentence, and the class repeats the same in concert, copying the model, either with closed books or with eyes upon the passages rendered. Again the teacher reads, and the class repeats, and thus continues to do until satisfied. If the teacher be a good model, the class will gain much by imitation; if not, then the method is not so safe.

VII. Repeating after each member of the class.

Note.—In this method the pupils successively assume the *rôle* of teacher: *i. e.*, A lines (reads line by line) a division of prose matter or poetry, and the class repeats the same line by line. Next B lines, and the class repeats. C and D follow, until each member of the class has lined a portion of the selection for the rest to repeat. This method keeps the whole class at work, and renders many of them laudably ambitious to become good models. (A line or couplet each, and the class repeat, is a variation of this method, keeping the whole class busy.)

VIII. By alternation—class and teacher.

Note.—The teacher reads the line, couplet, or stanza, and the class reads the next line, couplet, or stanza in concert. In this method, if the teacher reads clearly and forcibly, there is something contagious in it, and the class will do better for the example and comparison.

IX. By call by number.

Note.—Number the pupils of the class, and call them by these numbers in the succession in which you wish to hear them read. The one who is reading should cease the instant a new number is called by the teacher, even if in the midst of a sentence, phrase, or word, and the one whose number is called should commence immediately where the last one left off.

If the new number fails to commence aright, call another; if the place is still lost, call a third. Continue the exercise, if possible, until all the numbers have been called and have responded. There should be no talking or whispering during this exercise, as it would create unendurable confusion.

It **exercises** the memory of teacher and pupils, in order

that the former may know what numbers have been called and about how much each has read, and that the latter may be able to rehearse any errors in the review. Indolent and inattentive pupils should be called oftener, that they may learn to keep pace and place. This method develops the power of concentration.

X. Appoint a critic, or critics, whose business it is to point out and correct errors of each pupil in turn as he or she has finished reading a certain number of lines.

Note.—Appoint two critics, and name them "Critic No. 1" and "Critic No. 2." Divide the selection into portions of three lines each, in order that all may read, and request a member of the class to commence reading.

When the three lines are read the reader ceases, and it is the duty of Critic No. 1 to rise and enumerate and correct each and every mistake that he or she has observed. When done, Critic No. 2 rises, enumerates, and corrects all errors that he observed which Critic No. 1 overlooked.

After the appointed critics are done, let the remainder of the class signal any unmentioned error by raising the hand. The teacher then points to the one who shall be heard first, and all signaling the same mistake drop the hand; thus continue until all errors noticed have been corrected. If any errors remain unnoticed by the class, it is the teacher's duty to correct or point them out. · Recollect no criticisms are to be repeated, and no one to speak but in order. This method fixes the attention of the entire class, and renders them critically observant during each exercise.

Occasional Methods.

I. Reading to a mistake judged by the teacher.

Note.—Let the class read in the usual order of succession, each pupil stopping at the first error corrected by the teacher, and the next one in order correcting the mistake and reading on until he also is corrected. The fault in this method is that the best readers read longest, and those who need the most training are comparatively inactive.

II. Reading to a mistake judged by a pupil, who corrects the error, and proceeds to read from that point.

Note.—This method is very like No. I., except that the errors are discovered and indicated by the uplifted hands of pupils. If more than one hand is raised, the teacher points to or otherwise indicates which one is to read next. That pupil corrects the mistake and continues to read until another criticises and is appointed to read. This method tends to render pupils attentive, careful, and critical.

III. Reading any where the Reader is opened.

Note.—Let each pupil, when about to read, first close the book, then rise, open it, and read whatever his eye first rests upon. If any member of the class is unable to catch both words and meaning, the reader must repeat, reading over and over again what he has attempted to read, until it is at least clearly intelligible to all of the class. This method makes intelligible readers.

IV. Reading medley. All read at once in different places.

Note.—In this method each pupil should have a book; but if two must use *one*, let them read together. Arrange the class in single or double lines, so that you can pass near and speak or listen to a pupil at will. There should be at least as many lines in the selected poem as there are pupils in the class, and all lines equal in length. The best voices should be placed at the head and foot of the class. No. 1 commences to read; when he has finished one line, No. 2 begins at the *first line;* when he has done the line, No. 3 begins at the first line, each one in the class following in the same manner until the whole class are reading at once.

No two read the same line at the same time. No pupil is to stop, after he has begun reading, until the poem is finished. The surest way to start this exercise, if the teacher can endure the fatigue, is to pass from pupil to pupil, and read the first line of the poem with each one in class; then, if no one stops prematurely, the whole class will be reading when the teacher is through.

This method strengthens the voices of timid pupils who are unable to let out their voices to the fullest extent alone. It also renders pupils independent in recitation by the concentration necessary to read amid such a confusion of voices.

V. Reading two unlike pieces by alternation.

Note.—Select two contrasting pieces, and let the class read in concert a few lines of each, alternating from one to the other. If one is grave and the other brisk, let the number of lines of the brisk piece be two to one of the slow or grave piece. This method, as well as all other methods of contrast, enhance the power of personation, the life of drama or dialogue.

VI. Reading-match, choosing sides.

Note.—The teacher designates two of the class as leaders, who choose readers for their respective sides precisely as they used to do in "spelling down." The teacher may act as umpire, deciding mistakes. The contestants stand facing each other, if convenient, and No. 1 commences reading. When a mistake is observed, the umpire cries "Halt!" and the reader takes his seat. After No. 1 of the first division has read, No. 1 of the second division proceeds to read, and continues till called by the umpire. In this way the class is reduced until one remains alone. There is, however, the same objection to this method that there is to No. I. and to spelling down, both of which deprive the poorest pupils of the most exercise. To give the poor readers equal drill, this method can be conducted in the following manner:

Divide the selection into divisions of a certain number of lines, and allow each pupil to read a division, keeping a tally of the mistakes on each side, to compare when through the exercise.

The reading-match is exciting, and of great service when the class seems dull and listless.

VII. Reflection. "See thyself as others see thee."

Note.—In this method the teacher needs to bestow great care, and have an almost intuitive perception of the emotional nature of each pupil, otherwise grief, mortification, or anger may be displayed during the exercise. But if the teacher be kind-hearted and magnanimous, the pupils feel it, and will bear a great deal. There should be no ridicule or sarcasm in the mimicry, and then the looking-glass method will prove safe and profitable.

First, then, begin with the *bravest* scholars in the class, and not with those timid, shrinking ones who feel a lump in the throat whenever you speak to them. Tell them that you intend to read after them line by line, and that you intend to exaggerate their faults a little, so that they may see how they appear to other people. Call for volunteers to begin with, and the chances are you will have hands enough raised to select as you please. Take one of these brave ones aside, or facing the class, if you please, and let them read a line, and then imitate their manner and errors, if any. So continue until a stanza or prose division has been reflected line by line. If the class laugh, say, "Never mind; we'll see who'll laugh when your turn comes." Excuse this pupil, and call another, and another, until each one in class has had a peep in the glass—the faithful glass that, with hope to cure, portrays unconscious defects.

Many persons have mannerisms and faults of speech of which they seem entirely unconscious. Convince one that he is wrong, and there is hope of making him right.

VIII. Contrasting the pure with other qualities of voice.

Note.—Select a poem having decided rhythmical accent. Read the successive stanzas, alternating the qualities of voice. The pure tone should always be used as one of the qualities in every contrast. (See Qualities of Voice, p. 126.)

IX. A word each.
X. A sentence each.
XI. To a punctuation mark.
XII. A line.
XIII. A couplet. } Each in succession.
XIV. A stanza.

Note.—In each of these similar methods each pupil reads his allotted portion just as if he expected to continue reading, keeping the voice up on the last word, where the stress requires it, or letting it down. Herein lies the skill of these methods. The pupils must be attentive to keep the place, and should emphasize and accent as if to go on reading.

XV. Alternate repetition.

Note.—A reads a line, B repeats it, C reads the succeeding line, and D repeats it, etc.

XVI. Repeat and read a line each in succession.

Note.—A reads two lines; B repeats the last line that A

read, and one more; C reads the last line that B read, and one more, etc. Let each one leave off with the same inflection, emphasis, as if to continue.

XVII. Review and read an additional word each.

Note.—A reads the first word; B reads the first and second words; C the first, second, and third; D the first, second, third, and fourth, etc. When the repetition is too great, begin again. In prose composition six or eight lines is quite enough.

XVIII. Review and read an additional line each.

Note.—This method is executed like XVII.

XIX. All who have read, repeat all that has been read, and an additional word for each successive reader.

Note.—This method is similar to XVII. The whole class unite in the repetitions. A reads the first word of a stanza; A and B read the first and second words of the stanza; A, B, and C read the first, second, and third words; A, B, C, and D read the first, second, third, and fourth words, etc., until all the words of the stanza are read; then begin anew on the second stanza.

XX. is like XIX., except that lines take the place of words.

Note.—If the teacher wishes a whole class to learn a poem, this is a quick and sure way to accomplish it.

XXI. Let a pupil be appointed, from time to time, to select and read an entire selection to the class.

XXII. Let the teacher bring a selection and read it to the class for reproduction.

XXIII. Read from a periodical or other paper by passing it from one to another, if there be but one copy.

Note.—This makes intelligent readers, as all must be made to understand what is read before a reader is excused.

XXIV. Let the teacher read, making errors for the class to observe and criticise.

XXV. Reading high and low in contrast.

XXVI. Reading fast and slow in contrast.

Note.—Read alternate lines in the XXVth, and, by alternation, one line slow and two or three lines fast in the XXVIth. The former increases the *compass* of voice, and the latter helps regulate the *speed* of speech.

III. REVIEWS. (See Table 24.)

The review should begin by a careful description of the selections which have been read. First, the form, subject, or thought, objects, incidents, definitions, with the moral or personal application. Second, the errors committed by the pupils with regard to their reading position, articulation, pronunciation, phonic spelling, definitions, technical and received meaning of words, and elocution in general.

There are various ways of conducting the review, a few of which will be explained in this chapter. First method. Call on pupils, one by one, to give as full a review of all the items and errors named above as possible, independent of all prompting or questioning. Second method (adapted to large classes or short recitations). Divide the items under the head of review, and assign a portion to each pupil in class: *ex. gr.* In this review, A may talk of the form of the composition (see Table 24); B, of the subject or thought; C, of the class of poetry (whether epic, lyric, or dramatic); D, of the objects (whether natural or artificial, etc.); E, of the incidents narrated; and F, of the errors of the class, and so on. After these subjects have been given, call upon A, and require a complete and uninterrupted explanation of the subject. Ask no question, and allow no prompting until the pupil has finished and seated himself, or until the entire review is formally ended.

IV. A LINE, COUPLET, OR STANZA TO MEMORIZE.

The advantage of this exercise is not easily calculated. It stores the minds of pupils with the best thoughts of the best authors, expressed in choicest language. It is a source of enjoyment and means of entertainment during life. It creates a taste for a high order of literature, and inspires the young to seek noble companionship and to pursue lofty ambitions.

As you value truth and beauty, do not neglect this exercise. Choose judiciously, and give but a few lines each day, and the result will amply reward you.

Those poems or selections best calculated to answer this

purpose are pure in tone and replete with reflections, incidents, or examples of the cardinal virtues, faith, hope, patience, courage, generosity, gratitude, etc., etc.*

Suit the selections to the capacity of the learners by all means, for one is heartily tired of hearing Cato's or Hamlet's Soliloquy from children seven or eight years old. The fault with two thirds of school exhibitions, rehearsals, and even higher literary entertainments, is that the actors and speakers affect pieces or themes beyond their comprehension. There are high-toned selections suited to every understanding, if but found in time, and treasured up for occasions of need. †

V. EXAMINATION OF THE ADVANCE LESSON.

The lesson to be read at the next recitation should be examined and the difficulties removed before any time is wasted in erroneous study. It is certainly indispensable with young classes who are unable to consult the dictionary and reference books.

All the words should be properly pronounced before they are committed.

Older classes should be directed where to look for information desired, and thus be materially assisted without breaking the spirit of the first "Rule for Teachers"—"Never tell a pupil what he can discover for himself." (Primary Methods, page 66.)

* According to the ancients, the cardinal virtues are prudence, justice, temperance, and fortitude.

† There is a school in New England where for a number of years the pupils (over twelve years of age) have been required to commit forty lines a day; and, judging from the persons pursuing this course, it must be acknowledged a successful mental discipline. The lines should be read only *once* before an effort be made to recite them. This exercises the power of concentration, and pupils trained to reproduce a composition from once reading can readily give the substance of a lecture or sermon.

MANUAL OF READING.

TABLE NO. 25. COMPOSITION.

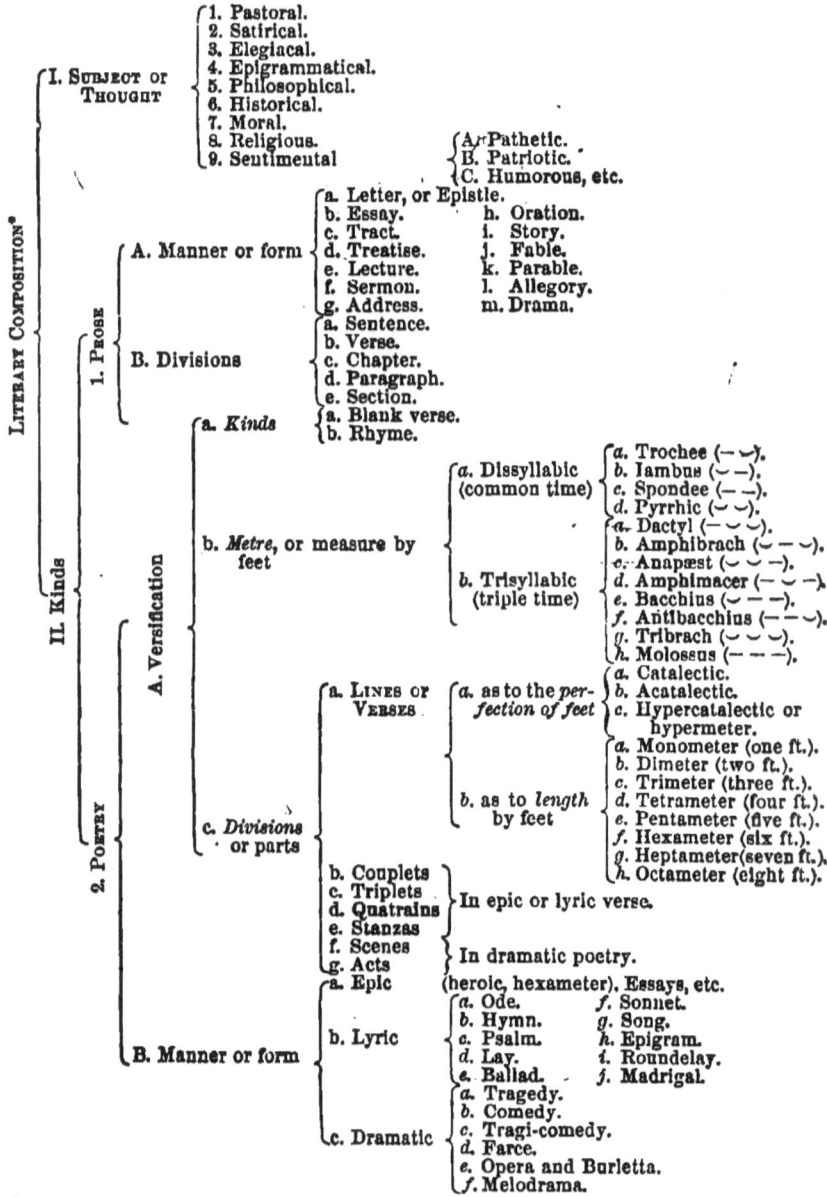

* Didactic, descriptive, narrative. See Note, page 1.

LITERARY COMPOSITION.*

A COMPOSITION is a written or literary work, and may be prose or poetry. The subject or thought of a composition may be pas'toral, satir'ical, ele'giacal, epigrămmăt'ical, philosoph'ical, histor'ical, mor'al, relig'ious, sentiment'al, etc.

1. Pastoral. Descriptive of country life.
2. Satirical. Exposing or censuring human weakness or folly; full of satire or invective; as, Byron's "English Bards and Scotch Reviewers."
3. Elegiacal. Expressive of sorrow or lamentation; funereal, mournful, pertaining to sad reflection; as, Gray's "Elegy in a Country Church-yard."
4. Epigrammatical. Short and witty; ending with a turn or point of wit, concise, poignant.
5. Philosophical. Pertaining to or proceeding from philosophy, physics, metaphysics (natural or mental philosophy, psychology, philology, etc.).
6. Historical. Pertaining to that which exists or has existed; containing history. Biographical: a species of historical writing which gives an account of the life and character of some particular person; when such an account has been written by the person in question, it is called *auto*biographical.
7. Moral. Relating to duty or obligation; pertaining to the conduct or manners of men, as social beings, in relation to each other as respects right and wrong; not depending on human laws, but conscience.
8. Religious. Teaching or setting forth religion.

---

* Composition is sometimes called *didactic*—giving instruction, teaching; sometimes *descriptive*—having the quality of representing, describing; and sometimes *narrative*—relating to the particulars of an event or transaction; a particular and continued account of any thing.

These pages are added to assist in reviewing the selections. (See Class Methods, page 85.)

9. **Sentimental.** Abounding in sentiments or reflections; with thoughts prompted by passion or feeling. Pathetic, patriotic, and humorous productions belong to this class.

(*a.*) **Pathetic.** Affecting or moving the tender emotions, as grief, pity.

(*b.*) **Patriotic.** Actuated or prompted by the love of one's country.

(*c.*) **Humorous.** Full of humor; playful; exciting laughter.

PROSE.

Prose is discourse or composition not metrical; *i. e.*, not in verse, or without poetic measure.

I. *Form or Manner.*

In form or manner it may be a letter or epistle, an essay, tract, treatise, lecture, sermon, address, oration, story, fable, parable, allegory, or drama.

1. A letter or epistle is a written or printed message; a short communication with regard to friendship, business, science, or belles-lettres.*

2. An essay is a short composition or informal treatise upon any particular subject; as, Bacon's "Essays."

3. A tract is a short written or printed discourse or treatise, usually on practical religion; as, "A Call to Prayer."

4. A treatise is a composition explaining or discussing any particular subject, and is longer, more studied, and methodical than an essay; as, Wilson's "Treatise on Punctuation."

5. A lecture is a formal or methodical discourse upon any subject (moral, social, scientific, philosophical, etc.), and is intended for instruction; as, "Lectures on Anatomy."

6. A sermon is a religious discourse, to be delivered from the pulpit or to a congregation; as, Christ's "Sermon on the Mount."

---

* Letters of friendship include those of condolence, congratulation, inquiry, explanation, advice, etc. Letters of business and law are letters of administration, of attorney, of credit, of license, of marque, of marque and reprisal, letters close, letters patent, overt, or open, etc. (*See* Quarto Dictionary.)

7. An address is a formal speech or message of respect, congratulation, thanks, petition, etc.; as, Lincoln's "Inaugural Address."

8. An oration is an elaborate discourse or speech in writing which has been spoken, or is proposed to be spoken on some *special* occasion, as a funeral, celebration, or anniversary; as, Antony's "Oration over the Body of Cæsar," Webster's "Oration at the Laying of the Corner-stone of Bunker Hill Monument."

9. A story is a narrative or recital, and more especially a fictitious narrative, less elaborate than a novel; as, "The Story of Ruth."

10. A fable is a fictitious story or tale intended to enforce some useful truth or precept; as, "The Fable of the Fox and the Grapes."

11. A parable is a fable of something in real life or nature from which a moral is drawn for instruction; as, "The Parable of the Vineyard," "The Parable of the Tares."

12. An allegory is a figurative application of real facts; a sentence or discourse in which the principal subject is described by another subject resembling it in its qualities, properties, and circumstances; as, Bunyan's "Pilgrim's Progress."*

II. *Divisions.*

The divisions of prose composition are sentences, verses, chapters, paragraphs, sections, etc.

1. A sentence is an assemblage of words logically and grammatically joined so as to make complete sense; as, "Insincerity is very troublesome to manage."—TILLOTSON.

2. A verse, in prose, is a short division of composition, as a verse in the Bible. "Blessed are the merciful, for they shall obtain mercy."—*Matt.* v., 7.

3. A chapter is a division of a book or treatise, as a chapter in the Bible.

4. A paragraph is a distinct part of a discourse or chapter,

---

* A parable must be literally possible, while an allegory may not. The story of the vineyard could be literally true, but when Christ says, "I am the vine," the expression is allegorical.

relating to a particular subject, and comprises one or more sentences. It is indicated by a break in the text, or the commencement of a new line begun farther from the margin than the other lines, and formally by the sign (¶) placed at or before it.

5. A section is a distinct portion of a book, writing, or discourse, and may be more or less than a chapter.

POETRY.

Poetry is metrical composition "produced and embellished more or less by a creative imagination, the end of which is to afford intellectual pleasure by exciting elevated, agreeable, or pathetic emotions."—WORCESTER.

In its accepted sense, poetry may be blank verse or rhyme.

1. Blank verse is metrical composition without rhyme. It is usually the heroic verse of five feet without rhyme.

Example:

"From the vale
. Of cold oblivion comes the breathing throng
Up to the paths of life, and, one by one,
Strive to unravel with their feeble hands
Existence' tangled knot, but find no clew,
And, wearied with the fruitless toil, sink back,
And darkness closes o'er them."—MRS. AREY.

2. Rhyme is the correspondence of sound in the last syllable or syllables of two lines or verses of poetry, in immediate succession or close proximity. Poetry possessing such terminal sound is called rhyme.

Rhymes may consist of single syllables, as *blind, find;* of two syllables, as *sound'ing, bound'ing;* of three syllables, as *beau'teous, du'teous;* of four syllables, as *quiv'eringly, shiv'eringly.**

Example of successive Rhyme:

"The smile is the bud of the full-blown laughter,
The bud comes first and the bloom comes after;
Down in the heart there's a genius lingers,
With feathery ends to his tickling fingers."—GANYARD.

---

* To constitute rhyme, the vowels, or, in case of double rhymes, the *accented* vowels, must be identical, and so must the sounds following these vowels, but the consonants preceding them in the same syllable must be different.

ADVANCED CLASS METHODS. 93

Example of alternate Rhyme:
"The twilight hours like birds flew by,
　As lightly and as free;
Ten thousand stars were in the sky,
　Ten thousand in the sea;
And every wave with dimpled face
　That leaped up in the air,
Had caught a star in its embrace,
　And held it trembling there."—CLARK.

Example of irregular Rhyme:
"And brushing ankle-deep in flowers,
He heard behind the woodbine veil
The milk that bubbled in the pail,
And buzzing of the honeyed hours."—TENNYSON.

Versification (Metre or Measure).

Versification is the art of constructing metrical composition, or poetry. This art lies in the harmonious arrangement of a certain number of long and short, or of accented and unaccented syllables.

The Greeks and Romans based their versification chiefly upon quantity. In their language, the length and brevity of syllables were so fixed and uniform in pronunciation that one long syllable was equal to two short ones. This gave license to as many as seventeen, and to no less than thirteen syllables in a line of hexameter, which, in musical time, was equal to twelve *long* syllables. In order to ascertain the exact time of verse, and the proper combinations of long and short quantities or syllables, a metre or measure was instituted, called a *metrical foot.* A line of hexameter must contain six of these feet. (See Epic Verse, p. 97.)

Modern poetry is measured by time and accentuation, which produce greater rhythmical effect than did the quantity in the Greek and Latin.

Metrical feet were dissyllabic or trisyllabic divisions of a line of poetry. A dissyllabic division consists of two syllables or their equivalent, the time being quadruple. A trisyllabic division consists of three syllables or their equivalent, the time being triple.

There are four species of dissyllabic feet, namely—

1. Trochee, the first syllable accented; as, HEED'less.

2. Iambus, the second syllable accented; as, inspire'.
3. Spondee, both syllables accented; as, a'men'.
4. Pyrrhic, both syllables unaccented; as, ible, in risible.
There are eight species of trisyllabic feet, namely—
1. Dactyl, the first syllable accented; as, cheer'fully.
2. Amphibrach, the second syllable accented; as, reluc'-tant.
3. Anapæst, the third syllable accented; as, importune'.
4. Amphimacer, with the accent on the first and third syllables; as, con'stant love'.
5. Bacchius, with the accent on the second and third syllables; as, the man'-child'.
6. Antibacchius, with the accent on the first and second syllables; as, strong'mind'ed.
7. Tribrach, three equal and unaccented syllables.
8. Molossus, three equal and accented syllables; as, faith, hope, love.

It is no easy task to find English examples of these Greek and Latin feet. The pyrrhic and tribrach can not be properly represented. The most common of these species are the trochee, iambus, anapæst, and dactyl.

(*Trochee.*)   Tell' me | not' in | mourn'ful | num'bers, |
          "Life' is | but' an | emp'ty | dream'!"
          For' the | soul' is | dead' that | slum'bers, |
          And' things | are' not | what' they | seem'.
                                Longfellow.

(*Iambus.*)   When free'|dom from' | her moun|tain height' |
          Unfurl'd' | her stand'|ard to' | the air', |
          She tore' | the az'|ure robe' | of night', |
          And set' | the stars' | of glo'|ry there'. | —Drake.

(*Anapæst.*)   'Tis the last' | rose of sum'|mer, left bloom'|ing alone'; |
          All her love'|ly compan'|ions are fa'|ded and gone'; |
          No flower' | of her kin'|dred, no rose'|bud is nigh', |
          To reflect' | back her blush'|es, or give' | sigh for sigh'. |
                                Moore.

(*Dactyl.*)   Bird' of the | wil'derness, |
          Blithe'some and | cum'berless, |
          Sweet' be thy | ma'tin o'er | moor'land and | lea'!
          Em'blem of | hap'piness, |
          Blest' is thy | dwell'ing-place: |
          O' to a|bide' in the | des'ert with | thee'!—James Hogg.

Metrical Feet.

(*Trochee.*) {TRO'chee | TRIPS' from | LONG' to | SHORT;
From long to long in solemn sort.
(*Spondee.*) SLOW' SPON'|DEE' STALKS'; | STRONG' FOOT'! | yet ill able
(*Dactyl.*) EV'er to | COME' up with | DAC'tyl tri|SYL'lable.
(*Iambic.*) IAM'|bics MARCH' | from SHORT' | to LONG', |
(*Anapæsts.*) With a LEAP' | and a BOUND' | the swift AN'|apæsts THRONG'. |
(*Amphi-brach.*) {One SYL'la|ble LONG', with | one SHORT' at | each SIDE',
AMPHI'brach|ys HASTES' with | a STATE'ly | STRIDE.
(*Amphi-macer.*) {FIRST and LAST | BE'ing LONG', | MID'dle SHORT' | AM'phiMA'-|cer,
STRIKES' his THUN'|DER'ing HOOFS' | LIKE' a PROUD' | HIGH'-bred RA'|cer.—COLERIDGE.

Divisions of Verse.

The divisions common to verse are lines or verses, couplets, triplets, quatrains, and stanzas, in epic or lyric poetry; acts and scenes in dramatic poetry.

A line or verse of poetry consists of a certain arrangement of long and short, or accented and unaccented syllables, according to established rules; a measured line of poetry, as,

"Idleness ever despaireth, bewaileth."—OSGOOD.

In scanning, or applying the measure of feet to a verse, if a line is found wanting a syllable, it is said to be catalectic; if the number of syllables is exact and proper, acatalectic; if redundant in syllables, hypercatalectic or hypermeter.

(*Catalectic.*) Slack'en not | sail' yet, at | in'let or | isl'and ; |
Straight' for the | bea'con steer, | straight' for the | high'land. |
MRS. SOUTHEY.
(*Acatalectic.*) Thy sports' | are fled,' | and all' | thy charms' | withdrawn'. |
GOLDSMITH.
(*Hypercatalectic.*) Full ma'|ny a gem' | of pur'|est ray' | serene,' |
The dark,' | unfath'|omed caves' | of o'|cean bear'. |
GRAY.

A line of poetry is also known by the number of feet it contains. A line of one foot is called monometer; of two, dimeter; of three, trimeter; of four, tetrameter; of five, pentameter; of six, hexameter; and of eight, octameter.

(*Monometer.*) "There we go,
To and fro,
With our knacks
At our backs."—CHALKHILL.

(*Dimeter.*) "Alas! for the | rarity
Of Christian | charity
Under the sun!"—HOOD.

(*Trimeter.*) "Thou high | and ho|ly One, |
Whose care | for sire | and son |
All nature fills—
While day | shall break | and close, |
While night | her cres|cent shows, |
O let | Thy light | repose |
On these our hills!"—PIERPONT.

(*Tetrameter.*) "Labor is | rest from the | sorrows that | greet us; |
Rest from all | petty vex|ations that | greet us; |
Rest from sin- | promptings that | ever en|treat us; |
Rest from world | sirens that | lure us to | ill."—OSGOOD.

(*Pentameter.*) "What stron|ger breast-|plate than | a heart | untainted."
SHAKSPEARE.

(*Hexameter.*) "I wan|der with | the waves, | and with | them rise | and fall." |
WHITTIER.

(*Heptameter.*) "Now glo|ry to | the Lord | of Hosts, | from whom | all glo-|
ries are." |—MACAULAY.

(*Octameter.*) "Hear the | bells from | bluff and | prairie, | through the | hush
of | Sabbath | air."—E. D. PROCTOR.

A couplet consists of two lines of rhyme.
"Keep cool; don't strive for sudden wealth too fast;
Fortunes quick made are seldom known to last."—S. A. DIX.

A triplet consists of three lines or verses rhyming together.
"Up from the earth curled leaves were coming,
Bees in the morning sunshine humming,
Away in the woods the partridge drumming."—ALICE CAREY.

A quatrain consists of four lines of poetry with alternate rhyme (the first line rhyming with the third, and the second with the fourth), and sometimes mixed rhyme (the first rhyming with the fourth, and the second with the third).

Alternate-rhymed Quatrains:
"Be kind when you can in the smallest of duties;
Don't wait for the larger expressions of love,
For the heart depends less, for its joys and its beauties,
On the flight of the eagle than coo of the dove."—ELIZA COOK.

A stanza is a distinct division of poetry, composed of a certain number of adjusted verses or lines, as

"When ranting round in pleasure's ring,
   Religion may be blinded;
Or, if she gie a random sting,
   It may be little minded;
But when on life we're tempest-driven,
   A conscience but a canker,
A correspondence fixed wi' heaven
   Is sure a noble anchor."—BURNS.

Form or Manner.

As to form or manner, all poetry is epic, lyric, or dramatic.

Epic poetry is of the narrative kind, and details external circumstances and events. It is sometimes called heroic verse, because it is used in narrating heroic actions and exploits.

In English, German, and Italian, this verse is iambic of ten syllables (five feet); in French it is iambic of twelve syllables (six feet); and in classic poetry it is hexameter, or verse consisting of six feet, equivalent to twelve syllables. Iambic of twelve syllables is also called Alexandrine, from an old poem written in French on the life of Alexander. The first four feet in a line of heroic or hexameter may be dactyls or spondees; the fifth must be a dactyl, and the sixth a spondee.

"A needless Alexandrine ends the song,
That, like a wounded snake, drags its slow length along."—POPE.

"Where men of judgment creep and feel their way,
The positive pronounce without delay;
Without the means of knowing right from wrong,
They always are decisive, clear, and strong."—COWPER.

Lyric poetry expresses internal emotions and thoughts, and was originally confined to such verse as was sung, or adapted to musical recitation, accompanied by the lyre or harp.

There are a variety of lyric compositions, differing somewhat in their uses, length, etc. The most prominent are

E

the ode, hymn, psalm, lay, ballad, sonnet, song, epigram, and roundelay.

1. An ode is a short song or poem. In the modern sense of the word, "the ode appears to be distinguished by greater length and variety, and by not being necessarily adapted to music. It is distinguished from the ballad and other species of lyric poetry by being confined to the expression of sentiment or of imaginative thought on a subject not admitting of narrative except incidentally."—BRANDE. As, Collins's "Ode on the Passions."

Odes are sacred, as in hymns and psalms; heroic, when praising heroes, martial exploits, or heroic deeds; moral and philosophical, as in odes on virtue, friendship, or humanity.

2. A hymn is a song of praise, adoration, or thanksgiving; as, Milton's "Hymn on the Nativity."

3. A psalm is a sacred or holy song; a poem for praise or worship to God; as, the Psalms of David.

4. A lay is an ancient elegiac kind of French lyric poetry; a species of narrative poetry among the ancient minstrels; as, "The Lay of the Last Minstrel," by Scott.

5. A ballad is a popular narrative song, often of a sentimental kind, written in simple, homely verse; as, "The Ballad of the Hours," by Longfellow.

6. A sonnet is a short poem—especially a short poem consisting of fourteen lines, comprising two quatrains and two tercets, the lines being adjusted by a particular rule; as, Shakspeare's Sonnets.

7. A song is a short poem fitted to be sung; as, Byron's "Song of the Greek Poet."

8. "An epigram is a short poem treating only of one thing, and ending with some lively, ingenious, and natural thought. Epigrams were originally inscriptions on tombs, statues, temples, triumphal arches, etc."—WEBSTER.

9. "A roundelay is an ancient poem consisting of thirteen verses, of which eight are in one kind of rhyme and five in another. It is divided into couplets, at the end of the second and third of which the beginning of the poem is repeated, and that, if possible, in an equivocal or punning sense."
—WEBSTER.

10. "A madrigal is a little amorous poem, sometimes called a pastoral poem, not confined to the scrupulous regularity of a sonnet or the subtlety of the epigram, but containing some tender and delicate, though simple thought."—WEBSTER.

Dramatic composition is that form or manner of poetry which is adapted to scenic representation. The species of this kind of composition are tragedy, comedy, tragi-comedy, farce, opera, burletta, and melodrama.

1. Tragedy represents the virtues, crimes, and sufferings of human beings in such a manner as to excite pity, indignation, grief, or horror; as, Shakspeare's "Julius Cæsar," Otway's "Venice Preserved."

2. Comedy represents the humors, follies, or pleasures of mankind; as, Shakspeare's "Merry Wives of Windsor."

3. Tragi-comedy is a representation of mingled tragedy and comedy; as, Shakspeare's "Much Ado about Nothing."

4. Farce is a brief dramatic representation of ludicrous qualities highly exaggerated. It frequently consists of one or two acts, and never more than three. "Farce is that in poetry which grotesque is in a picture."—DRYDEN.

5. Opera is the words of a musical drama. It consists of airs, choruses, etc., accompanied with instruments, and enriched with magnificent scenery and other decorations, to represent some passionate action; as, "Il Trovatore."

6. Burletta is a comic or farcical opera; as, "Hiawatha" (an operatic burlesque on the poem by that name).

7. Melodrama is a drama "in which songs are intermixed, and effect is sought by startling, exaggerated, or unnatural sentiment or situation."—WEBSTER.

A full dramatic composition (a drama, opera, or the like) is divided into five parts, each of which is called an *act*. These acts are subdivided into parts called *scenes*.

A scene "is so much of a play as passes without change of locality or time, or important change of character; a subdivision of an act."—WEBSTER.

An act is "one of the larger or principal divisions of a play or other dramatic work, in which a certain definite part of the action is completed."—WEBSTER.

MANUAL OF READING.

TABULAR VIEW, NO. 26. GESTURE.*

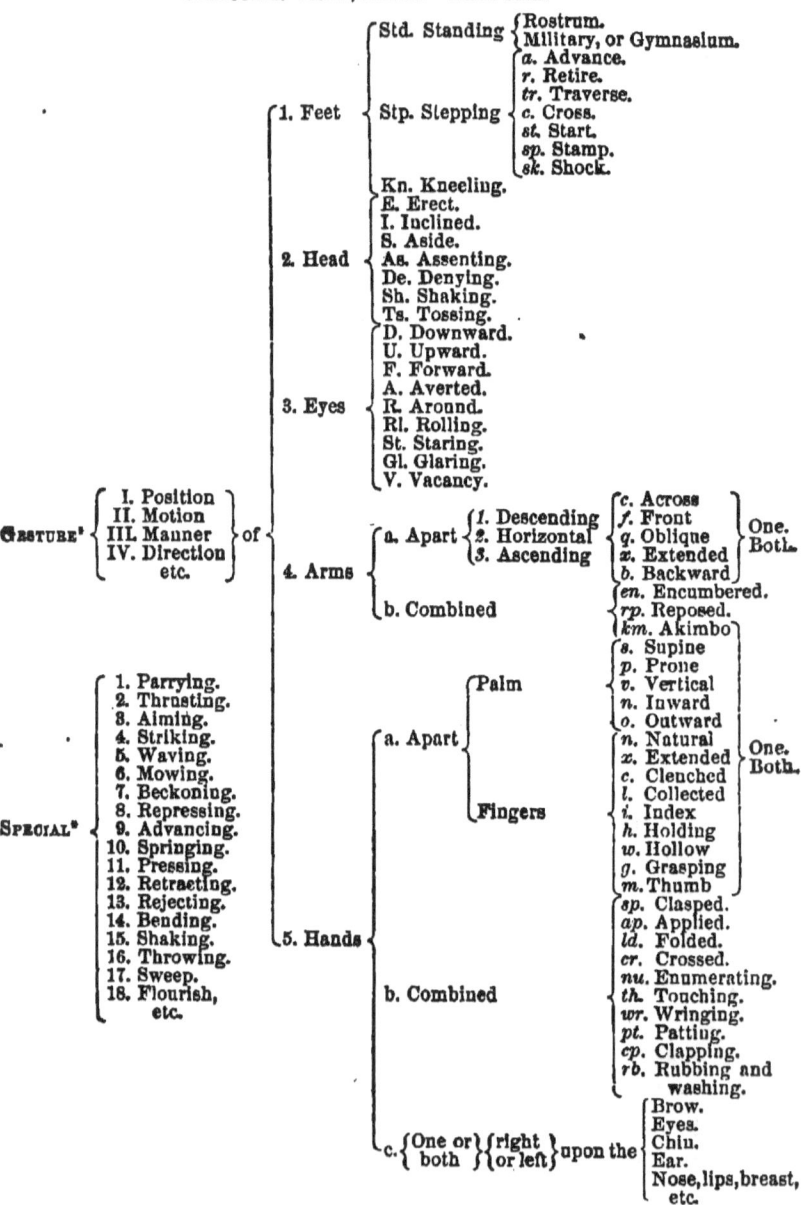

* The abbreviations for gesture conform with those found in other works, so as to avoid confusion.

PART III.
GESTURE.

GESTURE is visible expression independent of vocality. In oratory it includes posture, gesticulation, and facial expression. By gesture the condition or emotion of mind, as joy, sorrow, pain, revenge, hope, and despair, is plainly revealed and universally understood. It is a voluntary or involuntary common language; voluntary when the outward signs are subject to the will, and involuntary when unassisted or uncontrolled by the will.

1. POSTURE may be defined as the position, attitude, or disposition of the human figure when motionless or at rest; as a recumbent attitude, a sitting posture, a stooping position, an attitude of defiance.

2. GESTICULATION is the movement of the body or limbs; as bowing, pointing, fencing. It includes speed, manner, and direction of movement.

The movement as to speed may be rapid, moderate, or slow; as to manner, direct or rotary, single or double; and as to direction, descending, horizontal, or ascending; across, front, oblique, extended, or backward.

The manner is direct when the climax of gesture is attained in a straight line, and rotary when attained through a curved line. It is single when one hand or arm is employed in the action, and double when both are employed in the action.

Feet.

The movement of the feet may be described as,
1. Advancing—stepping forward.
2. Retiring—stepping back.
3. Traversing—stepping to the right and left of the original position.

4. Starting—suddenly jumping up as if frightened.
5. Stamping—lifting and forcibly returning a foot to the floor.

Head.

The head also is expressive in position and motion:
1. Erect, it indicates dignity, confidence, courage, honor.
2. Thrown back—pride, vanity, mirth.
3. Inclined forward—humility, diffidence, shame, grief.
4. Inclined aside—languor, indifference.
5. Assenting or nodding—agreement, consent, acceptance.
6. Denying or shaking—dissent, denial, disapproval.
7. Tossing—disdain, scorn, anger.

Arms.

The arms assume an indefinite number of motions and positions, some of which will be fully described in the article "How to Explain Direction" (page 104). In attitudes of repose, the arms are,
1. Encumbered or folded—inclosing each other.
2. Reposed—one arm lying over the other at the girdle.
3. Akimbo—see cut 4, p. 28.

The special actions of the arm are known as,

1. Parrying.	7. Beckoning.	13. Rejecting.
2. Thrusting.	8. Repressing.	14. Shaking.
3. Aiming.	9. Advancing.	15. Throwing.
4. Striking.	10. Springing.	16. Sweep and
5. Waving.	11. Pressing.	Flourish.
6. Mowing.	12. Retracting.	

Hands.

There are three principal positions of the hand with regard to the palm, viz., supine, prone, and vertical. *Supine*, with the palm up; *prone*, with the palm down; and *vertical*, with the palm perpendicular. Besides these there are *inward*, with the palm toward the speaker, and *outward*, with the palm turned from the speaker and the thumb downward.

With regard to the fingers, the hand is said to be,
1. Natural—the hand relaxed, as when hanging at the side.

2. Extended—with the fingers more or less separated.
3. Clenched—with the fingers closed firmly in the palm.
4. Collected—finger-ends all touching the end of the thumb.
5. Index—pointing with the forefinger while the others are closed.
6. Holding—the thumb and forefinger pressed together.
7. Hollow—with the palm up and the fingers curved.
8. Grasping—as if seizing something.

Combined, the hands are,

1. Clasped—fingers interlaced and closed.
2. Applied—palms and fingers laid together.
3. Folded—all the fingers of one hand closed across the other between the thumb and forefinger.
4. Crossed—one hand laid across the other flatly, as on the breast.
5. Enumerating—placing the index finger of one hand successively upon a finger or fingers of the other hand.
6. Touching—the finger-tips of one hand lightly touching those of the other.
7. Wringing—the hands clasped, and moving up and down.
8. Patting—gently applying the hands several times in succession.
9. Clapping—joining the palms forcibly several times in quick succession.
10. Rubbing—chafing the inner surfaces of the hands together.
11. Washing—rubbing the hands within each other, as if washing or oiling them.

The hands are sometimes placed upon the person to express sense, emotion, or reason. The hands are placed over the eyes to keep out the light or to assist vision in overcoming distances or darkness. The hands touch the closed eyes to express blindness or weak vision; they cover the eyes in shame and horrible delirium; are pressed upon the head in distress, pain, and bewilderment, and upon the heart in extreme joy, tenderness, and anxious expectation. The hand is placed by the ear to assist hearing, strokes the chin in thought, and presses the mute lips to enjoin silence and secrecy.

How to Explain Direction of Movement.

Were it possible to be stationed in the centre of a square room, direction in gesture, or calisthenics, could easily be explained. However, the following may answer the purpose. Standing at the centre of the room facing the wall, call attention to four perpendicular lines about you which contain the twelve principal points of direction. The first line is in front of you, reaching from floor to ceiling, and any gesture made toward this line is called *front*. The second line, on either side of you, is the perpendicular line in each corner of the room formed by the joining of the front and side walls. Any gesture toward either of these lines is called *oblique*. The third line, on either side of you, is the perpendicular line extending from floor to ceiling at your right hand and at your left. Any gesture to the right or left of you toward these lines is called *extended;* and the fourth and last line is the line on either side formed by the joining of the back and side walls. Any gesture toward these lines, or back of the extended, is called *back oblique,* or *backward*. We have now learned all the perpendicular lines—one *front*, two *oblique*, two *extended*, and two *backward*. Each of these lines has three distinct points with regard to the degree of elevation from the shoulder at the climax of gesture or action.

Any gesture which, *at the climax*, brings the arm or hand on a line horizontal with the shoulder, is called *horizontal;* below the horizontal, *descending;* and above the horizontal, *ascending*. Hence we have three points *front*, three *oblique*, three *extended*, and three *backward*, the first in each being *descending*, the second *horizontal*, and the third *ascending*.

There are teachers who fail to obtain *full* statements from their pupils, hence the following Review of Direction:

1. Front. Any gesture made directly before a person is called " front."

2. Extended. Any gesture made directly to the right or left is called " extended."

3. Oblique. Any gesture made between front and extended is called "oblique."

4. Backward. Any gesture made back of the extended is called "backward."

5. Descending. Any gesture whose climax is below the horizontal line of the shoulder is called "descending."

6. Horizontal. Any gesture made with the climax on a line with the shoulder is called "horizontal."

7. Ascending. Any gesture whose climax is above the horizontal line of the shoulder is called "ascending."

How to Teach Declamatory or Emphatic Gesture.

The twelve principal points of direction being thoroughly understood, it may be well to explain a method of acquiring emphatic gesture rapidly. A gesture of this kind must first be accomplished in parts, then united, and rounded off smoothly and gracefully. The first gesture to be made is,

I. DESCENDING FRONT. *First Step.*—Assume the speaking, or rostrum position; bring the arm from the side to horizontal front, *cutting* the air—i. e., with the arm straight and thumb uppermost; drop the hand to the side, and repeat four times. If the arm comes to the side in a stiff, awkward manner, assume the position again, and, when ready to drop the arm, take from it all the will force, and it will fall easily to the side of its own weight. This is the first step toward one emphatic gesture, and, when accomplished satisfactorily, proceed to the

Second Step.—From the horizontal front bring the hand near the head (so that the finger-tips point to the edge of the hair on the forehead), making a curve from the elbow to the finger-tips, and keeping the arm well in front. You are now ready to make the climax of gesture toward any one of the twelve points of direction. When so much of the gesture can be accurately and rapidly made, proceed to the

Third Step.—Bring the hand to the point called descending front, with the hand supine (palm up)—this must be at the climax of gesture—then drop the arm to the side, and you have completed one entire gesture. Repeat six or eight times.

II. Horizontal Front.—Take rostrum position, raise the hand and arm to horizontal front, and then to the head, as in second step, "Descending Front." When ready for the climax of action, throw the hand out horizontally front, with the hand supine; drop the hand, and you have completed the second entire gesture.

III. Ascending Front.—Proceed as before to the curve, and make the climax by throwing the hand ascending front, palm supine as before, dropping the hand easily to the side.

IV. Descending Oblique.—Proceed as in No. II., making the climax of gesture toward the point called descending oblique. Make the remaining points of direction in the same manner, changing the climax of gesture to

V. Horizontal Oblique.
VI. Ascending Oblique.
VII. Descending Extended.
VIII. Horizontal Extended.
IX. Ascending Extended.
X. Descending Backward.
XI. Horizontal Backward.
XII. Ascending Backward.

Thus far the gestures have been angular, having three pauses in each—one at the horizontal front, one at the head or curve, and one at the climax of gesture.

Explanation of Pauses.

The first (or pause occurring at horizontal front) is at the point in the gesture where the hand ceases to cut the air, and is brought to the supine more or less gradually; the second (or pause at the head) is a halt in the gesture to prepare for the utterance of the emphatic word. Sometimes it is necessary to wait while speaking several words before the word of principal emphasis occurs. At the instant when the most emphatic word is spoken the hand sweeps to the climax of gesture. Should the entire gesture occur on one word, then the gesture is continuous to the climax, and sometimes to the position of repose.

Example. "Away with such a thought!"

Here the entire gesture is on the word *away*, and hence

is made without pause at the head, and with an exceedingly short one at the climax.

The pupil must omit the first pause as soon as he has learned to turn the hand to the supine.

Beginning at the first gesture (descending front), make no pause until you arrive near the head in the curve; then make the climax of gesture descending front. Repeat several times.

Practice each gesture in this way until it is easy to omit the first pause, and to make a slight halt at the climax.

These exercises can be accomplished much more easily while counting thus: One, *two*, THREE, down; one, *two*, THREE, down, etc. Count one at the beginning of the gesture, *two* at the head, and THREE at the climax, letting the hand fall to the side at the word *down*. Make the word *three* emphatic, thus constantly applying the rule—"Make the climax of gesture on the most emphatic word, and drop the hand on the next emphatic word following."

When practicing to omit the first pause, count one, two, while bringing the hand slowly and steadily to the head. It is well to practice this *slowly*, as there is sometimes great strength expressed in carrying the arm, with the words, steadily to a climax.

Having completed the lesson with the right hand, repeat it with the left; and having mastered both singly, give them simultaneously, omitting the gesture backward, as they can not be made with the right and left hand at the same time. All emphatic gestures begin and continue the same up to the curve near the head; from there the hand may take any one of the points of direction, and be supine, prone, or vertical, as the case demands.

The next lesson should be to make the gestures with the hands prone. First, make the twelve points of direction with the right hand prone, then with the left hand prone, and finally with both hands prone. Second, make the twelve points with the right and then left hand vertical, then both vertical, and this completes exclamatory or emphatic gesture. All other emphatic gestures are but modifications or variations of these. A gesture may be made without approaching the head so nearly, making it less emphatic. It may reach the climax in a curve instead of a straight line, which makes it more graceful, and at the same time less forcible, or it may come under the head of special gesture, as flourishing, chopping, etc.; still there is an analogy. The climax of the gesture must be on the horizontal line of the shoulder, or above or below that line, and it will be also front, oblique, extended, or backward.

FACIAL EXPRESSION.

Facial expression is the language portrayed by the face.

The Brows,

1. When natural, express veneration, tranquillity.
2. When knit, express jealousy, anger, remorse, hatred.
3. When elevated, express admiration, wonder, fear, terror, desire, joy.

The Lips or Mouth,

1. When open, express mirth, love, pity, desire, terror, anger, fear, admiration, wonder, surprise.
2. When closed lightly—tranquillity.
3. When compressed—perplexity, defiance, hatred, intense scorn.
4. When the corners are drawn down—pride, scorn, contempt, hatred.
5. When pouting—petulance, discontent, boasting.
6. When smiling—approval, cheerfulness.

The Nose,

1. When expanded, expresses courage, anger.
2. When drawn up or wrinkled—disgust, contempt, mirth.
3. When contracted—pain, melancholy, fear.

The Eyes,

1. Looking downward, express grief, perplexity, diffidence, shame, humility, disappointment.
2. Upward or raised—joy, delight, hope, pride, admiration.
3. Forward—determination, courage.

4. Averted—disgust, aversion, listening.
5. Around—tranquillity, satisfaction, self-complacency.
6. Rolling the eyes expresses despair, rage, madness, jealousy.
7. Glaring—madness, revenge, distraction, pain, rage, jealousy.
8. Staring—boasting.
9. Vacant—despair.
10. Fixed and wide—fear, terror, despair, consternation.
11. Flashing—malice, anger

GENERAL RULES AND SUGGESTIONS.

1. Know what you are going to say. Commit the oration or declamation thoroughly, or, if the effort is to be extemporaneous, master the subject in all its relations before attempting to speak in public.

2. Without attracting any attention, breathe deep and long before and while speaking; it prevents embarrassment and redness of face, besides preparing the vocal organs for effort.

3. Speak with a view to being heard by the persons farthest from you; and, if the room echoes, speak slowly.

4. Walk upon the platform with a firm, easy tread.*

5. Stand with one foot a little in advance of the other, at an angle of 45 degrees.†

6. In advancing or retiring, preserve the angle, whether the step be long or short.

7. Let the weight rest upon one foot, so that the other can be moved at pleasure.

8. In shifting the weight from one foot to the other, avoid losing height by dropping one hip.

9. In repose—*i. e.*, when no action is required—the hands may (one or both) be at the girdle, hang at the side, or one

---

* Young orators sometimes keep their usual gait until near the desired place upon the platform, then take one long final step, or two or three shorter ones, as they wheel to a speaking position.

† There seems to be a difference of opinion as to the number of degrees which should be formed by the angle of the feet. Less than a right angle is preferred by many.

hand may be placed upon the hip, with the elbow pressed back. Some speakers preserve the grace of attitude and throw one hand behind them, with the palm out. To adhere to any one position, however graceful, during an entire speech, would be in bad taste.

10. Look about you, over the audience, before beginning to speak.

11. Do not bow abruptly or nod the head, but bend the body and head simultaneously; then step forward and commence speaking.

Note.—An occasion of great ceremony, as at a formal convention or college commencement, requires a bow first to the presiding officer. This should be done when going upon the platform, and before turning to the audience.

12. Look from manuscript or book, if one is used, as much as possible.

Note.—The less a speaker confines his eyes to the manuscript, the more eloquent he can be. While some speakers confine themselves entirely to paper, others refer only to the heads of discourse, or speak entirely from memory. It is needless to add that the latter hold an audience much better than the former.

13. Gesture should be decided, and not weak and uncertain.

14. When the gesture requires a glance, look toward the object of which you speak, *not after, but before or while speaking of it.* First the look, then the action and words in quick succession.

15. Make no gesture without a reason, and avoid excess of action.

16. Make the *climax* of gesture on the most emphatic word, and let the hand fall easily to the side on the next emphatic word thereafter. Having attained the climax, do not shake the hand or otherwise *emphasize* the climax, but hold the hand still until ready to resume the position of repose. Otherwise the gesture is weakened.

17. Do not occupy the hands by twisting any article of apparel, as the watch-chain, coat, or dress.

18. Do not thrust the hands into the pockets, or flourish a handkerchief more than is absolutely necessary.

19. Do not lean the weight upon a desk, chair-back, or other article of furniture.

20. Make no gesture when the eyes are fastened upon the manuscript or book.

21. Do not walk to and fro upon the platform like a caged panther, sway backward or forward, toss or shake the head *regularly*, or make any other monotonous recurrent movement or gesture.

22. Do not turn the back to the audience when speaking, but show at least a three-quarter's view of the chest.

23. Make gestures from within outward as much as is consistent with the action required.

24. In personating two characters, as in dialogue, turn the face to the right when one person speaks, and to the left when the other speaks. If there be explanations by the author, read or speak them in a lower tone of voice, with the face front.

25. In personating more than two characters, select a style of general appearance and quality of voice for each, and resume their respective signs when they speak.

26. The final bow may be made simultaneously with a short backward step as you turn to leave the platform. Let the weight be carried with the retiring foot, so that the other be free to move away.

Note.—1st. Take the *speaking* position, and, without moving the feet, bend *steadily* down until you have counted four. Resume the original upright position while counting four more.

2d. Take the *gymnasium* position, and bow while counting, as before.

3d. Step back, and bow while counting four or eight. See Rule No. 26.

The first form of bowing may very properly introduce a speech, and the third close the speech.

EXAMPLES FOR PRACTICE.

1. R. H. S., right hand supine.
2. R. H. P. " " prone.
3. R. H. V. " " vertical.
4. B. H. S., both hands supine.
5. B. H. P. " " prone.
6. B. H. V. " " vertical.

D. f. Descending front.
H. f. Horizontal "
A. f. Ascending "
D. o. Descending oblique.
H. o. Horizontal "
A. o. Ascending "
D. e. Descending extended.
H. e. Horizontal "
A. e. Ascending "
D. b. Descending backward.
H. b. Horizontal "
A. b. Ascending "

1, R. H. S.

D. f. This sentiment I will maintain | with the last breath of LIFE.*

H. f. I appeal | to YOU, sir, for your de *cis* ion.

A. f. I appeal | to the great Searcher of HEARTS for the truth of what I ut ter.

D. o. Of all mistakes, | NONE are so *fa* tal as those which we incur through prejudice.

H. o. Truth, honor, | JUS tice, were his *mo* tives.

A. o. Fix your eye | on the prize of a truly NO ble am *bi* tion.

D. e. A WAY | with an idea so absurd!

H. e. The breeze of morning | wafted IN cense on the *air*.

A. e. In dreams through camp and court he bore | the trophies of a CON queror.

D. b. A WAY | with an idea so abhorrent to humanity!

H. b. Search the records of the remotest an TI quity for a *par* allel to this.

A. b. Then rang their proud HURRAH!

2. R. H. P.

D. f. Put DOWN | the unworthy feeling!

H. f. Re STRAIN the unhallowed pro *pen* sity.

D. o. Let every one who would merit the Christian name | re PRESS | such a feeling.

H. o. I charge you as men and as Christians | to lay a re STRAINT on all such dispo *si* tions!

A. o. Ye gods, | with HOLD your *ven* geance!

D. e. The hand of affection | shall smooth the TURF for your last *pil* low!

H. e. The cloud of adver | sity threw its gloom over all his PROS pects.

A. e. So darkly glooms yon thunder-cloud that swathes | as with a purple SHROUD Benledi's distant *hill*.

---

* See Rule 16.

3. R. H. V.

H. f. Arise! meet | and re PEL your *foe!*
A. f. For BID it, Almighty *God!*
H. o. He generously extended the arm of power | to ward OFF the *blow.*
A. o. May Heaven a VERT the ca *lam* ity!
H. e. Out of my SIGHT, | thou serpent!
H. b. Thou tempting fiend, a VAUNT!

4. B. H. S.

D. f. All personal feeling he de POS ited on the *al* tar of his country's good.
H. f. Listen, I im PLORE you, to the voice of *rea* son!
A. f. HAIL! universal *Lord.*
D. o. Every personal advantage | he sur REN dered to the common *good.*
H. o. WEL come once more to your early *home!*
A. o. HAIL! holy *Light!*
D. e. I utterly re NOUNCE | all the supposed advantages of such a station.
H. e. They yet slept | in the wide a BYSS of possi *bil* ity.
A. e. Joy, joy | for EVER!

5. B. H. P.

D. f. Lie LIGHT ly on him, *earth*—his step was light on thee.
H. f. Now all the blessings of a glad father LIGHT on *thee!*
A. f. Blessed be Thy NAME, O Lord, Most *High.*
D. o. We are in Thy sight | but as the worms of the DUST!
H. o. May the grace of God | abide with you for EVER.
A. o. And let the triple rainbow rest | o'er all the mountain TOPS.
D. e. Here let the tumults of passion | forever CEASE!
H. e. Spread wide a ROUND the heaven-breathing *calm!*
A. e. Heaven | opened WIDE her ever-during *gates.*

6. B. H. V.

H. f. HENCE, hideous *spectre!*
A. f. AVERT, O *God,* the frown of thy indignation!
H. o. Far from OUR *hearts* be so inhuman a feeling.
A. o. Let me not | NAME it to *you,* ye chaste stars!
H. e. And if the night have gathered aught of evil or concealed, dis‹ PERSE it.
A. e. Melt and dis PEL, ye spectre *doubts!*

Note.—Begin to raise the hand on the dotted words, make the climax of gesture on the words in small capitals, and drop the hand upon the syllables in italics.

TABLE NO. 27. VOCAL GYMNASTICS.

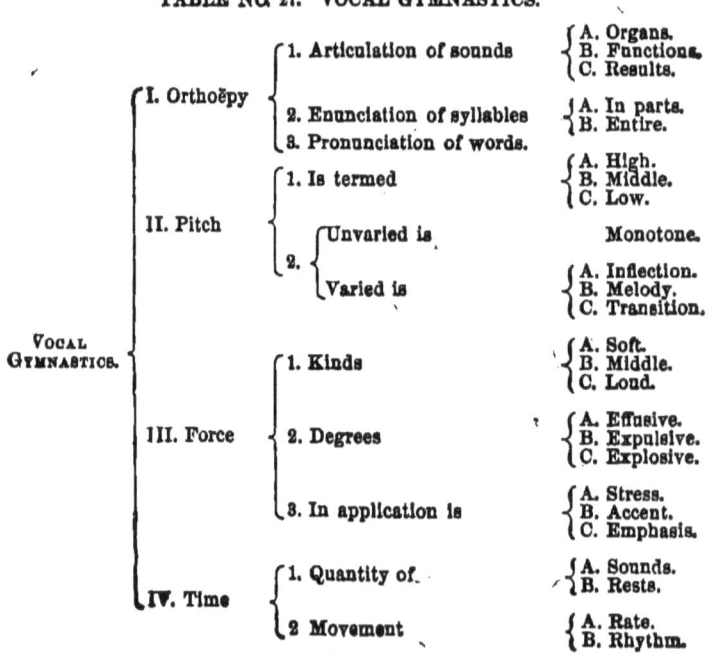

VOCAL GYMNASTICS.
- I. Orthoëpy
  - 1. Articulation of sounds
    - A. Organs.
    - B. Functions.
    - C. Results.
  - 2. Enunciation of syllables
    - A. In parts.
    - B. Entire.
  - 3. Pronunciation of words.
- II. Pitch
  - 1. Is termed
    - A. High.
    - B. Middle.
    - C. Low.
  - 2.
    - Unvaried is Monotone.
    - Varied is
      - A. Inflection.
      - B. Melody.
      - C. Transition.
- III. Force
  - 1. Kinds
    - A. Soft.
    - B. Middle.
    - C. Loud.
  - 2. Degrees
    - A. Effusive.
    - B. Expulsive.
    - C. Explosive.
  - 3. In application is
    - A. Stress.
    - B. Accent.
    - C. Emphasis.
- IV. Time
  - 1. Quantity of
    - A. Sounds.
    - B. Rests.
  - 2. Movement
    - A. Rate.
    - B. Rhythm.

PART IV.
ELOCUTION.

READING is the art of receiving or imparting ideas by means of written or printed characters. It is silent or vocal, sentential or oratorical.

Sentential reading has regard to the sense or thought of the composition; oratorical reading expresses not only the thought, but the emotion of the thought. To this end elocution is a means.

Elocution is the vocal delivery of extemporaneous or written composition, and includes vocal gymnastics and gesture.*

VOCAL GYMNASTICS.

Vocal gymnastics is the science and the art of speech. It includes orthoëpy, pitch, force, and time in the first, and orthophony in the second portion of the definition. Science teaches us to know, art to do. Science is classified knowledge, art is the *use* of classified knowledge.

The *science* of speech is the philosophy of the human voice—its relations, principles, and laws.

The *art* of speech is the use of these scientific facts.

1. ORTHOËPY treats of correct pronunciation. It includes articulation, enunciation, and pronunciation.

2. PITCH is any degree of elevation or height. In oratory, pitch is the position of voice upon the diatonic scale.

3. FORCE is the result of action. In oratory, force is the degree of intensity or energy with which words or their components are uttered.

4. TIME is a measured portion of duration. Time in oratory is the measure of rate or speed of utterance.

5. *Orthophony* is the training of the vocal organs in orthoëpy, pitch, force, and time.

* Gesture is not discussed as a science in this Manual, but has been treated with a view to assist the teacher or student in its application. See Gesture, p. 101.

MANUAL OF READING.

TABLE NO. 28. ORTHOËPY.

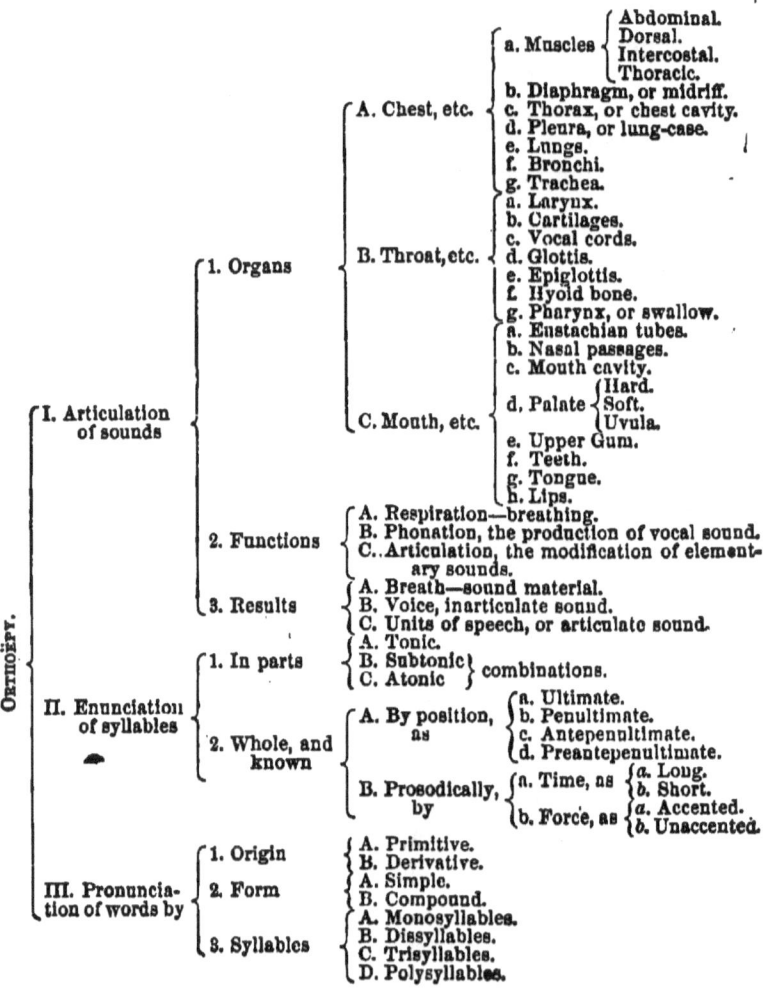

ORTHOËPY.

ORTHOËPY treats of correct pronunciation, or the distinct and proper utterance of combined elements of language. First, we must consider the *articulation* of single elements; second, the *enunciation* of combined elements in whole syllables, or in parts of syllables; third, the *pronunciation* of words.

Though these three terms are often regarded as synonymous, yet a distinction is to be made in their use. In speaking of the general manner of delivery, *elocution* may be used instead of *enunciation;* as, "His elocution is good," not "His *enunciation* is good."

Articulation, resulting as it does from certain definite and unvarying configurations or movements of the vocal organs, is in its nature fixed; whereas *pronunciation*, dependent as it is upon good usage, custom, or fashion, is subject to change from time to time. One unit of speech or sound may be substituted for another in words of the same origin and meaning, as *lände* for *länd, honde* (in Chaucer's time) for *hănd* (in our time), *myselve* for myself, etc. Sometimes the sounds are changed when the orthography is unchanged, as ēither and nēither for ēither and nēither.

Articulation, in the science of elocution, is the distinct utterance of the elementary sounds of a language.* This implies *organs,* their *functions* or *offices,* and the *results.* The organs of articulation may be classed in three groups; those of the *chest,* those of the *throat,* and those of the *mouth.* In the production of words, the first group performs the labor known as *respiration,* which furnishes breath, or material for sound; the function of the second group is *phonation,* or *sound-making,* and results in voice or sound; the function of the third group is *articulation,* or *sound-modification,* which results in units of speech or *articulate* sound.

* Utterance does not necessarily mean articulation; as, "He uttered a sigh," "He uttered a moan." A sigh or moan is not articulate.

I. FIRST GROUP—CHEST ORGANS.

The *organs* of respiration, their *functions*, and *results:*

1. *The muscles:*

    a. The abdominal (in front) give the first impulse toward the production of sound, and, by contracting, assist the diaphragm in an upward movement.

    b. The dorsal (in the lower part of the back) act in concert with the abdominal muscles in giving an upward movement during violent use of the voice, as shouting, etc.

    c. The intercostal (at the lower part of the chest), and,

    d. The thoracic and *pectoral* (at the upper part of the chest), dilate and contract the chest in breathing or vocalizing.

2. *The diaphragm,* or midriff (a muscular and tendinous partition which separates the thorax, or great chest cavity, from the abdomen), gives an upward impulse, acting upon the pleura, or lung-case.

3. *The thorax,* or chest cavity (the region of body between the neck and stomach), continues the great work of respiration by contracting and expanding, and gives depth and resonance to the voice, as well as voice-material, or breath.

4. *The pleura,* or *lung-case* (a membrane covering the lungs), receives from the diaphragm and muscles an impulse, which it communicates to the lungs, causing it to expel the air from its cells into the bronchi.

5. *The lungs* (a lobed and spongy body filled with minute divisions and subdivisions of the bronchi) act as an air receiver, subject to the action of the pleura.

6. *The bronchi* (two main branches of the trachea, or windpipe, with their divisions and subdivisions) distribute the air inhaled through the trachea to the lungs, and convey that expelled by the organic impulse back through the trachea, larynx, and mouth.

7. *The trachea,* or windpipe (a series of cartilaginous or gristly rings forming the great air-channel to and from the lungs), serves to conduct the breath through the bronchi to and from the lungs in respiration, phonation, and articulation.

II. SECOND GROUP—THROAT ORGANS.

The *organs* of phonation, their *functions*, and *results:*

1. *The larynx*, or Adam's apple (a cartilaginous box on the top of the trachea), expands and contracts, rises and sinks, thus enlarging or diminishing its capacity. It is depressed to produce *grave* sounds, and raised to produce *acute* sounds.

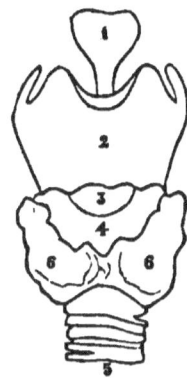 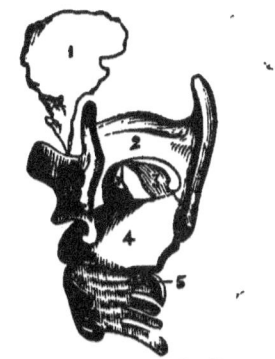

Fig. 1. Front view of the Larynx and a part of the Trachea.
1. Epiglottis.
2. Thyroid cartilage.
3. Crico-thyroid cartilage.
4. Cricoid cartilage.
5. Trachea.
6. Thyroid gland.

Fig. 2. Back view of the Larynx and upper part of the Trachea.
1. Epiglottis.
2. Thyroid cartilage.
3, 3. Arytenoid cartilages.
4. Cricoid cartilage.
5. Trachea.

2. The *cartilages* of the larynx:

a. The cricoid (situated immediately over the upper ring of the trachea, resembles in form a seal ring, from which it takes its name, the seal being back, and the narrow part of the ring in front), by its form and position, admits of the elevation and depression of this part of the larynx, thus helping to render tone acute or grave.

b. The thyroid (in form of a buckler or shield, much bent, and by its two main plates forming the sides or walls of the larynx) usually determines the capacity of the voice, and, with other parts of the larynx, renders the voice compact and sonorous.

c. The arÿt'enoid (two in number, so called from a fancied resemblance in shape to a pitcher, ladle, or funnel, fill the space back of the thyroid and cricoid cartilages, and are connected with both) serve as points of support and tension for the vocal cords or ligaments.

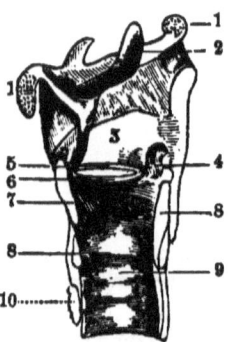
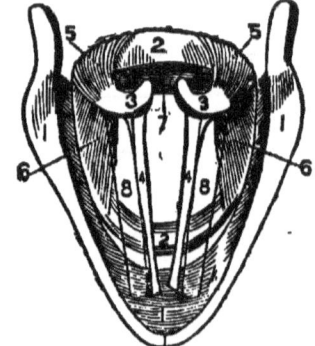

Fig. 3. Vertical section of the Larynx and a part of the Trachea.

1, 1. Hyoid or lingual bone, below which is seen the thyro-hyoid membrane extending to the thyroid cartilage.
2. Epiglottis.
3. One wing of the thyroid cartilage.
4. Arytenoid cartilage of one side.
5. Superior, or false vocal chord of one side.
6. Inferior, or true vocal chord of one side.
7. Thyroid cartilage in front.
8, 8. Cricoid cartilage.
9. Upper ring of the trachea.
10. Thyroid gland.

Fig. 4. Interior of the Larynx, seen from above.

1. Thyroid cartilage.
2. Cricoid cartilage.
3, 3. Arytenoid cartilages.
4, 4. Inferior, or true vocal chords.
5. Posterior crico-arytenoid muscles.
6. Lateral crico-arytenoid muscles.
7. Arytenoideus muscle.
8, 8. Thyro-arytenoid muscles, within the dotted lines.

3. *The vocal chords,* or *ligaments* (extending across the upper part of the larynx and forming the lips of the glottis), vibrate with the action of the current of air expelled from the lungs, and produce vocal sound, and, by tension and remission, produce various degrees of pitch.

4. *The glottis* (the small chink or opening between the vocal chords, forming the mouth of the larynx) opens and contracts, thus deciding in part the gravity or shrillness of tone. It dilates in low sounds, and contracts in high sounds.

5. *The epiglottis* (the valve or lid of which caps the glottis), when the larynx is elevated, as in the act of swallowing, covers the glottis, or orifice of the windpipe, and prevents strangulation. Usually it is erect, and allows free ingress and egress to the breath.

6. *The hyoid,* or *U-like bone* (a small crescent-shaped bone

ORTHOËPY.

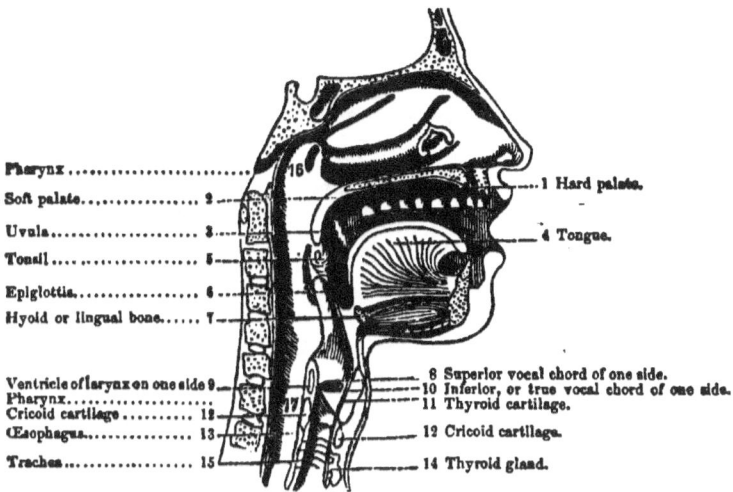

Pharynx .....
Soft palate 2
Uvula 3
Tonsil 5
Epiglottis 6
Hyoid or lingual bone 7
Ventricle of larynx on one side 9
Pharynx .....
Cricoid cartilage 12
Œsophagus 13
Trachea 15

1 Hard palate.
4 Tongue.
8 Superior vocal chord of one side.
10 Inferior, or true vocal chord of one side.
11 Thyroid cartilage.
12 Cricoid cartilage.
14 Thyroid gland.

Fig. 5. Section of the Head and Neck, showing the Organs of Speech.

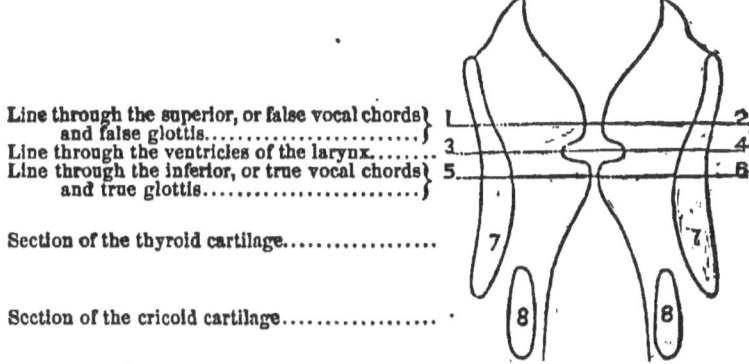

Line through the superior, or false vocal chords and false glottis .....
Line through the ventricles of the larynx 3
Line through the inferior, or true vocal chords and true glottis 5

Section of the thyroid cartilage 7

Section of the cricoid cartilage 8

Fig. 6. Transverse section, showing the cavity of the Larynx, with the true vocal chords nearly parallel, or in a position to vibrate.

lying at the root of the tongue, between the larynx and the mouth), forms a point of tension for the muscles which connect the larynx with the mouth, and aids in giving pitch.*

7. *The pharynx*, or *swallow* (a dilatable bag situated immediately behind and above the larynx, affects the charac-

* The hyoid bone. "Situated in an almost horizontal position behind and rather below the lower jaw, it performs the triple office of a basis of the tongue, a point of support to the larynx, and a fulcrum by which the contractions of the intrinsic muscles of the tongue and the larynx may be impressed on these organs."

F

ter of sound by giving it resonant space. A large pharynx usually indicates a deep tone of voice, and a small one a comparatively high pitch.

8. *The thyroid gland* (so called, although "it has no excretory duct; a firm, vascular substance, lying like a cushion, in two lobes, across the upper part of the trachea") is supposed to check the vibration of sound, and prevent its descent. When enlarged, this gland produces goître, or swelled neck.

III. THIRD GROUP—MOUTH ORGANS.

The *organs* of articulation, their *functions*, and *results*.

1. *The Eustachian tubes* (canals leading from the tympana, or drums of the ears, to the pharynx) help to render the voice clear and free.*

2. *The nasal passages* (the innermost parts of the nostrils united into one resonant channel, and opening into the back part of the mouth behind the "veil," or pendant and movable part of the palate) give resonance to the voice, and serve as air-channels when the mouth is closed, as in ordinary breathing.

3. *The mouth cavity* (oval in shape, bounded in front by the lips, behind by the soft palate, above by the hard palate or roof, below by the tongue, and on the sides by the cheeks and teeth), by its arched structure, moulds sound, and gives it scope and reverberation, sweetness and smoothness.

4. *The palate* (divided into the hard palate, or the roof of the mouth; [2] the veil, or soft palate—the pendant and movable membranous curtain separating the mouth from the pharynx; and [3] the uvula, a small round tag or process hanging from the middle of the lower border of the soft palate) defines the volume of sound.

5. *The teeth* help to give a clear and distinct character to enunciation.

6. *The tongue* (composed of muscular fibres, and having a

---

* The whole cavity of the head, its hollows and cells about the face and forehead, are subservient to the resonance of the voice. Organic malformation, snuff-taking, colds, or catarrh, at once prove how much the clear, pure, ringing tones depend upon the proper condition of these cavities.

ORTHOËPY. 123

very flexible tip) modifies vocal sound, and renders it articulate, changes the size of the mouth cavity, directs sound, and, by its various positions and movements, assists in producing the guttural, nasal, and oral qualities of voice.

7. *The lips* project, convey, and modify sounds very materially.

Review of Respiration, or Breathing.

The muscles of the chest—the intercostal, thoracic, and pectoral—compress and expand the thorax, or great chest cavity, thus expelling and receiving breath, and furnishing a constant supply of material for sound.*

Review of Phonation.†

The lungs being filled with breath, or material for sound, the abdominal muscles contract and elevate the diaphragm, which instantly communicates the received impulse to the pleura, or lung-case, which in its turn expels the breath from the lungs into the bronchi, thence into the trachea and larynx, where, by the action of the muscles at this point, it is rendered vocal, or is converted into sound.

Review of Articulation, or the Production of Speech-sounds.

The breath, converted into voice by the action of the larynx, passes out to the mouth, where, by the various posi-

---

* The sound of the human voice, as well as all mechanical or musical sounds, may be *discrete* or *concrete*. Discretes are successive detached notes or sounds; concretes are smooth and united sounds—a continuous stream of gliding sounds.

† The movement of the shoulders up and down, in respiration, indicates some organic derangement or artificial restriction. In ancient times, this was considered a great blemish in oratory, and aspirants to oratorical honors, subject to the habit, were wont to practice with a sword or other sharp instrument hung over the shoulder, so that the slightest upward movement was instantly checked, and the pupil put on his guard continually. Breathe horizontally, or down and outward. Keep the mouth closed when sleeping, and at other times when not speaking. Mr. George Catlin, the well-known Indian traveler, has written an entire volume upon this subject. He attributes lung diseases to the pernicious habit of breathing through the mouth. He cured himself of the habit by wearing a sort of clasp on the lips while sleeping. A small bit of isinglass-plaster answers as well.

tions or motions of the palate, tongue, teeth, and lips, it is rendered articulate, *i. e.*, made into distinct sounds called "units of speech," each of which is readily distinguished from all the others.

Thus elements of speech may be traced from the first impulse that begins them to the last and least modification that perfects them.

VOICE.

VOICE is sound produced by the forcible passage of air through the larynx.

The human voice, independent of articulation, has several native and acquired qualities, as compass, volume, and (when emitted in successive impulses, or notes) rate, or time. See Note, p. 123.

Compass and volume (or pitch and force) are attributes common to all voices. Pitch is caused by variations in the condition and dimensions of the glottis, and also by the length of the vocal tube—the larynx being raised for high notes, and depressed for low ones.

The voice varies in force from a whisper to a shout, just as the breath varies from soft breathing to panting. The degree of loudness of the voice is in proportion to the expulsive effort, and the resistance which the air meets in its passage from the lungs through the vocal tube. If little resistance be given to the outward rush of air, an aspirated or whispered sound is the result.

Compass of voice is the range of its capabilities upon the diatonic scale, above or below which it can not go easily. The usual compass of cultivated voices is three octaves.*
In ascending the scale, there is a point where the voice is said to "break." This point is about two octaves above the lowest note of the voice. The notes of the voice above this point are called *falsetto*, and those below, *natural*.

In music, the lowest octave of male voices is called *bass;* the middle, or second octave, *tenor;* and the highest octave, *treble*. The corresponding octaves of female voices are called *contralto*, *mezzo-soprano*, and *soprano*.† The natural pitch of women's and boys' voices is one octave above that of men. The treble corresponds with the falsetto, and the tenor and bass with the orotund, in man's voice; and the

* It is said that the ear can perceive nine octaves.
† The bass is often called by its Italian name, *basso;* the tenor, *baritone;* and the treble, *tenore*.

soprano corresponds with the falsetto, and the contralto with the orotund, in woman's voice.

QUALITIES OF VOICE.

Quality is the nature of a thing relatively considered. Quality of voice is the kind or property of the voice. There are eight of these organic, habitual, or assumed qualities. They are aspirate,* pure, orotund, pectoral, guttural, nasal, oral, and falsetto.

Every person's voice is characterized by one or more of these qualities. The pure, orotund, pectoral, and aspirate can not be united, but the nasal will unite with any other quality except the oral and guttural. Thus one may speak in the nasal pure, the nasal orotund, or the nasal aspirate.

The pure and orotund are far more pleasing than the remaining qualities, so that the former may properly be classed as agreeable, and the latter as disagreeable qualities, or vices.

1. The *aspirate* is known as a whisper and half whisper. The whisper is the least audible articulate sound, being midway between breath and vocality. It might be called articulated breath.

Example. "The foe! They come! They come!"—BYRON.

The half whisper is more vocal than the whisper, being midway between that and full vocality. These two varieties of sound arise from a relaxed condition of the vocal chords, caused by fear, weakness, awe, secretiveness, anger, or any violent emotion which prevents deep and full inspiration. The parts are temporarily paralyzed, and allow more breath to escape from the lungs than is rendered vocal by the larynx.

Examples.

(*Asp.*) "And then we thought on vengeance, and all along our van, 'Remember Saint Bartholomew!' was passed from man to man."
MACAULAY.

"To bed, to bed; there's knocking at the gate.
Come, come, come, come, give me your hand!"—*Macbeth.*

---

* The aspirate can hardly be said to have a place under voice, since it has no vocality; but, having tone, it has a place among qualities.

2. The *pure* is the full, distinct tone, which, above all others, is agreeable to the ear. In this quality the inspirations are deep and full, and the breath is given out slowly, the whole being converted into the greatest possible amount of sound. It is in strong contrast with the aspirate, which takes in a small supply of air and sends out much, thereby making little vocality.*

Example.   "The quality of mercy is not strain'd;
It droppeth, as the gentle rain from heaven
Upon the place beneath: it is twice bless'd;
It blesseth him that gives, and him that takes:
'Tis mightiest in the mightiest; it becomes
The throned monarch better than his crown:
His sceptre shows the force of temporal power,
The attribute to awe and majesty,
Wherein doth sit the dread and fear of kings;
But mercy is above this sceptred sway;
It is an attribute to God himself:
And earthly power doth then show likest God's,
When mercy seasons justice."—SHAKSPEARE.

3. The *orotund* is the *intensity and dignity* of the pure tone, known by its depth, rounded fullness, and power. "It is the pure tone rounded in the mouth and deepened in the chest."

Example.   "'On the earl's cheek the flush of rage
O'ercame the ashen hue of age;
Fierce he broke forth: 'And darest thou, then,
To beard the lion in his den,
The Douglas in his hall?
And hop'st thou hence unscathed to go?
No! by St. Bride of Bothwell, no!
Up drawbridge, groom!   What!   warder!   ho!
Let the portcullis fall!'"—SCOTT.

4. The *pectoral*, or hollow tone, arises from feeble organs, ill health, diffidence, constraint, or the like, but it is oftener the result of weak action of the abdominal muscles in giving the primary impulse to vocal expression. Its pitch is low, with the resonance in the chest.

---

* That vocal utterance which produces smoothly and without apparent effort the greatest number of distinct sounds with the least amount of breath, or material for sound, is the most perfect for emotional speaking, for it allows an uninterrupted climax.

Examples.

"You may, if it be God's will, gain our barren and rugged mountains; but, like our ancestors of old, we will seek refuge in wilder and more distant solitudes, and, when we have resisted to the last, we will starve in the icy wastes of the glaciers. Ay, men, women, and children, we will be frozen into annihilation together ere one free Switzer will acknowledge a foreign master!"

"The skies they were ashen and sober,
The leaves they were crisped and sear,
The leaves they were | withering and sear.
It was | night | in the lonesome | October
(Of my most immemorial year).
It was hard | by the dim | Lake of Auber,
In the misty mid-region of Wier.;
It was down by the dank tarn of Auber,
In the ghoul- | haunted woodland of Wier."—POE.

5. The *guttural*, or rough, grating voice, seems to issue from an obstructed throat. "The immediate organic cause of this bad quality of tone is an improper pressure of the muscles around the larynx and the root of the tongue, causing the voice, in the one case, apparently to issue from the pharynx, or swallow, instead of the larynx; and, in the other, to originate in the upper part of the throat only, cut off from communication with either the chest or mouth."—RUSSEL. It expresses hate, contempt, malignity, rage, etc.

Example. "The *curse* my noble father laid on thee
When, thou *didst crown* his warlike brows
With *paper*."—SHAKSPEARE.

6. The *nasal* is a tone which seems to come through the nose. Organically it is made by allowing the voice to drift with force against the nasal passages while they are partly closed, and the veil of the palate is too low. It is voice with little or no resonance in the nose.

Example. "I tell you what, I'll build one shay to beat the taoun,
'N the keounty, 'n all the kentry raoun';
It shall be so built that it couldn' break daoun."
                                            O. W. HOLMES.

7. The *oral* is a voice seemingly distant, as if coming from another room, a box, or closet, and partakes of ventriloquy in its effect. It can be produced by making the mouth-cavity high and narrow, pressing the cheeks closely against the well-opened teeth while speaking, and forcing the sound upward as it escapes. The veil of the palate is high in producing the oral.

Example. "Then fear not, doubt not, which thou wilt,
We'll try this quarrel hilt to hilt."—SCOTT.

8. The *falsetto.* In the falsetto voice, the vocal ligaments do not meet in their entire length, either a posterior or an anterior portion of them remaining apart.* It arises from feebleness, fatigue, indifference, affectation, and the like. In music, this voice is called treble, and begins about two octaves above the lowest note of the voice, where, in ascending the musical scale, the voice is said to "break." All notes above this "break" are falsetto, and those below, natural. In producing this quality, the veil of the palate is high, and the uvula is contracted into the veil and completely hidden from sight. It expresses irritability, scolding, invective, etc.

Example.

"Billy! where are you, Billy? I say, come home to your best of mothers.
I'm scared when I think of them Cabroleys, they drive so;
They'd run over their own sisters and brothers.
Or maybe he's stole by some chimney-sweeping wretch, to stick in narrow flues and what not,
And be poked up behind with a picked pointed pole, when the soot has ketched and the chimbly's red hot.
Oh, I'd give the whole wide world, if the world was mine, to clap my two longin' eyes on his face;
For he's my darlin' of darlin's, and if he don't soon come back, you'll see me drop stone dead on the place."—HOOD, *The Lost Heir.*

Nasal sound-units (m, n, ng) are emitted through the nose, while the *quality* of voice known as nasal is produced when the nasal passages are partially closed.

TABLE NO. 29. ELEMENTS OF LANGUAGE.

ELEMENTS OF LANGUAGE.*

- **I. Sounds**
  - 1. In Number 34 or 36.
    - A. Tone
      - a. Tonic.
      - b. Subtonic.
      - c. Atonic.
  - 2. As to
    - B. Organic Construction
      - a. Oral-larynguals.
      - b. Labials.
      - c. Linguals.
      - d. Palatals.
  - 3. In
    - A. Pitch
    - B. Force
    - C. Time
    - (See Tables.)

- **II. Signs**
  - 1. In Number 26.
  - 2. In Script called
    - a. Round hand.
    - b. Running hand.
    - c. Epistolary hand.
    - d. Court hand.
    - e. German text, etc.
  - 3. Print
    - A. Form (capital and small)
      - a. Romanic.
      - b. *Italic.*
      - c. 𝔒𝔩𝔡 𝔈𝔫𝔤𝔩𝔦𝔰𝔥.
      - d. 𝔊𝔢𝔯𝔪𝔞𝔫 𝔗𝔢𝔵𝔱, etc.
    - B. Size
      - a. Brilliant (the smallest).
      - b. Diamond.
      - c. Pearl.
      - d. Ruby.
      - e. Agate.
      - f. Nonpareil.
      - g. Minion.
      - h. Brevier.
      - i. Bourgeois.
      - j. Long Primer.
      - k. Small Pica.
      - l. Pica.
      - m. English.
      - n. Great Primer.
      - o. Paragon.
      - p. Canon
      - (the largest that has a specific name).
    - C. Names
      - a.
      - bee.
      - cee.
      - dee.
      - e.
      - ef.
      - gee.
      - aitch.
      - i.
      - jay.
      - kay.
      - el.
      - em.
      - en.
      - o.
      - pee.
      - qu.
      - ar.
      - es.
      - tee.
      - u.
      - vee.
      - double-you.
      - eks.
      - y.
      - zee.

* See Tables No. 1 and No. 2.

ELEMENTS OF LANGUAGE.

LANGUAGE is the expression of thought and feeling. It may be *oral*, or expressed by *sensible signs*.

Oral language is expression by *vocal sounds—articulate*, as in speech; or *inarticulate*, as in sighs, sobs, groans, etc.

Sensible sign-language is expression by *gesture*, as in the language of mutes, etc., or by *letters*, which appeal to the sense of sight, as in written or printed composition.

Every indivisible portion of language is a primary element or unit of language, and every unit has a sound, or a sign and name. In written or printed language every *sign* (letter of the alphabet) has a *name*, and represents one or more units of sound; but, unfortunately, every *unit* of *sound* has not a *name* nor a visible *sign*. The sign *h*, for instance, has a *sound*, as heard in hat, and a *name*, *aitch;* but the sound of *a*, as heard in *ăt*, has no *name*, neither has it a sign distinguishing it from *a*, as heard in the words *fāte, fär, fȧll*. Diacritical marks, which indicate the precise sound required, are sometimes used in dictionaries and spelling-books; but these marked letters scarcely assume the dignity of distinct signs, and are so seldom found in print as to furnish quite inadequate assistance to native or foreign students in the acquisition of the English language. The letter *a*, for example, may stand for any one of seven sounds, unless it receive some one of the following marks, ā, ă, ä, ạ, ạ, å, â, to indicate the required sound, and, since these added marks are neither in general use in scientific or literary works, nor uniform in dictionaries, thousands of words must be arbitrarily learned. Again, as if to add to confusion, there are from one to fourteen single and compound *signs* to represent a solitary sound, and there are some sounds without any signs. (See Table, "Elements of Language." Note the pure sounds or units of speech, the sounds that are common to several signs, and their equivalents, etc.) There are about thirty-six sound-units, twenty-six sign-units, and twenty-six names for the signs.

1. *A unit of sound* is an indivisible portion of spoken language, and appeals to the ear.

2. *A letter* or *sign-unit* is an indivisible portion of written or printed language, and appeals to the eye (or, in case of blindness, to the sense of feeling).

Signs are known by their *form*, as R o m a n i c, 𝔒𝔩𝔡 𝔈𝔫𝔤𝔩𝔦𝔰𝔥, *Italic*, 𝔊𝔢𝔯𝔪𝔞𝔫-𝔗𝔢𝔵𝔱, etc., each having twenty-six capitals, and twenty-six corresponding small or "lower-case" letters.

Printed signs are distinguished by their comparative *size*, as brilliant (the smallest), diamond (the next larger size), pearl, ruby, agate, nonpareil, etc., up to canon (the largest which has a name) (see Table No. 29). Besides being distinguished by *form* and *size*, signs have each a *name* (twenty-six in number), a, bee, cee, dee, ee, ef, je, aitch, etc. (see Table No. 29). These names are expressions used in speaking of the alphabet as initials, as R. H. Smith, LL.D.

UNITS OF SPEECH (see Table, p. 8).

A unit of speech or sound-unit is an indivisible portion of spoken language. The various positions and motions of the organs of speech so modify vocalized breath as to produce at least thirty-four distinct sounds or units of speech.

Those sound-units, produced with no obstruction of the vocal tube (trachea, larynx, and mouth), are called *vowels* or *tonics*; those formed with the vocal tube entirely or partially *closed* at some point, are called consonants, or sub-tonics and atonics. The three points or stations where the vocal tube is closed or obstructed are at the lips, at the front palate (or roof near the front teeth), and at the back palate. Those units formed by the obstruction at the lips are called *labials*, those formed by an obstruction at the front palate (or by the teeth and tongue) are called *linguals*, and those formed at the back palate are called *palatals*, or, less properly, *gutturals*.

Rem. 1. "Professor Willis, in experimenting on the nature of sound, discovered that in placing a reed in a common organ-pipe, the length of which could be varied at pleasure, and forcing the air through it with a pair of bellows, he ob-

tained, according to the length of the pipe (going from the sound produced by the shortest to that produced by the longest), the following series of sounds, as expressed by the italicized vowels of the given words, viz.: 1. mē; 2. māte; 3. mär; 4, mąw; 5. mōw; 6. my̆rrh; 7. mǫod; and that, continuing to lengthen the pipe, the *same* sounds were still heard, but *in an inverse order*—7, 6, 5, 4, 3, 2, 1; and that, still further increasing its length, the same identical sounds again occurred, but *in the first order;* and so on throughout."
—*Cambridge Phil. Transactions*, vol. iii., p. 231-262.

Rem. 2. "The natural order of the primary vowels, as determined mechanically, is I, E, A, O, U, or U, O, A, E, I (*i. e.*, ē, ā, ä, ō, oo, or oo, ō, ä, ā, ē), as heard in the English words field, vein, far, owe, ooze. This order should be well impressed upon the memory."—HALDEMAN's *Latin Prosody.*

Rem. 3. "The closeness of ē and oo approximates them to the nearest consonant, into which they are apt to fall; the first into the semi-vowel *y*, and the last into the semi-vowel *w*." *Ah*, however, from its extreme openness, is farthest removed from the consonants.

Besides the formation names (labials, etc., see Table, p. 9), sound-units are classed and named with reference to their tone or vocality, as, 1. Tonics; 2. Sub-tonics; and, 3. Atonics; or, 1. Vocals; 2. Sub-vocals; 3. Aspirates.

1. A *tonic* is a full tone modified, but not interrupted in the vocal tube, and capable of indefinite prolongation.

2. A *sub-tonic* is a sound which has less perfect vocality than the tonic, and, being more or less interrupted in its passage through the vocal tube, has less capacity for prolongation.

3. An *atonic* is an articulate breath-sound.*

The tonics comprise all the sounds of the vowels a, e, i, o, u (w and y have no tonic sounds not found among the pure sounds of the vowels). Phonologists differ very materially as to the number of sounds in the English language, so that

---

* It is a *sound*, or it could not be heard, and it is *articulate*, or we could not understand what is said; *i. e.*, it has a characteristic formation, yet it is not *vocal*, or it would be capable of variations in pitch. Atonics can not be said to have pitch.

no system can be free from objection, however carefully prepared.

In describing the sound-units called tonics, those which require no change in the position of the organs of speech, from their beginning to their close, are called *pure* or *simple* tonics (see Table No. 2), while those that require a change of position in the organs of speech during their formation are called diphthongal tonics.

The diphthongal tonics have a radical or beginning, and a vanish or close. The sound of a letter which can not be distinguished from another sound, already attributed to some letter as one of its pure sounds, is said to be common, *i. e.*, common to two or more sign-units or letters (see Table No. 2). The sounds of *a*, as in *all*, and *o*, as in *old*, when not so closely joined to a succeeding sound as to prevent their *completion*, have each a *vanish*, or closing sound, distinct from the *radical*, or opening sound.

But, since the vanish is often omitted in unaccented syllables and at other times, they are classed with the simple vowels, and not with the diphthongs (see *Principles of Pronunciation in* WEBSTER, § 44, 50).

THE TONIC OR VOWEL SOUNDS. (See Table No. 6.)

Webster.	Worcester.	
		A has four pure sounds and three common:
ā (āē)	ā (āī)	as in ale, or long a, ⎫
ă	ă	" at, or short a, ⎪
ä	ä	" far, or Italian a, ⎬ pure sounds.
ạ	ȧ	" all, or broad a, ⎭
â (ĕ)	â	" dare, many (like short ĕ prolonged, called common).
ȧ	ȧ	" ask, past, or intermediate (between short and Italian a).
ǫ (ŏ)	a	" what (like short ŏ, common).
		E has two pure sounds and four common:
ē	ē	as in eve, or long e, ⎫ pure sounds.
ĕ	ĕ	" end, or short e, ⎭
ẽ (ũ)	ê	" her, or e before r, trans-fer (common).
ê (â)	ê	" where (common).
ę (ā)	e	" eight (common).
	e (ĭ)	" pretty (common).
		I has one diphthongal sound, one pure, and two common:
ī (āē)	ī (ūē)	as in ice, or long i (diphthongal).
ĭ	ĭ	" it, or short i, pure sound.

ORTHOËPY.

Webster.	Worcester.	
ī (ē)	ī	as in marine, or the French sound of i, like ē long (common).
ĭ (ŭ)	ĭ	" sir, fir, or the sound of u short (common).
i	i (y)	" union.
		O has three pure sounds and three common:
ō	ō	as in old, or long o, ⎫
ŏ	ŏ	" lot, or short o, ⎬ pure sounds.
ǫ	ǫ	" do, move, or long close o, ⎭
ô (å)	ō (å)	" orb, form, like a broad (common).
ó (ŭ)	ó (ŭ)	" sŏn, óther, like short u (common).
ọ (ụ)	o (ù)	" wǫlf, wǫman, like ŭ in full (common).
		U has two pure sounds, four common, and one diph-
ū (ēǫ)	ū (ēō)	as in lute, or long u (diphthongal). [thongal:
ŭ	ŭ	" up, or short u, ⎫ pure sounds.
ụ	ů	" full, or obtuse u, ⎬
ü (ǫ)	ü (ō)	" rule, sure (see Rule, p. 1), (common).
ů	u	" urge (common).
u	u (ĕ)	" bury (*berry*) (common).
u	u (ĭ)	" business (bizness) (common).
		W has one vowel sound, common:
w (ǫ)	w	as in now (like o in do).
		Y has three sounds, common:
y (ī)	y	as in by (like long ī).
y (ĭ)	y	" sylph (like short ĭ).
y (ŭ).	y	" myrtle (like short ŭ).

· Beside the sounds already named, we have combined—

oo (ǫ), as in moon (like o in *do*).
oo (ụ), as in foot (like *u* in *full*).
oo (ō), as in floor (like o in *more*).
oo (ŭ), as in flood (like *u* in *up*).
ou or ow (ŭụ), as in our, flower (a union of *u* in up and *u* in full).
oi or oy (aī), as in oil, boy (a union of *a* in ball and *i* in pin).

SUB-TONICS AND ATONICS.   BY ORGANIC FORMATION.

Labials.

Those sounds whose peculiar characteristic is formed by the position or action of the lips are called *labials.* They are the sounds of m, p, b, v, f, w.*

1. M is produced by closing the lips and sending vocalized breath through the nose.

2. P is produced by forcing breath suddenly through the closed lips.

3. B is produced by closing the lips and making a vocal sound in the throat before opening them.

---

* The sounds of m, b, p are nearly alike; m is produced with the mouth passage closed, and p is a whispered b; n, d, t, and ng, g, k, have the same or corresponding differences.

4. F is produced by placing the under lip against the edges of the upper incisor teeth, and audibly breathing through them.

5. V is produced by placing the organs in the same position as for the sound of f, and making vocal the breath as it escapes.

6. W is produced by nearly closing the lips, making a sound in the throat, and forcing it through them.

Linguals.

Those sounds whose peculiar characteristic is caused by the special position or action of the tongue are called linguals. They are n, d, t, *th*, th, s, z, r, l.

1. The sound of *n*, as in *noon*, is produced by placing the tip of the tongue against the interior upper gums, so as to close the vocal tube, and emitting vocal sound through the nose.

2. The sound of *d*, as in *did*, is produced by closing the vocal tube as before, and forcing *vocal sound* through the obstructions in the mouth.

3. The sound of *t*, as in *tent*, is produced by closing the vocal tube, as described in No. 1, and forcing *breath* through the obstruction.

4. The sound of *th*, as in *th*is, is produced by placing the rim of the tongue against the edges of the upper teeth, and emitting vocalized breath between them.

5. The sound of *th*, as in *thin*, is produced by joining the teeth and tongue, as before, and emitting breath instead of vocal sound.

6. The sound of *s*, as in *son*, is produced by pressing the sides of the tongue against the teeth in such a way as to leave a small passage down its centre, and forcing breath through this channel, causing it to escape the teeth in a hiss.

7. The sound of *z*, as in *zone*, is formed by vocalizing the breath as it escapes, instead of emitting it, as in *s*.

8. The sound of *r*, as in *run*, is produced by bringing the sides of the tongue against the teeth, elevating the tip toward the centre of the roof of the mouth, but leaving it free to vibrate, and emitting vocal sound.

9. The sound of *l*, as in *lull*, is formed by placing the tip of the tongue against the front roof of the mouth, and emitting vocal sound over the sides of the tongue.

Palatals.

Those sounds whose peculiar characteristic is caused by the position or action of the palate are called palatals. They are *ng, g, k, c,* or *sh, z, h, y;* with the consonant triphthongs *ch* and *j.**

1. The sound of *ng* as in *sing,* or *n* in *ink,* is formed by raising the base of the tongue against the palate, so as to close the vocal tube at that point, and emitting vocal sound through the nose with the lips open.

2. The sound of *g,* as in *go,* is produced by closing the vocal tube at the palate and nasal passages (thus confining the vocal sound in the throat), and suddenly expelling the breath by way of the mouth.

3. The sound of *k,* as in *kite,* is formed by closing the vocal tube at the palate and nasal passages, and forcing out a puff of unvocalized breath.

4. The sound of *sh* as in *shall,* or *c* as in *ocean,* is formed by bringing the sides of the tongue in contact with the roof of the mouth, and sending a breath-sound through the opening thus formed. It is a sound midway between *s* and *y.* (See WEBSTER's *Principles of Pronunciation.*)

5. The sound of *z* (*zh*), as in *azure,* differs from sh only in being vocal.

6. The sound of *h,*† as in *hat,* is an emission of unvocalized breath, through whatever position of the mouth-organs the succeeding element requires, the organs being always placed to form the next succeeding letter before the *h* is produced.

7. The subtonic sound of *y,* as in *yes,* is a sound approximating the vowel *e,* the sound of *y* being less pure in vocality because of a greater obstruction of the vocal tube. The tongue is closer to the roof of the mouth in producing *y* than in producing *e.*

---

* Ch and j are triphthongs (see Tables Nos. 3 and 6).

† H is not included with labials or linguals, and has been placed among the palatals.

138 MANUAL OF READING

TABLE NO. 30. PITCH.

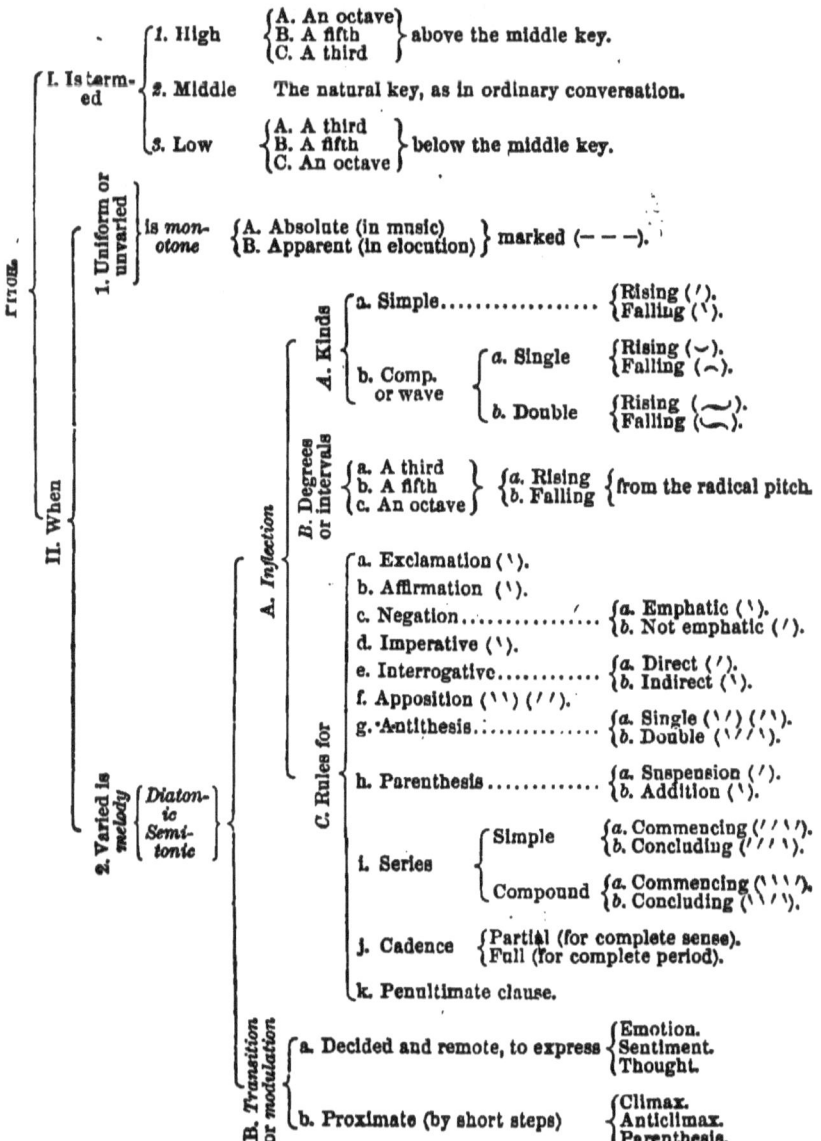

PITCH.

PITCH is the degree of elevation of the voice, or its position upon the diatonic scale.

A *scale* is a series of sounds arranged in continuous ascent or descent, by measured intervals from any pitch or key-note.

It is diatonic or semitonic. The former ascends or descends mostly by *whole* tone intervals, two half tones occurring once only in every seven.

The semitonic or chromatic scale* ascends and descends altogether by *half-tone* intervals.†

An *interval* is the distance between any two points of the scale.

A note is a sound at any given point in the scale.

Key-note is the *first* note. A key is said to be high, middle, or low, according as it is above, on, or below the natural or ordinary elevation.

A *high key* is any key above the middle or natural voice, and is used in calling, shouting, commanding, etc.

A *middle key* is the one used in common conversation, and, owing either to the structure of the vocal organs or to habit, it varies with different people. It is used in narrative or unimpassioned language.

A *low key* is any key below the middle or natural voice, and is used in expressing revenge, solemnity, etc.

The high and low keys are more commonly heard at a third, a fifth, or an octave above or below the middle key.

When the voice *slides* from one note of the scale to another, higher or lower, the distance is called a *concrete* interval; when the voice *steps* from one note to another more re-

---

* "The name chromatic is derived from the fact that the intermediate tones were formerly written and printed in colors."—WEBSTER.

† The diatonic scale is represented by the successive white keys of a piano; the semitonic by the white and black keys successively.

mote without a continuous sound, the interval is called *discrete*. Hence the interval between the first and second notes of a scale may be either a discrete or a concrete interval of a tone. The distance from the first note to the third of a scale is called a discrete or a concrete interval of a third, and the difference between the first and fifth is called a discrete or a concrete interval of a fifth, etc.

HIGH KEYS.

A *third* above is a key three notes above the middle key, and is used to make a number of people hear at the same time.

A *fifth* above is a key five notes above the middle key, and is used in lively and humorous delivery.

An *octave*, or *eighth* above, is a key eight notes above the middle key, and is used in spirited declamation.

LOW KEYS.

A *third* below is a key three notes below the middle key, and is used in expressing dignified sentiment.

A *fifth* below is a key five notes below the middle key, and is used in giving utterance to solemn and impressive thought.

An *octave*, or *eighth* below, is a key eight notes below the middle key, and is used in language of deep solemnity.

MONOTONE.

In elocution, monotone is voice seemingly unvaried in pitch. It expresses awe, reverence, solemnity, sublimity, grandeur, majesty, power, splendor, amazement, all vastness and force, and all preternatural emotions. It is also used in legal and statistical statements, where emotion is unnecessary. In music, monotone is absolute or uniform sameness of sound.

VARIATIONS OF PITCH.

A change or variation of pitch on a single note or syllable is *inflection;* on successive notes or syllables it is *melody*.

MELODY.

Melody is a pleasing succession of sounds in varied pitch. In reading or speaking, melody consists principally of inflections and transitions of pitch, or modulation.*

Melody is diatonic or semitonic, the former being the progression of pitch through the interval of a whole tone, the latter through that of a half tone or semitone. Diatonic melody is used in narration, or to express simple thought; semitonic to express supplication, entreaty, etc.

Examples of Diatonic Melody.

"The cynic is one who never sees a good quality in a man, and never fails to see a bad one. He is the human owl, vigilant in darkness and blind to light, mousing for vermin, and never seeing noble game. The cynic puts all human actions into only two classes, openly bad and secretly bad. He holds that no man does a good thing except for profit. It is impossible to indulge in such habitual severity of opinion upon our fellow-men without injuring the tenderness and delicacy of our own feelings. A man will be what his most cherished feelings are. If he encourages a noble generosity, every feeling will be enriched by it; if he nurse bitter and envenomed thoughts, his own spirit will absorb the poison, and he will crawl among men a burnished adder, whose life is mischief, and whose errand is death."—BEECHER.

Examples of Semitonic Melody.

"Pity the sorrows of a poor old man,
Whose trembling limbs have borne him to your door."
THOMAS MOSS.

"The poor man alone, when he hears the poor moan,
Of his morsel a morsel will give.
Well-a-day!" THOMAS HOLCROFT.

---

* Melody differs from harmony in that the latter is a pleasing union of melodies, while the former is a succession of sounds constituting *one* melody.

INFLECTION.

Inflection is the variation of pitch on a single note or sound; a bending or turning of the voice either upward or downward on a single sound or syllable.

Inflections are distinguished as *simple* and *compound;* the latter are more commonly known as *waves.* When any of these variations in pitch (whether simple or compound) end in an upward turn of voice, they are called *rising* inflections, and when they end in a downward turn of voice they are termed *falling* inflections.

As in discrete sounds, the *beginning* of an inflection is known as its "*radical,*" and the end as its "*vanish,*" or *close.*

A *simple inflection* is a single upward or downward movement of voice in reading and speaking, and is distinguished as rising (indicated by this mark, ╱) or falling (indicated by this mark, ╲), according as its vanish is above or below its radical.

A *simple rising inflection* is a single upward slide of the voice, and suggests incomplete sense.

It is used in direct (and, in case of repetition, in indirect) interrogation, in unemphatic negation, and in exclamations of inquiry; as,

(*Direct Interrogation.*) Have you read the story of Rúth?

(*Indirect Interrogation.*) What did you sáy?

(*Unemphatic Negation.*) I would rather nót.

(*Exclamation of Inquiry.*) Áh! Halló! (meaning "Is that trúe?" in the first, and "It's you, is ít?" in the last interjection.

A *simple falling inflection* is a single downward slide of the voice, and suggests complete sense. It is used in exclamation, affirmation, emphatic negation, and in all imperative expressions; as,

(*Exclamation.*) Truth is etèrnal.

(*Negation.*) I tell you I will nòt.

(*Imperative.*) Get thee hènce! Leave mè! Gò!

A *compound inflection,* or *wave,* is the union of two or more simple inflections upon a single sound or syllable, and expresses surprise, scorn, contempt, sarcasm, mockery, raillery, irony, wit, admiration, sorrow, and often a contrast of meaning. Example: Is that the lăw? Waves are classed as single or double.

A *single wave* is the union of two simple inflections, and a double wave is the union of more than two simple inflections.*

Single waves are termed equal when the ascent and descent are equal, otherwise unequal.

A *single rising wave* begins with the simple falling inflection, and ends with the simple rising inflection; as,

(*Equal Wave.*) Gŏne to be friĕnds!

(*Unequal Wave.*) Must I budge? must I observe you?

A *single falling wave* begins with the simple rising inflection, and ends with the simple falling inflection; as,

(*Equal Wave.*) So, you have cŏme.

(*Unequal Wave.*) "Tell me I hate the bowl?
I loathe, abhor—my very soul
With strong disgust is stirred
Whene'er I see, or hear, or tell
Of the dark beverage of hell."

A *double rising wave* is a union of three simple inflections, beginning and ending with an upward turn of voice; as, in the play of *Julius Cæsar*, where Cassius says to Brutus, "You love me not!" Brutus replies, "I do not love your *faults;*" and in *The School for Scandal*, where Sheridan makes Sir Peter say to Lady Teazle, in the quarrel scene, "Oons, madam! if you had been born to this, I should not wonder at your talking thus; but you forget what your situation *wãs* when I married you." To which she replies, "No, no, I don't; 'twas a very disagreeable one, or I should never have married *yŏu*."

A *double falling wave* is the union of three simple inflections, beginning and ending with a downward turn of voice; as,

They cry for *pĕace*, when there is no peace.

---

* The Irish tone is replete with the simple falling wave, and the Scotch with the simple rising wave.

DEGREES OF INTERVALS.

A *degree* or *interval* of inflection is the space upon the scale swept by the voice at one turn or slide.

The intensity of the speaker decides the *length* of intervals, which is never less than a quarter tone, and seldom exceeds an octave.

These intervals are commonly a third, a fifth, or an octave; *i. e.* they include a variation of three, five, or eight notes from the radical or opening pitch.

The *rising third* is used in moderate interrogation, emphasis, and expressions of surprise; as,

(*Interrogation.*) Is it yours?
(*Emphasis.*) No, it is not mine, but Mary's.

The *falling third* expresses emotions of mockery, derision, impetuosity, and courage; as,

(*Mockery.*) "What drugs, what charms, what conjuration, and what mighty magic."—SHAKSPEARE.

(*Derision.*) "O excellent interpreter of the laws! corrector and amender of our Constitution!"—CICERO.

(*Courage.*) "Hurrah! the foes are moving. Hark to the mingled din
Of fife, and steed, and trump, and drum, and roaring culverin!"—MACAULAY.

The *rising fifth* expresses emotions of wonder, admiration, inquiry, doubt, and interrogation, and emphasis stronger than is expressed by the rising third; as,

(*Interrogation* ("I said an elder soldier, not a better.
and *Emphasis.*) Did I say better?"—JULIUS CÆSAR.

(*Strong Emphasis.*) "Fail!
In the lexicon of youth, which Fate reserves
For a bright manhood, there is no such word
As—*fail!*"—BULWER's Play of *Richelieu*.

The *falling fifth* expresses determination, indignant rebuke, and excessive grief; as,

(*Determination.*) "'To arms! to arms!' cried Mortimer,
And couched his quivering lance."—GRAY.

(*Rebuke.*) "Yet this is Rome,
That sat on her seven hills, and from her throne
Of beauty ruled the world."—MITFORD.

(*Suppli-cation.*)
> "Grant me another year, God of my spirit,
> But a day to win something to satisfy
> This thirst within. I would know something here.
> Break for me but one seal that is unbroken,
> Speak for me but one word that is unspoken."—WILLIS.

A *rising octave* expresses the most forcible interrogation and emphasis, contempt, mirth, raillery, and astonishment; as,

(*Interrogation.*) You come to teach the people?

        Gesler.   "You look upon your boy
        As though instinctively you guessed it.

(*Astonish-ment.*)
    Tell.   Look upon my *boy?* What mean you?
        Look upon my boy as though I guessed it—
        Guessed the trial you'd have me make?"—KNOWLES.

A *falling octave* expresses intense scorn and indignation; as,

        You pretend to teach a British general!

SPEECH OF LORD CHANCELLOR THURLOW IN REPLY TO THE DUKE OF GRAFTON.

1. MY LORDS,—I am amazed at the attack the noble duke has made upon me. Yes, my lords, I am *amazed* at his grace's speech. The noble duke can not look before him, behind him, or on either side of him, without seeing some noble peer who owes his seat in this house to his successful exertions in the profession to which I belong.

2. Does he not feel that it is as honorable to owe it to these as to being the accident of an accident! To all these noble lords the language of the noble duke is as applicable and as insulting as it is to myself. But I do not fear to meet it single and alone. No one venerates the peerage more than I do; but, my lords, I must say that the peerage solicited me—not I the peerage.

3. Nay, more; I can and will say, that as a peer of Parliament, as speaker of this right honorable house, as keeper of the great seal, as guardian of his majesty's conscience, as lord high chancellor of England—nay, even in that character alone in which the noble duke would think it an affront to be considered—as a MAN, I am at this moment as respect*-*

ble, I beg leave to add, as much respected, as the proudest peer I now look down upon.

The duke had, in the House of Lords, reproached Lord Thurlow with his plebeian extraction and his recent admission to the peerage. Lord Thurlow rose from the woolsack, and, fixing on the duke almost the look of Jove when he grasps the thunder, he spoke as above; and the effect of his speech was so great that it gave him an ascendency, both within the walls of the House and out of them, which no other chancellor ever possessed. It should be given with great and increasing energy.

RULES FOR INFLECTION.*

Rule 1. Exclamations usually take the falling inflection; as,

"Hurrāh! hurrāh! a single field hath turned the chance of wār;
Hurrah! hurrah! for Ivry, and Henry of Navarre."—MACAULAY.

Rule 2. An affirmative clause or sentence takes the falling inflection; as,

"The earth is the Lord's, and the fullness thereof; the world, and they that dwell therein."—*Psalm* xxiv.

Note.—Indifferent answers to questions take the rising inflection; as when, in reply to the question "Which do you prefer?" one says, "I have no chóice."

Rule 3. A negative clause or sentence requires the rising inflection, unless made emphatic for the sake of force; as,

---

* A few rules for inflection are here introduced, which may prove valuable in the hands of judicious teachers. No one of them should be given without explanation and example suited to the comprehension of all the pupils in the class.

Children upon the play-ground, or in unchecked conversation, give the most appropriate and natural inflections possible. They find no difficulty in expressing emotions of joy or sorrow, hope or fear, forgiveness or retaliation, whenever these emotions are excited. These are true models of expression. But as soon as they learn to conceal their feelings, and to read or speak the thoughts of others, they lose this property of intonation, and acquire mannerisms. After this, much time and money is often required to teach them how to do mechanically what was once so natural and involuntary.

In giving the following rules and illustrations, the teacher should be sure that the class understands them, and can make practical application of them to examples selected from the book. Unnecessary pauses and undue emphasis should be avoided. Let the examples be smoothly and continuously rendered, so that every sentence may be borne, as it were, on a wave of sound.

(*Unemphatic.*) O ño! that is not the lãw!
(*Emphatic.*) I say that is ŇOT the law!

Note.—When a negative phrase or clause is contrasted with an affirmative one, whether first or last in the order of construction, the rule is the same; as, "I said thĩs book, not thãt;" or, "I did not say this book, but thàt." "It was blãck, not white;" or, "It was not white, but blãck."

Rule 4. An imperative sentence takes the falling inflection; as,

"Strikẽ! till the last armed foe expireš;
Strikẽ! for your altars and your fireš."

"Go to the añt, thou sluggaṙd; consider her ways, and be wise."—*Bible.*

"Hencẽ! horrible shadoẁ!"

Rule 5. A direct interrogation, or a question that can be answered by Yes or No, takes the rising inflection; as,

"To purchase heaven has gold the powér?
Can gold remove the mortal hoúr?
In life can love be bought with gold?
Are friendship's pleasures to be sold?"

Note.—When, by strong emphasis on the first or auxiliary verb, a direct question anticipates an affirmative reply, it takes a falling inflection; as, "*Is* this truè? *Can* you believe it? *Has* not reason prevailed?"

Rule 6. An indirect interrogation, or a question that can not be answered by Yes or No, takes the falling inflection; as,

"Who shall ascend into the hill of the Loṙd, and who shall stand in his holy placè?"—*Bible.*

Note 1.—If the question be repeated, it takes the rising inflection; as, "Which way did you sáy?"

Note 2.—Sometimes the meaning of a question is decided by an inflection, making it direct or indirect; as, "Will you read Popé or Miltoǹ?" Ans. "Pope." It is a direct question when both nouns receive the rising inflection; as, "Will you read Popé or Miltón?" "Yes."

Rule 7. Words or phrases in apposition take the same inflection; as,

"Absaloḿ, my són, was my staff."

"Victoria is the daughter of Edwaṙd, duke of Kent."

"We will go to Brooklyn, the City of Churches."

Rule 8. Words or phrases in contrast or antithesis take opposite inflection; as,

(*Single Antithesis.*)
"They sang of love, and not of fame—
Forgot was Britain's glory;
Each heart recalled a different name,
But all sang 'Annie Laurie.'"—BAYARD TAYLOR.

(*Double Antithesis.*) "The difference between a madman and a fool is, the former reasons justly from false data, and the latter erroneously from just data."

"Prosperity gains friends; adversity tries them."

"It is harder to avoid censure than to gain applause."

Rule 9. Words or phrases in a parenthesis, suspending the sense, take the rising inflection; as,

"But here's a parchment with the seal of Cæsar.
I found it in his closet: 'tis his will.
Let but the commons hear this testament
(Which, pardon me, I do not mean to read),
And they would go and kiss dead Cæsar's wounds,
And dip their napkins in his sacred blood—
Yea, beg a hair of him for memory,
And, dying, mention it within their wills,
Bequeathing it as a rich legacy
Unto their issue."—SHAKSPEARE.

Rule 10. Words or phrases in a parenthesis, making addition to the complete sense, take the falling inflection; as,

"In fact, there's nothing that keeps its youth,
So far as I know, but a tree and truth.
(This is a moral that runs at large;
Take it.—You're welcome.—No extra charge.)"—HOLMES.

Note.—When the sense is reopened by the parenthetical addition, the voice is kept up at the close of the parenthesis.

SERIES.

A series is a succession of particulars, at least three in number. Series are classed as simple and compound, either of which may be a commencing or a concluding series.

A SIMPLE series is one whose members are single in word or idea; as,

In my garden are apples, | peaches, | plums, | and pears.|

A series is COMPOUND when the members comprise several words, or convey more than one idea; as,
"From every battle-field of the Revolution—from Lexington and Bunker Hill—from Saratoga and Yorktown—from the fields of Eutaw—from the cane-brakes that sheltered the men of Marion, the repeated, long-prolonged echoes came up, 'THE UNION: IT MUST BE PRESERVED.'"—BANCROFT.

A series is COMMENCING when the sense is not complete at the close of the series; as,
Men, | women, | and children | *were seen in the park.*

A series is CONCLUDING when the sense is complete with the series; as,
I saw in the park men, | women, | and children.|

Rules for the Inflection of Series.

Rule 11. A *simple commencing* series should have the rising inflection on every member but the penultimate, or last but one; as,
(*Nouns.*) Mary, | Sarah, | James, | and John | were at the fair last week.
(*Adjectives.*) A beautiful, | accomplished, | and amiable| lady | lives in the house on the hill.*
(*Verbs.*) He sees, hears, and feels as well as ever he did.

Rule 12. A *simple concluding* series takes the rising inflection on every member but the ultimate, or last; as,
At the fair last week I saw Mary, Sarah, James, and John.
In the house on the hill lives a lady, beautiful, accomplished, and amiable.
He can still hear, see, and feel.

Rule 13. A *compound commencing* series takes the falling inflection on every member but the ultimate, or last, which takes a strong rising inflection; as,
(<) "From every valley in our land, | from every cabin on the pleasant mountain sides, | from the ships at our wharves, | from the tents of the hunter in our westernmost prairies, | from the living minds of the living millions of American freemen, | from the thickly coming glories of fu-

* A series of adjectives takes the noun as one of its members, in the application of the rule for inflection.

turity, | the shout went up, like the sound of many waters, 'THE UNION: IT MUST AND SHALL BE PRESERVED.' "—BANCROFT.

<small>Commence this series in moderate time and force, and increase in volume to the last member of the series, which receives a full rising inflection.</small>

Rule 14. A *compound concluding* series takes the falling inflection on every member but the penultimate, or last but one; as,

".We hold these truths to be self evident: that all men are created equal; | that they are endowed by their Creator with certain inalienable rights; | that among these are life, liberty, and the pursuit of happiness; |"—*Const. of U. S.*

Rule 15. *A long Series.*—When a series exceeds five members, divide it into two or more shorter series, and read each division according to the rule which would apply to the entire series; as,

In him was genius, | judgment, | memory, | learning, || circumspection, | reflection, | application.

The series, as a whole, would follow the rule for simple concluding series (No. 12), hence each of the shorter series should be read according to that rule.

Rule 16. *Antithetical Series.*—When each member of a series contains an antithesis, the rule for antithesis should be applied to each member, and the whole series should be read according to the rule for that particular series; as,

"Talent is power, tact is skill; | talent is weight, tact is momentum; | talent knows what to do, tact knows how to do it; | talent makes a man respectable, tact will make him respected; | talent is wealth, tact is ready money. |"—*London Atlas.*

"I have spoken but of feelings and associations common to all ages, and all generations of men; | to the rude and the polished; | to the barbarian and the civilized; | to the bond and the free; | to the inhabitant of the dreary forests of the north and the sultry regions of the south; | to the worshiper of the sun, and the worshiper of idols; | to the heathen, dwelling in the darkness of his cold mythology; | and to the Christian, rejoicing in the light of the true God. |"—STORY.

These examples follow the rule for compound concluding

series (No. 14), while each antithesis follows the rule (No. 8) for antithesis.

Rule 17. *Irregular Series.*—When a series is mixed in form, being part simple and part compound, read it according to the rule for compound series, with such inflections upon the members of the simple series as shall not interfere with the whole.

" Oh for a prophet's eye to look into the future! If it be the destiny of America *to administer* with fidelity, wisdom, and success her free institutions ; | *to spread* them over the whole continent, filling it with a numerous, enlightened, industrious, moral, and contented people — one in name, one in government, one in power; | *to build* up here an empire, the last and the noblest offspring of Time, | this whole accumulated greatness will constantly tend to exalt higher and higher in the estimation of mankind him who will forever be deemed the founder of it all."—FRANCIS C. GRAY.

This is a concluding series of three members (beginning with "to administer," "to spread," "to build"), and contains three simple series, one in the first, and two in the second member of the series.

SENTENTIAL INFLECTIONS, OR CADENCES.

Cadence is the falling of the voice in reading or speaking, especially at the end of a sentence.

The sentential inflections arise from the construction of sentences. They are the closing slides, or cadence, and the rising slide upon the last clause before the cadence called the penultimate slide.

Rule 1. The full cadence of complete sense, at the close of a full period, is made by three "concretes,"* gradually descending in their radical pitch ; as,

"The mean of true valor lies between the extremes of cowardice and rashness."—CERVANTES.

(cowardice ^{and} rash$_{ness.}$)

---

* Sounds, it must be remembered, are *discrete* when separate or detached, and *concrete* when blended or united in succession, so as to discover no joinings. The former are illustrated by touching successive keys of the piano, and the latter by sliding the hands along the strings of a violin while drawing the bow.

Rule 2. "The partial cadence of complete sense, but incomplete period, has the rising ditone* on the first and second of the three closing syllables, and the concrete of the second with a downward vanish on the third."—RUSSEL.

"Feelings come and go like light troops following the victory of the *present*; but principles, like troops of the line, are undisturbed and stand fast."—RICHTER.

Rule 3. The penultimate is the upward slide of voice before the full cadence; as,

"He who considers himself a paragon of wisdom is sure to commit some superlatively stupid act."—TIECK.

Transition or Modulation.

Transition or modulation is a changing of the pitch-note to a higher, or lower degree of elevation, in obedience to emotion, sentiment, or thought. It is generally attended with a change of both force and time.

Modulation may be decided and distant, or proximate, by short steps. The decided transition is a sudden change from one key to another several notes above or below that key. It is used to express a contrast, or change of emotion, sentiment, or thought.

(*ff. High.*) "GIVE ME ANOTHER HORSE! BIND UP MY WOUNDS!
 HAVE MERCY, JESU! (*pp. Low.*) Soft, I did but dream."
SHAKSPEARE.

(*High.*) {" Try not the pass!" (*m.*) the old man said.
 "Dark lowers the tempest overhead;
 'The roaring torrent's deep and wide!"
(*Medium.*) And loud that clarion voice replied,
(*High.*) "Excelsior!"—LONGFELLOW.

The proximate transition is a change from one key to another not far distant, which may be continued from word to word, or phrase to phrase, up or down the scale, as emotion or thought indicates. It is used to express climax and anticlimax. One step below is used in parenthetical words or passages, also to place unimportant allusions and explanations in the background, so to speak, of the main thought.

(*Climax.*) "If I were an American, as I am an English-

---

* An interval comprehending two whole tones.

man, while a foreign troop was landed in my country, I never would lay down my arms—NEVER, NEVER, *never.*"

(*Parenthesis.*) "That patriotism which (*catching its inspiration from God*) animates and prompts to deeds of self-sacrifice, of valor, of devotion, and of death itself—that is public virtue, that is the noblest, the sublimest of all public virtues."

There is a transition of syllables which seems very nearly related to inflection. These turns of voice correspond with compound inflections or waves so precisely as to be called inflections by those who have not compared them. Thus the compound rising wave of a third may take the notes mi, do, mi ( ) concretely.

Give this turn or slide to one syllable or sound, and it is inflection; when, however, it be given to three successive syllables or monosyllables, it is not inflection, but transition; for a syllable being *one impulse* of voice, a turn or slide of voice can not be given to more than one syllable concretely, but will be divided into as many *discretes* as there are syllables. If this be true of the syllables of a word, it is also true of successive syllables that do not belong to one word, and would include an unlimited number of inflections, while it destroyed the simplicity of transitions.

Examples.

TABLE NO. 31. FORCE.

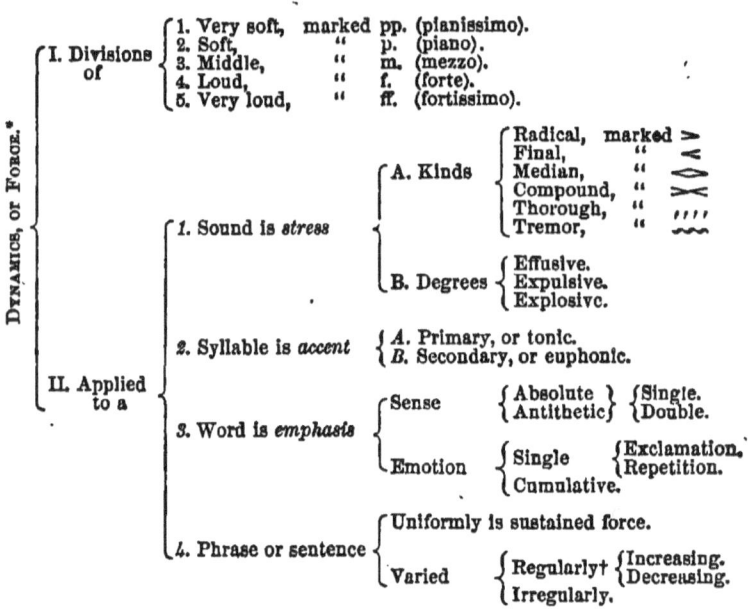

DYNAMICS, OR FORCE.

- I. Divisions of
  1. Very soft, marked pp. (pianissimo).
  2. Soft,   "   p. (piano).
  3. Middle,   "   m. (mezzo).
  4. Loud,   "   f. (forte).
  5. Very loud, "   ff. (fortissimo).

- II. Applied to a
  - 1. Sound is *stress*
    - A. Kinds
      - Radical, marked >
      - Final,   "
      - Median, "
      - Compound, "
      - Thorough, "
      - Tremor, "
    - B. Degrees
      - Effusive.
      - Expulsive.
      - Explosive.
  - 2. Syllable is *accent*
    - A. Primary, or tonic.
    - B. Secondary, or euphonic.
  - 3. Word is *emphasis*
    - Sense
      - Absolute } Single.
      - Antithetic} Double.
    - Emotion
      - Single { Exclamation.
               { Repetition.
      - Cumulative.
  - 4. Phrase or sentence
    - Uniformly is sustained force.
    - Varied
      - Regularly† { Increasing.
                   { Decreasing.
      - Irregularly.

* Volume is force and quantity combined.
† Regularly increasing and decreasing in force to the close or to the middle of a phrase or sentence producing climax and anti-climax. See Table No. 10, note 16.

DYNAMICS, OR FORCE.

DYNAMICS treats of the power or force of sounds.

Force is the result of action. In elocution, force is the degree of energy with which words are spoken. *Degrees* of force depend upon the intensity of the given power. They are indefinite in number, but *three* are deemed sufficient for reference. 1st, soft or weak; 2d, middle or moderate; and, 3d, heavy or strong.

Note.—Force should not be confounded with loudness, because sound can be produced with great force in a whisper as well as in a shout.

1. Soft or weak utterance is the result of little exertion, whether arising from organic weakness or from sentiment. It expresses pity, admiration, endearment, tenderness, grief, and the like.

(*Pity.*) "Give me three grains of corn, mother,
　　　Only three grains of corn;
　　It will keep the little life I have
　　　Till the coming of the morn.
　　I am dying of hunger and cold, mother,
　　　Dying of hunger and cold;
　　And half the agony of such a death
　　　My lips have never told."—MRS. EDMUND.

(*Endearment.*) "Look at me with thy large brown eyes,
　　　Philip, my king,
　　Round whom the shadowing purple lies
　　　Of babyhood's royal dignities.
　　Lay on my neck thy tiny hand,
　　　With love's invisible sceptre laden.
　　I am thine, Esther, to command
　　Till thou shalt find a queen handmaiden,
　　　Philip, my king."—MISS MULOCK.

(*Whisper.*) "Breathe it not aloud; the wild winds must not hear it."

2. Middle or moderate utterance is the result of little energy or exertion. It expresses reverence, and is used in narration and description.

(*Narrative.*) "The Irish peasant has at all periods been

peculiarly distinguished for unbounded but indiscriminate hospitality. To be in want or misery is the best recommendation to his disinterested protection; his food, his bed, his raiment are equally the stranger's and his own; and the deeper the distress, the more welcome is the sufferer to the peasant's cottage."—SIR J. BARRINGTON.

(*Description.*) "Methought I saw a thousand fearful wrecks,
A thousand men that fishes gnawed upon,
Wedges of gold, great anchors, heaps of pearl,
Inestimable stones, unvalued jewels,
All scattered in the bottom of the sea.
Some lay in dead men's skulls; and in those holes
Where eyes did once inhabit, there were crept
(As 'twere in scorn of eyes) reflecting gems
That wooed the slimy bottom of the deep,
And mocked the dead bones that lay scattered by."
SHAKSPEARE, *Dream of Clarence.*

(*Reverence.*) "The nation rises up at every stage of his coming; cities and states are as pall-bearers, and the cannon beats the hours in solemn progression; dead, dead, dead, he yet speaketh. Is Washington dead? Is Hampden dead? Is David dead? Is any man that ever was fit to live dead? Disenthralled from the flesh, and risen to the unobstructed sphere where passion never comes, he begins his illimitable work. His life is now grafted upon the Infinite, and will be fruitful as no earthly life can be. Pass on. Four years ago, oh Illinois, we took from your midst an untried man from among the people. Behold, we return him to you a mighty conqueror, not thine any more, but the nation's; not ours, but the world's. Give him place, oh ye prairies! In the midst of this great continent his dust shall rest, a sacred treasure to myriads, who shall pilgrim to that shrine to kindle anew their patriotism. Ye winds, that move over the mighty spaces of the West, chant his requiem! Ye people, behold the martyr, whose drops of blood, as so many articulate words, plead for fidelity, for law, for liberty."—BEECHER'S *Sermon on Lincoln.*

(*Whisper.*) "And the bridemaidens whispered, ' 'Twere better by far,
To have matched our fair cousin with young Lochinvar.' "
SCOTT.

3. Heavy or strong utterance is the result of great energy or exertion. It expresses anger, defiance, and command. It is used in calling, shouting, rage, and fear.

Ex. (*Anger.*) "So you will fly out! can't you be cool like me? What good can passion do? Passion is of no service, you impudent, insolent, overbearing reprobate! There you sneer again! Don't provoke me! but you rely upon the mildness of my temper, you do, you dog: you play upon the meekness of my disposition! yet take care; the patience of a saint may be overcome at last! But mark! I give you six hours and a half to consider of this: if you then agree, without any condition, to do every thing on earth that I choose, why—confound you, I may in time forgive you."— SHERIDAN, *The Rivals.*

(*Defiance.*) "I loathe you with my bosom! I scorn you with mine eye!
    And I'll taunt you with my latest breath, and fight you till I die!
    I ne'er will ask for quarter, and I ne'er will be your slave,
    But I'll swim the sea of slaughter till I sink beneath the wave."—*The Seminole's Reply.*

(*Command.*) "Once more unto the breach, dear friends, once more,
    Or close the wall up with our English dead!
    In peace, there's nothing so becomes a man
    As modest stillness and humility;
    But when the blast of WAR blows in our ears,
    Then imitate the action of the tiger;
    Stiffen the sinews, summon up the blood,
    Disguise fair nature with hard-favored rage:
    Now set the teeth, and stretch the nostrils wide;
    Hold hard the breath, and bend up every spirit
    To his full height! On, ON, you noble English,
    Whose blood is fet from fathers of war-proof—
    Fathers that, like so many Alexanders,
    Have in these parts from morn till even fought,
    And sheathed their swords for lack of argument.
    I see you stand like greyhounds in the slips,
    Straining upon the start: the game's afoot;
    Follow your spirit; and upon this charge
    Cry, GOD FOR HARRY, ENGLAND, AND ST. GEORGE!"
                                    SHAKSPEARE.

(*Calling.*) "How yet resolves the governor of the town?
    This is the latest parle we will admit.
    Therefore to our best mercy give yourselves;

>Or, like to men proud of destruction,
>Defy us to our worst; for, as I am a soldier
>(A name that in my thoughts becomes me best),
>If I begin the battery once again,
>I will not leave the half-achieved Harfleur
>Till in her ashes she lie buried.
>The gates of mercy shall be all shut up;
>And the flushed soldier, rough and hard of heart,
>In liberty of bloody hand shall range,
>Mowing like grass your fresh, fair virgins
>And your flowering infants.
>   Therefore, you men of Harfleur,
>Take pity of your town and of your people
>While yet my soldiers are in my command."
>   SHAKSPEARE, *Henry V.*

(*Shouting.*) "'JUMP, far out, boy, into the wave!
>Jump, or I fire!' he said;
>'This chance alone your life can save.
>JUMP! JUMP!' The boy obeyed."—GEO. P. MORRIS.

(*Rage.*) "Mind and charge home,
>Or, by the fires of heaven, I'll leave the foe,
>And make my wars on you: look to't! come on!"

(*Fear, intense Whisper.*) "Hark! I hear the bugles of the enemy! They are on their march along the bank of the river. We must retreat instantly, or be cut off from our boats. I see the head of their column already rising over the height. Our only safety is in the screen of this hedge. Keep close to it; be silent; and stoop as you run. FOR THE BOATS! FORWARD!"

Additional force may be given to a sound, syllable, word, phrase, or sentence.

It receives the name *stress* when applied to a sound, *accent* when applied to a syllable, and *emphasis* when applied to a word, phrase, or sentence.

Accent produces *rhythm*, stress expresses more or less of the *emotional* condition of the speaker, while emphasis makes plain the *meaning* of the author.

STRESS.

Stress is the special application of force to some part of an accented sound or syllable.* The degrees of stress are

* See Accent, p. 162.

three—effusive, expulsive, and explosive (*i. e.*, moderate, full, and abrupt).

1. Effusive stress is a moderate use of breath or voice material while producing sounds, and indicates a placid emotional condition, an unruffled temper; as,

> "Where, where will be the birds that sing
> A hundred years to come?
> The flowers that now in beauty spring
> A hundred years to come?"

2. Expulsive stress is produced by forcibly expelling the breath while speaking or producing sounds, and indicates a more positive emotional condition or earnestness of purpose; as,

"There! there is the liquor which God, the eternal, brews for all his children! Not in the simmering still, over smoking fires, choked with poisonous gases, and surrounded with the stench of sickening odors and rank corruption, doth your Father in heaven prepare the precious essence of life, pure cold water; but in the green glade and glassy dell, where the wild deer wanders, and the child loves to play, there God himself brews it!"—PAUL DENTON.

3. Explosive stress is a degree of force produced by projecting the breath abruptly or violently, and indicates an intense emotional condition; as,

> "See, Boy Briton, see, boy, see!
> They strike! HURRAH! the fort has surrendered!
> Shout! shout, my warrior boy!
> And wave your cap, and clap your hands with joy!
> Cheer answer cheer, and bear the cheer about—
> HURRAH! HURRAH!"—WILSON.

Kinds of Stress.

Every sound or syllable must have a *beginning*, a *middle*, and an *end*, and force applied to these divisions in various ways produces six kinds of stress; viz., radical, final, median, compound, thorough, and intermittent (or tremor). It is called,

1. RADICAL when the force gradually diminishes from the beginning to the end of the sound or syllable. When intense, it expresses command, anger, defiance ($\breve{\text{a}}, \breve{\text{e}}, \breve{\text{i}}, \breve{\text{o}}, \breve{\text{u}}$).

(*Effusive.*) "Can storied urn or animated bust
  Back to its mansion call the fleeting breath?
 Can honor's voice provoke the silent dust,
  Or flattery soothe the dull, cold ear of death?"—GRAY.

(*Expulsive.*) "Then shook the hills with thunder riven,
 Then rushed the steed to battle driven;
 And louder than the bolts of heaven,
  Far flashed the red artillery."

(*Explosive.*) "The combat deepens. On, ye brave,
 Who rush to glory or the grave.
 Wave, Munich, all thy banners wave,
  And charge with all thy chivalry!"—CAMPBELL.

2. FINAL, when the force gradually increases to the end of the sound or syllable, and closes abruptly. It expresses contempt, scorn, impatience, determination, or revenge (a, e, i, o, u).

(*Effusive.*) "Click, click, click! how the needles go."
(*Expulsive.*) "Come back! come back! he cried, in grief."
(*Explosive.*) "Speak! speak! thou fearful guest,
 Who, with thy hollow breast still in rude armor dress'd,
 Com'st to haunt me!"

3. MEDIAN, or middle stress, when the force is greatest at the middle of the sound or syllable. It is smooth-flowing, and expresses reverence, patriotism, and affection (a, e, i, o, u).

(*Effusive.*) "There's a land far away, 'mid the stars, we are told,
 Where they know not the sorrows of time;
 Where the pure waters wander through valleys of gold,
  And life is a treasure sublime."—CLARK.

(*Expulsive.*) "Now glory to the Lord of Hosts, from whom all glories are,
 And glory to our sovereign liege, King Henry of Navarre!
 Now let there be the merry sound of music and of dance,
 Through thy corn-fields green and sunny vines, O pleasant
  land of France."—MACAULAY.

(*Explosive.*) "'Charge, Chester, charge! on, Stanley, on!'
 Were the last words of Marmion."—SCOTT.

4. COMPOUND, when the force is least in the middle of the sound or syllable, *i. e.*, the force gradually decreases to

the middle and then increases to the end. It is the radical and final stress united on one syllable or sound (ā, ē, ī, ō, ū). It expresses sarcasm, irony, extreme surprise, petulance, and provocation.

"Gone to be married! gone to swear a peace!
False blood to false blood joined! gone to be friends!
Shall Louis have Blanche, and Blanche these provinces?"
SHAKSPEARE.

5. THOROUGH, when the successive syllables have little apparent increase or diminution of force. It is often produced with beating regularity, like staccato in music, and expresses command or hilarity, and is used in calling, warning, and threatening (ā, ē, ī, ō, ū).

(*Effusive.*) "Good-by, proud world! I'm going home.
Thou'rt not my friend, and I'm not thine."
EMERSON.

(*Expulsive.*) "If men, when Wrong beats down the Right,
Would strike together and restore it;
If Right made Might in every fight,
The world would be the better for it."—CLARK.

(*Explosive.*) "Flashed all their sabres bare,
Flashed as they turned in air,
Sab'ring the gunners there;
Charging an army, while
All the world wondered:
Plunged in the battery smoke,
Right through the line they broke;
Cossack and Russian
Reeled from the sabre-stroke
Shattered and sundered.
Then they rode back, but not,
Not the Six Hundred."—TENNYSON.

6. TREMOR, when the voice moves unevenly or trembles on the syllables. It is an intermittent stress, and expresses feebleness, tenderness, admiration, and subdued grief or joy (ã, ẽ, ĩ, õ, ũ).

(*Effusive.*) *Grief.*
"'And shall I never see thee more,
Mine own delightful home!
Nor fetterless as the free winds
Among thy green fields roam?

Those singing brooks! and shall their tones
Be never in mine ear?
And those dear voices, I could die
But only once to hear.
O mother, mother!' "—Mrs. Case, *Joan of Arc in Prison.*

(*Expulsive.*) *Age.*
"If they should fire on Pickens, let the colonel in command
Place me upon the ramparts with the flag-staff in my hand.
No odds how hot the cannon smoke, or how the shells may fly,
I'll hold the stars and stripes aloft, and hold them till I die."
Bayard Taylor.

(*Explosive.*) *Intense Grief and Supplication.*
" 'O spare my child! my joy, my pride!
O give me back my boy!' she cried.
'My child, my child!' with sobs and tears,
She shrieked upon his calloused ears."—Mackay.

*Accent.**

Accent is superior force applied to one or more syllables of a word, to distinguish them from others in the same word, as *mu'*sic al, con ver'ti *bil'*i ty. It is primary and secondary.

1. Primary when the force is greater upon one syllable than upon any other in the word, as *cir'*cum stances.

2. Secondary accent is force upon one or more syllables of long words, less strongly marked than the primary, as cir'cum *stan'*ces. The first syllable receives the primary and the third the secondary accent.

The position of accent often decides the meaning of a word, as in per'fume, per fume'. This belongs to a class of words that are used as nouns and as verbs. The nouns take the accent on the first, and the verbs on the last syllable.

Emphasis.

Emphasis is force upon one or more words, to distinguish them from other words in the same sentence.

Emphasis is of sense, absolute or antithetic; and of emotion, single or cumulative.

* See Stress, page 158.

Emphasis of sense brings out the meaning, and emphasis of emotion the feeling of the author.

1. It is *absolute* when used to express sense; as, Go *now!* "In all ages *Love* is the truth of life."—ROBERTSON.

2. Antithetic when used on words in contrast and comparison; "I said an *elder* soldier, not a *better*." You may *ride*, but I shall *walk*.

3. Single emphasis of emotion is force upon single words to express strong feeling; as,

"RISE, fellow-men, our country yet remains!"

4. Cumulative emotional emphasis is superior force on a succession of words; as,

"HEAVEN for HARRY, ENGLAND, and ST. GEORGE!"
"The Union: it MUST and SHALL BE PRESERVED."

Force upon an entire phrase or sentence should be considered separately with regard to its increase or diminution, called climax and anticlimax.* The conditions are more or less in accordance with the following statements.

1. Force may be unchanged throughout an entire period.
2. It may increase to the end of a clause or sentence.
3. It may decrease to the end of a clause or sentence.
4. It may increase to the middle, and decrease to the end.
5. It may decrease to the middle, and increase to the end.
6. It may vary irregularly throughout the sentence.

(*Slow, with* ⎫ 1. "When Ajax strives some rock's vast weight to throw,
even force.)⎭ The line too labors, and the words move slow."—POPE.

(<) 2. "In a clamorous appealing to the mercy of the fire,
  In a mad expostulation with the deaf and frantic fire."—POE.

(>) 3. "The loud wind dwindled to a whisper low,
  And sighed for pity as it answered 'No.'"—MACKAY.

(><) 4. "How the danger sinks | and swells,
(><)   By the sinking or | the swelling
  In the anger of the bells."—POE.

(<>). 5. "If I were an American, while a foreign troop were landed in my country, I never would lay down my arms—NEVER, NEVER, *never*."—LORD CHATHAM.

(*Irregular.*) 6. "Keep yourself from opportunities, and God will keep you from sin. Idleness is the sepulchre of a living man."

---

* *Volume* is force and quantity combined. Full volume is made of much force, and long time or quantity.

164   MANUAL OF READING.

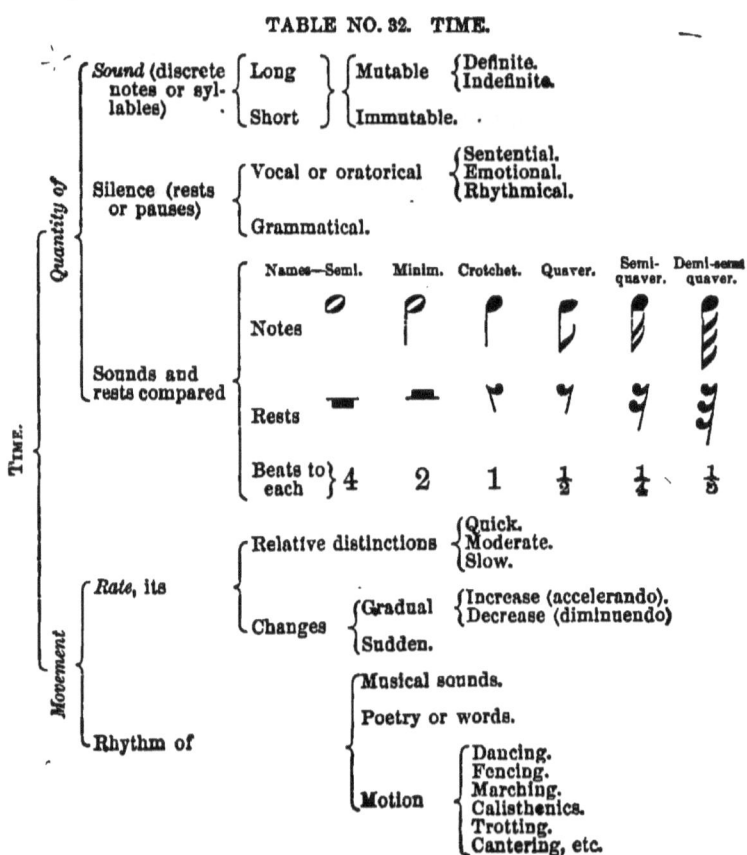

TABLE NO. 32. TIME.

TIME.

TIME is a measured portion of duration. In elocution, time is a measure of the speed of utterance. As a measure of speed of utterance, the duration or quantity of single sounds and rests, and the movement of successive sounds and rests, must be considered.

QUANTITY.

Quantity is the duration or length of single sounds and rests. Some sounds are naturally and necessarily longer than others; and while a few, both long and short, can be prolonged, others can not: hence they may be classed as immutable (those that can not be prolonged) and mutable (those that can be prolonged.) The latter, being capable of definite or of indefinite prolongation, have received the names "*definite*" and "*indefinite*" *mutable elements*.

1. The immutable elements of our language are the abrupts (see Table No. 7), p, t, k, b, d, g, which can not be prolonged.

2. The *mutable* elements are most strongly represented in the long vowel sounds, because they are capable of agreeable prolongation—(see Table No. 6)—ē, ā, ä, a̤, ō, o̤, ī, ū.

3. The *definite mutable elements* are the short vowels (see Table No. 6), ĭ, ĕ, ă, ŏ, ŭ, ů, and continuants (Table No. 7), r, l, m, n, ng, w, y, h, wh, because, though capable of slight prolongation, it is seldom in good taste or agreeable to the ear to add to their usual length.

Examples.

(*Immutable.*) "*Would you make men trustworthy? Trust them. Would you make them true? Believe them. We win by tenderness; we conquer by forgiveness.*" — ROBERTSON.

(*Mutable.*)
"Hail, holy Light! Offspring of heaven first-born,
Or of the eternal co-eternal beam,
May I express thee unblamed? Since God is light,
And never but in unapproached light
Dwelt from eternity, dwelt then in thee,
Bright effulgence of bright essence increate."—MILTON.

(*Definite Mutable.*)
"Up! comrades, up! in Rokeby's halls
Ne'er be it said our courage falls!"—SCOTT.

Rests or Pauses.

A pause is a suspension. In spoken or written language, pauses are signs of the divisions of discourse, and may be classed as vocal or oratorical, and as grammatical.

A vocal or oratorical pause is a suspension of voice for the purpose of obtaining breath, or to convey to the auditors the emotion or meaning of the speaker. They may, but often do not, coincide with grammatical pauses. Those vocal pauses that make plain the *meaning* of the author or speaker are called sentential; those that express his *feelings* are called emotional; and those necessary to metrical composition or verse are called *rhythmical* pauses.

Rules for the Use of Sentential and Emotional Pauses.

A sentential or emotional pause should be made—
1. Before infinitive phrases.
2. " prepositional phrases.
3. " relative pronouns.
4. " adjectives following their nouns.
5. " the conclusion or closing half of a sentence.
6. " an ellipsis, or in place of the omitted word.
7. " a word or phrase of concentrated emphasis.

Examples.

1. (*Infinitive Phrase.*) It is noble | *to say little and perform much.*

2. (*Prepositional Phrase.*) Never measure other people's corn | *by your own bushel.*

3. (*Relative Pronoun.*) He laughs best | *who* laughs last.

4. (*Adjective.*) Dim miniature of greatness | *absolute!*
5. (*Conclusion.*) The man who spares vice | *wrongs virtue.*
6. (*Ellipsis.*) I fondly dream had I been thou—but what could that have done?
7. (*Emphasis.*) The Union | MUST be preserved.

A sentential or emotional pause should be made—
1. After the nominative or subject phrase.
2. " the objective phrase in inverted sentences.
3. " each member of a series.
4. " and between words in apposition.
5. " and before a word or phrase in parenthesis.
6. " and before a quotation.
7. " the completion of sense.
8. " emphatic words or subjects.
9. " each member of a sentence.

Examples.

1. (*Nominative Phrase.*) "*All high poetry* | is infinite."— SHELLEY.
2. (*Objective Phrase.*) "*A word once spoken* | a coach and six horses can not bring it back."—CONFUCIUS.
3. (*Members of a Series.*) "Here is your unadulterated ale of Father Adam; better than *Cognac*, | *Hollands*, | *Jamaica*, | *strong beer*, | or *wine* of any price; here it is by the hogshead or the single glass, and not a cent to pay."—HAWTHORNE.
4. (*Apposition.*) *John Chrysostom Wolfgang Gottlieb Mozart'*, | *the great German composer'*, was born in Salzburg, January 27, 1756.
5. (*Parenthesis.*) God is thanked | (*perhaps unconsciously*) | for the brightness of earth on summer evenings, when a brother and sister, who have long been parted, pour out their heart-stores to each other, and feel their course of thoughts brightening as it runs.
6. (*Quotation.*) Longfellow says: | "*Silently, one by one, in the infinite meadows of heaven, blossom the lovely stars, the forget-me-nots of the angels;*" | and who can forget it?

7. (*Complete Sense.*)
"Count that day lost whose low-descending sun
Views from thy hand no worthy action done." |

8. (*Emphasis.*)
"*Strike* | till the last armed foe expires!
STRIKE | for your altars and your fires!
Strike | for the green graves of your sires!
God and your native land!"—HALLECK.

RHYTHMICAL PAUSES.

Rhythm is regularly recurring accent in motion or sound, as in music, poetry, dancing, fencing, calisthenics, marching, and the like.*

Rhythmical pauses are those cessations of sound necessary to metrical composition.

They are termed *final*, *cæsural*, and *demi-cæsural*. Final pauses occur at the close of lines of poetry, the cæsural in the middle of the lines, and the demi-cæsural subdivide the cæsural divisions.

The final Rhythmical Pause:
"How dear to my heart are the scenes of my childhood,|
When fond recollection presents them to view!|
The orchard, the meadow, the deep-tangled wildwood,|
And every loved spot which my infancy knew!"|
WORDSWORTH.

The Cæsural Pause:
"When the humid shadows gather | over all the starry spheres,
And the melancholy darkness | gently weeps in rainy tears,
'Tis a joy to press the pillow | of a cottage-chamber bed,
And listen to the patter | of the soft rain overhead."
COATES KINNEY.

The Demi-cæsural Pause:
"There's a land | far away, 'mid the stars, | we are told,
Where they know not the sorrows of time—
Where the pure | waters wander through val|leys of gold,
And life is a treasure sublime."—J. G. CLARK.

The Final, Cæsural, and Demi-cæsural Pause:
"Knowledge comes, | but wisdom lingers, | and he bears | a laden breast,|
Full of sad ex|perience moving| toward the stillness | of his rest."|
TENNYSON.

* Notice the distinction between rhythm and metre. Metre is applied to words only, while rhythm is applied to motion and to sound, which includes words.

Rule for the final Rhythmical Pause.

If the final pause be necessary to the sense, it may be a breathing pause; if not, it should be a suspension of voice without taking breath.*

Final Breathing Pause:
"Launch thy bark, mariner!
 Christian, God speed thee;|
Let loose the rudder-bands,
 Good angels lead thee!|
Set thy sails warily;
 Tempests may come.
Steer thy course steadily;
 Christian, steer home."|—Mrs Southey.

Final Pause of Suspension:
"Yet not to thine eternal resting-place |
Shalt thou retire alone, nor couldst thou wish |
Couch more magnificent. Thou shalt lie down |
With patriarchs of the infant world, with kings,
The powerful of the earth—the wise, the good—
Fair forms, and hoary seers of ages past,|
All in one mighty sepulchre."—W. C. Bryant.

GRAMMATICAL PAUSES, OR PUNCTUATION MARKS.

Grammatical pauses, or marks of punctuation, are visible signs made in written or printed composition to indicate more plainly the meaning of the author's words.
The principal signs are the
(,) Comma.
(;) Semicolon.
(:) Colon.
(.) Period, denoting a full stop, and abbreviations; as, H. for Henry, Mr. for Mister.
(?) Interrogation Point, showing that a question is asked.

* In reading poetry there are two common errors. First, that of running one line into another without pause; the second, that of taking breath at the end of each line. The true artist heeds neither the presence nor absence of grammatical pauses or punctuation, particularly in reading blank verse. The voice should poise, as it were, upon the last word of the line, but, unless the sense requires it, not long enough to take breath.

II

(!) EXCLAMATION POINT, which follows expressions of strong emotion.

The remaining signs in common use include the

(-) HYPHEN, used to connect compound words and to separate the syllables of a word; as, wild-wood, con-stan-cy.

(—) DASH, denoting a sudden pause, or change of subject, and sometimes for a parenthesis.

(———) (* * *) ELLIPSIS, showing the omission of letters in a word, or words in a sentence; as, M———y for Mary, I go to * * * to-morrow.

[( )] PARENTHESIS, inclosing an explanatory phrase or sentence.

([ ]) BRACKETS, or crotchets.

(" ") QUOTATION MARKS, showing that the exact words of another are used.

(') APOSTROPHE, denoting the possessive case, or that one or more letters in a word have been omitted; as, 'pon, sigh'd, man's life.

(∧) CARET, showing that by mistake one or more letters have been omitted; as, boded, God love.
               ∧   ∧
                n   is

(}) BRACE, used to connect several words with a common term.

(¨) DIÆRESIS, placed over the latter of two vowels to indicate a division of syllables between them; as, aërial (a-e-rial).

(☞) INDEX, referring to an important statement.

(¶) PARAGRAPH, indicating the commencement of a new subject.

(§) SECTION, used to divide a chapter or a book into parts.

(*) ASTERISK,
(†) OBELISK, or DAGGER,
(‡) DOUBLE DAGGER,
(§) SECTION,
(‖) PARALLELS,
(¶) PARAGRAPH,
Letters and figures,
} refer to notes in the margin, or at the bottom of the page.

MOVEMENT.

Movement, in this connection, means the motion or progression in time, and includes *rate* and *rhythm*. The rate or speed of movement is classed as quick, moderate, and slow.

Quick or rapid movement is used to express haste, alarm, confusion, terror, joy, mirth, humor, and animation; as,

"Away! away! our fires stream bright
 Along the frozen river,
And their arrowy sparkles of brilliant light
 On the forest branches quiver."—BRYANT.

Moderate movement is the speed used in simple narration, description, or didactic thought; as,

"Oh, Maggie Bell, sweet Maggie Bell,
'Twere better for me had thy funeral knell
Been tolled ere we parted, upon the old bell;
'Twere better for me, and better for thee,
Had I been content with a simple lot,
With honest toil and a humble cot;
Had I but made *thee* my honor and fame,
My world and my fortune, ambition and aim,
Thy love would have been all these to me."

Slow movement expresses emotions of sublimity, grief, pathos, melancholy, reverence, deep repose, grandeur, majesty, vastness, power, splendor, adoration, and horror; as,

"When Ajax strives some rock's vast weight to throw,
The line too labors, and the words move slow."—POPE.

"He is gone on the mountain, he is lost to the forest,
Like some summer-dried fountain when our need was the sorest;
The fount reappearing from the rain-drops shall borrow,
But to us comes no cheering, to Duncan no morrow.
The hand of the reaper takes the ears that are hoary,
But the voice of the weeper wails manhood in glory;
The autumn winds rushing waft the leaves that are serest,
But our flower was in flushing when blighting was nearest.
Like the dew on the mountain, like the foam on the river,
Like the bubble on the fountain, thou art gone and forever."
                                                SCOTT.

SELECTIONS

FOR THE LITTLE FOLKS.

THE simplest matter is often hardest to read. Let the best reader try his skill upon lessons prepared for children, or any simple narration, and he will discover the difficulties which the young reader encounters. First, the words must *mean* something; and if a long word occurs now and then, do not wait for the child to study it out until he has forgotten the story, but help him by speaking the word, or even the entire phrase, if necessary. He will then keep the meaning in mind, and become interested in learning. It is no wonder a child reads stupidly such unsatisfactory and unmeaning phrases as "I go up," "You go down," when what he goes up *for*, or *how*, or *when*, or *where*, is wholly unknown.

In order to obtain a variety of new selections suited to a natural style of reading, special permission has been obtained to copy from three monthly magazines, viz., "The Nursery" and "Our Young Folks," published in Boston, and "The Little Corporal," published in Chicago. Many of the selections found in this volume can not be copied without permission from the owners of the copyrights.

The selections for "little folks" are simple enough for any child that can recognize common monosyllables at sight. Hard words, particularly proper names, will soon be learned as sight-words.

Those who expect to instruct children will do well to practice these selections.

JOHNNY'S FIRST SNOW-STORM.—*From the Nursery.*

Johnny Reed was a lit'tle boy who nev'er saw a snow'-storm till he was six years old. Before this, he had lived in a warm coun'try, where the sun shines down on beau'tiful or'ange-groves, and fields al'ways sweet with flow'ers. In the win'ter, *there*, rain falls in'stead of snow.

But now he had come to vis'it his grand-moth'er, who lived where the snow falls in win'ter. And Johnny was stand'ing at the win'dow when the snow came down.

"Oh mamma!" he cried, joy'fully, "do come quick, and see all these lit'tle white birds fly'ing down from heaven!"

"They are not birds, Johnny," said mamma, smiling.

"Then maybe the lit'tle an'gels are dan'cing, and los'ing their feath'ers! Oh! do tell me what it is: is it sug'ar? Let me taste it," said Johnny.

But, when he tasted it, he gave a lit'tle jump, it was so cold.

"It is snow, Johnny," said his moth'er.

"And what is snow, moth'er?"

"The snow-flakes, Johnny, are little drops of wa'ter that fall from the clouds. But the air through which they pass is so cold, it freez'es them, and they come down turned to snow. In the sum'mer, here, it is too warm for snow, but the win'ter is very cold."

As she said this, she brought out an old black hat from the clos'et.

"See, Johnny, I have caught a snow-flake on this hat. Look quick through this glass, and you will see how beau'-tiful it is."

Johnny looked through the glass. There lay the snow-flake like a love'ly lit'tle star.

"Twin'kle, twin'kle, little star," he cried, in delight. "Oh! please show me more."

So his mamma caught sev'eral more. They were all beau'-tiful, yet no one was shaped like anoth'er.

The next day Johnny had a fine play in the snow, and, when he came in, he said, "I love snow; and I think snow-balls are a great deal pret'tier than or'anges."

THE SNOW MAN.—*From the Little Corporal.*

In the blinding, whirling snow,
  Jolly snow-birds now are we!
Roll his body while we go;
  Plant him up against a tree!

Fix him up a pair of hands;
  Then a pair of funny legs;
Count how many feet he stands—
  Ain't he shaky on his pegs!

Nimble fingers, how they fly!
  Laughing cheeks are cherry red!
Punch him here and there an eye—
  What a precious pumpkin head!

Ringing shouts are in the air—
  Now he's done, except the nose!
Pop him here and pop him there—
  One, two, three, and down he goes!

JINGLE, JINGLE!—*From the Nursery.*

Jingle, jingle! up and down,
Sleighs are flying through the town
Jingle, jingle! don't you hear
Merry sleigh-bells far and near?

Get a sleigh that's large and wide;
Let the children have a ride—
Henry, Ellen, Tom, and Ann,
George and Jane, and little Fan.

Yes, there's room enough for all:
Bring another blanket-shawl;
Tuck them in. Away we go,
Jingle, jingle! through the snow.

Jingle, jingle! now we meet
Faces gay and horses fleet;
And we laugh, and shout, and sing,
While the merry sleigh-bells ring.

LEARNING TO FLY.—*From the Nursery.*

When the little chicks were three weeks old, their mother thought they were strong enough to learn to fly. So she flew up on a bush. Then she looked, and called for the little ones to come. One bold little chick flew up a short way, and then fell to the ground.

The sun was going down, and it was time for all little chicks to go to bed. Their mother flew up on the roost and waited for them.

Then the little chicks all began to cry, and kept looking up to their mother, as if to say, "We can not fly up so high. Oh dear! what shall we do? Do help us up."

But their mother kept cheering them by little soft sounds, which meant "Come up, my darlings! Come up, my dear little chicks! It is not so hard as you think it is. Just try."

By-and-by they had all flown up to the roost—all but one poor little chick. This one was smaller than the rest, and its wings were not so much grown. So it just ran off alone in the corner, and seemed very sad. Then Lucy took it in her hands, and put it up on the roost.

One little chick flew up on its mother's back. Then they all shut up their eyes and went to sleep.

MIND YOUR STEPS.—*From the Nursery.*

George caught sight of a big brown but'terfly. "I will have that fellow!" said George. So off he dashed after the but'terfly, hat in hand. Down in the hol'low, up on the hill, over the lawn—away he went at full speed. "Now I've got him!" said George, making a swoop with his hat.

Well, George did not get the but'terfly, but he got a fall. I wonder if the but'terfly laughed to see him sprawl'ing on the ground?

If but'terflies can laugh, I think this one did, for he looked on very sau'cily while George was pick'ing him'self up, and then whisked away over the fields, as much as to say, "Would you like to try anoth'er race with me, my young friend? Good-by! I must leave you."

HANG UP THE BABY'S STOCKING.

Hang up the baby's stocking;
  Be sure that you don't forget
The dear little dimpled darling—
  He never saw Christmas yet.
But I have told him all about it,
  And he opened his big black eyes,
And I am sure he understood me,
  He looked so funny and wise.

Dear, dear, what a tiny stocking!
  It doesn't take much to hold
Such little pink toes as baby's
  Away from the frost and cold.
But then, for the baby's *Christmas*,
  It never will do at all:
Why, Santa Claus won't be looking
  For any thing half so small.

I know what we'll do for the baby—
  I have thought of the very best plan—
We will borrow a stocking of grandma,
  The longest that ever we can,
And you will hang it by mine, dear mother,
  Right here in the corner—so—
And write a letter to Santa,
  And fasten it on the toe.

Write, "This is the baby's stocking,
  That hangs in the corner here;
You never have seen him, Santa,
  For he only came this year;
But he is just the blessedest baby!
  And now, before you go,
Just cram his stocking with goodies
  From the top clear down to the toe."

FRETTING JENNIE.

Little Jennie, fretful,
    Sitting in a tree,
Worried at the buzzing
    Of a humble-bee.

Said she had a headache,
    Wished it would be still;
Knew it buzzed on purpose
    To defy her will.

Buzzing bee was happy,
    Busy at its work,
Gathering stores of honey—
    Never thought to shirk;

Never thought of Jennie,
    Fretting in the tree,
It was such a happy,
    Busy little bee.

Jennie grew more fretful
    When it answered not,
Said 'twas really hateful—
    That was what she thought.

Still the bee kept buzzing,
    Glad its sphere to fill;
Discontented Jennie
    May be fretting still.

Are there not some Jennies,
    Boys and girls, you know,
Who to fret at others
    Are not slack or slow?

Forth to duty, children!
    Like the busy bee,
Minding not cross Jennie,
    On her fretting tree.

OLD HERO.—*From the Nursery.*

Ann and her little sister Mary went out to the pasture one bright summer day to see the old horse. The horse stood in the shade of the great elm-tree, and, as the two girls came up, he put his head over the fence, as though he was glad to see them.

"Let me feed him," said Mary; and she plucked a bunch of clover to give to the horse.

But when she held it to his mouth, he reached out for it with his upper lip, and gave a slight snort that startled the little girl. She drew back timidly.

"Don't be afraid," said Ann. "He will not hurt you. Good old horse! See me pat him on the head." Then little Mary took courage, and let the old horse eat the clover from her hand.

Now I must tell you something about this old horse. Mary's father, who was a doctor, bought him when he was a colt, and named him Hero. For many and many a year he carried the doctor on his rounds, and served the whole family faithfully.

He was older than the oldest of the doctor's children, and was such a gentle, steady, useful creature that they all became much attached to him.

By-and-by Hero grew so old that he was not able to do his usual work. One day a man said to the doctor, "That horse is of no use to you now. Sell him to me. I will give you twelve dollars for him. I want him to work in my tread-mill."

Wasn't there an outcry in the house when the folks heard this! The idea of selling old Hero to be worked in a tread-mill! That was too bad. But the doctor's answer to the man settled the matter very soon.

"My friend," said he, "there is not money enough in your town to buy this horse for a tread-mill."

Soon after this old Hero got so lame that he was not fit to work at all. Then somebody said, "That horse is good for nothing. I would kill him if I were you."

There was another outburst in the family when the doctor told this. "Papa," said Mary, with her lip quivering, "if you let old Hero be killed, you will be a cruel man."

"That's just what I think," said the doctor. "No, old fellow," said he, patting Hero, "you shall not be killed. You shall have no more work to do. You shall take your ease. You shall have the best stall in the stable, and we will take care of you as long as you live."

So, after that, Hero was one of the family pets.

In the summer his shoes were taken off, and he was put in the richest pasture to roam at will.

He lived upon the fat of the land, and grew so strong and hearty, that, when I last saw him, the old, broken-down horse was frisking about like a young colt.

I wish that all horses could have such a happy old age.

THE FIRST SNOW.—*From the Nursery.*

Drop, pretty snow-flakes, one by one;
Don't be afraid of the noon-day sun.
Build up your palaces crystal white,
Aladdin-like, in a single night.

Hide the old fences under your veil;
Cover the dimples of hill and of dale;
Don't let the trees go naked, but place
On their shivering limbs a web of your lace.

Visit the martin-house if you will,
Or lodge all night on my window-sill;
Call on the well-sweep, and wreathe it about
With fringes, as well as the water-spout.

Give to the door-bell a fleecy cap;
Lend the salt hay-cocks an ermine wrap;
And drift just enough to make the world look
As if it had stepped from a fairy brook.

THE MOTHER-BIRD.—*From the Nursery.*

"Peep, peep, peep!" says she;
"One, two, three, one, two, three
Little birds who wait for me!

"One is yellow, two are brown,
And their throats are soft with down;
On each head a scarlet crown.

"Mother-bird is flying fast;
Soon your hunger will be past:
Here is mother, come at last.

"Peep, peep, peep!" says she:
"And can it be?—ah! can it be?
No little ones are here for me."

In vain her cry, in vain her quest.
A thoughtless boy has robbed her nest:
She looks around with aching breast.

In reviewing a piece of this kind, there is an opportunity for the teacher to impress the mind of the pupil with a desire to protect and care for animals, and to abhor cruelty.

WHAT THE FLOWERS WISHED.—*From the Nursery.*

A FABLE.

On the edge of a stream grew a Lily, a Rose, a Daisy, and a Violet.

"I would like," said the Lily, "to bloom in the pal'-ace of the king; to be seen by the lords and ladies in their fine dress'-es of vel'-vet, silk, and gold."

"As for me," said the Rose, "I would like to be taken by some learn'ed flor'-ist, who would look at me through his eye-glass, and then have me dried, and placed where I would be seen and known to fame."

"I do not care for kings and learn'ed men," said the Daisy. "What I would like would be to be put among the flowers of a wreath for the gold'en locks of some fair young girl."

And what said the Violet when it was her turn to speak? She said, "Let the good God do with me as he will!"

The son of the king gathered the Lily.
An old flor'-ist plucked the Rose.
A young girl with gold'en locks took the Daisy.
Then along the bor'der of the stream came a poor child, thin, sick'ly, and burnt by the sun. Her feet were bare, and

her dress was patched and rag'-ged. She gath'-ered the Vio'let.

On the even'-ing of that day the Lily was put on a table in the palace of the king. Great lords and ladies praised the Lily's beauty, and the queen stooped to breathe its per'-fume.

The Rose was put by the flor'-ist between two leaves of gray paper; and then some heav'-y books, which crushed it by their weight, were put on it; and thus it had the fame it had longed for.

The Daisy shone like a star on the brow of the young girl with golden locks as she led the dance in a light'-ed hall.

Mean'-while, on some straw in a barn, where she had been told to lie down, the poor child who had plucked the Violet pressed it to her lips, and said in her heart, "How good is God to scatter his flowers on the earth, where we all can pluck them."

And if they had told the Violet that she might change her lot for that of the Daisy, the Rose, or the Lily, the Violet would have said, "I prefer to stay where I am."

WHO KILLED TOM ROPER?—*From the Temperance Speaker.*

Who killed Tom Roper?
"Not I," said New Cider:
"I couldn't kill a spider—
   I didn't kill Tom Roper."

"Not I," said Strong Ale:
"I make men tough and hale—
   I didn't kill Tom Roper."

"Not I," said Lager Bier:
"I don't intoxicate. D'ye hear?
   I didn't kill Tom Roper."

"Not I," said Bourbon Whisky:
"I make sick folks spry and frisky;
The doctors say so—don't they know
What quickens blood that runs so slow?
   I didn't kill Tom Roper."

"Not I," said sparkling old Champagne:
"No poor man e'er by me was slain;
I cheer the rich in lordly halls,
And scorn the place where the drunkard falls—
    I didn't kill Tom Roper."

"Not we," said various other wines:
"What! juice of grapes, product of vines
Kill a man! The Bible tells
That wine all other drink excels—
    We didn't kill Tom Roper."

"Not I," said Holland Gin:
"To charge such a crime to me is sin—
    I didn't kill Tom Roper."

"Not I," spoke up the Brandy strong:
"He grew too poor to buy me long—
    I didn't kill Tom Roper."

"Not I," said Medford Rum:
"He was almost gone before I come—
    I didn't kill Tom Roper."

"Ha! ha!" laughed old Prince Alcohol:
"Each struck the blow that made him fall;
And all that helped to make him toper,
MY AGENTS WERE to kill Tom Roper."

PLAYING SCHOOL.—*From the Nursery.*

"Oh! I am tired of run'ning about!" said Ruth May to her little cousins, who had come to spend a day with her. "Suppose we find a shady place and play school?"

"Oh yes!" they all cried. "That will be nice fun."

"And, Ruthie," said George, "you must be the teacher, because you are the oldest."

"Well, so I will," said Ruth. "But, when I am teacher, you must not call me Ruthie; you must all say *Miss* May very politely."

"Oh yes! we had better begin right off," said Dora, a bright little girl of five years. "Miss May, will you please show us where the school-room is?"

"Yes, dear," said Ruth. "On the bench under the old apple-tree at the end of the orchard: that will be just the place. I will run in for some books, and then we will all go there."

So here they are under the tree; Miss May with a long rod, "to keep roguish children in order," as she says.

Bessie, a little girl of three years, when she sees this, says, "You wouldn't really hurt us with it, would you, Cousin Ruth?"

"Oh no, darling!" replied Ruth. "I shall only tingle your fingers a little bit, just for fun."

I think she will have to try it on George's fingers first, for he is slyly pulling Dora's hair as she slips down from the seat, and holds up her hand to know if she may speak.

"What is it, Dora?" says the teacher.

"Please, Miss May, I know my lesson," answers Dora.

"Very well, dear. Now I will hear you spell. George may begin. Spell bird, George."

"B-w-r-d," says George. "Halloa! there's one on the end of that branch. Wouldn't I like to catch him!"

"For shame, sir!" says Ruth. "Go to the foot of the class. Now, Dora, let me hear you spell it."

"B-i-r-d, bird," Dora says, very promptly.

Then Ruth gives little Bessie the word "cat" to spell. She thinks a minute, and then says,

"C-a-t, pussy," which makes them all laugh.

"You mean cat, darling," Ruth says; "but that is very well for such a little girl."

Then they read and count, and so go on playing, till by-and-by a voice from the other side of the fence says suddenly,

"Please, ma'am, may I come to school too? I'll be good."

All turn to see whose voice it is, when who should appear but Ruth's father, who is coming to see where they all are.

"Oh, Uncle John!" the three little ones call out, "how you did startle us!"

"And how funny it would be for a big man to come to school!" says little Bessie, with a merry laugh.

"Do you think I am too big, Bess?" Uncle John says. "Well, then, come here, and you shall ride to the house on my shoulder, for I hear the dinner-bell ringing."

"Who would have thought it was so late!" says Ruth. "School is dismissed. Pick up your doll, Dora; and, George, bring the books. Haven't we had a nice time?"

"Yes, indeed!" says Dora; "and we've really learned something too."

LITTLE BOY'S POCKET; OR THE YOUNG PHILOSOPHER.
From Hearth and Home.

Do you know what's in my pottet?
  Such a lot of treasure's in it!
  Listen, now, while I bedin' it.
  Such a lot of sings it hold,
  And all there is, you sall be told
Every sin dat's in my pottet,
  And when, and where, and how I dot it.

First of all, here's in my pottet
  A beauty shell: I picked it up;
  And here's the handle of a tup
  That somebody has broke at tea;
  The shell's a hole in it, you see;
Nobody knows that I have dot it—
I keep it safe here in my pottet.

And here's my ball, too, in my pottet,
  And here's my pennies, one, two, fre,
  That Aunty Mary gave to me;
  To-morrow-day I'll buy a spade,
  When I'm out walking with the maid;
I can't put *dat* here in my pottet,
But I can use it when I've dot it.

Here's some more sins in my pottet!
  Here's my lead, and here's my string,
  And once I had an iron ring,
  But through a hole it lost one day;
  And this is what I always say—
A hole's the worst sin in a pottet—
Have it mended when you've dot it.

AUNT MARY'S BULLFINCH.—*From the Nursery.*

Edith has been to see her aunt Mary's new bird. Aunt Mary brought it from Ger′many. It is a bull′finch.

Aunt Mary's bird is what they call a "pip′ing bull′finch;" by which we mean that it has been taught to pipe or sing tunes.

Aunt Mary took Edith on her knee, and told her about these pip′ing bull′finches.

"There are men," said Aunt Mary, "who spend a great deal of time in teach′ing these birds to sing tunes, and then sell them for a high price.

"It must be fun′ny, must it not? to see a school of bull′-finches learn′ing to sing! Shall I tell you how they are taught?

"First of all, they are tak′en when they are quite young, not more than ten days old; and they have great care giv′en to them till they are about two months old, when they grow to be quite tame.

"Soon they begin to whis′tle; and then their mas′ter knows it is time to begin to teach them. What does he do then, do you think? Does he fetch out prim′ers and spell′-ing-books, and pen′cils and slates? Oh no! noth′ing of the kind.

"He di-vides his lit′tle school into class′es of about six birds in each, and shuts them up in a dark room, where they are left for some time with-out any food. The poor lit′tle birds won′der what it all means, and grow quite sad.

"Then their mas′ter comes in, and begins play′ing over and over one tune on what is called a bird-or′gan; that is, a kind of ti′ny or′gan, the notes of which are very like those of a bull′finch.

"Soon the lit′tle birds begin to lis′ten; and after the same air has been played over I am sure I can not tell you how many times, some of the birds try to sing the air.

"As soon as they do this, some food is given to them as a reward, and the light is let in; and so, at last, they begin to find out what their mas′ter wants them to do.

"The same thing goes on day after day for a long time,

till they sing quite bold′ly, and then the class′es are bro′ken up, and each bird is put under the care of a boy, who plays that one tune over all day long, so that the bull′finch may learn it well.

"These little birds remem′ber their teach′ers a long time, and often seem very fond of them.

"In his wild state the bull′finch is quite a good sing′er, and it is fun′ny to watch him while he is sing′ing. He puffs out his feath′ers, and moves about his head, as if try′ing to do his best; but, when he sees some one look′ing at him, he will fly off."

This was the end of Aunt Mary's sto′ry; and then her little bull′finch sang the tune of "Sweet Home." Edith was much pleased, and went home and told her moth′er all about the pip′ing bull′finch.

LITTLE MARY'S BOUQUET.—*From the Little Corporal.*

"To-morrow is little Mary's birth-day," said the gardener, as he examined his flowers. "She must have a nice bouquet."

"To-morrow is little Mary's birth-day," whispered the flowers to one another. "To-morrow! to-morrow!"

"My buds are all ready," said the rose.

"So are mine," said the sunflower.

The pansies smiled at the thought, but the sunflower held his head so high that he did not see them.

"I'd rather stand in this garden than be put in the queen's bouquet," said a tall hollyhock.

"I've no flowers to spare for any one," said the moneywort, anxiously counting her buds.

"Don't be a miser," said the ragged robin. "They may have all of mine."

"I would like to go to little Mary," said the mignonette.

"My dear child, don't think of such a thing," said a gay tulip, spreading her petals. "You have no beauty."

"I know it," said the mignonette, mournfully.

"Never mind," said the rose; "you have perfume, and some think that better than beauty."

"Ah!" said the tulip.

"Why are you here, pray?" said a pert little lady's-slipper to a bright dandelion, as she gave her a sly kick.

"If it comes to that, why are *you* here?" said the dandelion.

"Because I was planted here," said the lady's-slipper. "*You* are *wild*, but I came in a paper bag, with my name on it, and was planted by the gardener."

"Perhaps I *am* a little wild," said the dandelion; "but I was planted here; and, besides, I can tell the time."

"I never heard of a dandelion's being planted," said the lady's-slipper.

"I never heard of a dandelion telling time," said a four-o'clock.

"At all events, I was blown here by some one who wanted to know what time it was."

"Did they find out?" interrupted the four-o'clock.

"And I thought, as I was here, I might as well grow," continued the dandelion. "I am good to eat, and I can be made into coffee."

"Don't say any thing about time, whatever you do," said the four-o'clock; "I am the only one who knows about time."

"Thyme! thyme!" said the summer savory. "There are plenty of sweet herbs better than thyme."

"What are you quarreling about, you foolish little things?" said the sunflower. "I can tell time; I go by the sun."

"What will you do to-morrow, when the clouds come over and hide the sun?" asked a poor-man's-weather-glass at his feet.

"I can guess at it," said the sunflower; "but you must be a very poor-man's-weather-glass to talk of clouds when the sky is so bright."

"I feel it in my fibres," said the weather-glass.

"For pity's sake, can any one tell me if it is four yet?" said the four-o'clock. "Here I have been gossiping, and forgetting all about it."

"I can see the clock," said a sweet pea, on tiptoe. "It is half past four."

"Dear me!" said the four-o'clock; "I promised these buds they should be out to-day, and now they will have to wait till four to-morrow morning, and then there will be no one to see them but the early birds. It is too bad."

"Only blame to yourself, madam," said a thistle.

The four-o'clock made no reply, for she knew she would suffer if she meddled with him. The next morning, early, the gardener came to make a bouquet. He made it of lovely pink sweet peas, purple pansies, rose-buds wet with dew, the modest mignonette, the spicy carnation, fragrant geranium leaves, and delicate heliotrope.

"Every bouquet should have a bit of yellow," said the gardener, as he added a dandelion. "There! that finishes it, and it is fit for a queen;" and he carried it away.

"Just to think! He took that saucy dandelion, and left me," said the lady's-slipper.

"What is a bouquet without me?" said the tulip, tossing her head. "No matter; I shall live the longer."

"So shall I," said ragged robin; but no one took any notice of him, because he was a ragged robin.

CHOICE OF TRADES.—*From the Festival.*
A RECITATION FOR LITTLE BOYS.

This recitation should be accompanied with appropriate action. Thus the farmer should make the motion for sowing, reaping, plowing, binding, and pitching away; the carpenter for planing, hammering, and sawing; the mason for bricklaying and smoothing; the smith for blows on the anvil, and the shoemaker for sewing shoes, etc.

First Boy. When I'm a man, a man,
I'll be a farmer if I can—and I can!
I'll plow the ground, and the seed I'll sow;
I'll reap the grain, and the grass I'll mow;
I'll bind the sheaves, and I'll rake the hay,
And pitch it up on the mow away,
      When I'm a man.

Second Boy. When I'm a man, a man,
I'll be a carpenter if I can—and I can!

I'll plane like this, and I'll hammer so,
And this is the way my saw shall go.
I'll make bird-houses, and sleds, and boats,
And a ship that shall race every craft that floats,
   When I'm a man.

Third Boy. When I'm a man, a man,
A blacksmith I'll be if I can—and I can!
Clang, clang, clang shall my anvil ring,
And this is the way the blows I'll swing.
I'll shoe your horse, sir, neat and tight,
Then I'll trot round the square to see if it's right,
   When I'm a man.

Fourth Boy. When I'm a man, a man,
A mason I'll be if I can—and I can!
I'll lay a brick this way, and lay one that,
Then take my trowel and smooth them flat;
Great chimneys I'll make; I think I'll be able
To build one as high as the Tower of Babel
   When I'm a man.

Fifth Boy. When I'm a man, a man,
I'll be a shoe-maker if I can—and I can!
I'll sit on a bench, with my last held so,
And in and out shall my needles go.
I'll sew so strong that my work shall wear
Till nothing is left but my stitches there,
   When I'm a man.

Sixth Boy. When I'm a man, a man,
A doctor I'll be if I can—and I can!
My powders and pills shall be nice and sweet,
And you shall have just what you like to eat;
I'll prescribe for you riding, and sailing, and such;
And, 'bove all things, you must never study too much
   When I'm a man.

Seventh Boy. When I'm a man, a man,
I'll be a minister if I can—and I can!
And once in a while a sermon I'll make
That will keep little boys and girls awake;

For ah! dear me! if the ministers knew
How glad we are when they get through!—
   When I'm a man.

Eighth Boy. When I'm a man, a man,
A teacher I'll be if I can—and I can!
I'll sing to my scholars, fine stories I'll tell;
I'll show them pictures, and, well—oh! well,
They shall have some lessons—I s'pose they ought;
But oh! I shall make them so very short,
   When I'm a man.

Ninth Boy. When I'm a man, a man,
I'll be a school-committee if I can—and I can!
'Bout once a week I'll come into school,
And say, "Miss Teacher, I've made a rule
That boys and girls need a good deal of play;
You may give these children a holiday"—
   When I'm a man.

Tenth Boy. When I'm a man, a man,
I'll be a president if I can—and I can!
My uncles and aunts are a jolly set,
And I'll have them all in my cabinet,
I shall live in the White House; and I hope you all,
When you hear I'm elected, will give me a call
   When I'm a man.

(All in concert, or, if they can not be trained to speak it in concert so as to make every word understood, let the best speaker step forward, and repeat alone in a distinct voice),

   When we are men, are men,
I hope we shall do great things; and then,
Whatever we do, this thing we say,
We'll do our work in the very best way;
And you shall see, if you know us then,
We'll be good, and honest, and useful men—
   When we are men.

MYSTERIES.—*From the Little Corporal.*

Where are you going, dear little feet?
  Restless, pattering things!
Bearing your burden, soft and sweet,
  Swift as the swallow's wings.

What are you doing, dear little hands?
  Busy from morn till night!
Counting the hours by golden sands,
  Charming with new delight.

What are you saying, dear little tongue?
  Chattering all day long,
Words that the wild birds teach their young,
  Sweeter than peach or song.

What are you seeking, wandering eyes?
  Gazing away to the West;
Watching the rosy, sunset skies,
  Where the day sinks to rest.

Ah! little tender baby soul,
  Wonderful dreams are yours!
Life must be sweet when life is new,
  Long as the world endures.

WATER.

Water! water! cries the bird,
  With his singing, gentle note:
And the liquid sound is heard
  Pouring from his little throat;
Water! water! clear and sweet!
    Te-weet! te weet!

Water! water! roars the ox,
  While it rushes at his side,
Down among the mossy rocks
  Rippling with its crystal tide;
Water! water! pure and true!
    Moo! moo!

Water! water! said the tree,
  With its branches spreading high;
Water! water! rustled he,
  For his leaves were very dry;
Water! water for the tree,
    Pure and free.

Water! water! said the flower,
  Whispering with its perfumed breath;
Let me have it in an hour,
  Ere I, thirsting, droop in death!
Water! water! soft and still,
    Is my will.

Water! water! said the grain,
  With its yellow head on high;
And the spreading, fertile plain,
  Ripening, joined the swelling cry;
Water for the grains of gold!
    Wealth untold!

Water! water! sparkling, pure,
  Giveth Nature every where—
If you drink it, I am sure
  It will never prove a snare.
Water is the thing for me—
    Yes, and thee.

Water! water! Young and old
  Drink it, crystal-like and sweet;
Never heed the tempter bold—
  Smash him underneath your feet!
Water! water! Youth, for thee—
    Thee and me.

TOMMY'S WEEK.—*From the Little Corporal.*

The first day, of course, was Sunday. Sunday always comes first in my weeks, though I have heard people say it came away down at the end, after Saturday. It came first in Tommy's week, but he didn't know much about it until he waked up one morning and found the sun shining very bright, and wondered why his mamma didn't get up and dress him. Then he crept out of bed, and went to the window, and stood there in his little night-gown watching an old robin that was feeding her babies with worms for breakfast. The baby robins opened their mouths very wide, and seemed to relish their breakfast, which reminded Tommy that he wanted his own. But when he turned around from the window, he saw his new red trumpet lying on the floor, and he picked it up and blew it very loud indeed. It waked up every body in the house. Bridget thought it was the milkman, and clattered out the door with one foot half way into her shoe; and Tommy's mamma opened her eyes very wide, and said,

"Why, Tommy Bancroft! didn't you know it was Sunday morning?"

And that was the first Tommy ever remembered about Sunday. After breakfast Uncle Jim didn't go to the city, but sat and read with his pretty new slippers on, and Tommy was dressed up in his white linen clothes and buttoned gaiters, and had his yellow hair curled into queer little curls that didn't stay in very well, and went with his mamma to a great house with a bell on the top of it. They called it a church. Tommy's mamma told him he mustn't talk in church. There were a great many other people there, and nobody talked at all except one man in a kind of a box high up at one end, and that man talked all the time. Tommy thought perhaps he didn't know any better. There was a little girl in the next seat with a blue and white feather in her hat. She looked at Tommy a good deal, and Tommy looked at the feather. He wondered if it was a rooster's feather. He thought he should like to have a rooster with such feathers. Then the little girl's hat began to move about, then there were two hats and two blue and white feathers—Tommy saw them; then three hats, then four, then the whole air was full of them, and Tommy laid his head down in his mother's lap, and didn't remember any more.

They must have gone home after a while, for Grandma Bancroft was there to dinner, and she had her black velvet bag with beads around the bottom. Tommy liked to play with the beads, and sometimes Grandma Bancroft used to open the bag and give him some caraway seeds, or red and white peppermint candies. This time she gave him two raisins, and asked him if he could tell her about the sermon.

"They didn't have any of them fings to *my* church," said Tommy, innocently.

He thought about it while he was eating his raisins, and then he said,

"Was that what the men passed around in the boxes, gamma? I didn't take any of that. Wish't I had."

Grandma tried to explain about the sermon, and told the little boy how the minister was trying to tell the people how to be good. But Tommy didn't understand.

"He didn't speak to me 'tall," he insisted; "kept talkin' to himself all the time. Course if he talked to me I should understood him; *what you s'pose?*"

But by-and-by mamma took Tommy on her lap and told him all about Samuel, the little boy that talked with God; and about David, the shepherd-boy that slew the great giant; and about Jesus, the dear Savior, who lived and died to save just such boys as he; and then Tommy felt very good and very loving, and meant to mind his mamma as long as he lived, and always let the baby have his red ball and his trumpet, and say please to Bridget, and not cry when his face was washed. He said his little prayer very earnestly and heartily, though he was sound asleep two minutes afterward. And after that, Sunday always came regular in Tommy's week.

Monday.

Monday was Tommy's own day, and he liked it the very best of all. First, because it was washing day, which was the very reason mamma *didn't* like it at all. He knew it was Monday the very minute he woke up, because there was his red plaid dress and gingham apron for him to wear. He always wore that dress washing days, and baking days, and days when mamma was too busy to look after him; and Tommy's heart always gave a great jump of delight when he saw it, for he knew he could dig in the dirt with the fire-shovel, and nobody would say,

"*Why, Tommy Bancroft, look at your new clothes.*"

When his mamma dressed him, she said,

"I can't stop to curl your hair this morning, because it's *washing day,*" and then Tommy was gladder yet. When he was a man he meant to have all his hair cut close to his head, so nobody could curl it; it always made him so cross to have it pulled.

After breakfast mamma tied his old straw hat under his chin, and told him to run and play like a good boy. Tommy went straight out to the sink-drain in the back yard. There was quite a little river of soap-suds running through it, and Tommy fished in it a while with the handle to his mother's parasol that he found on the hall-table. She shouldn't have left it there, you know. Then he thought he would build a dam across the drain, and he threw down the parasol, and went in to get the fire-shovel to dig with. Bridget was cross, and said she wanted the shovel herself— did he think she was going to put in coal with her fingers? Then he thought he would take a case-knife, and, while he was looking for one, he spied his mother's silver pie-knife in the spoon-basket; it was broad and flat, pretty much like a shovel, and Tommy thought he could make it do.

"Course she'd let me take it; won't hurt it 'tall," said Tommy to his conscience; but he was very careful to keep it out of Bridget's sight as he trudged back to the drain. He found a nice, soft place to dig dirt in the middle of one of mamma's flower-beds; it was full of little sticks to show where the seeds were planted a few days before, but they had not come up, and Tommy thought it must be because there was too much dirt. He pulled off his hat for a cart, and it was splendid fun to load it up with the pie-knife, and drag it to the drain by the ribbons. Pie-knives are not made to dig in the dirt with, and pretty soon it began to curl up at the point, and then the handle doubled down sideways, and Tommy threw it down with the parasol, saying to himself, "I guess Uncle Jim can fix it."

While he was squatted up in the very middle of the

drain, somebody emptied another tub full of suds, and it came swashing along, and washed Tommy and the dam away together. He gave one little squeal of astonishment; but, though he was very wet and muddy, he only put on his dirty little hat and started after the gray kitten that was watching a bird under the raspberry bushes. He chased her three times around the garden and twice under the fence, but he couldn't catch her, though he tore the brim half off from his hat, and did something to the skirt of his plaid dress that made it hang down around his feet. Then he went into the coal-cellar, and climbed up and down the great mountain of coal, and played he was a traveler climbing up some icy mountains, like some men Uncle Jim read about. When he was tired of this he thought it must be dinner-time, he was so hungry; so he started for the house. There was an elegant carriage at the gate, and he wondered if his Aunt Sue hadn't come to bring him the velocipede she promised him. He went to look for his mamma, but she wasn't in her room, or the dining-room, or the nursery. So he walked straight into the parlor, and there was his pretty mamma, in her nice ruffled morning dress, and there were two strange ladies and the *minister's wife!*

Dear! dear! how his mamma looked! She felt as if she should faint away; and the strange ladies said, "Is this your youngest, Mrs. Bancroft?" and tried not to laugh; but the minister's wife said, "*Come here, Tommy,*" and then she gave right up and laughed till the tears ran down her cheeks. Tommy's mamma laughed too, though she looked at first as if she was going to cry; and Tommy stood there with his old torn skirt hanging down over his muddy little trowsers and stockings, his old torn hat-brim flopping about his shoulders, and his hands, and face, and long yellow hair all black and grimy with coal-dust, and wasn't one bit ashamed!

Tuesday.

If it had not rained that day it never would have happened; but before Tommy had half finished his breakfast, Uncle Jim got up and walked to the front window, and remarked that "it was raining cats and dogs."

Tommy looked up, with his mouth full of bread and butter, to see if Uncle Jim was really in earnest; but as he looked perfectly sober, he immediately scrambled down from his chair and rushed to the window, expecting to see a shower of black and white kittens, with a smart sprinkling of curly dogs. What he really saw was a very muddy river rushing along through the gutter; two men, with tin pails and short pipes, tramping down the street; and a miserable-looking dog, with a bone in his mouth, picking his way through the mud. He looked as if he might have rained down; but Tommy knew he didn't, because he knew where he lived up the alley, and he had often seen him sneaking around the back door after bits which Tommy threw away when he took his lunch out of doors. Just at that instant Uncle Jim came in from the back hall, and said, in a very dreadful voice,

"Now, then, Tommy Trotter, where are my rubbers?"

When any thing was lost in that house, they always asked Tommy about it. It was a habit they had of supposing that Tommy had had it, especially if it was something he never ought to touch.

Tommy forgot all about the cats and dogs, and looked at Uncle Jim, and said quickly, "I d'n know."

That was a habit Tommy had, and he always said "*I d'n know*" before he stopped to think. But he did know very well, and so he said,

"Oh yes, Uncle Jim. They're over to Billy's house, in the big *troft* where the horse drinks. Me and Billy sailed 'em for boats, all full wid oats, and they sinked down to the floor of the water."

"Why, Tommy Bancroft," said his mamma, looking greatly troubled, "what shall I do with you?"

Uncle Jim looked at him very soberly, and said,

"Well, young man, here I am, two miles from my office, and no rubbers. I should like to know what you mean to do about it. You ought to buy me some more. I shall catch my death of cold, and *then* how'll you feel, sir?"

Tommy's face brightened in a minute.

"Oh, I'll buy you some more," said he, and trotted away

to get his bank, which had a loose floor, so that whatever you put in at the top could be easily shaken out at the bottom, an arrangement Tommy found very satisfactory. The first thing that came out was a quarter, very new and crisp; but Tommy's heart never faltered.

"There," said he, "you can buy you some more rubbers, and I won't never sail 'em in the troft."

"Very well," said Uncle Jim, putting the money in his pocket, and going into the hall.

"Uncle Jim," called Tommy, "if there's any change left, you buy me some pea-nuts, will you?"

Uncle Jim nodded and said, "I shouldn't wonder," as he strode out into the rain.

Tommy's mamma gave the baby her breakfast, talked a while with Bridget about supper, dusted the parlor, and watered the ivy in the bay-window, and then she put the baby on the floor in the dining-room, and gave her some clothes-pins and a tin pan to play with. Tommy had his Noah's ark, but he had to keep it on the table, because the baby put the camels and elephants into her mouth whenever she got a chance, and once she sucked all the paint off from Shem, Ham, and Japheth, and made herself quite sick. Ellen was ironing in the kitchen, and Mrs. Bancroft said,

"Now, Ellen, it is such a rainy day nobody will be in, and I am going up to look over the winter clothing, and put it away. The children will do very well in here, but you must keep your door open, and look in once in a while."

"Yes'm," said Ellen; "Tommy's gettin' right handy to mind the baby, when he tries."

"Oh, I'll tend to her," said Tommy, who was trying to stand Mrs. Noah on the ridge-pole of the ark; "Ellen needn't mind about us at all."

So Tommy's mamma went away up stairs, and Ellen hurried with her ironing, looking out once in a while through the rain to see if the grocer's young man was not coming for his orders. When he did come she shut the dining-room door, because the baby was always frightened at the grocer's young man, though Ellen herself did not seem at all afraid of him. It was just at this moment that Tommy spied a bottle of mucilage on the clock-shelf over the table, and it struck him instantly what a fine thing it would be to fasten on the elephant's trunk and Noah's head again. It was quite easy to reach it and pull out the cork; but there did not happen to be any brush, so Tommy was forced to use one of his fingers, which answered very well, only he had to wipe it frequently upon his apron. Noah's head refused to stick, and so did the elephant's trunk, though he tried it on most all the animals.

Then he concluded he would paste up hand-bills, as he had seen men do on the street. So he got baby's little, soft, white hair-brush, and poured out some of the mucilage in the seat of Uncle Jim's table-chair. Then he dipped the brush, and stuck pieces of the morning paper on the walls, on the doors, on the stove, and, last of all, he happened to remember how he had seen a funny man walking through the streets with hand-bills on his hat and his back; so he pasted some papers on the baby's back, and on the top of her poor little bald head. Baby had no hair to speak of, but she did not at all fancy this way of dressing it, so she set up a loud scream of anger, and at that very moment came a ring at the door-bell.

"Dear! dear!" said Tommy's mamma, peeping out at her chamber window, "if there isn't Miss Dilly Dean, come to spend the day."

Mamma hurried down to the door to receive Miss Dilly, who stood in the hall, with the inky water running off from her umbrella, and making a little black river on the oil-cloth.

"You didn't look for me to-day, I'm sure," said Miss Dilly, "but I thought I should be sure of a good long visit all to myself, because it rained so."

Ellen went back to try to hush the baby, and Tommy stood in the door with the hair-brush in his hand, while mamma said,

"Well, come right into the dining-room, Miss Dilly, and dry your feet; we keep a fire there on account of the baby."

And Tommy kept on staring at Miss Dilly's funny little

curls, until mamma pushed Uncle Jim's chair to the grate, and said,
"Sit right down here, Miss Dilly;" and Miss Dilly sat down.

Mamma began to pick up things about the room, and by-and-by she found the empty mucilage bottle, and she said, "Why, Tommy Bancroft! where's my mucilage?"

Then Tommy put his finger in his mouth, and looked at Miss Dilly harder than ever, and said, "*She's sittin' on it.*"

Miss Dilly jumped up as spry as a kitten, and the chair jumped too; and Miss Dilly's best alpaca dress was just about ruined.

I don't know just what Tommy's mamma said to him, but, whatever it was, she put him to bed afterward to think about it. And that was what happened on Tuesday.

Wednesday.

The next day must have been Wednesday, but Tommy did not remember much about it, for, long before morning, he began to feel very sick. He had bad dreams. First, he thought an elephant picked him up with his long, crooked finger, and tucked him away in one corner of his big mouth, and Tommy felt very hot and uncomfortable in there. And then he thought that he had swallowed the elephant, and found him very cold and heavy, and altogether too large for his quarters. And the next Tommy knew, his mamma was standing by his crib with a lamp in her hand, looking very anxious, and that set Tommy to crying. He cried so long and so loud that Uncle Jim came to see what was the matter. Uncle Jim looked very sleepy; said he guessed Tommy would be all right in the morning; most likely he had eaten something. Now that was one of Uncle Jim's aggravating ways; whenever Tommy was sick, he always insisted it was because he had "*eaten something,*" as if boys were not always eating something. When he had said this, he felt as if he had done his whole duty, and went back to bed contentedly; but Tommy's mamma soothed, and petted, and fussed over him until morning, when she told Uncle Jim that, in her opinion, Tommy was a very sick boy, and must have the doctor at once. Uncle Jim finished his breakfast, and then went into the bedroom chewing his toothpick. He sat down by the bed and took Tommy on his knee.

"Well, sir," said he, briskly, "are you going to the city with me to-day?"

Tommy tried to smile, but he only sneezed five times in succession.

"My dear child, where's your handkerchief?" exclaimed Uncle Jim, groping about in a bewildered fashion, as if he supposed little boys had half a dozen pockets in their night-gowns, and carried handkerchiefs in them all. Mamma rushed to the rescue, but by that time Uncle Jim had solved the difficulty by wiping Tommy's nose with the corner of the white counterpane.

"It is only a cold," he said, putting him back in bed, "but, if it will be any satisfaction to you, I'll have the doctor come around and look at him. I wouldn't worry about him, though."

As if the dear little woman could help it.

Doctor Smith was out of town, so Uncle Jim sent Doctor Brown, a very pompous individual, but quite good-natured. He looked at Tommy, and Tommy's mamma watched him very suspiciously. He looked at his tongue, and felt of his pulse; then rubbed his hands together, and asked,

"Has he eaten any thing to disagree with him, madam?"

"*Not a thing,*" said Mrs. Bancroft, positively; "I'm very particular about his diet."

Then the doctor looked closely at Tommy's face, which was quite red and blubbery, partly with the cold and partly with crying so much; he looked behind his ears and under his chin; lifted the yellow hair from his neck, and said,

"Hm—m! has your son ever had the measles, madam?"

"Never," said Mrs. Bancroft, faintly.

"Then he has them now, madam," said the doctor, blandly. "A very clear case, and coming out finely." And he nodded his head at Tommy, as if it was a delightful thing to have the measles.

Then they all went out; but presently the doctor came back with a spoonful of nice red jelly, and said,

"Here, my little man, is something nice for you; let me see you take it."

Tommy had never been deceived about medicine, so he sat up directly and took it in his mouth; but it tasted very badly, and he would have spit it out, only the doctor looked very fierce, and said "*Swallow it, quick!*" in such a dreadful voice that Tommy dared not do any thing else.

Then the doctor went away laughing, as if it was a good joke to cheat a little boy; but Tommy lay down on his pillow with his honest little heart full of indignation. By-and-by he said,

"Mamma, don't doctors have to tell the *troof* like other folks?"

Tommy's mamma wished him to respect the doctor, but she thought it a great deal more important that he should respect the truth, so she told him that *every body* was bound to speak the truth, and that it was not right to deceive sick people or cheat little boys.

Tommy grew worse instead of better. There were the little red spots on his neck, but no more measles came out, and his mamma began to grow alarmed. She wondered if the doctor knew so very much. He wasn't *her* doctor, and she had not a particle of confidence in the good sense of any other doctor in the world but her doctor. What if Tommy should die? And then she remembered all his naughty little pranks, and wondered how she could have been so vexed with him about the mucilage, and thought, if he only got well, she should never be vexed with him again. About noon she sent Ellen for Uncle Jim, and begged him to telegraph to New York for Tommy's papa to come straight home. Uncle Jim sat down by Tommy again, and began to question him. Uncle Jim was a very obstinate man, and he still believed Tommy had "*eaten something.*"

"Where was he yesterday?" he asked.

"In the house all day," said mamma; "don't you remember how it rained?"

"He was over to Billy's, ma'am, about tea-time," said Ellen; "you mind you said he might go and play in the barn."

"Oh yes," said mamma, "I had forgotten; but it was only half an hour or so, and he had on his rubbers."

"Did you play in the water, Tommy?" asked Uncle Jim.

"N-no," said Tommy, faintly; "only we tried to catch it in our moufs, where it runned down the roof, and it went down our backs, and felt awful funny."

"I should think so," said Uncle Jim; "and what else did you do?"

"Noffin; only played."

"Played what? What did you *eat?*" persisted Uncle Jim.

"Noffin," said Tommy, "only I was Billy's horse, and—oh yes, Uncle Jim, he gave me some *shopped feed.*"

"Chopped feed! what on earth was that?" asked Uncle Jim, glancing triumphantly at mamma.

"Why, turnuts and oats, shopped in a pail, and water mixed in," said Tommy, with the pride of an inventor.

"Raw turnips and oats! there's a delightful mixture for you," exclaimed Uncle Jim; "and you ate that stuff, did you, Tommy?"

"Y-e-e-s," said Tommy, faintly, as if it was not quite pleasant to remember; "I used to like *turnuts.*"

Mamma looked perfectly horrified; Ellen pulled the corner of her apron and giggled as loud as she dared; but Uncle Jim leaned back in his chair and laughed a great, hearty, ringing laugh, until you would have thought the windows rattled.

"Any thing more, Tommy?" he said, at last; "did you take any condition-powders?"

"No," said Tommy, "but Billy rubbed my neck with *gogling oil,* 'cause I had the—the *marrow bones.*"

"Gargling oil! That accounts for the measles," said Uncle Jim, laughing again; and then he wiped his eyes, and told Ellen to bring him a glass of warm water, with a teaspoonful of mustard in it.

"Now, Tommy," said he, "I want you to drink this all down—every drop."

"Is it good?" wailed Tommy.

"Not very," said Uncle Jim, taking a little sip; "it isn't very bad, either, and if you will drink it all before I count ten, I'll buy you a jack-knife."

Tommy drank very fast, and Uncle Jim had only counted eight when the last drop was swallowed, and Tommy asked, with a shudder, when he should have the knife.

"To-night," said Uncle Jim, watching Tommy curiously. Perhaps you have taken warm water with mustard in it. If you have, you know just what happened, and why Tommy lay upon his pillow, about ten minutes afterward, looking red about the eyes and white about the mouth, but feeling a great deal better.

"Now, youngster," said Uncle Jim, "I'm going straight after that knife, but I sha'n't get back till tea-time; so, if you go to sleep, the time will pass before you know it."

Tommy did go to sleep, and slept so long his mamma began to worry again, but, by the time Uncle Jim came home, a sturdy little voice shouted from the bedroom,

"Uncle Jim! where's my knife?"

"Ah!" said Uncle Jim, "I believe I have mistaken my profession. I should have been a doctor."

Thursday and Friday.

Yes, and a good long night between them. We must take them all together, on account of what happened. It would never do to make two stories out of Tommy's visit to his grandmother. You see, there was something else besides the visiting, and it came right in the middle, between Thursday and Friday. That was when he was in the old— But wait till I tell you the beginning of it.

Tommy was standing on a cricket by the west window, flattening his nose against the pane, and making snail-tracks all over the glass with his tongue, when grandma drove up, with Dolly and the red wagon. Dolly was the horse; and she and grandma had come to take Tommy out to the farm in Pearfield, you know, where his grandparents lived, to stay two whole days. And he wasn't going as a baby, with somebody to take care of him, but as a young gentleman who could look out for himself.

"Nobody ain't goin' wiv me," said he to Ellen, triumphantly. "I'm jes goin' all myself, alone; me 'n gamma."

It was the grandest thing that ever was heard of to go

off as his father did, kissing them all good-by, and, perhaps, seeing his mother cry a little.

If she felt ever so much like crying, she could only cry with laughter when Tommy came down from the garret, covered with cobwebs and dust, and presented himself in the parlor, dragging an old blue umbrella and a carpet-bag bigger than himself.

"There, my fings are all ready," said he.

Grandma laughed heartily too; yet she made no objection to the outfit of the young traveler, but stowed the bag and umbrella into the wagon, while Tommy was lifted into the seat, and Dolly's head was turned toward Pearfield.

The journey was not a long one, and only one thing worth mentioning happened on the way. They were passing a great clover-field, just by the edge of the pine woods, when Tommy cried out,

"Oh! gamma, gamma, I see a bear, a sittin' right up on the end of his tail."

Grandma looked where Tommy pointed, and Dolly stopped to look too.

"Don't you see him?" cried Tommy.

"No."

"Put on your speckatles, then."

The spectacles were put on, and, after a long while, she saw what the sharp young eyes had spied so quickly, an old woodchuck sitting at the mouth of his hole. Just as Tommy was proposing to capture him in the carpet-bag, he whisked out of sight; and Dolly started off at a brisk pace, which she kept up without stopping till she reached her own hitching-post at grandpa's gate.

Grandpa himself was there to meet them, and lifted the funny little boy and his funny big baggage out of the red wagon. When he heard about the bear, he told Tommy that there were plenty of such bears in his fields, and that perhaps they would go and catch one after dinner.

"In the carpet bag?" asked Tommy.

"Yes."

"We must have the 'breller to spear him wiv."

"Of course."

Long before grandpa was ready to go, Tommy was parading the yard, spearing imaginary bears with his umbrella, and putting them into his bag. He had just caught a fine large one, when he heard a loud rumble, and, looking up, saw a man run a great yellow stage out of the barn on the other side of the street. Tommy ran to the fence, and, squeezing his chubby face as far as possible between the pickets, watched the man while he washed the coach, greased the wheels, one at a time, and finally lit his pipe and went away. When he was quite out of sight Tommy unlatched the gate and went over to the coach. Finding one of the doors open, he climbed up the iron steps, tugging the bag and umbrella after him, to try a short ride by stage —a standing-still ride, of course. He played that he was papa going to New York; then that the great hole under the seat was a den full of bears; and then that he was the bear himself. He crawled into the den. It was a funny place, with nice straw on the floor, and a long curtain of leather in front. He lay very still in there, and softly growled to his make-believe cubs to look out for that terrible hunter, Tommy.

Now you know that bears are very sleepy fellows, and it is not strange that this little wild animal by-and-by fell asleep in his den.

Meantime grandma had looked out of the front door, and, not seeing Tommy any where, thought that he had gone with grandpa to the field; while grandpa himself had forgotten the young bear-hunter altogether, and had gone to the field alone.

After a time the stage-driver came, harnessed his four horses to the coach, and drove it away. He stopped at the store to get the mail-bag and take in several passengers. There was a fat woman with a baby, an Irish servant-girl, a one-legged little French peddler, and a stiff old gentleman with a gold-headed cane. With this load the yellow stage started for Ryetown, twelve miles away, and Tommy still asleep under the seat.

When he awoke he couldn't tell where he was, and wondered what made his bed rock and bounce about so. Then he heard the people talking right over his head. He peeped under the leather curtain, and saw several pairs of shoes. Too frightened to know what he did, he lifted the curtain and gave one desperate spring, thrusting his curly head, all covered with straw, right between the old gentleman's legs.

If a real bear had jumped out he could not have made more confusion. The old gentleman sprang to his feet, smashing his hat over his eyes by striking against the top of the coach; the Irish girl screamed "Murther!" and tried to leap out of the window; the fat woman fainted and dropped her baby; the little Frenchman jumped up and down on his one leg till he lost his balance and tumbled over; and Tommy clung with both hands to the old gentleman's pantaloons, and screamed with all his might.

I can not begin to describe what followed, or record the questions with which Tommy was assailed, in English, Irish, and French, to all of which he could only say that his grandpa owned Dolly and kept bears, and that he was a bear himself when he went to sleep. Of course there was nothing to do but take the little bear to Ryetown, and send him back by Friday's coach. So he cried himself to sleep that night in the Ryetown hotel, and early the next morning was lifted into the yellow stage again. All the way back the driver wondered what he should do with the boy when he got to Pearfield; but there was no need of worrying about that, for every body in town knew that he was lost, and dozens of people were looking for him in every direction. You can guess whether any body was glad when the little runaway was set down at grandpa's gate, umbrella, carpet-bag, and all.

Grandma's eyes looked very red, and her voice trembled when she said,

"Why, Tommy, Tommy, you poor, dear child, where *have* you been?"

"Oh, ever'n ever so far!" said the young adventurer, with a sigh; "way, way over most to the 'lutionary war. Has gampa caughted my bear?"

Saturday.

Nothing would induce Grandma Bancroft to keep Tommy another night, though he begged hard to be allowed to stay and spear one of those bears.

"I shouldn't be easy a minute with him in the house," said grandma; "not if he was locked into the room and the windows nailed up; something would be sure to happen to him."

So Dolly was harnessed to the red wagon, and Tommy was sent home, with his big "*carper bag*" filled with doughnuts, and caraway cakes, and great white hickory nuts, and a few little red apples, that were beginning to get tough and wrinkly in the skin.

His mamma was delighted to see him, but she grew very pale, and hugged Tommy hard, when she heard how the little fellow had been lost a whole night.

"And just to think that I was sleeping comfortably here at home, and my poor darling away among strangers," said she, mournfully, as if she thought it was very cruel of her.

"Ho!" said Tommy, "I wasn't 'fraid 'tall. I cried a little, 'cause I fought gamma'd be a wantin' me."

He was very well satisfied to be at home, however, and climbed into his crib more pleasantly than usual, for mamma had promised him that in the morning he would find something very nice in the chair beside it. He thought it would be very hard to wait so long, but it only seemed a minute or so before he waked up and heard the robins singing with all their might out in the cherry-trees. Mamma was brushing her hair, moving about very softly, so as not to wake baby, and Tommy sat right up and looked about him, rubbing his eyes with his little fat fists. Sure enough, there was "*something*" on the chair where he had left his little plaid dress and ruffled panties. A new dress?—no, not a dress at all, but the prettiest little suit; jacket and pants of soft gray cloth, buttoned with shining pearl buttons, and trimmed with braid. Tommy could hardly believe his eyes; but he was on the floor in a twinkle, laughing and chuckling, and trying to put his pants right on over his long night-gown. Mamma was almost as much pleased as Tommy was, and she helped the little fellow to dress, and swung the mirror back that he might see himself from head to foot.

"Just like a man," giggled Tommy, thrusting his hands into his pockets; and baby lifted her precious little head from the pillow, and stared at him with her great blue eyes, as if she wondered who that boy was.

"She don't know me," said Tommy, in still greater delight. "*She* won't never have pants, will she?" he added, in a tone that was partly pity and partly triumph.

When he went out to breakfast, Uncle Jim pretended not to know him, and said, "Good morning, sir! very fine weather we are having."

And then he asked mamma if she expected Tommy home pretty soon.

"Why, Uncle Jim," said Tommy, showing two great dimples in his hard red cheeks, "*I'm Tommy!* Don't you see I'm got pants?"

"You Tommy?" said Uncle Jim, looking very much astonished; "I should think not; you're a young gentleman; Tommy's a little girl, and wears dresses."

"I ain't never goin' to be a girl any more," said Tommy; "pretty soon I'll have boots, and long sleeves to my shirt."

Tommy was quite indignant because his mamma pinned a napkin around his neck at the table, but Uncle Jim begged her to pin *his* napkin around his neck, and informed Tommy that gentlemen often did so at restaurants. So Tommy was consoled.

"I suppose you won't care about eating pea-nuts and candy any more," said Uncle Jim, as he went away.

Tommy was walking about with his hands behind him, trying to make his shoes squeak. He stopped and looked at Uncle Jim to see if he was in earnest. There was a twinkle in his eye that reassured Tommy, so he went on squeaking his shoes, and wondering what Billy would say to him. He determined to go over immediately and see; but mamma spoiled that plan by telling him not to go outside the gate on any account, or do any thing to soil his new clothes, because his papa was coming home that very morning, and Tommy must look very nice. Tommy forgot Billy, and jumped around on one foot for joy, and wondered if his papa would know him in his pants and jacket.

"Maybe he'll think it's Uncle Jim," said Tommy to himself, and then he put on his uncle's rainy-day hat, and marched up and down the porch. When he got tired of this, he went into the kitchen to see Bridget, and discovered, to his great delight, that it was baking day, and all manner of nice-looking and nice-smelling things were being made. Generally, Bridget sent Tommy out of the kitchen quick as a wink, but to-day she was pleased with his new clothes, and she was going to ride with her cousin in the afternoon, so she said, "La sakes! just to look at the fine young gintleman! Would you be plazed to take a sate, sir?"

Tommy giggled, and sat down in the chair by the end of Bridget's table. He sat very still for a few minutes, watching Bridget's bare red arms as she beat the eggs for a plum-pudding.

"Oh, Bridget!" he said, suddenly, "you're got holes in your elabows," and then Bridget laughed till she got two more holes right in the middle of her round fat cheeks.

After a while he forgot about being a gentleman, and began to tease Bridget for raisins, and currants, and bits of citron, and tastes of jelly, and lumps of sugar. He put the nutmeg-grater in his pocket, and at last, in leaning upon the table to see just how Bridget made the scallops on the pies, he managed to plant his elbow right in the middle of a cranberry pie, all ready for the oven. Tommy screamed, and so did Bridget; Tommy in dismay, and Bridget in anger, which only made matters worse, as anger always does, for when Bridget jerked Tommy up from the table with a shake that landed him on his feet in the chair, he staggered and tottered, and fell over backward plump into the great bread-pan, which stood there, full to the brim with a mountain of white, puffy dough. Oh dear! but that was a fix to be in! and by the time Bridget had pulled Tommy out with her great floury hands, rubbed his elbow with a towel, and scraped his pants with a big knife, you may be sure the new clothes were a sight to see.

Mamma thought she should cry at first, it was such a disappointment, you see; but one look at Tommy's miserable face made her so sorry for her poor little man that she comforted him very bravely, washed his sticky hands, and let him keep on his pants, though they did look funny behind, especially when they came to dry, as if Tommy had been pasted up somewhere and just broken loose. Tommy went out in the yard again, and Lion, the big dog, got up from his rug by the door, and came smelling around him, as if he suspected a strange boy had come into the yard. He didn't seem to approve of the new clothes at all, for he went back to his rug with a growl of disgust, which amused Tommy very much. He followed Lion, and curled himself up beside him, and laid his head on his shaggy side.

"Are you tired, Tommy?" asked his mamma, looking out at the window.

"Oh no," said Tommy, "I'm just a finkin."

It was very warm and sunny, so Tommy's mamma let him keep on "*finkin*," and when his papa came home he found him there fast asleep.

Perhaps you think that was enough for one week, but it wasn't, for Tommy's papa brought him a music box that would play three tunes, and a set of toy horsemen that rode up and down to the tune of Captain Jinks when you turned the handle to the box they stood upon, so of course he had to go over after dinner to show his treasures and his new clothes to Billy. The result was dreadfully disappointing so far as the new clothes were concerned, for that young gentleman sniffed up his nose at them in decided disapproval.

"Ho!" said Billy. "They're most like a girl; only come to your knees, and no *galluses*. I don't have *my* clothes that way."

Tommy stared with his big eyes, and wondered what "galluses" might be, but had not a doubt that there was but one proper way to make clothes, and that was just like Billy's. Now Billy's mamma never troubled herself about the spring fashions, or any other fashions. She had half a dozen boys, and when the older ones outgrew their clothes, she just cut off the legs a little, patched the knees and elbows, and passed them on down the row. Billy's present pants happened to be a little long, and a little *baggy*, but that was a fault time would remedy; so, after inspecting them a moment, Tommy unbuckled his little trowsers at the knee, and stretched and smoothed them down over his scarlet stockings. It was no use; at the very best, they would not reach his ankles.

"Tell ye what," said Billy, "if ye had some *galluses*, them pants would reach down."

"Y-e-s," said Tommy, in bewilderment.

The inventive Billy went directly to work, and manufactured a pair of suspenders out of some old red reins. The short trowsers were unbuttoned from the jacket, and let down to a desirable length, the "galluses" fastened on with pins and twine, and then Billy surveyed his work with triumph.

To be sure there was a noticeable gap between the top of the trowsers and the bottom of the jacket, but the red suspenders bridged it over, and Billy remembered to have seen the same lack upon Jake, the hostler; so both boys were satisfied.

"There, now!" said Billy; "now you look something like."

He didn't say like what, and Tommy didn't ask, but they played with the soldiers till Ellen rung the bell for tea. Then papa and mamma, looking out at the parlor window, saw a funny little figure coming across the yard, with gray trowsers dragging over its feet, red suspenders stretching down in front across a puff of plaid flannel shirt, and a gay little plaid banner streaming bravely out in the rear. Tommy's papa laughed and shouted, and felt like rolling on the floor, and he called Uncle Jim, and he laughed too; but, though Tommy went to the window the minute he got in, to see what the fun was, he couldn't see any thing at all.

HEEDLESSNESS, OR THE CONCEITED LITTLE GRASSHOPPER.

There was a little grasshopper
　Forever on the jump;
And, as he never looked ahead,
　He often got a bump.

His mother said to him one day,
　As they were in the stubble,
"If you don't look before you leap,
　You'll get yourself in trouble."

This silly little grasshopper
　Depised his wise old mother,
And said he knew what best to do,
　And bade her not to bother.

He hurried off across the fields—
　An unknown path he took—
When, oh! he gave a heedless jump,
　And landed in a brook.

He struggled hard to reach the bank—
　A floating straw he seizes—
When quick a hungry trout darts out,
　And tears him all to pieces.

MORAL.

Good little boys and girls, heed well
　Your mothers' wise advice:
Before you move, look carefully;
　Before you speak, think twice.

SELECTIONS

FOR THE YOUNG FOLKS.

COLUMBIA'S UNION PARTY.—*From the School Festival.*

CHARACTERS:

    COLUMBIA.   BROTHER JONATHAN.
    UNCLE SAM.   DISTRICT OF COLUMBIA.
    THE THIRTY-SEVEN STATES.

[COLUMBIA *dressed in national colors ;* UNCLE SAM *in Continental uniform ;* BROTHER JONATHAN *as an old-time Yankee ; each* STATE *wears a circlet, with the initials of her name.* STATE *characteristics should be represented as far as possible in the dress of each state ; thus,* MICHIGAN *should have copper chains and other ornaments;* NEVADA, *of silver;* CALIFORNIA, *of gold ;* DELAWARE *may be in Swedish dress. The stage should be adorned with flags, stars, and shields.* COLUMBIA *must have a raised central seat, and there should be a table for receiving the gifts.* DISTRICT OF COLUMBIA *should receive and arrange them.*]

Enter UNCLE SAM.

Columbia. Uncle Sam! welcome to my Union party.
Uncle Sam. Thanks, fair Columbia; hope you're well and
    hearty.
Col. Quite well, good uncle; I'm rejoiced you're here—
It will be such support to have you near.

Enter BROTHER JONATHAN.

And Brother Jonathan I hope to see—
Brother Jonathan. Wal, neow, Columby, shake hands;
    here I be.
How big a party will ye have, d'ye s'pose?
And will the young folks poke fun at my clothes?

Col. No, no, dear brother—not one bit of danger;
You will not meet to-day a single stranger.
Only the children, coming home once more
To see their mother, now she's ninety-four.
Almost a hundred! Jonathan, alas!
Our days are as the grass—like sands they pass!
  Bro. J. Oh sho! Columby, now don't cry no more—
Somebody's knockin'; I'll go 'tend the door.

   Enter DISTRICT OF COLUMBIA.

 Col. Oh! 'tis my little District; she's so near,
She is the very first one to appear.

Enter New England States; UNCLE SAM *receives them, and presents them to* COLUMBIA; *each salutes her, kisses her hand, and then is placed on one side of* COLUMBIA.

 Maine. I touch this sacred hand with loving lips.
Receive from me a model of my ships.
 New Hampshire. I bring a sceptre that a king might own,
Made from free pines from our Mount Washington.
 Vermont. And I a crown-wreath fit to deck a queen,
Made by Green Mountain girls, of laurels green.
 Massachusetts. I bring you fabrics rich, of varied stock,
From hills and vales that end at Plymouth Rock.
 Bro. J. (aside). Old Massachusetts never went out yet
But what she bragged on Plymouth Rock, you bet.
 Connecticut. I bring my fair, pure laws to show to you;
Mother Columbia, see, *they are not "Blue!"*
 Rhode Island. I'm little Rhody, and I bring you this:
Mother Columbia, bend and take—a kiss.
 Col. By-and-by, daughters, we will talk some more.
Hark! Jonathan, pray don't neglect the door.
 Bro. J. Yes, yes, Columby, I'll 'tend; don't you worry.
I'll see who's thumpin' out there, in a hurry.

   Enter NEW YORK: UNCLE SAM *presents her.*

 Uncle S. This is New York, the grand, proud Empire State.
 New York. I came alone, because I *have no mate!*

Bro. J. You jest hold on, and give the West fair chance,
And Illinois will jine ye in the dance.
Uncle S. "Hold on" New York ne'er does, but Illinois
May catch up, if she can—she has her choice.
Bro. J. Wal, here's New Jersey, fit to stand beside her,
With, sure's you live, a jug of Newark cider!
Pennsylvania. And I, Penn's Keystone State, with loyal
    soul,
Offer Columbia samples of my coal.
Col. Jonathan, the door.
Bro. J. Wal, neow, I dew declare,
Ef here don't come eour little Delaware!
And she's got on the same old Swedish dress
She wore in sixteen thirty-seven, I guess!
Col. My eldest daughter, and my little pet,
Say, do you love your dear old mother yet?
Delaware. Yes, true and dear, Columbia, as when
I was thine only child, and loved thee then.
Maryland. I bring a heavy offering in my hand:
'Tis useful iron ore, from Maryland.
Bro. J. Neow, ra'ally, Columby, that ain't bad—
No knowin' how soon you'll need an iron-clad.
East and *West Virginia.* We went where sad Mount Ver-
    non's willow weeps,
To bring thee flowers from where thy hero sleeps.
Col. It is an omen good that thus ye came—
One memory, one love, almost one name.
Uncle S. See, for thy blessing three now bend and wait:
Georgia, "Palmetto," and the "Old North State."
Georgia. I've sweet potatoes, best the South can yield.
North and *South Carolina.* We've rice and cotton from
    sea-isle and field.
Mississippi and *Alabama.* More cotton from the Gulf's
    rich shores we bring;
Thine is the cotton, though the cotton's king.
Florida. I offer garlands from the land of flowers,
Culled in my lowland swamps and live-oak bowers.
Bro. J. Wal, I remember when them beowers was holes
To hide away the skulkin' Seminoles;
K

And when the harnsome flowers you had were fewer'n
Creek Injins in them swampy lands o' yourn.
 Louisiana. Wrought in fit forms Columbia's lips to greet,
We bring bright samples of our sugars sweet.
 Bro. J. (*in a whisper*). Neow, Rhody, since you're standin'
in there handy,
You jest neow, on the sly, pass reound that candy!
Knock, knock; I'm comin'; wonder who you be?
 Col. I welcome Texas! my "Lone Star" I see.
 California. O'er the Pacific Railroad vast I came.
 Bro. J. Wal, you're a shiner! Tell us what's your name?
 Col. I know my darling from Pacific shore.
 Cal. Receive these chains of gold; this golden ore.
 Arkansas and *Missouri.* Within your courts are gifts that
we bestow,
Our flocks and herds that loudly bleat and low.
 Bro. J. Neow, Uncle Sam, you've got to help 'tend door,
Here's Western gals comin', half a score.
To laugh at me they'll to each other beckon—
But 'taint no wuss to *guess* than 'tis to *reckon;*
An' *ef* they hint at soup of codfish-tails,
I'll jest hand out to them 'bout *prairie whales.*
 Uncle S. Oh, Jonathan, don't be so sensitive;
Our family motto should be, live—let live.
 Col. And, Jonathan, I'm sure it is small loss
Whether they ride a ho*rr*se, or you a *hoss.*
Just *let* them *reckon,* or, perhaps, *allow;*
You *calc'late* and *guess*—now that you know.
Since we're in sections, why, of course, we're sectional;
But, seems to me, we all may be affectional.
 Bro. J. Here's Tennessee, with old Kentuck to back her.
 Tennessee and *Kentucky.* Take, if perchance you choose,
some fine tobacco. [brook it?
 Col. (*angrily*). What! if *I chew!* What insult! Shall I
 Bro. J. Wal, no; I'd "put it in my pipe and smoke it."
 Uncle S. They only meant, Columbia, did you choose
To see their product men will have and use.
 Col. My children, your old mother made mistake;
Give me your hand—receive a cordial shake.

Ohio. Fair mother, see my wealth of golden corn.
Indiana and *Illinois.* And ripened grains from our broad prairies shorn.
Michigan. See, I from Lake Superior's distant shore
Bring, green and shining, precious copper ore.
Iowa and *Wisconsin.* We, from our mines, bring wedges of our lead,
For bullets that we pray you ne'er may need.
Minnesota, Oregon, and *Kansas.* We bring not here our gift your halls to cumber,
But send to us for lots of grain and lumber.
Nevada and *Nebraska.* We are your youngest; open wide your hands,
We'll fill them with our shining silver sands.
Col. A stranger comes; pray, Jonathan, go meet her.
Bro. J. Wal, neow, I guess that' she's a curi's creetur,
Rigged out in snow-shoes, seal-skin, furs—I'll ask her
To give her name. She says she's Miss Alaska.
Col. Uncle Sam, bring her in; although you bought her,
She shall be welcome here as any daughter.
Alaska. Thanks, dear Columbia; and I'll guard your gates
When hostile hordes pour down—through Behring's Straits!
Bro. J. Hallo, there! what's that thumpin' now ag'in?
Col. I know! my boys in the last Western train.
They come to swell my Union Party's glories
By bringing news from my rich territories.

Enter boys from WASHINGTON, IDAHO, MONTANA, DAKOTAH, UTAH, COLORADO, ARIZONA, NEW MEXICO, INDIAN TERRITORIES. *These should be in backwoods dress, and with rifles. They sing:*

TUNE: "When Johnny comes marching home."

The boys they come marching from the West;
   Hurra! hurra!
Montana, Dakotah, and the rest;
   Hurra! hurra!
With Washington, Colorado,
   New Mexico and Idaho;
And we all feel gay to visit Columbia.

The boys they come marching from the West;
  Hurra! hurra!
From Utah and Indian, and the rest;
  Hurra! hurra!
Through grand primeval wilds we come,
Arizona our farthest home,
And we all feel gay to visit Columbia.

Uncle S. (*addressing the States*). Now, my fair nieces, hear
  a word from me:
I'd call, if you were boys, for three times three;
But gentle maidens' voices lovelier sound
When sweetly sending music-strains around.
So let's all sing, while gay we gathered are,
The grand old song of "Hail Columbia."
  [*All sing "Hail Columbia."*

COLUMBIA'S ADDRESS:
Thanks, children—love is strong and words are weak;
My love, your loyalty, no words can speak.
And *do* you love me so, and I so old?
  Bro. J. Of course they dew; must you ag'in be
  told?
  Uncle S. Hush, Jonathan; don't interrupt the address.
  Bro. J. You're right—Columby's got the floor, I guess.
  Col. Well-nigh a hundred am I. I rejoice
To see each daughter's face, and hear her voice;
And I rejoice, too, at the manly strain
That sounds from Western mount, and shore, and plain.
I'll happier grow as on my swift years run—
Each daughter fair, and brave and strong each son.
Continue true and loyal unto me,
And kind and loving to each other be;
Sound welcome o'er the earth, that all may come,
And find in your broad lands an ample home.
Bid all men hasten from oppression's ban,
And don't be shy of poor *John Chinaman;*
Don't have him *brought* as merchandise, but then
Welcome him as you do all fellow-men.

Love virtue, truth, and honor, and fair Fame
Shall wreathe bright garlands for each shining name.
There, introduce, shake hands, acquainted be,
And then we'll all sit down to Union tea.

PANTOMIME.—*Let there be a general introducing one to another, but only with motions, keeping perfect silence. Then, when* UNCLE SAM *offers his arm to* COLUMBIA, BROTHER JONATHAN *to* NEW YORK, *let all choose partners, and march around and off the stage, to the tune of "Yankee Doodle."*

THE TEA-KETTLE'S PARTY.—*From Our Young Folks.*

The Tea-kettle danced and sang, and sang and danced, until Mary, the cook, thought it would dance itself off the range; but she didn't know that it felt awfully jolly, and was telling its neighbor, the Saucepan (who was boiling potatoes for the dinner), that it intended to give a party.

"Why shouldn't we have a party?" sang the Kettle. "We've worked hard enough, goodness knows, for some weeks past. What with Thanksgiving, Christmas, and New-year's-day, we're nearly worn out. Let's rest a day or two, and then have a party ourselves."

The Saucepan rattled its lid in hearty applause, and held out its handle in token of ready acquiescence.

The Poker and Shovel, who had been listening, cried, "That's an excellent idea!" and so the matter was settled.

That evening, after the servants had gone to bed, the Tongs, who was the best walker, on account of the length of his legs, went round with the invitations. Of course none of the China family were invited, because they lived in the dining-room, and very rarely associated with the inhabitants of the kitchen. The Tins glowed with delight when they heard of the party, and the young Pans and small Pipkins raised such a clatter that the Rolling-pin gave them several round raps to silence them.

At last the long-looked-for evening arrived. All the family had retired, and the kitchen was put in perfect order. The Broom had swept the floor until not a grain of dust could be found on it, and the Tins had polished themselves until they shone again.

The Kettle was so excited that, although it was a winter evening, she was in a state of profuse perspiration, and the Saucepan had her round hat placed on one side of her head in the most knowing manner.

The first arrivals were the Tins. They lived up town, and were obliged to slide down the walls, but this did not dim their lustre in the least.

"You all look as though you were brand-new out of the store," said the good-natured Kettle to them.

Then came the guests who resided in the closets. First the Frying-pan and the Griddle stepped out, their broad faces shining with good-humor, and looking as though they fed on the fat of the land.

Next came the Coffee-pot, with the Quart-measure leaning gracefully on his arm, accompanied by her daughter, Miss Pint. Then came the Gridiron and the Dish-pan, the latter wearing an elegant waterfall made out of the dish-cloth. The next couple were the Hash-chopper (oh! such a sharp fellow) and the Fluting-iron, who wore her hair in the fashionable style, waving down her back; and they were followed by the two large wooden Spoons. Some Earthen Dishes and a number of Pipkins arrived soon after, and the party commenced.

The Kettle proposed a waltz, and although, on several occasions, the Dinner-pot had called her black, she kindly forgave him, and, taking his arm, prepared to lead off the dance. An old Guitar in the corner struck up a merry tune, and a small Waiter behind the stove played upon the tambourine.

The Poker grasped the Shovel round the waist and hopped into the middle of the room, the Broom slid off with the Window-brush, the Coffee-pot danced with the Quart-measure, and the Griddle pulled the Dish-pan about so rudely that her waterfall fell off, and was found by the cook on the hearth in the morning. The Tins jingled and tinkled, and even the Nutmeg-grater, a rough old fellow, could not resist the music, but seized the Apple-corer, and danced away as merrily as the rest.

After the waltz they had a polka, then a quadrille; then the Tongs danced the Sailor's Hornpipe in a manner wonderful to behold. When he ceased every one applauded; even the Covers on the range rattled as loudly as possible to show how pleased they were.

After the hornpipe the Kettle made a steaming bowl of punch, and the Broom proposed the health of the hostess. The hostess said she was strictly temperate, never drank any thing but water, but never refused to assist in making punch for those who liked it. In water, therefore, she returned the toast, and hoped they might all meet again soon and spend another pleasant evening; she loved and esteemed her friends, and would like to see them often.

"I'm most steamed," whispered the Iron-stand, "for I hang from the mantel right over the range."

"Joke!" cried one of the little Pipkins, and laughed until he cracked his sides.

The company then dispersed; and the girls, coming in next morning, never dreamed that the Tea-kettle had been having a party.

THE WHITE GIANT.—*From Our Young Folks.*

One afternoon, about a hundred years ago, a boy was sitting in his grandmother's kitchen, apparently doing nothing in particular, but really holding a very remarkable conversation with—whom do you think?—a white giant!

Now on the face of it, nothing would seem more unlikely than that a giant should be found in a plain little Scotch kitchen not more than eight feet high from the bare floor to the unplaned rafters; all the more so when a horse-shoe hung by the chimney-side, and the old lady's Bible, with her silver-bowed spectacles on the top of it, lay on the shelf. Nevertheless, there was the giant; and there, gazing intently on the place of his imprisonment, were the only two eyes in all Scotland that were able to find him out.

Indeed, I must tell you that the giant, in his proper state, was quite invisible; but, when he did appear in plain view, it was in the shape of a very old man with long white hair and beard, which seemed to encircle him like a garment, unless, indeed, they flowed down and mingled with his garment; and all—hair, beard, and robe—were whiter than snow. Therefore he is called the white giant.

And this is the way in which he made himself known to the boy.

Sitting by the fire, James had noticed that the lid of the tea-kettle was in a singular state of agitation. It would rise and fall, and flutter up and down in a very excited manner; and, coming as he did of a race that had believed for centuries in witches and goblins, and many supernatural creatures, the boy naturally began to suspect that some imprisoned force or other was beneath it, struggling to get free.

"Who are you?" said he, very quietly; "and what do you want, that you are so restless and excited?"

"Space, freedom, and something to do!" cried the captive giant from within.

"Softly! you have not told me yet who you are," said James.

"No matter who I am. I'm pressed down here into nothing at all, and I am a great strong giant that wants room to work and be free."

"Well, well! there's work enough to be done," said James. "Never was a race that wanted more done for it. But what can you do?"

"Try me and see. No one can do more. I will carry your ships, draw your carriages, and lift all your weights. I will plow your fields, sow the grain, and reap and thresh the harvests. I will hew away mountains and build roads. I will turn all the wheels in all your factories. I will weave your cloths, and print your books, and carry them to the ends of the earth. In short, I will do every thing that strength can do, and you shall be the brain that directs. I will be the faithful servant to fulfill all your commands."

"Here's a singular treasure-trove to be found in an old copper tea-kettle!" cried James, rubbing his eyes to be sure he was not dreaming.

"Only shows the use of having your eyes open," replied his strange companion. "I am one of the forces that were created to work for you; but you have a fancy for drudgery, it seems, and prefer to dig and weave for yourselves."

"Indeed, we prefer no such thing," said James, laughing. "We are told that it is one of our great vices to require other people to work for us while we sit idle."

"That is very true when it is your brethren that you are enslaving," replied the giant; "but you have not found out half the servants that were ordained to work for you since the foundation of the world, or else you would not be delving in the ditches and drudging with your hands, instead of letting your brains grow, that you may direct us. What do you mean by letting little children toil in your miserable factories, and become dwarfed in body and soul, when here am I, and a hundred other giants like myself, any one of whom could do the work of ten thousand of those babies, and never feel it—and you give us no work to do?"

"You are a kind-hearted old genie, I am sure," said the boy; "and, if I live, *my* work shall be to introduce you to the acquaintance of men. But tell me something of your history. Where have you been all these years, that no one has found you out?"

"Where I am now, and in similar places, though not always so tightly pressed. And, indeed, I have not been idle, though my appetite for work has never been half supplied. I am one of the elder children of the flood, and began my work in the world before your race appeared upon it. Before the rain began her ministry, I arose from my hidden retreats in the earth, and watered the earliest of gardens. Ever since then I have been carrying on a great system of irrigation; rising from the ocean into the sky, sailing in great fleets laden with treasure toward the mountain-sides where my bounties have been bestowed; sinking then, in a slightly altered form, into the earth, and visiting the roots of all the trees with supplies of food—creeping up through all their veins and into their broad green leaves, whence I escape into the air again. You see I have had something to do. But all this quiet work is only half enough for me. Work is my nature; so do not be afraid of overtasking me. I can not have too much."

"Indeed you are a grand old fellow, and I am proud of your acquaintance," cried James. "Now I seem to remember having seen you in April days, or sometimes in August or September, floating in the sky, but I never thought to become so much better acquainted with you in my grandmother's kitchen."

"James, James! what are ye doing?" cried the old lady from her straight-backed chair. "Here ye've done naething a' the day but tilt the cover of the kettle, like a lazy lout that ye be. Gae to your tasks noo, like a mon, and be of some use in the warld."

"Ah! grandam," said James, "I have been doing a thousand days' work, sitting here by the ingleside."

"Dinna be fooling, bairn! Dinna be fooling, ye idle dreamer! Wark and ye'll thrive; be lazy and ye'll come to naught."

Nevertheless, James's dreams came to more use than many another man's work, because he had the faculty of thinking to a purpose; and, in the many talks he held with the friendly old giant, he learned, one after another, the secrets of his power. When lessons were over, the giant told wonderful stories to his young disciple; and perhaps I can repeat one of them in a few words:

"In old times there was a long-continued contest between the land and the sea. At first the sea had been the monarch, and ruled over the whole surface of the globe. At length the land appeared, claiming a large part of his domain, and this enraged the sea, who beat wrathfully with whole armies of billows upon her shore, and threatened to conquer back all that he had lost.

"Presently came the children of the land: first, the little grasses, that, tenderly embracing their mother, protected her from being quite carried away by the rude invading sea; and at length the taller trees, the great pines and oaks, that added greatly to her beauty and glory.

"Then a new thought occurred to the land, and she sent out these her greater children to subdue the sea on his own domains. They rode triumphantly over the billows, and, aided by the friendly winds, plied diligently from place to place, increasing every where the wealth and glory of their mother. But the sea arose in his wrath, and often ingulfed these faithful children of the land, or broke their bones, and cast them up upon her lap in bitter scorn and defiance.

"Then the land resolved to take a more exquisite revenge than ever before. And she called forth a mighty spirit from the bosom of the sea himself—a weird, white, gigantic genie, who had been the eldest child of the flood. She gave him an armor of iron scales which the sea could not break, and upon him she laid her spells, and he went obediently to and fro at her bidding. Thus the land was at last triumphant, as organized brain always will be over brute natural force; and the children of men passed over land and sea in safety toward their goal of perfect knowledge.

"But part of that is prophecy," said the white giant, when he had finished the story.

"It shall be fact before many years," said James. "And you, my good giant, are the genie who shall finish the tale."

Soon swift cars were running to and fro the whole length of the kingdom, propelled by the giant's arms. Soon, too, the tasks of the little children at the factories were done by the same old worker, who could drive a million spindles at a stroke quite as easily as a child could move one; and if the children were still employed, it was only to keep the giant supplied with work enough, which indeed was no easy task.

His good-nature was equal to all the tasks which could be imposed upon him. If you have ever seen his white beard rising above the chimney of some factory on a winter morning, or puffing out of the escape-valve of some little tug, you may almost have mistaken him, in the wavy, graceful lines of his white drapery, for a sunny cloud—which, indeed, would not be the greatest of mistakes.

Before long the great ocean-going ships had the giant established in their holds, and their ponderous wheels moved by his iron arms, so that, independently of wind or tide, they could hold their course night and day, and, like swiftly-moving shuttles, weave the continents together with bands of neighborly good-will.

IN SCHOOL DAYS.—*From Our Young Folks.*

J. G. WHITTIER.

Still sits the school-house by the road,
  A ragged beggar sunning;
Around it still the sumachs grow,
  And blackberry vines are running.

Within, the master's desk is seen,
  Deep scarred by raps official;
The warping floor, the battered seats,
  The jack-knife's carved initial;

The charcoal frescoes on its wall;
  Its door's worn sill, betraying
The feet that, creeping slow to school,
  Went storming out to playing.

Long years ago a winter sun
  Shone over it at setting,
Lit up its western window-panes,
  And low eaves's icy fretting.

It touched the tangled golden curls,
  And brown eyes full of grieving,
Of one who still her steps delayed
  When all the school were leaving.

For near her stood the little boy
  Her childish favor singled,
His cap pulled low upon a face
  Where pride and shame were mingled.

Pushing with restless feet the snow
  To right and left, he lingered;
As restlessly her tiny hands
  The blue-checked apron fingered.

He saw her lift her eyes; he felt
  The soft hands light caressing,
And heard the tremble of her voice,
  As if a fault confessing.

"I'm sorry that I spelt the word:
  I hate to go above you,

Because"—the brown eyes lower fell—
"Because, you see, I love you!"
Still memory to a gray-haired man
That sweet child-face is showing.
Dear girl! the grasses on her grave
Have forty years been growing.
He lives to learn, in life's hard school,
How few who pass above him
Lament their triumph and his loss,
Like her—because they love him.

NEW GOWNS.—*From Our Young Folks.*

Once upon a time there lived a beautiful lady, who had the loveliest dresses—such as never were seen before. First, she had a long robe of rich green velvet, embroidered all over with flowers of every color; its train was decked with silver spangles, and sparkling ribbons of silver flowed from the wide and flashing silver girdle at her waist down to her feet, and here and there masses of feather trimming, of the richest green, decorated the seams and hems, and green plumes waved around her snowy tresses; for she was old as she was beautiful, showing age alone in these glittering coils of blanched hair. Whenever she moved, the silver girdle, wide as a breastplate, swayed and shimmered about her, and the green plumes bent slowly and gracefully. Nothing, men thought, could be more beautiful than her garment; but she was a woman, and got very tired of it. Now the lady had two old uncles—Uncle Jack and Uncle Sol; they did not agree at all, and, when one refused what she wanted, the other was sure to give it to her. So, when she got weary of her green robe, she told Uncle Sol she wanted a change of raiment.

"Fy! fy!" said the portly old gentleman, who wore a yellow coat, somewhat spotted, and had fire-red hair; "how long have you worn that gown, my dear? I know very well, for I gave it to you; no, indeed. Do you see me getting new coats? The idea is absurd!"

He turned his face away from her, and she was so angry she ran straight off to find Uncle Jack.

Uncle Jack was a funny old man with keen gray eyes, and his long hair and wavy beard were like drifted snow. All his clothes were white, and trimmed with crystal buttons, and in his hand he carried a tiny slender spear of crystal, on whose tip glittered a diamond point, clear and cold as a star; it was an enchanted spear that never broke or wore out, and he could work wonders with it.

"Oh, Uncle Jack!" said the lady, "do give me something new to wear; I am so tired of green and silver!"

"Why, my! I think your dress is very fresh and rich yet."

"That's what Uncle Sol says."

"Oho! the gruff old rascal has been denying you what you wanted, has he? I'll see to your dress, my dear!"

With that, Uncle Jack took up his magic wand, and lightly touched the feather trimming and the plumes, and all at once they flashed into the most gorgeous colors—scarlet glowing like coals, yellow as fierce as July sunshine, masses of deep gleaming garnet, and spots of dusky purple and light vivid crimson on the trimming, while the plumes waved with here and there a golden spire, or a feather of flame, interspersed with dark velvety green, pallid yellow, or shining brown.

"There!" said Uncle Jack, "are you satisfied?"

The lady looked at her face in one of the broad burnished silver ribbons, and smiled, for she was lovely as a dream; all the air about her seemed steeped in sunshine, and in her girdle and her sashes the splendid colors floated and flowed like jewels poured out. Uncle Jack laughed to see her so pleased.

But after a while the velvet gown began to fade and grow threadbare; its folds and edges showed dull brown; the embroidery of blossoms, and leaves, and berries, that had strewed it with many a gay wreath and graceful tendril, or starred it with tiny flowers, was all frayed away and fallen off. The silver ribbon still shone, but the robe itself had become a dead brownish-yellow, and the glorious plumes had dropped one little featherling after the other, till of them and of the trimming there was nothing left but bare gray stems and tracery.

The lady wept bitterly. Uncle Sol had turned the cold shoulder toward her, and she was half afraid of Uncle Jack, he had so lately clothed her in magnificent robes.

There was, however, no one else to help her, so she called loudly for him, and he came.

There was a sly smile in his keen gray eye as he looked at the lady. "Rags and tags, hey, madam? Well for you that Uncle Jack lives within hearing."

So saying, he passed his wand across her again, and about her shoulders and waist hung trails of exquisite lace of the most delicate tracery and purest whiteness, and a white tissue robe fell softly over the worn velvet, and hid it with a sheeny mist. The plumes were covered and tipped with lacework too, and the beautiful lady smiled again to see how delicately fair her robes showed in the morning light. But hardly had she enjoyed their grace and purity for an hour or two when along came the other old uncle.

"Ho! ho!" laughed Uncle Sol; "here you are in another new gown! In white lace, like a young girl at her wedding! This is too absurd for a woman of your age. I can't allow it!"

Now Uncle Sol's magic was in his face; if he once looked hard and long at any thing it ran away, and now he stared fixedly at the lovely lace raiment. Horrible to relate, it ran away as he looked in streams of gray shreds, and even drops like tears, till the beautiful lady stood weeping bitterly in her old brown gown, and the gray sticks of her feathers looking worse for the silver ribbons.

Now she began to sob and wail; the plumes, featherless as they were, rustled in her hair like a storm of pitiful whispers and sighs, and the silver girdle and breastplate heaved up and down till it grated on her brown robe heavily, and frayed it still more.

"Oh, Jack! dear Uncle Jack!" she cried; "come! do come!"

In he bustled and hustled with a great crackling and whistling, for he was very busy and hard at work. Up went both his withered hands in surprise.

"What a sight to behold! all that lace gone! My dear,

you cost too much; you are so tall and large, one needs stores as broad and deep as the sky to clothe you!"

The lady drew herself up and looked at Uncle Jack. Now, indeed, she was a piteous sight; all her fair face and dingy robe marred with tears and shreds, her beauty worn with grief and rage, and her broad shoulders wearing no trace of their late filmy covering.

"Look at me, Uncle Jack!"

That was enough.

"Poor child! poor child!" said he, pitifully. "I will give you a garment that Uncle Sol may stare at as much as he likes, but it will take a long while to make it."

So off went Uncle Jack into upper air, and borrowed of the sprites, who prepare wool and crystal in those high dwellings, their most spotless and heavy fleeces. These he floated softly down upon the beautiful lady till they rested upon her brown mantle and covered it completely, hiding even the holes about her sides and elbows; then he waved his wand till the stainless wool grew into a lovely robe, so white and sparkling that, if one but looked upon it, the water would stand in his eyes. Another touch of the diamond-tipped spear, and the silver ribbons turned to polished steel; steel bound the girdle and breastplate with a broad bright edge. The lady was more splendid than ever; one thing alone was wanting—a new set of plumes.

"Whew! whew!" said Uncle Jack; "must I travel up stairs again?" and off he went to borrow dew-crystal of the sprites who had already lent him wool; they were kindly sprites indeed, for they showered the bright, clear drops he wanted all over the feather trimming, and the plumes also, and, as they clung to the delicate stems and tendrils, Uncle Jack pointed his spear-tip at them, and they changed to diamonds. How they sparkled, and danced, and shone! how every sigh that fluttered about made the myriad rainbows thrill and quiver! how blinding was the blaze of their splendor! how glorious the lady in her jewels and her brilliant robe! She looked as a queen might, adorned for her bridal, and from her clear bright girdle and ribbons shone back all the stars of heaven.

"There!" said Uncle Jack; "I think I have done well for you; you can defy Uncle Sol now as to the gown. I won't answer for the diamonds—he hates jewelry; but don't come screaming after me again for a long time, my lady! I have business on hand;" and off he went.

The beautiful lady smiled, and all the wonderful brilliants about her rustled, and flashed, and blazed for joy. Poor lady! it was but the very next morning Uncle Sol looked at her over his shoulder. "Ridiculous old creature!" growled he. "*I* know when she was born, if nobody else does; and for a person whose years are more than she likes to make known to be wearing jewelry, and *such* jewelry, is enough to make one laugh. No, never can I allow it!"

So saying, he stared at the diamonds with all his might and main. How they burned under his gaze! how every tiny speck shot out a blaze of anger and splendor! Their glory was blinding, but it was brief. Presently they began to drop from the plumy stems—tinkle, tinkle, tinkle! faster and faster, with a sweet and bright sound like the ring of fairy sleigh-bells, or the laugh of fairy babies, down they showered, tumbling on the beautiful lady's shoulders, over her steel ribbons, and on her beaming girdle and breast-plate—tinkle, tinkle, tinkle! ringing their tiny peals of delicate music, and glittering where they fell. Alas! in a moment more they were but tears.

Uncle Jack no longer listened to the lady's calls; her jewels were gone, and who could replace them? She wore the stainless robe without ornaments save the steel and steel-bound silver of her ribbons and girdle; and, being careless, in a few months the white garments gathered stains and grew threadbare, and was no longer fair to see.

Then she bethought herself of Uncle Sol, who had ceased turning his face away from her, and made friends with him once more, so that he again clothed her with soft and fresh green garments, with newer and even more exquisite trailing embroideries and misty green trimmings; he renewed her graceful plumes, and changed ribbons and girdle to shining silver once more. So it came to pass that the beautiful lady was never at a loss for robes between the two old uncles. And so it hath been, and shall be while the world endures.

Ah! if only I had an Uncle Jack and an Uncle Sol, I should never again say I had nothing to wear, and sigh over my lack of gowns.

LECTURE ON HEAT.—*From Our Young Folks.*
BY MY LORD HIGH FIDDLESTICK.

"His name is Force," squeaked the little traveler; "but, for the sort of person that he is, I can not say, your royal highness, seeing that he is sometimes as great as a giant, and at others as fine as a thread; only that he is the worst-used and best-natured individual in your majesty's dominions; for there is not a ship or a house, a road or a garden made, or a dinner got, or so much as a cup of water drawn, without his help. He is wanted to do every thing every minute of the day all over the earth, and he does it without grumbling; and now, mark how he is paid! Every time that he gives any body a neighborly lift, from sawing a stick of wood to dragging a train, he disappears. He is destroyed. All day long he is smashed, blown up, choked, your royal highness, under your royal highness's very nose —under every body's nose—made away with, done for, murdered, used up, in a hundred thousand places all at once, by Christians and heathens all alike—which your majesty will see is quite improper. For if it is so very bad to choke, blow up, and murder a man once, how much worse to do all these things to a person all the time! and if your highness would protect even a thief from such abuse, how is it that there is nobody to say a word for poor Force, who wags your very heads for you? and whose blame is it?"

When the little traveler said "Whose blame is it?" he looked hard at the king. The king was quite thrown out of countenance—for here was a very bad case, you see, made out against somebody—and he looked severely at the Lord High Fiddlestick, because it was understood that, when any thing happened to be right, the credit was due to the king; but, when any thing was wrong, the blame fell to my Lord High Fiddlestick. As the king looked severe, the courtiers looked severe also, and as if— Come, now, this was really *too* bad, and a *little* the worst thing they had heard yet about my Lord High Fiddlestick. But my Lord High Fiddlestick only crossed his pink slippers comfortably one over the other, and said,

"Your majesty, there is no one to blame here. The gentleman is quite right and entirely wrong."

The little traveler jumped up. He was wrapped from head to heels in a large overcoat full of pockets. Out of one pocket he took a bit of iron and a hammer. He laid the iron on the table, and pounded it with the hammer.

"There!" he said; "Force did that; but now where has he gone, my Lord High Fiddlestick?" Then he pulled at his mustache, and stamped his foot, and got out a saw and a piece of wood, and had off an end of the wood before you could wink. "Force did that too," said the little traveler; "but, if he did not die in doing it, can you tell where he is now, my Lord High Fiddlestick?" Then he drew out a pistol, and, aiming at the third leg of the king's extension table, sent a bullet at it as savagely as if it had been the Lord High Fiddlestick himself.

"Force did that too," screamed the queer, angry little man, "and now where is he? I am not to be put off with a riddle about being quite right and entirely wrong. If he is dead, as you are to blame for whatever happens in this country, you ought to be hung at once; and if he is not dead, I will trouble you to show him to me."

"Good Mr. Traveler," answered my Lord High Fiddlestick, picking up the saw, "will you feel of that? It is cold, is it not? and the wood—that is cold too. Well, now, suppose you saw us off another bit of wood. Thank you. Feel now of the wood. Is it cold, just as it was before? No? You mean to say that it is warmer? Touch the saw. That is warmer too. Very good. Here are your iron and your hammer. Will your majesty touch them? You see they are cold enough. Now, my friend, favor us with a little more of that lively pounding which you say your friend Force died to do. How are your iron and hammer? I declare!—feel, your majesty—they are both warm. Now for the pistol. Here is a target—but stop! feel the bullet. It is cold, of course. Fire away! Very good! But the bullet! feel it, Mr. Traveler. Your majesty perceives that it is quite hot—this bullet, which was cold a moment ago!"

"What if it is?" growled the traveler.

My Lord High Fiddlestick put his hands in the pockets of his green satin gown and laughed.

"Ah! Mr. Traveler, you have not learned all the old tricks of your friend Force. Just now he pounded a cold bit of iron with a cold hammer. Then he was gone, nowhere to be seen—dead, you said; but you found heat in the iron and the hammer. You sawed a cold piece of wood with a cold saw. That done—whisk! Force was lost; but there was heat in the wood and saw. You fired your cold bullet at a cold target. Off went force, but there was heat again in the bullet. Whenever you lose force you find heat. What does that mean? You say that Force is sometimes a giant. Did it ever occur to you that he may be a giant with two heads under his hood? Let us follow this giant a little farther. He is pulling a train at the rate of thirty miles an hour. You put on the brakes, the train stops. Force is gone from the engine, but what do you find at the wheels, where the brake rubbed on them? Why, so much heat that you see fire and sparks; and the engine-driver sends a man to rub grease on the wheels of the train. Why? Because, if the wheels turn around with difficulty, the engine can not pull the train so fast; Force, who should give all his attention to urge the engine, must give a part of his strength to the wheels; and just as much as he gives to the wheels, just so much is lost to the engine."

"As if every school-boy did not know that!" growled the little traveler.

"Wait a minute," said my Lord High Fiddlestick. "You say every school-boy knows that; but, when Force goes to the wheels, what shape does he take? He is there turning the wheels in spite of themselves, and the engine is missing him, and these ungreased wheels show that he is there. How? By their heat. You miss Force from the engine. The last time he was seen he was going to the ungreased wheels. You go to the wheels. You see no Force there, but a stranger; but if it is the giant Force that you have lost from the engine, this stranger will be a giant; if Force is at his pigmy tricks, the stranger will be a dwarf; and, in either case, he will tell you his name is Heat. While you are staring at him, you observe something familiar about him, and you say, 'Pray, Mr. Heat, have I not seen you before somewhere about the engine? You are the fireman, perhaps!' 'Exactly,' answers Heat. 'I was in the fire under the boiler.' Under the boiler! Why, that is where our lost Force came from. Put it all together. You put heat under the boiler, and force comes out and pulls the train. You miss Force, and, when you go to look for him, you find Heat in his place. Is it not reasonable, good Mr. Traveler, to think that, as Heat can turn into Force, Force can turn back into Heat again?"

"Your royal highness," cried the little traveler, jumping up in a great rage, "I hope your royal highness won't listen to such stuff as this. Heat a person, indeed! Heat is a fluid, and it is called caloric. I see my Lord High Fiddlestick is laughing, but he won't laugh long. Here is the dictionary, and the word in it to prove what I say; and the ungreased wheels were hot because they turned so hard that some of their caloric was squeezed out of them; and when the hammer came down hard on the iron, some of the caloric was squeezed out of that, and all the old philosophers say so; and, if you want us to believe that force is not burned in the fire, and blown off from the engine, and crushed under the wheels, but is turned into heat, you must make us swallow the dictionary and the old philosophers first."

"I see I must tell you a little story," answered my Lord High Fiddlestick, gently. "As my friend Count Rumford and your friend Force were one day boring a cannon, Count Rumford tried to pick up some of the brass chips that Force had just cut off, and discovered that they were hotter than boiling water. Brass is not generally hotter than boiling water. Before we go farther, perhaps you will tell us, Mr. Traveler, what had happened to these chips."

"Why, the boring had squeezed so much caloric fluid into these chips," answered the traveler.

"Then, of course," said my Lord High Fiddlestick, "if the brass chips held so much more heat-fluid than they ever held before, they must be altered in some way. If you were going to put say a quart of heat-fluid in chips that only held a pint before, you must alter your chips. But Count Rumford found that the chips were not altered; that is, if you are right, Mr. Traveler, a pint could hold a quart; and he thought that was tougher to swallow than the old philosophers. So he took a hollow tube of brass called a cylinder. In it he put a flat piece of hard steel. The steel was almost as large as the cylinder, so that it could just turn around the steel. He put the cylinder in a box filled with water. A horse was made to turn the cylinder round and round. The piece of steel rubbed hard all the time on the bottom of the brass cylinder. The brass grew warm and the water grew warm. Count Rumford and a great many people stood watching it curiously. The cylinder turned and turned, all the time growing hotter. The water all the time grew hotter too; and, at the end of two hours and a half, the water was so hot that it boiled. Now, Mr. Traveler, what makes water boil?"

"Heat," answered the little man, sulkily.

"Well, there was no heat here," cried my Lord High Fiddlestick — "only force; and force made the water boil. Own up, Mr. Traveler. It begins to look as if Heat and Force were the same person."

"I shall not own any thing of the sort," answered the little man. "Pray, my Lord High Fiddlestick," catching up the hammer and bringing it down hard on the iron, "*how* did force turn into heat then?"

"This iron," said my lord, "is made of what we call atoms—tiny particles too small to be seen separately."

"Bosh!" snorted the traveler.

"These atoms," said the Lord High Fiddlestick, "are held fast together by a liking they have for each other—an attraction that we call cohesion. Force strikes this iron with the weight of the hammer. He jars the iron; he jars, he stirs the atoms; they can stir, although their band of cohesion holds them so close that they look as if they were stuck tight together. The hammer is down. You would say Force is dead. I say he has gone in among those atoms; he is carrying on the stir and jar from one atom to the other. 'Stop!' says Cohesion, trying to hold them fast. 'Go on!' cries Force. The atoms of iron can not get away from one another, but they can move. Force makes them move and struggle. When you struggle you get warm. When the atoms of iron struggle, they make what my friend, Lord Bacon, calls the fire and fury of heat. They actually get farther away from each other; and this is why philosophers will tell you that heat makes a body larger.

"This hard, solid iron is actually a little larger than when it was cool, because the atoms have succeeded in getting farther from each other. Now all the king's horses, and all the king's men, if you could set them to tug on each side of this little bit of iron, have not strength to do that. It required a great force, stronger than all the king's horses and men. But who did pull the atoms? Heat. Then heat is force, or perhaps I should say motion; for, when we struck this iron with the hammer, and it became warmer, what had happened really? Why, the motion of the arm and hammer that struck it went in among the atoms of iron, and they moved and pulled a little way from each other. What we call Heat was really their motion; and so—"

"Stuff!" interrupted the traveler. "When a man comes down to atoms, he must be hard up for proofs."

"Comes down to atoms!" exclaimed my Lord High Fiddlestick, opening a window. Outside, the sill was covered with fresh-fallen snow, which my Lord High Fiddlestick scraped up in his hands. "Can any thing be softer than this snow?" he asked. "Well, the pull and strain that brought the water-atoms together to make such snow as I hold here, would pitch a ton of stone over a precipice two thousand feet deep. Come *down* to atoms, indeed! Pray, let me show you a few of the things that atoms can do."

"My lord," interrupted the king, in a hurry, "I observe that dinner is ready, and the beefsteak on the table. If the steak gets cold, according to your philosophy, it will grow smaller, and then, perhaps, there will not be enough to go round. Let us go to dinner, and hear what the atoms can do another time, my Lord High Fiddlestick."

BIRDS AND THEIR WAYS.—*From the Little Corporal.*

About the second week of March, here in Northern Illinois, I hear somebody singing up in the air, "Ka-wet! ka-wet!" His back is as blue as the violets, and his breast looks as red and warm as a little red cloud at sunrise.

The trees are bare, the grass is dry, and Bluebird's voice is a little sad at first, but by the middle of April he is all over it, for he takes him a mate; then he is very busy trying to find a place for the nest that is to hold the wee ones.

One day I saw a pair of bluebirds sitting on the stakes of a rail fence. Bluebird flew down to a hole in one of the rails; he went in, examined its sides with his black bill, turned around in it, then, flying up to the top of a stake, warbled "Ka-wet! que-we-o-it!"—my dear, come look at it. Mrs. Bluebird answered "Ka-wet!"—yes, dear. They examined and consulted a long time, but it would not do to put their nest there; the room was too small, and the roof very poor. I saw them there no more. The mates sometimes choose a hole in a tree, where a busy woodpecker once made his nest. They carry in grass, wool, and feathers, and arrange a soft, warm nest. The female lays from four to six pale blue eggs. Two broods a year are raised. Bluebirds live upon worms, beetles, and other insects that would destroy our fruit and gardens.

Generally, within two weeks from the time I first hear the plaintive salutation of the bluebird, a chorus of spring voices are in my ear. The red-winged blackbirds are chatting in the tree-tops; the crow blackbird throws in an occasional note of reproof; the meadow-lark sings "E-chee-a-chirp-pa" in the richest of voices; the snowbird trills in the hazel bush; the wild ducks are quacking on the streams; the soft piping of the nuthatch sounds from the woods; the belted kingfisher darts chattering by, and the plover flies over, crying sharply "Kill-deer! kill-deer!"

But whose voice is this I hear a few days before the coming of April? He calls from the trees, just at evening, "Quit! quit! quit!" The night is cold and frosty, but with the early morning light a rich bugle-voice breaks out in "Ka-i-a ka-e-ore quit! cho-wo que-we que-wit! tka-a-ru ka-we-wa ka-we-wa tkeep!" Robin knows *how* to sing. I once heard four singing in one bur-oak at a time.

Look at Robin when he is on the ground. He gives a hop or two, then runs a few feet straight forward in a very careless way. He stops, turning one eye up as if he needed to keep watch of the weather, while with the other he looks sharply at the ground. Now he finds a bug or grub, now a May-beetle, and a little farther on he pulls up a cut-worm. He is very useful, for he eats up some of the worst enemies of the fruit and grain.

The first day of last May, as I passed a thorn-tree, a bright eye peered from behind a branch. A moment after, two brown wings were spread, and away went Mrs. Robin. Robin himself sat near by, on a crab-apple-tree, jerking his tail, and eying me anxiously. Here was a nest with four blue eggs.

Soon the bluejays became too inquisitive, and I often saw Robin dart out bravely and drive them off. After a few days I found the nest deserted, one egg gone, and the rest cold. I am afraid Bluejay took that egg.

But the robins were not discouraged. They built another nest on the branch of a bur-oak a short distance from the first nest. They left this one also, and without using it at all.

A third nest was made in a black oak, whose boughs touch our house. Mrs. Robin constructed it chiefly of dried grass, and plastered the inside with mud. When the mud was dry, she lined it smoothly with fine soft grass, and the nest was ready for use.

The eggs were laid, and for about two weeks patient Mrs. Robin kept them warm under her red breast. The sweet June days came, and the wild roses showed their bright buds. Robin, meantime, sang his richest songs on the boughs near by. He became almost as tame as a chicken, hopping around us when we were out of doors, and singing, with his bill just apart, quaint little strains that could hardly be heard. The robin does not open his bill so widely as some little birds, if he sings ever so loud and clear.

One day I saw Mrs. Robin standing on the side of the nest. She peered into it, and put her bill down one, two, three times. Just then her mate alighted near by, with his beak full of worms and soft insects. The young birds were out of the shells, and the mother was feeding them. What funny babies they were, with only a small number of curious feathers, looking just like the little plumes you have seen on some seeds floating about in the air. At the least sound their hungry bills would fly open, as if they expected that it was going to rain worms. Robin did not get much time to sing then, for they kept him as busy as a bee. In less than two weeks they were pretty well feathered out, and their tails an inch and a half long.

Then there was a time of wild excitement in the oak. The old birds called loudly, and the young ones answered "Pe-ip?"—I fly! The little robins found out then what their wings were made for. For a day or two they staid quietly in the trees, and their parents carried them food. Then they hopped on the ground after Mr. and Mrs. Robin.

About this time Mrs. Robin left her husband to provide for all three youngsters, and went off somewhere. Sometimes they tried to feed themselves. One would think he saw a worm on the ground, and, putting down his head, would nearly fall over trying to get it. I saw them pick up little sticks, and drop them. In less than three weeks from the time they left the nest they looked as large as Robin, and he thought them big enough to get their own living. They were very handsome, but they did not look just like the old robins. Their backs had a great many little black and white streaks, and the red of their breasts was full of black spots.

Robin still gathered worms, but he would not give them to these young ones. I followed him, and found Mrs. Robin, with another brood of little birds, in the very nest that was built on the branch of the bur-oak after the first one was broken up.

HANDY ANDY.
SAMUEL LOVER.

SCENE FIRST. *The Dining-room.*

THE first time Andy was admitted into the mysteries of the dining-room, great was his wonder. The butler took him in to give him some previous instructions, and Andy was so lost in admiration at the sight of the assembled glass and plate that he stood with his mouth and eyes wide open, and scarcely heard a word that was said to him. After the head man had been dinning his instructions into him for some time, he said he might go until his attendance was required. But Andy moved not; he stood with his eyes fixed by a sort of fascination on some object, that seemed to rivet them with the same unaccountable influence which the rattlesnake exercises over its victim.

"What are you looking at?" said the butler.

"Them things, sir," said Andy, pointing to some silver forks.

"Is it the forks?" said the butler.

"Oh no, sir. I know what forks is very well; but I have never seen them things afore."

"What things do you mean?"

"These things, sir," said Andy, taking up one of the silver forks, and turning it round and round in his hand in utter astonishment, while the butler grinned at his ignorance, and enjoyed his own superior knowledge.

"Well!" said Andy, after a long pause, "evil be from me if ever I seen a silver spoon split that way before."

The butler laughed a horse-laugh, and made a standing joke of Andy's split spoon; but time and experience made Andy less impressed with wonder at the show of plate and glass, and the split spoons became familiar as "household words" to him; yet still there were things in the duties of table attendance beyond Andy's comprehension: he used to hand cold plates for fish, and hot plates for jelly, etc. But "one day," as Zanga says, "one day" he was thrown off his centre in a remarkable degree by a bottle of soda-water.

It was when that combustible was first introduced into

Ireland as a dinner beverage that the occurrence took place, and Andy had the luck to be the person to whom a gentleman applied for some soda-water.

"Sir?" said Andy.

"Soda-water," said the guest, in that subdued tone in which people are apt to make known their wants at a dinner-table.

Andy went to the butler. "Mr. Morgan, there's a gintleman—"

"Let me alone, will you?" said Mr. Morgan.

Andy manœuvred round him a little longer, and again essayed to be heard.

"Mr. Morgan!"

"Don't you see I'm as busy as I can be? Can't you do it yourself?"

"I dunno what he wants."

"Well, go and ax him," said Mr. Morgan.

Andy went off as he was bidden, and came behind the thirsty gentleman's chair with "I beg your pardon, sir."

"Well!" said the gentleman.

"I beg your pardon, sir, but what's that you axed me for?"

"Soda-water."

"What, sir?"

"Soda-water; but perhaps you have not any."

"Oh, there's plenty in the house, sir. Would you like it hot, sir?"

The gentleman laughed, and, supposing the new fashion was not understood in the present company, said, "Never mind."

But Andy was too anxious to please to be so satisfied, and again applied to Mr. Morgan.

"Sir," said he.

"Bad luck to you! can't you let me alone?"

"There's a gintleman wants some soap and wather."

"Some what?"

"Soap and wather, sir."

"Bother take you! soda-wather, you mane. You'll get it under the sideboard."

"Is it in the can, sir?"

"The curse of Crum'll on you! in the bottles."
"Is this it, sir?" said Andy, producing a bottle of ale.
"No, bad 'cess to you! the little bottles."
"Is it the little bottles with no bottoms, sir?"
"I wish *you* were in the bottom of the say!" said Mr. Morgan, who was fuming and puffing, and rubbing down his face with a napkin, as he was hurrying to all quarters of the room, or, as Andy said, in praising his activity, that he was "like bad luck, every where."

"There they are," said Morgan at last.

"Oh! them bottles that won't stand," said Andy; "sure them's what I said, with no bottoms to them. How'll I open it? it's tied down."

"Cut the cord, you booby!"

Andy did as he was desired; and he happened at the same time to hold the bottle of soda-water on a level with the candles that shed light over the festive board from a large silver branch, and the moment he made the incision, bang went the bottle of soda, knocking out two of the lights with the projected cork, which, performing its parabola the length of the room, struck the squire himself in the eye at the end of the table, while the hostess at the head had a cold bath down her back. Andy, when he saw the soda-water jumping out of the bottle, held it from him at arm's length, every fizz it made exclaiming "Ow! ow! ow!" and at last, when the bottle was empty, he roared out, "Oh Lord! it's all gone."

Great was the commotion; few could resist laughter except the ladies, who all looked at their gowns, not liking the mixture of satin and soda-water. The extinguished candles were relighted, the squire got his eye open again, and the next time he perceived the butler sufficiently near to speak to him, he said, in a low and hurried tone of deep anger, while he knit his brow, "Send that fellow out of the room;" but within the same minute resumed the former smile, that beamed on all around as if nothing had happened.

SCENE SECOND. *The Post-office.*

"Ride into town and see if there's a letter for me," said the squire one day to our hero.

"Yis, sir."

"You know where to go?"

"To the town, sir."

"But do you know where to go in the town?"

"No, sir."

"And why don't you ask, you stupid thief?"

"Sure, I'd find out, sir."

"Didn't I often tell you what you're to do when you don't know?"

"Yis, sir."

"And why don't you?"

"I don't like to be throublesome, sir."

"Confound you!" said the squire; though he could not help laughing at Andy's excuse for remaining in ignorance.

"Well," continued he, "go to the post-office. You know the post-office, I suppose?"

"Yis, sir; where they sell gunpowdher."

"You're right for once," said the squire; for his majesty's post-master was the person who had the privilege of dealing in the aforesaid combustible. "Go, then, to the post-office, and ask for a letter for me. Remember, not gunpowder, but a letter."

"Yis, sir," said Andy, who got astride of his hack, and trotted away to the post-office. On arriving at the shop of the post-master (for that person carried on a brisk trade in groceries, gimlets, broadcloth, and linen-drapery), Andy presented himself at the counter and said,

"I want a letther, sir, if you plaze."

"Who do you want it for?" said the post-master, in a tone which Andy considered an aggression upon the sacredness of private life; so Andy thought the coolest contempt he could throw upon the prying impertinence of the post-master was to repeat his question.

"I want a letther, sir, if you plaze."

"And who do you want it for?" repeated the post-master.

"What's that to you?" said Andy.

The post-master laughed at his simplicity, and told him he could not tell what letter to give him unless he told him the direction.

"The directions I got was to get a letther here—that's the directions."

"Who gave you those directions?"

"The masther."

"And who's your master?"

"What consarn is that o' yours?"

"Why, you stupid rascal, if you don't tell me his name, how can I give you a letter?"

"You could give it if you liked; but you're fond of axin' impident questions, bekase you think I'm simple."

"Go along out o' this! Your master must be as great a goose as yourself, to send such a messenger."

"Bad luck to your impidence! is it Squire Egan you dar to say goose to?"

"Oh, Squire Egan's your master, then?"

"Yis; have you any thing to say agin it?"

"Only that I never saw you before."

"Faith, then you'll never see me agin, if I have my own consint."

"I won't give you any letter for the squire, unless I know you're his servant. Is there any one in the town knows you?"

"Plenty," said Andy; "it's not every one is as ignorant as you."

Just at this moment a person to whom Andy was known entered the house, who vouched to the post-master that he might give Andy the squire's letter. "Have you one for me?"

"Yes, sir," said the post-master, producing one; "fourpence."

The gentleman paid the fourpence postage, and left the shop with his letter.

"Here's a letter for the squire," said the post-master; "you've to pay me elevenpence postage."

"What 'ud I pay elevenpence for?"

"For postage."

"Saint Pathrick! Didn't I see you give Mr. Durfy a letther for fourpence this minnit, and a bigger letther than this? and now you want me to pay elevenpence for this scrap of a thing! Do you think I'm a fool?"

"No, but I'm sure of it," said the post-master.

"Well, you're welkim to be sure, sure; but don't be delayin' me now; here's fourpence for you, and gi' me the letther."

"Go along, you stupid thief!" said the post-master, taking up the letter, and going to serve a customer with a mousetrap.

While this person and many others were served, Andy lounged up and down the shop, every now and then putting in his head in the middle of the customers, and saying, "Will you gi' me the letther?"

The squire in the mean time was getting impatient for his return, and, when Andy made his appearance, asked if there was a letter for him.

"There is, sir," said Andy.

"Then give it to me."

"I haven't it, sir."

"What do you mean?"

"He wouldn't give it to me, sir."

"Who wouldn't give it to you?"

"The owld chate beyant in the town—wanting to charge double for it."

"Maybe it's a double letter. Why didn't you pay what he asked, sir?"

"Arrah, sir, why would I let you be chated? It's not a double letther at all; not above half the size o' one Mr. Durfy got before my face for fourpence."

"You'll provoke me to break your neck some day, you vagabond. Ride back for your life, you omadhound, and pay whatever he asks, and get me the letter."

"Why, sir, I tell you he was sellin' them before my face for fourpence a piece."

"Go back, you scoundrel, or I'll horsewhip you; and if you're longer than an hour I'll have you ducked in the horsepond."

Andy vanished, and made a second visit to the post-office. When he arrived two other persons were getting letters, and the post-master was selecting the epistles for each from a large parcel that lay before him on the counter; at the same time many shop-customers were waiting to be served.

"I'm come for that letther," said Andy.

"I'll attend to you by-and-by."

"The masther's in a hurry."

"Let him wait till his hurry's over."

"He'll murther me if I'm not back soon."

"I'm glad to hear it."

While the post-master went on with such provoking answers to these appeals for dispatch, Andy's eye caught the heap of letters which lay on the counter; so, while certain weighing of soap and tobacco was going forward, he contrived to become possessed of two letters from the heap; having effected that, he waited patiently enough till it was the great man's pleasure to give him the missive directed to his master.

Then did Andy bestride his hack, and, in triumph at his trick on the post-master, rattle along the road homeward as fast as the beast could carry him.

He came into the squire's presence, his face beaming with delight, and an air of self-satisfied superiority in his manner quite unaccountable to his master until he pulled forth his hand, which had been grubbing up his prizes from the bottom of his pocket, and, holding three letters over his head, while he said, "Look at that!" he next slapped them down under his broad fist on the table before the squire, saying,

"Well, if he did make me pay elevenpence, by gor, I brought your honor the worth o' your money, any how!"

SCHOOL.—*From Merry's Museum.*

BEFORE SCHOOL.

"Quarter of nine! Boys and girls, do you hear?"
"One more buckwheat, then; be quick, mother dear."
"Where is my luncheon-box?" "Under the shelf,
Just in the place where you left it yourself."

"I can't say my table!" "Oh, find me my cap!"
"One kiss for mamma, and sweet sis in her lap."
"Be good, dear." "I'll try." "Nine times nine's eighty-one."
"Take your mittens!" "All right." "Hurry up, Bill; let's run."
With a slam of the door, they are off, girls and boys,
And the mother draws breath in the lull of the noise.

AFTER SCHOOL.

"Don't wake up the baby! Come gently, my dear."
"Oh, mother! I've torn my new dress; just look here!
I'm sorry; I only was climbing the wall."
"Oh, mother! *my* map was the nicest of all!"
"And Nelly, in spelling, went up to the head!"
"Oh, say! can I go on the hill with my sled?"
"I've got such a toothache!" "The teacher's unfair!"
"Is dinner most ready? I'm just like a bear!"

Be patient, worn mother, they're growing up fast;
These nursery whirlwinds, not long do they last;
A still, lonely house would be far worse than noise—
Rejoice and be glad in your brave girls and boys.

SECOND LECTURE ON HEAT.
BY MY LORD HIGH FIDDLESTICK.

The king, the court, and the little traveler were assembled to hear what atoms can do. The king looked very serious: he was thinking that atoms were a bore, but that it was his duty to encourage them. The courtiers looked very serious too: they were thinking, each one, that, if he was king, he would have any body hung that dared to talk about atoms. A table stood before the Lord High Fiddlestick; on the table stood a copper basin filled with pounded ice and salt, and two strong bottles of iron, each closed by a screw firmly fixed in the neck.

"Your majesty," said my Lord High Fiddlestick, taking up one of them, "these iron bottles are half an inch thick, and, as you see, they are firmly fastened at the top. They are filled with water, and I am going to place them in this pounded ice and salt, and freeze the water, to show you what atoms can do. But I should like first to explain, as well as I can, how water freezes. The water is made up of atoms, or tiny particles of vapor, which are held together, like the atoms of iron, by cohesion. But water is always much warmer than iron, and, you remember, we found out that heat is motion; so, when I say that, I mean that the atoms of water have much more motion than the atoms of iron. The iron has so little heat-motion that cohesion can hold its atoms tight and firm, and we call the iron hard and solid. The water-atoms have so much heat-motion that cohesion can hardly hold them in its grip, and the atoms roll over each other so loosely that we call water a liquid. I place these bottles in this ice and salt. The water-atoms are chilled, and begin to huddle together. The motion of heat will keep the atoms apart as long as it can, but as the atoms grow colder—that is, as they lose their heat—they lose their motion, and press closer together, till you may say the heat-motion is gone entirely; the dancing water-atoms cling together hard and stiff, and the water now takes up less room in the bottles than it did at first. Almost every thing, when freezing, becomes smaller, and stays smaller till it is warmed again; but this is not the case with water, luckily for the fishes—for, if the ice remained smaller, it would sink to the bottom, warm water would rise, be frozen, and sink in its turn, till the lake or river was frozen solid. But 'No,' say the water-atoms, 'we know better; we draw together, close and hard, till we freeze, and then, crack! we stretch out on every side—we grow larger and lighter, and make a warm roof for every thing below.' Now, your majesty, while I have been talking, the ice-atoms in the bottle have been stretching and pressing out. 'We will have more room,' say they. 'You can't have it,' answer the rigid iron-atoms, piled on each other half an inch thick. Which is the strongest? There go the bottles, broken from top to bottom! And now, Mr. Traveler, what do you think of the soft water-atoms, that can break iron?"

The traveler said nothing. "Very curious," observed his majesty.

"Your royal highness," cried my Lord High Fiddlestick, much delighted, "do you remember how just two weeks ago the Pink Page forgot to turn off the water? Just what has happened now in these bottles happened then in the pipes: the water froze, the ice-atoms tried to stretch themselves, the pipes would not stretch, and were broken as the bottles are. When a thaw came, it was nothing but dribble and leak all over the palace; and your majesty will recollect that the queen's pink satin gown, which the Dame of the Slippers had carelessly left in the powder closet, was quite ruined."

"The Pink Page deserves to be hung, and you too, since you knew all about it," growled the king.

"Your majesty, I should like to show you some more atom-work," said the Lord High Fiddlestick, in a flurry.

"If flooding the palace is atom-work, I should say I had seen enough," grumbled the king; but the Lord High Fiddlestick pretended not to hear, and took out from a refrigerator a large block of ice.

"Your majesty," he said, "here, as you see, is a block of ice. In front of it I place a glass, and before the glass a white screen. Here I have what is called an electric lamp. I am going to send a warm beam from this lamp through the ice, as I have not a sunbeam handy. If any thing happens in the ice, it will be reflected in this glass; but this is a peculiar glass: whatever is reflected in it will be made larger, and its image cast on the screen, so that you can all see it."

"Likely story!" growled the traveler; "as if any thing worth seeing could happen in that piece of ice."

"We know," continued the Lord High Fiddlestick, "that the ice-atoms came close together, but we do not know whether they scrambled together, and are now lying head and shoulders, or came in order; but we can take down the block of ice, and find of what it is built, as we could take down a house. I send a beam through the ice—the light passes through. But there was Heat in the beam; he has found work to do, and he stays among the ice-atoms. He is going from atom to atom, and urging them apart; they are all in motion, and the solid block is coming down in water—melting, as you would say. We are taking down the ice now; look on the screen."

The king and the courtiers looked. "Oh la!" screamed every body. The sour little traveler had determined not to look; but he was so curious to know why every body cried "oh la!" that he could not help turning his head, and seeing the stars and sprays of the ice-atoms.

"Very fine," remarked the king; "but handsome is that handsome does! I should think better of these stars and sprays if they had not flooded my palace."

My Lord High Fiddlestick knew better than to remind the king that, if the Pink Page had been as orderly as the ice-atoms, the palace would not have been flooded. Instead, he brought out a little furnace filled with live coals, on which stood a tea-kettle filled with boiling water.

"Your majesty has seen," he said, "that water-atoms can break iron, and are, in fact, 'giants in disguise.' We have seen, also, that they are orderly giants, and, at the word of command, fall into stars and sprays, as the soldiers of your majesty's regiments fall into line. Now we have the water-atoms and our old friend Heat here in this furnace. He is at his usual work, fighting with Cohesion, and pushing the water-atoms apart. Cohesion presses down with all its weight, but Heat is quite strong enough to lift it. Then the water-atoms spring apart in fine steam particles. The water needs now much more room than it did in the beginning. The water-atoms are greatly heated—that is, they are in furious motion, and are stretching and pushing for more room; and once more we see here that Heat is Force. This water, which would yield to the finger when cold, is now strong. It whirls, and spins, and presses so hard that, if there were no spout through which it could escape, and the cover of the kettle were fitted tight, it would burst the kettle. These atoms, your majesty, will push and drag tons. They will saw, and grind, and punch, and plane stone and iron. They—"

"Yes," cut in the traveler; "but what could your wonderful atoms do without the fire?"

"Just so," answered my Lord High Fiddlestick, with a benevolent smile. "Just what I am coming at. We can hear the roaring of the wheels and hammers in his majesty's iron-mill near by. What is making that noise? Force, you say. He is twisting, and turning, and rolling, and pounding iron; and every time he turns a wheel, or brings down a hammer, he dies, 'poor fellow!' So we go there to mourn over him, and we find, as I said before, Heat in the wheels, and in the instruments with which Force worked, and in all the places where he has been. You know that Force can take more shapes than one, and you begin to suspect that Heat always comes where Force disappears—that Heat is only one of his shapes. You ask, 'Why, where did Force come from?' 'From the steam,' says somebody. But what is steam? Why, water-atoms pulled apart from each other, and set in violent motion. But why does this water not keep still, like other water? Because it is heated. Getting heat is getting motion.

"But all this motion and strength of the wheels comes from the motion of the water, and all this strength and motion of the water comes from the heat of the fire! Yes. Why, then, all this force comes from Heat; and, Mr. Traveler, your friend Force only gave you one of his names. His proper name is Heat, Motion, Heat; and, when he has done his work, he does not die, but only slips back into his old shape of Heat again."

"My lord," exclaimed the king, "I am delighted! I have learned a great deal; but it is always necessary to think of what we learn, or our ideas will be jumbled in our brains like fruit in a pudding."

So the king and the courtiers went away, stretching and yawning, to think over what they had learned from the Lord High Fiddlestick.

LIFE.—*From January and June.*

BENJAMIN F. TAYLOR.

The pulses of great Nature never beat more audibly and musically than just about "the leafy month of June;" life, every where life, in field and flood, in earth, and air, and sky.

Life in all forms; life with a sweet breath in it, life with a song in it, life with a *light* in it. Life tied up in little bags of most Quakerish-looking silk by that sly spinner, the spider; life done up in gray bundles, and hung upon appletrees; deposited in little brown paper cups, or packed away in little clay cells by gentry in yellow jackets, and gentry with delicate waists, whose only foible consists in their not being always and altogether like Job and Moses; life hidden in the hearts of ripening plums and reddening cherries—find a sweeter cradle any where, if you can; life rocked in shells, put up in mother-of-pearl, set in ivory, chased with gold, consigned to little graves every where; laid away in "patent burial-cases"—just where Fisk got the idea—and fastened to rails and fence-posts; life that, by-and-by, shall spread wings damp with the imprint of this great stereotyping establishment of the Almighty; life standing "on end" in little boats, and rising into the air, taking to bugling as soon as it is born, and evincing, by the presentation of "bills" at most unseasonable and unreasonable hours, a decided talent for ledger literature; life sheltering itself beneath the leathern umbrella of the mushroom, reveling in the rose's red heart, drilled into the solid rock, domiciled in mud hovels, along rafters and beneath eaves, "playing in the plighted clouds," "laid" in a manger, peeping from holes, floating in the air, swinging in the wind, skulking under the chips, burrowing in the earth, darting along rail fences, opening nankeen throats from little baskets of twigs, floating in tatters of green baize on the ponds, advocating Solomon on birch, "poor Will" talking Greek, "*brekekek koax, koax*," and practicing hydropathy, "*k'chug;*" life in bags and boxes, bundles and blankets; in silks, satins, and shells; in "tights," and flounces, and feathers, and flannels; life full dressed and in dishabille; life knocking from the centre of fallen logs; knocking from the other side of shells white and blue, and mottled and dappled; and June is

"The delegated voice of God"

to bid them "come in, come up, come down, come out," and *be*, and do, and suffer; conjugating and inflecting the great active verb—"Live."

Turn over the loam in the fields, and you turn out turtle's eggs by the score. Go "across lots" to the neighbors', and you find the pearly treasures of the whistling quail by the dozen. Tap a sand-hill lightly with the toe of your boot, and you will see the ladies to whom Solomon referred sluggards by the myriad. Shake a bush, and you shake out a bird, or a peep, or a bug, or a bud, or something that's "all alive." Pluck a leaf, and you may find in it a crystal drop - such as one might dream Queen Mab would shed if "in the melting mood;" but the sun shall "set" on it a few days, and out will come a thing all legs, or wings, or stings—something to hum or drum—to fly, or creep, or crawl; something to *be* something and somebody, and count just as many in the great census of creation as he who called the shades of Ashland his, or she who journeyed of old to see Solomon—count just as many, "in words and figures following," to wit, (1) *one*.

THE GUARD ON THE RHINE.—*Translated from the German.*

There swells a cry as thunders crash,
As clash of swords and breakers dash—
To Rhine, to Rhine, to the German Rhine.
Who will protect thee, river mine?
Dear fatherland, let peace be thine—
Brave hearts and true defend the Rhine.

To millions swiftly came the cry,
And lightnings flashed from every eye:
Our youth, so good and brave, will stand
And guard thee, holy border land.
Dear fatherland, let peace be thine—
Brave hearts and true defend the Rhine!

And though my heart should beat no more,
No foreign foe will hold thy shore;
Rich, as in water is thy flood,
Is Germany in hero-blood.
Dear fatherland, let peace be thine—
Brave hearts and true defend the Rhine!

Up looked he to the heavens blue,
Where hero-dead our actions view;
He swore, and proudly sought the strife,
"The Rhine is German as my life."
Dear fatherland, let peace be thine—
Brave hearts and true defend the Rhine!

While yet one drop of blood throbs warm,
To wield the sword remains one arm,
To hold the rifle yet one hand,
No foeman steps upon the strand.
Loved fatherland, let peace be thine—
Brave hearts and true defend the Rhine!

The oath resounds, the billows run,
Our colors flutter in the sun;
To Rhine, to Rhine, to the German Rhine,
We will protect thee, river mine.
Dear fatherland, let peace be thine—
Brave hearts and true defend the Rhine!

A SINGING LESSON.
JEAN INGELOW.

A nightingale made a mistake—
  She sang a few notes out of tune—
Her heart was ready to break,
  And she hid from the moon.
She wrung her claws, poor thing,
  But was far too proud to weep;
She tuck'd her head under her wing,
  And pretended to be asleep.

A lark, arm-in-arm with a thrush,
  Came sauntering up to the place;
The nightingale felt herself blush,
  Though feathers hid her face.
She knew they had heard her song,
  She felt them snicker and sneer;
She thought that this life was too long,
  And wished she could skip a year.

"Oh, nightingale," cooed a dove,
  "Oh, nightingale, what's the use?
You, a bird of beauty and love,
  Why behave like a goose?
Don't skulk away from our sight
  Like a common, contemptible fowl;
You bird of joy and delight,
  Why behave like an owl?

"Only think of all you have done—
  Only think of all you *can* do;
A false note is really fun
  From such a bird as you!
Lift up your proud little crest;
  Open your musical beak;
Other birds have to do their best,
  But *you* need only *speak*."

The nightingale shyly took
  Her head from under her wing,
And, giving the dove a look,
  Straightway began to sing.
There was never a bird could pass—
  The night was divinely calm—
And the people stood on the grass
  To hear that wonderful psalm.

The nightingale did not care—
  She only sang to the skies;
Her song ascended there,
  And there she fixed her eyes.
The people who listened below
  She knew but little about—
And this tale has a moral, I know,
  If you'll try to find it out.

THE SOLDIER'S REPRIEVE.*

"I thought, Mr. Allan, when I gave my Bennie to his country, that not a father in all this broad land made so precious a gift—no, not one. The dear boy only slept a minute—just

* Arranged by C. W. Sanders.

one little minute, at his post; I know that was all, for Bennie never dozed over a duty. How prompt and reliable he was! I know he only fell asleep one little second—he was so young, and not strong, that boy of mine! Why, he was as tall as I, and only eighteen! and now they shoot him because he was found asleep when doing sentinel duty! Twenty-four hours, the telegram said—only twenty-four hours! Where is Bennie now?"

"We will hope with his heavenly Father," said Mr. Allan, soothingly.

"Yes, yes, let us hope; God is very merciful!"

"'I should be ashamed, father!' Bennie said, 'when I am a man, to think I never used this great right arm'—and he held it out so proudly before me—'for my country when it needed it! Palsy it rather than keep it at the plow!'

"'Go, then—go, my boy,' I said, 'and God keep you!' God has kept him, I think, Mr. Allan!" and the farmer repeated these last words slowly, as if, in spite of his reason, his heart doubted them.

"Like the apple of his eye, Mr. Owen; doubt it not."

Blossom sat near them, listening with blanched cheek. She had not shed a tear. Her anxiety had been so concealed that no one noticed it. She had occupied herself mechanically in the household cares. Now she answered a gentle tap at the kitchen door, opening it to receive from a neighbor's hand a letter. "It is from him," was all she said.

It was like a message from the dead. Mr. Owen took the letter, but could not break the envelope on account of his trembling fingers, and held it toward Mr. Allan with the helplessness of a child.

The minister opened it and read as follows:

"DEAR FATHER,—When this reaches you I shall be in eternity. At first it seemed awful to me; but I have thought about it so much now that it has no terror. They say they will not bind me nor blind me, but that I may meet my death like a man. I thought, father, it might have been on the field of battle, for my country, and that, when I fell, it would be fighting gloriously; but to be shot down like a dog for nearly betraying it—to die for neglect of duty! Oh, father, I wonder the very thought does not kill me! But I shall not disgrace you. I am going to write you all about it, and when I am gone you may tell my comrades. I can not now.

"You know I promised Jemmie Carr's mother I would look after her boy, and when he fell sick I did all I could for him. He was not strong when he was ordered back into the ranks, and the day before that night I carried all his luggage, besides my own, on our march. Toward night we went on double-quick, and though the luggage began to feel very heavy, every body else was tired too; and as for Jemmie, if I had not lent him an arm now and then, he would have dropped by the way. I was all tired when we came into camp, and then it was Jemmie's turn to be sentry, and I would take his place; but I was too tired, father. I could not have kept awake if a gun had been pointed at my head; but I did not know it until—well, until it was too late."

"God be thanked!" interrupted Mr. Owen, reverently. "I knew Bennie was not the boy to sleep carelessly at his post."

"They tell me to-day that I have a short reprieve—given to me by circumstances—'time to write to you,' our good colonel says. Forgive him, father, he only does his duty; he would gladly save me if he could; and do not lay my death up against Jemmie. The poor boy is broken-hearted, and does nothing but beg and entreat them to let him die in my stead.

"I can't bear to think of mother and Blossom. Comfort them, father! Tell them that I die as a brave boy should, and that, when the war is over, they will not be ashamed of me, as they must be now. God help me; it is very hard to bear! Good-by, father! God seems near and dear to me; not at all as if He wished me to perish forever, but as if He felt sorry for his poor, sinful, broken-hearted child, and would take me to be with Him and my Savior in a better—better life."

A deep sigh burst from Mr. Owen's heart. "Amen!" he said, solemnly; "Amen!"

"To-night, in the early twilight, I shall see the cows all coming home from pasture, and precious little Blossom standing on the back stoop, waiting for me; but I shall never, never come! God bless you all! Forgive your poor Bennie."

Late that night the door of the "back stoop" opened softly, and a little figure glided out, and down the footpath that led to the road by the mill. She seemed rather flying than walking, turning her head neither to the right nor the left, looking only now and then to heaven, and folding her hands as if in prayer. Two hours later, the same young girl stood at the Mill Dépôt watching the coming of the night-train; and the conductor, as he reached down to lift her into the car, wondered at the tear-stained face that was upturned toward the dim lantern he held in his hand. A few questions and ready answers told him all; and no father could have cared more tenderly for his only child than he for our little Blossom. She was on her way to Washington, to ask President Lincoln for her brother's life. She had stolen away, leaving only a note to tell her father where and why she had gone. She had brought Bennie's letter with her: no good, kind heart, like the President's, could refuse to be melted by it. The next morning they reached New York, and the conductor hurried her on to Washington. Every minute, now, might be the means of saving her brother's life. And so, in an incredibly short time, Blossom reached the capital, and hastened immediately to the White House.

The President had but just seated himself to his morning's task of overlooking and signing important papers, when, without one word of announcement, the door softly opened, and Blossom, with downcast eyes and folded hands, stood before him. "Well, my child," he said, in his pleasant, cheerful tones, "what do you want so bright and early in the morning?"

"Bennie's life, please, sir," faltered Blossom.

"Bennie? Who is Bennie?"

"My brother, sir. They are going to shoot him for sleeping at his post."

"Oh yes," and Mr. Lincoln ran his eye over the papers before him. "I remember. It was a fatal sleep. You see, child, it was at a time of special danger. Thousands of lives might have been lost for his culpable negligence."

"So my father said," replied Blossom, gravely; "but poor Bennie was so tired, sir, and Jemmie so weak. He did the work of two, sir, and it was Jemmie's night, not his; but Jemmie was too tired, and Bennie never thought about himself, that he was tired too."

"What is this you say, child? Come here; I do not understand;" and the kind man caught eagerly, as ever, at what seemed to be a justification of an offense.

Blossom went to him; he put his hand tenderly on her shoulder, and turned up the pale, anxious face toward his. How tall he seemed, and he was President of the United States too! A dim thought of this kind passed through Blossom's mind, but she told her simple and straightforward story, and handed Mr. Lincoln Bennie's letter to read.

He read it carefully; then, taking up his pen, wrote a few hasty lines, and rang his bell.

Blossom heard this order given: "SEND THIS DISPATCH AT ONCE."

The President then turned to the girl and said, " Go home, my child, and tell that father of yours, who could approve his country's sentence, even when it took the life of a child like that, that Abraham Lincoln thinks the life far too precious to be lost. Go back; or—wait until to-morrow; Bennie will need a change after he has so bravely faced death; he shall go with you."

"God bless you, sir!" said Blossom; and who shall doubt that God heard and registered the request?

Two days after this interview the young soldier came to the White House with his sister. He was called into the President's private room, and a strap fastened "upon the shoulder." Mr. Lincoln then said: "The soldier that could carry a sick comrade's baggage, and die for the act so uncomplainingly, deserves well of his country." Then Bennie and Blossom took their way to their Green Mountain home. A crowd gathered at the Mill Dépôt to welcome them back; and, as Farmer Owen's hand grasped that of his boy, tears flowed down his cheeks, and he was heard to say fervently, "THE LORD BE PRAISED!"

THE SMACK IN SCHOOL.
J. W. PALMER.

A district school, not far away,
'Mid Berkshire Hills, one winter's day,
Was humming with its wonted noise
Of threescore mingled girls and boys;
Some few upon their tasks intent,
But more on furtive mischief bent.
The while the master's downward look
Was fastened on a copy-book;
When suddenly, behind his back,
Rose sharp and clear a rousing smack,
As 'twere a battery of bliss
Let off in one tremendous kiss.
"What's that?" the startled master cries;
"That, thir," a little imp replies,
"Wath William Willith, if you pleathe;
I thaw him kith Thuthanna Peathe."
With frown to make a statue thrill,
The master thundered, "Hither, Will!"
Like wretch o'ertaken in his track,
With stolen chattels on his back,
Will hung his head in fear and shame,
And to the awful presence came—
A great, green, bashful simpleton,
The butt of all good-natured fun.
With smile suppressed, and birch upraised,
The threatener faltered: "I'm amazed
That you, my biggest pupil, should
Be guilty of an act so rude;
Before the whole set school to boot—
What evil genius set you to 't?"
"'Twas she herself, sir," sobbed the lad;
"I did not mean to be so bad;
But when Susannah shook her curls,
And whispered I was 'fraid of girls,
And dursn't kiss a baby's doll,
I couldn't stand it, sir, at all,

But up and kissed her on the spot.
I know—boo-hoo—I ought to not,
But, somehow, from her looks—boo-hoo—
I thought she kind o' wished me to!".

THE BRIDAL WINE-CUP.

"Pledge with wine—pledge with wine," cried the young and thoughtless Harvey Wood; "pledge with wine," ran through the bridal party.

The beautiful bride grew pale—the decisive hour had come. She pressed her white hands together, and the leaves of the bridal wreath trembled on her brow; her breath came quicker, and her heart beat wilder.

"Yes, Marion, lay aside your scruples for this once," said the judge, in a low tone, going toward his daughter; "the company expect it. Do not so seriously infringe upon the rules of etiquette; in your own home, do as you please; but in mine, for this once, please *me*."

Every eye was turned toward the bridal pair. Marion's principles were well known. Harvey had been a convivialist, but of late his friends noticed the change in his manners, the difference in his habits; and to-night they watched him to see, as they sneeringly said, if he was tied down to a woman's opinion so soon.

Pouring a brimming cup, they held it with tempting smiles toward Marion. She was very pale, though more composed; and her hand shook not, as, smiling back, she gracefully accepted the crystal tempter, and raised it to her lips. But scarcely had she done so, when every hand was arrested by her piercing exclamation of "Oh, how terrible!"

"What is it?" cried one and all, thronging together, for she had slowly carried the glass at arm's length, and was fixedly regarding it as though it were some hideous object.

"Wait," she answered, while a light, which seemed inspired, shone from her dark eyes; "wait, and I will tell you. I see," she added, slowly, pointing one jeweled finger at the sparkling ruby liquid, "a sight that beggars all description; and yet listen: I will paint it for you if I can. It is a lovely spot; tall mountains, crowned with verdure, rise in awful sublimity around; a river runs through, and bright flowers grow to the water's edge. There is a thick, warm mist, that the sun seeks vainly to pierce. Trees, lofty and beautiful, wave to the airy motion of the birds; but there—a group of Indians gather; they flit to and fro with something like sorrow upon their dark brows. And in their midst lies a manly form—but his cheek, how deathly; his eye wild with the fitful fire of fever. One friend stands behind him—nay, I should say kneels; for, see, he is pillowing that poor head upon his breast.

"Genius in ruins—oh the high, holy looking brow! why should death mark it, and he so young? Look how he throws back the damp curls! See him clasp his hands! Hear his thrilling shrieks for life! Mark how he clutches at the form of his companion, imploring to be saved. Oh, hear him call piteously his father's name—see him twine his fingers together as he shrieks for his sister—his only sister —the twin of his soul—weeping for him in his distant native land.

"See!" she exclaimed, while the bridal party shrank back, the untasted wine trembling in their faltering grasp, and the judge fell, overpowered, upon his seat—"see! his arms are lifted to heaven—he prays, how wildly, for mercy! hot fever rushes through his veins. The friend beside him is weeping; awe-stricken, the dark men move silently away, and leave the living and the dying together."

There was a hush in that princely parlor, broken only by what seemed a smothered sob from some manly bosom. The bride stood yet upright, with quivering lip, and tears stealing to the outward edge of her lashes. Her beautiful arm had lost its tension, and the glass, with its little troubled red waves, came slowly toward the range of her vision. She spoke again; every lip was mute. Her voice was low, faint, yet awfully distinct! She still fixed her sorrowful glance upon the wine-cup.

"It is evening now; the great white moon is coming up, and her beams lie gently on his forehead. He moves not; his eyes are set in their sockets; dim are their piercing

M

glances; in vain his friend whispers the name of father and sister—death is there. Death—and no soft hand, no gentle voice to bless and soothe him. His head sinks back; one convulsive shudder—he is dead."

A groan ran through the assembly. So vivid was her description, so unearthly her look, so inspired her manner, that what she described seemed actually to have taken place then and there. They noticed, also, that the bridegroom hid his face in his hands, and was weeping.

"Dead!" she repeated again, her lips quivering faster and faster, and her voice more and more broken; "and there they scoop him a grave, and there, without a shroud, they lay him down in that damp, reeking earth—the only son of a proud father, the only idolized brother of a fond sister. And he sleeps to-day in that distant country, with no stone to mark the spot. There he lies—my *father's* son—my own *twin brother!* a victim to *this* deadly poison. Father," she exclaimed, turning suddenly, while the tears rained down her beautiful cheeks, "father, shall I drink it now?"

The form of the old judge was convulsed with agony. He raised not his head, but in a smothered voice he faltered, "No, no, my child—NO!"

She lifted the glittering goblet, and, letting it suddenly fall to the floor, it was dashed in a thousand pieces. Many a tearful eye watched her movement, and instantaneously every wine-glass was transferred to the marble table on which it had been prepared. Then, as she looked at the fragments of crystal, she turned to the company, saying, " Let no friend hereafter, who loves me, tempt me to peril my soul for wine. Not firmer are the everlasting hills than my resolve, God helping me, never to touch or taste the poison-cup. And he to whom I have given my hand, who watched over my brother's dying form in that last solemn hour, and buried the dear wanderer there by the river, in that land of gold, will, I trust, sustain me in that resolve. Will you not, my husband?"

His glistening eyes, his sad, sweet smile, was her answer. The judge left the room; and when, an hour after, he returned, and with a more subdued manner took part in the entertainment of the bridal guests, no one could fail to read that he, too, had determined to banish the enemy at once and forever from his princely home.

Those who were present at that wedding can never forget the impressions so solemnly made. Many from that hour renounced forever the social glass.

THE CHRISTMAS-TREE.—*Carrier's Address, Philadelphia Post.*

Hurra! hurra! for the Christmas-tree,
May it flourish for aye in its greenery.
When the winter comes with its whitening snow,
How proudly the Christmas-tree doth grow!
It spreadeth its boughs so broad and so fair,
And jolly and gay are the fruits they bear.
    Then hurra! hurra! for the Christmas-tree;
    Hurra! hurra! for its mirth and glee;
    When forests of oak have passed from the land,
    The jolly old Christmas-tree shall stand.
There are wonderful plants far over the sea,
But what are they all to the Christmas-tree?
Does the oak bear candies, the palm-tree skates?
But sugar-plums, trumpets, doll-babies, slates,
Picture-books, elephants, soldiers, cows,
All grow at once on the Christmas-tree boughs.
    Then hurra! hurra! for the Christmas-tree;
    Hurra! hurra! for its mirth and glee;
    When forests of oak have passed from the land,
    The jolly old Christmas-tree shall stand.
Oh, many the homes it hath happy made,
When the little ones under its leaves have played;
Oh, sweet are the pleasures around it that spring,
And dear are the thoughts of the past they bring.
Then long may it flourish, and green may it be,
The merry, mighty old Christmas-tree.
    Hurra! hurra! for the Christmas-tree;
    Long shall it flourish, green shall it be;
    When forests have passed away from the land,
    The jolly old Christmas-tree shall stand.

BARBARA FRIETCHIE.
John Greenleaf Whittier.

Up from the meadows rich with corn,
Clear in the cool September morn,

The clustered spires of Frederick stand,
Green-walled by the hills of Maryland.

Round about them orchards sweep,
Apple and peach tree fruited deep,

Fair as a garden of the Lord
To the eyes of the famished rebel horde,

On that pleasant morn of the early fall,
When Lee marched over the mountain-wall—

Over the mountains, winding down,
Horse and foot, into Frederick town.

Forty flags with their silver stars,
Forty flags with their crimson bars,

Flapped in the morning wind; the sun
Of noon looked down, and saw not one.

Up rose old Barbara Frietchie then,
Bowed with her fourscore years and ten;

Bravest of all in Frederick town,
She took up the flag the men hauled down;

In her attic window the staff she set,
To show that one heart was loyal yet.

Up the street came the rebel tread,
Stonewall Jackson riding ahead.

Under his slouched hat, left and right,
He glanced—the old flag met his sight:

"Halt!"—the dust-brown ranks stood fast;
"Fire!"—out blazed the rifle-blast;

It shivered the window, pane and sash;
It rent the banner with seam and gash.

Quick, as it fell, from the broken staff
Dame Barbara snatched the silken scarf;

She leaned far out on the window-sill,
And shook it forth with a royal will:

"Shoot, if you must, this old gray head,
But spare your country's flag!" she said.

A shade of sadness, a blush of shame,
Over the face of the leader came;

The nobler nature within him, stirred
To life at that woman's deed and word:

"Who touches a hair of yon gray head
Dies like a dog! March on!" he said.

All day long through Frederick street
Sounded the tread of marching feet;

All day long that free flag tossed
Over the heads of the rebel host.

Ever its torn folds rose and fell
On the loyal winds that loved it well;

And through the hill-gaps sunset light
Shone over it with a warm good-night.

Barbara Frietchie's work is o'er,
And the rebel rides on his raids no more.

Honor to her! and let a tear
Fall, for her sake, on Stonewall's bier.

Over Barbara Frietchie's grave,
Flag of freedom and union, wave!

Peace, and order, and beauty, draw
Round thy symbols of light and law;

And ever the stars above look down
On thy stars below in Frederick town!

DEATH OF LITTLE NELL.—*From the Old Curiosity Shop.*
CHARLES DICKENS.

By little and little the old man had drawn back toward the inner chamber while these words were spoken. He pointed there as he replied, with trembling lips,

"You plot among you to wean my heart from her. You will never do that—never while I have life. I have no relative or friend but her—I never had—I never will have. She is all in all to me. It is too late to part us now."

Waving them off with his hand, and calling softly to her as he went, he stole into the room. They who were left behind drew close together, and, after a few whispered words — not unbroken by emotion or easily uttered — followed him. They moved so gently that their footsteps made no noise, but there were sobs from among the group, and sounds of grief and mourning.

For she was dead. There, upon her little bed, she lay at rest. The solemn stillness was no marvel now.

She was dead. No sleep so beautiful and calm, so free from trace of pain, so fair to look upon. She seemed a creature fresh from the hand of God, and waiting for the breath of life—not one who had lived and suffered death.

Her couch was dressed with, here and there, some winter berries and green leaves, gathered in a spot she had been used to favor. "When I die, put near me something that has loved the light, and had the sky above it always." These were her words.

She was dead. Dear, gentle, patient, noble Nell was dead. Her little bird—a poor slight thing the pressure of a finger would have crushed—was stirring nimbly in its cage, and the strong heart of its child-mistress was mute and motionless forever.

Where were the traces of her early cares, her sufferings, and fatigues? All gone. His was the true death before their eyes. Sorrow was dead indeed in her, but peace and perfect happiness were born, imaged in her tranquil beauty and profound repose.

And still her former self lay there, unaltered in this change. Yes; the old fireside had smiled on that same sweet face; it had passed like a dream through haunts of misery and care; at the door of the poor schoolmaster on the summer evening—before the furnace-fire on the cold, wet night—at the still, dying boy, there had been the same mild, lovely look. So shall we know the angels in their majesty, after death.

The old man held one languid arm in his, and kept the small hand tight folded to his breast, for warmth. It was the hand she had stretched out to him with her last smile— the hand that had led him on through all their wanderings. Ever and anon he pressed it to his lips, then hugged it to his breast again, murmuring that it was warmer now—and, as he said it, he looked in agony to those who stood around, as if imploring them to help her.

She was dead, and past all help, or need of it. The ancient rooms she had seemed to fill with life, even while her own was ebbing fast—the garden she had tended—the eyes she had gladdened—the noiseless haunts of many a thoughtless hour—the paths she had trodden as if it were but yesterday, could know her no more.

"It is not," said the schoolmaster, as he bent down to kiss her on her cheek, and gave his tears free vent, "it is not in this world that heaven's justice ends. Think what it is compared with the world to which her young spirit has winged its early flight, and say, if one deliberate wish, expressed in solemn terms above this bed, could call her back to life, which of us would utter it!"

KATIE LEE AND WILLIE GRAY.

Two brown heads with tossing curls,
Red lips shutting over pearls,
Bare feet, white, and wet with dew,
Two eyes black, and two eyes blue—
Little boy and girl were they,
Katie Lee and Willie Gray.

They were standing where a brook,
Bending like a shepherd's crook,
Flashed its silver, and thick ranks
Of willow fringed its banks—
Half in thought and half in play,
Katie Lee and Willie Gray.

They had cheeks like cherries red;
He was taller 'most a head;

She, with arms like wreaths of snow,
Swung a basket to and fro
(As they loitered, half in play),
Chattering to Willie Gray.,

"Pretty Katie," Willie said—
And there came a dash of red
Through the brownness of the cheek—
"Boys are strong, and girls are weak,
And I'll carry, so I will,
Katie's basket up the hill."

Katie answered with a laugh,
"You shall carry only half;"
Then said, tossing back her curls,
"Boys are weak as well as girls."
Do you think that Katie guessed
Half the wisdom she expressed?

Men are only boys grown tall;
Hearts don't change much, after all;
And when, long years from that day,
Katie Lee and Willie Gray
Stood again beside the brook
Bending like a shepherd's crook,

Is it strange that Willie said,
While again a dash of red
Crowned the brownness of his cheek,
"I am strong, and you are weak;
Life is but a slippery steep,
Hung with shadows cold and deep.

"Will you trust me, Katie dear—
Walk beside me without fear?
May I carry, if I will,
All your burdens up the hill?"
And she answered with a laugh,
"No, but you may carry half."

Close beside the little brook
Bending like a shepherd's crook,

Working with its silver hands
Late and early at the sands,
Stands a cottage, where to-day
Katie lives with Willie Gray.

In the porch she sits, and, lo!
Swings a basket to and fro
Vastly different from the one
That she swung in years agone:
This is long, and deep, and wide,
And has—rockers at the side!

SHERIDAN'S RIDE.

THOMAS BUCHANAN READ.

Up from the South at break of day,
Bringing to Winchester fresh dismay,
The affrighted air with a shudder bore,
Like a herald in haste, to the chieftain's door,
The terrible grumble, and rumble, and roar,
Telling the battle was on once more,
And Sheridan twenty miles away.

And wider still those billows of war
Thundered along the horizon's bar,
And louder yet into Winchester rolled
The roar of that red sea uncontrolled,
Making the blood of the listener cold
As he thought of the stake in that fiery fray,
And Sheridan twenty miles away.

But there is a road from Winchester town,
A good, broad highway leading down;
And there, through the flush of the morning light,
A steed as black as the steeds of night
Was seen to pass as with eagle flight.
As if he knew the terrible need,
He stretched away with the utmost speed;
Hills rose and fell—but his heart was gay,
With Sheridan *fifteen* miles away.

Still sprung from those swift hoofs, thundering south,
The dust, like the smoke from the cannon's mouth,
Or the tail of a comet, sweeping faster and faster,
Foreboding to traitors the doom of disaster.
The heart of the steed and the heart of the master
Were beating, like prisoners assaulting their walls,
Impatient to be where the battle-field calls.
Each nerve of the charger was strained to full play,
With Sheridan only TEN miles away.

Under his spurning feet, the road
Like an arrowy Alpine river flowed,
And the landscape fled away behind
Like an ocean flying before the wind;
And the steed, like a bark fed with furnace ire,
Swept on with his wild eyes full of fire.
But, lo! he is nearing his heart's desire;
He is snuffing the smoke of the roaring fray,
With Sheridan only FIVE miles away.

The first that the general saw were the groups
Of stragglers, and then the retreating troops;
What was done—what to do—a glance told him both,
And, striking his spurs with a terrible oath,
He dashed down the line 'mid a storm of huzzas,
And the wave of retreat checked its course there, because
The sight of the master compelled it to pause.
With foam and with dust the black charger was gray—
By the flash of his eye and his nostril's play,
He seemed to the whole great army to say,
"I have brought you Sheridan, all the way
From Winchester down, to save the day!"

Hurra! hurra for Sheridan!
Hurra! hurra for horse and man!
And when their statues are placed on high,
Under the dome of the Union sky—
The American soldier's temple of fame—
There, with the glorious general's name,

Be it said in letters both bold and bright,
"Here is the steed that saved the day
By carrying Sheridan into the fight
From Winchester, twenty miles away!"

THE BOTTLE IMP.—*From the Little Corporal.*

JULIA M. THAYER.

"Come, little Hans," said the lame cobbler, with a good-natured wink, "run round the corner for father, and get the bottle filled; here's a penny for a ginger-snap; quick, now, before the mother gets back! he! he! he!" and he nodded and chuckled to himself, as if it were a rare joke to send the absent mother's darling on a fiend's errand, whither the angel of her prayers would hardly follow.

The little one hesitated, knowing, in his heart, that the mother would say "Nay, the child shall not meddle with hell-fire;" but was there ever a little one could resist a ginger-snap? Not Hans Christopher, certainly, for whom the cottage shelf seldom held such dainties.

"There goes the cobbler's boy to old Grinder's den, with a big black bottle," said the brisk little dress-maker over the way, glancing out of the window. "Now we'll not hear the rat-tat-tat of his hammer again for another fortnight. Mother, what think you will ever become of that man? He goes from bad to worse, that's certain; and the boy will be *ditto*, I suppose. None of my business? Of course not; it is none of my business that my own father and brother went the same way to destruction; it is none of my business that ten thousand fathers and brothers—" she stopped suddenly, for the old woman's sigh struck her to the heart.

Meantime little Hans came back, picking his way carefully over the rough paving-stones.

"Say, little one," and the dress-maker put her head out at the window, "what have you in that lovely junk bottle? Is it a nice sup of his infernal majesty's favorite bitters, seasoned with tears and curses? Your mother likes to have your father drink that, don't she? Take care! don't spill a drop of the precious stuff. I'll tell you what, little boy," and the tone sunk to an awful whisper, "there's an ugly little black imp shut up in that bottle; you let him out, and sometime he'll *tear the very heart out of your body!*"

She shut the window with a jerk; and little Hans, on wings of terror, flew back to the dingy shop.

"Oh, father," he shrieked, panting for breath, "don't let him out! don't let him out!"

"Who? What? The child's bewitched," said the cobbler, pausing in the act of drawing the cork.

"The—the—oh, father, she said there was a—imp—in the bottle, and he'd tear your heart to pieces! Don't! Oh, father, don't!" and he held up his little hands imploringly, while drops of perspiration beaded his face.

Such agony was distressing to witness, and Christopher set the bottle down to reason with the child.

"What is it, Hans? Who has been putting this nonsense into your head? Why, let me tell you, little man, this bottle is my comfort—my *angel;* just see, now, how he warms my stomach, and cheers my heart, and is, altogether, a very good friend. What could a poor man do without it, indeed? Here's to your health, little Hans." And the little boy, with horror, saw the fatal vessel uncorked, and lifted to his father's lips.

Shrinking back into the uttermost corner, and pressing his hands tightly over his heart, he gazed long and shudderingly; but no uncanny imp appearing to verify the dress-maker's assertion, with a child's light-heartedness he soon dismissed the horrid phantom from his imagination.

Not so Christopher. A new train of thought was awakened in his brain, now roused to unusual activity by the stimulating draught.

"An imp in the bottle, hah! that is an *idee*, truly," quoth he to himself. "An imp is a devil, and a devil is good for naught but to frighten women and children; let him come on! I'm not *a—feared!*" With that he took another draught of the liquid fire. "Go to blazes! can't a man have a drop of somethin' warm, but they must get up a scarecrow of some sort o' nother to it? Go — to — Good God! there he is now," shrieked the cobbler, gazing, with livid face and eyes starting from their sockets, into a dusky corner of the room.

"Get out! get out! you nasty, grinning, ill-mannered devil, you! Get out, I say!" flinging his hammer at the fiend, while boots, lapstone, and last went flying after.

But the creature moved not. He sat enveloped in a bluish smoke; his tongue darted forth flames, and the glance of his eyes burnt into the cobbler's very soul, who already felt those horrid claws tugging at his heart-strings.

"Come!" said the goblin.

Great drops of sweat rolled down the cobbler's face as he strove in vain to move his palsied limbs.

"Come!" and the black-faced imp began to leer, and chuckle, and dance about in horrid glee.

"I'm the bottle sprite—your comfort, your *angel*, your good friend, in whom you delight! Cheer up, and let's away; I've something to show you." With that he made a dive at Christopher, who, with superhuman effort, sprang from his bench, and struggled wildly toward the door. He missed it, and, after spinning round and round like a top, went sprawling to the floor, whence the bottle sprite lifted him by the hair of his head, and bore him off triumphantly through the roof—away, away into the fields of air.

At last he found himself set plump upon the roof of a vast distillery. He knew it by the pungent odors that filled his nostrils, and helped to restore his scattered senses. Squat before him was his black "angel," encircled still in the blue atmosphere of the nether world.

Christopher shrank away in horror, and covered his face with both hands.

"You loathe me—you shrink from me," hissed the imp; "me, who have cheered, and warmed, and comforted you so often! Is that fair?"

The cobbler felt his brain on fire—his throat parched—his blood like molten lead in his veins.

"Drink—give me drink!" he cried, in an agony of thirst; "devil or not, I *must* have drink."

The bottle sprite laughed mockingly, and again uttered the magic word "Come!"

They descended into the rooms below. There were huge vats and giant hogsheads of steaming liquor; there were loads upon loads of life-sustaining grain, toward which were lifted the empty, outstretched hands of famishing thousands; there were ponderous machines, and hundreds of men, toiling to convert the nutritious gift of the Creator into soul poison and body poison. And there, among all, and over all, and flitting hither and thither, like bats, squatting like toads, or creeping like reptiles, were myriads of uncanny imps—hate, envy, strife, anger, discord, cruelty—all baleful passions—all fearful and disgusting forms of devilishness. They swarmed round the vats, casks, and demijohns; they plunged and frolicked in the burning liquid; they clung to it, and followed it through all its changes, and whatever its destination.

"Ah! comrades, how are you?" cried Christopher's "angel," with a wicked grin. "You're at it, I see. You'll never perish here for lack of sustenance. It's *whisky* that does it, my hearties! Wherever *that* goes, *you* go; and wherever *you* go, tears, and curses, and broken hearts follow. Oh, you make a jolly world of it! Success to you! Do you see that cask of good old rye?" said the philosophic imp, turning to Christopher, who by this time had nearly forgotten his thirst in amazement. "I'll tell you what we are going to do with *that*. There's *murder* in that, and suicide. The man that drinks it will kill his own brother, and then go and hang himself. And, see here! this lovely bottle of Bourbon is for medicine. Some poor sick body'll take it for *tic douloureux*, or the like. What then? Why, there's a sleeping serpent in it, called *Appetite*, that will eat into that soul like a canker. Ah! good cobbler, if these liquors were only named according to their real uses, what an array we *should* have! but come!"

Away they sped, over prairies laughing in the sunshine, over waters dimpling in the breeze, over cities reeking with vile vapors, and bustling with all the activities of life. They reached the land of the vintage—a land of peace and beauty. A smiling sky looked down upon a smiling landscape; the song of the vintners floated far on the still summer air;

grapes hung in purple clusters from the vine, or stained the wine-press with their juices; rosy youths and maidens wrought amid the vineyards. "Here it begins," said the bottle imp; "more than half the want and woe over yonder. You wouldn't think it, would you, so calm a scene? Toil away, fair youths and simple maidens! prepare the seducing cup, sweet, and bright, and sparkling; so much the better—the less can men resist it. Oh, to see it fire the brain and stir the heart to madness! Oh, to see it drive reason from her throne, drown the voice of conscience, and stifle the sense of pity and affection! to see it steal the bread from the poor man's shelf—his food, and fire, and raiment—his honor, hope, happiness; and, last of all, his *soul!* ha! ha! Toil on, sweet people, dear people; the Evil One loves your work!"

The grimaces and contortions of the little chuckling fiend were horrible to witness, and the poor cobbler would fain have hidden away behind some friendly trellis; but no, the spell was on him, and he must away.

"That is as it was in the very, *very* olden time," continued the fiend, as they paused upon a city spire for Christopher to take breath. "We bottle imps were half asleep in those days. Men drank the pure juice of the grape; and, though we managed to creep in, very much to their undoing, it was nothing compared with these times—he! he! Now here's something precious to show you. Come!"

They descended, by what witchcraft the cobbler never knew, to dark, underground regions — vast vaults, where were ranged, on every side, in vessels of various sorts, what purported to be *pure* wines and liquors of every description, cobwebbed and mildewed with age.

"Now this beats the other place all to nothing, as you shall see," quoth the imp.

Presently a little weazen-faced old man appeared, bearing in his hand a lighted taper, which moved like a baleful star amid the darkness.

He went from cask to cask, from bottle to bottle; and ever, as he opened and closed each one, in went a horrid little image, compared with which the bottle fiends were beautiful.

Christopher's black "angel" was nearly beside himself with mirth. "Pop! there goes another," said he; "that's *arsenic;* and there's *opium*, and *copperas*, and *white lead*, and *vitriol*, and *nux vomica*, and *coculus indicus*, and a host of others. There's *gripes* for you, and scorching fevers, and nausea, and deadly stupor, and wild delirium—ha! ha! ha! what a jolly time they will have with all those poisonous devils. Come, let's see to it!"

But ah! what tongue can tell the heart-rending pictures poor Christopher was doomed to witness! He shrank in horror from each new scene, but, like one in a fearful nightmare, he was dumb and powerless.

Gifted with a strange *clairvoyance*, he saw the secret canker gnawing at the heart-strings of him who was given over to appetite. He saw the young wife turn in torturing misery from her husband's bloated visage; he saw the promising youth, yet encircled by his mother's prayers, lured by the sparkling wine-cup, break over all restraints, while the roses of joy and love fell blighted round his path; and the rainbow of hope, which once spanned his way, was shrouded in tempest and darkness. He saw that mother's heart torn with anguish as she laid her first-born in a drunkard's grave; he saw the upturned, pitiful faces of the drunkard's children, innocent, but accursed ; he saw brother smiting brother in his frenzy; and women, once tender and beautiful, besotted drunkards; and among all, and above all, the bottle imps still played their wild pranks, and chuckled, in hellish glee, over the ruin they had wrought.

Christopher saw all this, and it burned deeply into his soul. The sparkling glass, the well-filled demijohn, no longer charmed him. Oh, for some mighty talisman by which to exorcise all these demons, and sweep every vestige of them from the earth!

But still his lips were dumb. Then, with a wild longing, his heart turned toward *home.* "Come!" said the imp, as if divining his thoughts, and they swiftly neared the dingy shop.

How plainly, now, he beheld, through clapboard and rafter, the emptiness of the spot—the unlighted hearth, the scanty wardrobe, the stinted board; the lonely heart there, pining for affection; the well-nigh fatherless child, now clinging to him with winning confidence, now shrinking utterly away in pain and terror.

"Ah! but this is a fine place, isn't it?" said the bottle imp, delightedly; "not much elegance and beauty, or even comfort, here. A good many tears have been shed — a good many ghosts of dead hopes and joys are flitting round; but we'll do better than that! Only stick to the *bottle*, good Christopher, and *we'll* stay by you, never fear! Here are a few tools might yet be pawned for liquor; things aren't quite so rickety as they may be. And then the woman—she's a brave one — she works hard to keep things together, and wears a pretty bright face, but we'll break her heart yet— and the little one! for all her tender coddlings and fine teachings, just train him up to follow *your* footsteps, and won't he toss the first clod upon *her* grave?"

The poor cobbler wept and groaned in anguish of spirit, for, with all his faults, he heartily loved his wife and child, and thoroughly detested his own bad ways.

With one last, mighty effort, he broke the spell that bound him.

"Out, fiend! liar! devil!" he shrieked; "take that—and that!"

Crash—clatter—crash!

"What can be the matter?" exclaimed Madame Christopher, just hurrying in from her morning's scanty marketing.

"Oh, father, have you done it? have you smashed him?" shouted little Hans, capering with glee around the shining fragments of the "lovely junk bottle."

"Yes, my son, I have done it, and I *am done with it forever!*" said Christopher, gathering himself up slowly from the floor, and standing erect upon his lame leg.

"Do tell, mother! what do you think?" said the little dress-maker, one day. "Doesn't every thing go nicely over the way? Little Hans is as happy and well-dressed a boy as one often sees, and *Madame* steps around about her work as if she was fairly dancing to the *rat-tat-tat* of the cobbler's hammer."

RULES FOR LIFE.

1. Keep good company, or none.
2. Speak the truth, or nothing.
3. Make few promises, and keep them.
4. Drink no intoxicating liquors.
5. Never play at games of chance.
6. Never be idle.
7. Earn money before you spend it.
8. Do that first which needs doing most.
9. Make no haste to be rich.
10. Investigate affairs closely, and engage in them cautiously.
11. Lay your plans with prudence, and be prepared for emergencies.
12. In difficulties be patient, and overcome them by perseverance.
13. Say nothing that you would be ashamed to hear again.
14. When you retire at night, think over the events of the day, and avoid to-morrow the errors of to-day.

GERMAN QUOTATIONS AND PROVERBS.

1. By the street of By-and-by one arrives at the house of Never.
2. If you are an anvil, be patient; if you are a hammer, strike hard.
3. One to-day is better than ten to-morrows.
4. Once in people's mouths, 'tis hard to get out of them.
5. Procrastination of a good deed has often brought repentance.—GLEIM.
6. We must wait for the future, and enjoy or bear the present.—WILHELM VON HUMBOLDT.
7. Divide and command, a wise maxim; unite and guide, a better.—GOETHE.
8. We are accustomed to see men deride what they do not understand, and snarl at the good and beautiful because it lies beyond their sympathies.—GOETHE.

MISCELLANEOUS SELECTIONS.

FULL OF SNOW.
Rev. Joseph Cook.

Out in the wind and storm, upon a tree
All stripped and bare, sits drearily
    A bird's nest full of snow,
From which the bird has parted long ago.
From the cold nest no song of bird is flowing,
No cry for food from tender nestlings going,
        Full of snow.

Mourning and sad the barren branches wave
Around the nest—an unprotected grave;
    'Tis sad to see it so,
Braving the storm, from which it can not go;
Fetters of ice the driving sleet is leaving,
Yet still to that cold branch we see it cleaving
'Neath sun, and moon, and winter's heaving
        Full of snow.

Type of a wilder, colder winter's reign;
Semblance of deeper, soul in wailing, pain:
    For well this world I know,
That it is very wide, and full of woe.
Cold, cold as here to-night, 'round hearts are wailing
Winds of dark grief, the spirit's features paling,
And millions walk this journey, weary, failing,
        Full of snow.

God knows of griefs that we know not, alone,
God knows of nests from which the bird is flown—
    Of hidden, silent woe,
That we pass by, and lose in life's great flow.
God sees the stricken mourner's secret weeping;
God sees the dark, cold shadow silent creeping
O'er hearts that cold distrust, or hate, is heaping
        Full of snow.

What does the wide world know of real life?
Ours, as it is, an inner, silent strife;
    Of thoughts that ever flow
Deep in the secret soul—what does it know?

In each soul's realm of being there's an ocean
Ever unknown to man, and yet in motion,
Shoreless and deep, with storms that have their portion
    Full of snow.

Green vales but tremble o'er earth's inner groans,
Daisies bloom white above the battle's bones;
    We surface gazers do not know
The hidden caves the ocean laves below.
There is a night that never knows a breaking
This side God's heaven; sun's-rise, and yet no waking;
Sleep on the lids of joy, and moments flaking
    Full of snow.

Have ye not felt it who have laid God's boon,
The loved and lovely, in the tearless tomb,
    Whom God has made, that every hour to know
When from its resting-place the bird must go?
Have ye not felt it who alone are treading
Paths on which love no light is longer shedding,
Which dire desertion, day and night, is spreading
    Full of snow?

See! as I linger here, the clouds droop nigh,
Winds, storm, and night rush howling from the sky;
    Hopeful, though sad, O God, to thee I go,
For thou art God of spring as well as snow.
I know the time is short; if we are steady,
A home beyond Time's falling flakes is ready,
Where o'er the vales, around God's feet, shall eddy
    No more snow.

LABOR.

Mrs. Frances S. Osgood.

Pause not to dream of the future before us,
Pause not to weep the wild cares that come o'er us:
Hark how Creation's deep musical chorus
    Unintermitting goes up into heaven!
Never the ocean-wave stops in its flowing;
Never the little seed stops in its growing;
More and more richly the rose-heart keeps glowing
    Till from its nourishing stem it is riven.

"Labor is worship!" the robin is singing:
"Labor is worship!" the wild bee is ringing:
Listen! that eloquent whisper upspringing

Speaks to thy soul from out nature's great heart.
From the dark cloud flows the life-giving shower;
From the rough sod blows the soft-breathing flower;
From the small insect the rich coral bower;
    Only man, in the plan, ever shrinks from his part.
Labor is life! 'Tis the still water faileth;
Idleness ever despaireth, bewaileth;
Keep the watch wound, for the dark rust assaileth;
    Flowers droop and die in the stillness of noon.
Labor is glory! the flying cloud lightens;
Only the waving wing changes and brightens;
Idle hearts only the dark future frightens:
    Play the sweet keys wouldst thou keep them in tune!
Labor is rest from the sorrows that greet us;
Rest from all petty vexations that meet us;
Rest from the sin-promptings that ever entreat us;
    Rest from the world-sirens that lure us to ill.
* Work—and pure slumbers shall wait on thy pillow;
Work—thou shalt ride over care's coming billow.
Lie not down wearied 'neath woe's weeping willow!
    Work with a stout heart and resolute will.

Labor is health! Lo! the husbandman reaping,
How through his veins goes the life-current leaping!
How his strong arm, in its stalwart pride sweeping,
    True as a sunbeam the swift sickle guides!
Labor is wealth—in the sea the pearl groweth;
Rich the queen's robe from the frail cocoon floweth;
From the fine acorn the strong forest bloweth;
    Temple and statue the marble block hides.

Droop not, though shame, sin, and anguish are round thee,
Bravely fling off the cold chain that hath bound thee;
Look to yon pure heaven smiling beyond thee;
    Rest not content in thy darkness—a clod!
Work for some good, be it ever so slowly!
Cherish some flower, be it ever so lowly;
Labor—all labor is noble and holy;
    Let thy great deeds be thy prayer to thy God.

GETHSEMANE.

E. CLEMENTINE HOWARTH.

I think, could I behold the bowers
    Where my Redeemer bent the knee,
And breathe the fragrance of the flowers
    Of sanctified Gethsĕm'ane,

And with my sinful lips once press
　　The turf on which my Savior trod,
Anointed thus, then could they bless,
　　And praise, and serve thee, O my God.

I know not if the Kĕdron brook
　　Doth water still the solemn glade,
Nor if it bears aught of the look
　　It bore when there our Savior prayed;
But, though the Kedron floweth not,
　　And thou art bare of flower or tree,
To *me* thou art earth's holiest spot,
　　Oh sanctified Gethsemane!

There is a sad and soothing charm
　　Even in thy name, oh sacred earth,
That stills like drop of magic balm,
　　The turbid waves of passion's birth;
And thou hast ever power to set
　　My captive heart from fetters free;
I only sin when I forget
　　The sorrows of Gethsemane.

'Tis said that every earthly sound
　　Goes trembling through the voiceless spheres,
Bearing its endless echoes round
　　The pathway of eternal years.
Ah! surely, then, the sighs that He
　　That midnight breathed, the zephyrs bore
From thy dim shades, Gethsemane,
　　To thrill the world for evermore.

I know not, but I fain would trace
　　O'er burning deserts long and wide,
That I might look upon the place
　　Where my Redeemer lived and died;
And fallen tower and broken wall
　　Of his loved city I would see,
And thou, the holiest spot of all,
　　Oh sanctified Gethsemane!

A BALLAD OF SIR JOHN FRANKLIN.

GEORGE H. BOKER.

"Oh whither sail you, Sir John Franklin?"
　　Cried a whaler in Baffin's Bay.
"To know if between the land and the pole
　　I may find a broad sea-way."

"I charge you back, Sir John Franklin,
  If you would live and thrive;
For between the land and the frozen pole
  No man may sail alive."

But lightly laughed the stout Sir John,
  And spoke unto his men :
"Half England is wrong if he is right;
  Bear off to westward, then!"

"Oh whither sail you, brave Englishman?"
  Cried the little Esquimaux.
"Between your land and the polar star
  My goodly vessels go."

"Come down, if you would journey there,"
  The little Indian said,
"And change your cloth for fur clothing,
  Your vessel for a sled."

But lightly laughed the stout Sir John,
  And the crew laughed with him too;
"A sailor to change from ship to sled
  I ween were something new!"

All through the long, long polar day
  The vessels westward sped,
And wherever the sail of Sir John was blown,
  The ice gave way and fled—

Gave way with many a hollow groan,
  And many a surly roar,
But it murmured and threatened on every side,
  And closed where he sailed before.

"Ho! see ye not, my merry men,
  The broad and open sea?
Bethink ye what the whaler said—
  Think of the little Indian's sled!"
  The crew laughed out in glee.

"Sir John! Sir John! 'tis bitter cold;
  The scud drives on the breeze;
The ice comes looming from the north;
  The very sunbeams freeze!"

The drifting icebergs dipped and rose,
  And floundered down the gale;
The ships were stayed, the yards were manned,
  And furled the useless sail.

"The summer's gone, the winter's come,
　We sail not on yonder sea;
Why sail we not, Sir John Franklin?"
　A silent man was he.

The cruel ice came floating on,
　And closed beneath the lee
Till the thickening waters dashed no more—
'Twas ice around, behind, before—
　"My God! there is no sea!"

"What think you of the whaler now?
　What of the Esquimaux?
A sled were better than a ship
　To cruise through ice and snow."

The snow came down, storm breeding storm,
　And on the decks was laid,
Till the weary sailor, sick at heart,
　Sank down beside his spade.

"Sir John, the night is black and long,
　The hissing wind is bleak;
The hard, green ice is strong as death;
　I pr'ythee, captain, speak!"

"The night is neither bright nor short;
　The stinging breeze is cold;
The ice is not so strong as hope!
　The heart of man is bold!"

　　*　　*　　*　　*　　*　　*

"Hark! heard ye not the noise of guns?
　And there—there—there again!
'Tis some uneasy iceberg's roar
　As he turns in the frozen main."

"Sir John, where are the English fields,
　And where are the English trees?
And where are the little English flowers
　That open to the breeze?"

"Be still, be still, my brave sailors!
　You shall see the fields again,
And smell the scent of the opening flowers—
　"But when, Sir John; but when?"

"Oh when shall I see my orphan child—
　My Mary that waits for me?
Oh when shall I see my old mother,
　And pray at her trembling knee?"

"Be still, be still, my brave sailors!
    Think not such thoughts again!"
But a tear froze slowly on his cheek—
    He thought of Lady Jane.

Ah! bitter, bitter grows the cold;
    The ice grows more and more;
More settled stare the wolf and bear—
    More patient than before.

"Oh think you, good Sir John Franklin,
    We'll ever see the land?
'Twas cruel to send us here to starve,
    Without a helping hand!

" 'Twas cruel, Sir John, to send us here,
    So far from help and home,
To starve and freeze on this lonely sea!
I ween the Lords of the Admiralty
    Would rather send than come."

"Oh, whether we starve to death alone,
    Or sail to our own country,
We have done what man has never done:
The truth is found—the secret won—
    We passed the northern sea!"

*   *   *   *   *   *

Long years went by. Hope died in fear,
    But never relented the frost.
Some letters that stood for the brave and dear,
And some oars and bones told the story drear—
    Then we knew what the secret cost!

THE KING OF DENMARK'S RIDE.

Mrs. Caroline Norton.

Word was brought to the Danish king
    (Hurry!)
That the love of his heart lay suffering,
And pined for the comfort his voice would bring.
    (Oh ride as if you were flying!)
Better he loves each golden curl
On the brow of that Scandinavian girl
Than his rich crown-jewels of ruby and pearl;
    And his Rose of the Isles is dying.

Thirty nobles saddled with speed;
    (Hurry!)
Each one mounted a gallant steed
Which he kept for battle and days of need;

(Oh ride as though you were flying!)
Spurs were struck in the foaming flank,
Worn-out chargers staggered and sank;
Bridles were slackened, and girths were burst;
But, ride as they would, the king rode first,
    For his Rose of the Isles lay dying.

His nobles are beaten one by one;
    (Hurry!)
They have fainted, and faltered, and homeward gone;
The little fair page now follows alone.
For strength and for courage trying,
The king looked back at that faithful child,
Wan was the face that answering smiled.
They passed the drawbridge with clattering din,
Then he dropped, and only the king rode in
    Where his Rose of the Isles lay dying.

The king blew a blast on his bugle-horn:
    (Silence!)
No answer came, but faint and forlorn
An echo returned on the cold gray morn,
    Like the breath of a spirit sighing.
The castle portal stood grimly wide;
None welcomed the king from that weary ride;
For, dead in the light of the dawning day,
The pale, sweet form of the welcomer lay,
    Who had yearned for his voice while dying.

The panting steed with a drooping crest
    Stood weary;
The king returned from the chamber of rest,
The thick sobs choking in his breast,
    And that dumb companion eying,
The tears gushed forth which he strove to check;
He bowed his head on his charger's neck:
"Oh steed, that every nerve didst strain—
Dear steed! our ride hath been in vain
    To the halls where my love lay dying!"

OVER THE RIVER.

                      MISS PRIEST.

Over the river they beckon to me—
    Loved ones who've crossed to the farther side;
The gleam of their snowy robes I see,
    But their voices are drowned in the rushing tide.

There's one with ringlets of sunny gold,
   And eyes the reflection of heaven's own blue;
He crossed in the twilight gray and cold,
   And the pale mist hid him from mortal view.
We saw not the angels who met him there;
   The gates of the city we could not see:
Over the river, over the river,
   My brother stands ready to welcome me!

Over the river the boatman pale
   Carried another—the household pet:
Her brown curls waved in the gentle gale—
   Darling Minnie! I see her yet.
She crossed on her bosom her dimpled hands,
   And fearlessly entered the phantom bark;
We watched it glide from the silver sands,
   And all our sunshine grew strangely dark.
We know she is safe on the farther side,
   Where all the ransomed and angels be:
Over the river, the mystic river,
   My childhood's idol is waiting for me.

For none return from those quiet shores
   Who cross with the boatman cold and pale·
We hear the dip of the golden oars,
   And catch a gleam of the snowy sail,
And lo! they have passed from our yearning heart;
   They cross the stream, and are gone for aye;
We may not sunder the veil apart
   That hides from our vision the gates of day.
We only know that their barks no more
   May sail with us o'er life's stormy sea;
Yet somewhere, I know, on the unseen shore
   They watch, and beckon, and wait for me.

And I sit and think, when the sunset's gold
   Is flushing river, and hill, and shore,
I shall one day stand by the water cold,
   And list for the sound of the boatman's oar.
I shall watch for a gleam of the flapping sail;
   I shall hear the boat as it gains the strand;
I shall pass from sight with the boatman pale
   To the better shore of the spirit land;
I shall know the loved who have gone before;
   And joyfully sweet will the meeting be,
When over the river, the peaceful river,
   The Angel of Death shall carry me.

YOUNG LOCHINVAR.

SIR WALTER SCOTT.

Oh, young Lochinvar is come out of the West,
Through all the wide Border his steed was the best,
And save his good broadsword he weapons had none;
He rode all unarmed, and he rode all alone.
So faithful in love, and so dauntless in war,
There never was knight like the young Lochinvar.

He staid not for brake, and he stopped not for stone,
He swam the Esk River where ford there was none;
But, ere he alighted at Netherby gate,
The bride had consented, the gallant came late:
For a laggard in love and a dastard in war
Was to wed the fair Ellen of brave Lochinvar.

So boldly he entered the Netherby hall,
'Mong bridemen, and kinsmen, and brothers, and all.
Then spoke the bride's father, his hand on his sword
(For the poor craven bridegroom said never a word),
"Oh come ye in peace here, or come ye in war,
Or to dance at our bridal,-young Lord Lochinvar?"

"I long wooed your daughter, my suit you denied;
Love swells like the Solway, but ebbs like its tide;
And now I am come, with this lost love of mine,
To lead but one measure, drink one cup of wine.
There be maidens in Scotland more lovely by far,
That would gladly be bride to the young Lochinvar."

The bride kissed the goblet; the knight took it up,
He quaffed off the wine, and he threw down the cup;
She looked down to blush, and she looked up to sigh,
With a smile on her lips, and a tear in her eye.
He took her soft hand ere her mother could bar—
"Now tread we a measure!" said young Lochinvar.

So stately his form, and so lovely her face,
That never a hall such a galliard did grace;
While her mother did fret, and her father did fume,
And the bridegroom stood dangling his bonnet and plume,
And the bridemaidens whispered, " 'Twere better by far
To have matched our fair cousin with young Lochinvar."

One touch to her hand, and one word in her ear,
When they reached the hall door, and the charger stood near,
So light to the croup the fair lady he swung,
So light to the saddle before her he sprung—

She is won! we are gone, over bank, bush, and scaur;
They'll have fleet steeds that follow," quoth young Lochinvar.
There was mounting 'mong Græmes of the Netherby clan;
Fosters, Fenwicks, and Musgraves, they rode and they ran;
There was racing and chasing on Cannobie Lea,
But the lost bride of Netherby ne'er did they see.
So daring in love, and so dauntless in war,
Have ye e'er heard of gallant like young Lochinvar?

THE INQUIRY.
CHARLES MACKAY.

 Tell me, ye winged winds,
  That round my pathway roar,
 Do you not know some spot
  Where mortals weep no more?
 Some lone and pleasant dell—
  Some valley in the West,
 Where, free from toil and pain,
  The weary soul may rest?
(>) The loud wind dwindled to a whisper low,
And sighed for pity as it answered (>) "No!"

 Tell me, thou mighty deep,
  Whose billows round me play,
 Knowest thou some favored spot—
  Some island far away,
 Where weary man may find
  The bliss for which he sighs
 Where sorrow never lives,
  And friendship never dies?
The loud waves, rolling in perpetual flow,
Stopped for a while, and sighed to answer (<>) "No!"

 And thou, serenest moon,
  That with such lovely face
 Dost look upon the earth,
  Asleep in night's embrace,
 Tell me, in all thy round,
  Hast thou not seen some spot
 Where miserable man
  Might find a happier lot
Behind a cloud the moon withdrew in woe,
And a voice sweet, but sad, responded "No!"

 Tell me, my secret soul—
  Oh tell me, Hope and Faith,

Is there no resting-place
  From sorrow, sin, and death?
Is there no happy spot
  Where mortals may be bless'd—
Where grief may find a balm,
  And weariness a rest?
Faith, Hope, and Love—best boons to mortals given—
Waved their bright wings, and whispered "Yes, in heaven!"

WOUNDED.
J. W. Watson.

Steady, boys, steady!
Keep your arms ready!
God only knows whom we may meet here.
  Don't let me be taken!
  I'd rather awaken
To-morrow in—no matter where,
Than lie in that foul prison-hole—over there.

  Step slowly!
  Speak lowly!
These rocks may have life.
Lay me down in this hollow;
We are out of the strife.
By heavens! the foeman may track me in blood,
For this hole in my breast is outpouring a flood.
No! no surgeon for me: he can give me no aid;
The surgeon I want is a pickaxe and spade.
What, Morris, a tear? why, shame on ye, man!
I thought you a hero; but since you've began
To whimper and cry, like a girl in her teens,
By George! I don't know what it all means.

Well! well! I am rough; 'tis a very rough school,
This life of a trooper—but yet I'm no fool!
I know a brave man, and a friend from a foe;
And, boys, that you love me, I certainly know.
  But wasn't it grand,
When they came down the hill over sloughing and sand?
But we stood—did we not—like immovable rock,
Unheeding their balls and repelling their shock?
  Did you mind the loud cry,
  When, as turning to fly,
Our men sprang upon them, determined to die?
  Oh, wasn't it grand?

God help the poor wretches that fell in the fight;
No time was there given for prayer or for flight.
They fell by the score, in the crash, hand to hand,
And they mingled their blood with the sloughing and sand.
                Huzza!
Great heavens! this bullet-hole gapes like a grave.
A curse on the aim of the treacherous knave!
Is there never a one of ye knows how to pray,
Or speak for a man as his life ebbs away?
                Pray!
                  Pray!
Our Father! Our Father! Why don't you proceed?
Can't you see I am dying? Great God, how I bleed!
Ebbing away!
       Ebbing away!
            The light of day
            Is turning to gray.
                Pray!
                  Pray!
Our Father in Heaven—boys, tell me the rest,
While I stanch the hot blood from this hole in my breast.
There's something about forgiveness of sin—
Put that in! put that in! and then
I'll follow your words, and say an amen.

Here, Morris, old fellow! get hold of my hand;
And Wilson, my comrade—oh, wasn't it grand,
When they came down the hill like a thunder-charged cloud,
And were scattered like dust by our brave little crowd?—
Where's Wilson—my comrade—here, stoop down your head—
Can't you say a short prayer for the dying and dead?

      "Dear Christ, who died for sinners all,
        Hear thou this suppliant wanderer's cry;
      Let not e'en this poor sparrow fall
        Unheeded by thy gracious eye.
      Throw wide thy gates to let him in,
        And take him, pleading, to thy arms;
      Forgive, O Lord! his life-long sin,
        And quiet all his fierce alarms."

God bless you, comrade, for singing that hymn;
It is light to my path when my sight has grown dim.
I am dying—bend down till I touch you once more—
Don't forget me, old fellow! God prosper this war!
Confusion to enemies!—keep hold of my hand—
And float our dear flag o'er a prosperous land!

WE MEET AND WE PART.

From "The Mystic Star."

There's a world where all are equal—
  We are hurrying toward it fast—
We shall meet upon the level there
  When the gates of death are pass'd.
We shall stand before the Orient,
  And our Master will be there,
To try the blocks we offer
  By his own unerring square.
We shall meet upon the level there,
  But never thence depart;
There's a mansion—'tis all ready—
  For each faithful, trusting heart.
There's a mansion and a welcome;
  And a multitude are there
Who have met upon the level
  And been tried upon the square.
Let us meet upon the level, then,
  While laboring patient here;
Let us meet and let us labor,
  Though the labor be severe.
Already, in the western sky,
  The signs bid us prepare
To gather up our working-tools
  And part upon the square.

BABY BUNN.

Josie H.

  Winsome Baby Bunn!
Brighter than the stars that rise
  In the dusky evening skies;
Browner than the robin's wing,
Clearer than the woodland spring,
Are the eyes of Baby Bunn—
  Winsome Baby Bunn!

  Smile, mother, smile!
Thinking softly all the while
  Of a tender, blissful day,
When the dark eyes, so like these
Of the cherub on your knees,
  Stole your girlish heart away.
Oh, the eyes of Baby Bunn!

Rarest 'mischief will they do
When once old enough to steal
   What their father stole from you!
   Smile, mother, smile!

     Winsome Baby Bunn!
Milk-white lilies half unrolled,
Set in calyces of gold,
Can not make his forehead fair,
With its rings of yellow hair!
Scarlet berry, cleft in twain
By a wedge of pearly grain,
Is the mouth of Baby Bunn—
    Winsome Baby Bunn!

   Weep, mother, weep
For the little one asleep
   With his head against your breast!
Never in the coming years,
Though he seeks for it with tears,
   Will he find so sweet a rest.
Oh, the breath of Baby Bunn!
Oh, the scarlet mouth of Bunn!
One man wears its crown of thorns;
Drink its cup of gall must one!
Though the trembling lips shall shrink,
White with anguish, as they drink,
And the temple sweat with pain
Drops of blood, like purple rain—
   Weep, mother, weep!

     Winsome Baby Bunn!
Not the sea-shell's palest tinge,
Not the daisy's rose-white fringe,
Not the softest, faintest glow
Of the sunset on the snow,
Is more beautiful and sweet
Than the wee pink hands and feet
Of the little Baby Bunn—
    Winsome Baby Bunn!
Feet like these may lose the way,
   Wandering blindly from the right;
Pray, and sometimes will your prayers
Be to him like golden stairs
   Built through darkness into light.
Oh, the dimpled feet of Bunn,
   In their silken stockings dressed!
Oh, the dainty hands of Bunn,
   Hid like rose-leaves in your breast!

These will grasp at jewels rare,
But to find them empty air;
Those will wander on the way—
  Pray, mother, pray!

DRIFTING.
T. B. READ.

My soul to-day
Is far away,
Sailing the Vesuvian Bay;
  My winged boat—
  A bird afloat—
Swims round the purple peaks remote.

Round purple peaks
It sails, and seeks
Blue inlets and their crystal creeks,
  Where high rocks throw
  Through deeps below
A duplicated golden glow.

Far, vague, and dim
The mountains swim,
While on Vesuvius's misty brim
  With outstretched hands
  The gray smoke stands,
O'erlooking the volcanic lands.

Here Ischia smiles
O'er liquid miles;
And yonder, bluest of the isles,
  Calm Capri waits,
  Her sapphire gates
Beguiling to her bright estates.

I heed not if
My rippling skiff
Float swift or slow from cliff to cliff;
  With dreamful eyes
  My spirit lies
Under the walls of Paradise.

Under the walls
Where swells and falls
The bay's deep breast at intervals,
  At peace I lie,
  Blown softly by
A cloud upon this liquid sky.

MISCELLANEOUS SELECTIONS.

   The day so mild
   Is Heaven's own child,
With Earth and Ocean reconciled;
   The airs I feel
   Around me steal
Are murmuring to the murmuring keel.

   Over the rail
   My hand I trail
Within the shadow of the sail;
   A joy intense—
   The cooling sense—
Glides down my drowsy indolence.

   With dreamful eyes
   My spirit lies
Where summer sings and never dies;
   O'erveiled with vines,
   She glows and shines
Among her future oils and wines.

   Her children hid
   The cliffs amid,
Are gamboling with the gamboling kid,
   Or down the walls,
   With tipsy calls,
Laugh on the rocks like waterfalls.

   The fisher's child,
   With tresses wild,
Unto the smooth, bright sand beguiled,
   With glowing lips
   Sings as she skips,
Or gazes at the far-off ships.

   Yon deep bark goes
   Where Traffic blows
From lands of sun to lands of snows;
   This happier one
   Its course is run
From lands of snow to lands of sun.

   Oh happy ship,
   To rise and dip
With the blue crystal at your lip!
   Oh happy crew,
   My heart with you
Sails and sails, and sings anew!

No more, no more
The worldly shore
Upbraids me with its loud uproar;
With dreamful eyes
My spirit lies
Under the walls of Paradise.

TO A MOUSE,

ON TURNING UP HER NEST WITH THE PLOW,
November, 1785.

ROBERT BURNS.

Wee, sleekit, cow'rin', tim'rous beastie,
Oh what a panic's in thy breastie!
Thou need na start awa sae hasty,
   Wi' bickering brattle;
I wad be laith to rin and chase thee
   Wi' murd'ring pattle!

I'm truly sorry man's dominion
Has broken nature's social union,
And justifies that ill opinion
   Which makes thee startle
At me, thy poor earth-born companion,
   And fellow-mortal!

I doubt na, whyles, but thou may thieve;
What then? poor beastie, thou maun live!
A daimen icker in a thrave
   'S a sma' request:
I'll get a blessin' wi' the laive,
   And never miss't!

Thy wee bit housie, too, in ruin,
Its silly wa's the win's are strewin',
And naething now to big a new ane
   O' foggage green,
And bleak December's winds ensuin',
   Baith snell and keen.

Thou saw the fields laid bare and waste,
And weary winter comin' fast,
And cozie here, beneath the blast,
   Thou thought to dwell,
Till, crash! the cruel coulter passed
   Out through thy cell.

That wee bit heap o' leaves and stibble
Has cost thee mony a weary nibble!
Now thou's turned out, for a' thy trouble,
    But house or hald,
To thole the winter's sleety dribble,
    And cranreuch cauld!

But, Mousie, thou art no thy lane,
In proving foresight may be vain:
The best-laid schemes o' mice and men
    Gang aft a-gley,.
And lea'e us nought but grief and pain
    For promised joy.

Still thou art bless'd compared wi' me;
The present only toucheth thee;
But, och! I backward cast my e'e
    On prospects drear;
And forward, though I canna see,
    I guess and fear.

THE MISER'S DEATH.

OSBORNE.

Note.—In France, during the year 1762, a miser by the name of Foscue, having amassed enormous wealth by extortion and parsimony, was requested by the government to advance a sum of money as a loan. The miser refused, pretending that he was poor. In order to hide his money, he dug a deep cellar under his hut, the descent to which was by a ladder. To the trap-door above he attached a spring-lock. He entered, one day, to gloat over his gold; the trap-door fell, the spring-lock snapped, and he died miserably.

So, so! all safe! Come forth, my pretty sparklers!
Come forth, and feast my eyes! Be not afraid!
No keen-eyed agent of the government
Can see you here. They wanted me, forsooth,
To lend you, at the lawful rate of usance,
For the state's needs. Ha! ha! my shining pets,
My yellow darlings, my sweet golden circlets!
Too well I loved you to do that; and so
I pleaded poverty, and none could prove
My story was not true.

                    Ha! could they see
These bags of ducats, and that precious pile
Of ingots, and those bars of solid gold,
Their eyes, methinks, would water. What a comfort

Is it to see my moneys in a heap,
All safely lodged under my very roof!
Here's a fat bag—let me untie the mouth of it.
What eloquence! What beauty! What expression!
Could Cicero so plead? Could Helen look
One half so charming? (*The trap-door falls.*)

       Ah! what sound was that?
The trap-door fallen? and the spring-lock caught?
Well, have I not the key? Of course I have!
'Tis in this pocket. No. In this? No. Then
I left it at the bottom of the ladder.
Ha! 'tis not there. Where, then? Ah! mercy, Heaven!
'Tis in the lock outside!
       What's to be done?
Help, help! Will no one hear? Oh, would that I
Had not discharged old Simon! but he begged
Each week for wages—would not give me credit.
I'll try my strength upon the door. Despair!
I might as soon uproot the eternal rocks
As force it open. Am I here a prisoner,
And no one in the house—no one at hand,
Or likely soon to be, to hear my cries?
Am I entombed alive? Horrible fate!
I sink—I faint beneath the bare conception! (*Swoons.*)

(*Awakes.*) Darkness! Where am I? I remember now:
This is a bag of ducats—'tis no dream—
No dream! The trap-door fell, and here am I,
Immured with my dear gold—my candle out—
All gloom—all silence—all despair! What ho!
Friends! Friends? I have no friends. What right have I
To use the name? These money-bags have been
The only friends I've cared for, and for these
I've toiled, and pinched, and screwed, shutting my heart
To charity, humanity, and love!

Detested traitors! since I gave you all—
Ay, gave my very soul—can ye do naught
For me in this extremity? Ho! without there!
A thousand ducats for a loaf of bread!
Ten thousand ducats for a glass of water!
A pile of ingots for a helping hand!
Was that a laugh? Ay, 'twas a fiend that laughed
To see a miser in the grip of death!

Offended Heaven, have mercy! I will give
In alms all this vile rubbish; aid me thou

In this most dreadful strait! I'll build a church—
A hospital! Vain, vain! Too late, too late!
Heaven knows the miser's heart too well to trust him!
Heaven will not hear—why should it? What have I
Done to enlist Heaven's favor?—to help on
Heaven's cause on earth, in human hearts and homes?
Nothing! God's kingdom will not come the sooner
For any work or any prayer of mine.

But must I die here—in my own trap caught?
Die—die? and then! Oh mercy! grant me time—
Thou who canst save—grant me a little time,
And I'll redeem the past—undo the evil
That I have done—make thousands happy with
This hoarded treasure—do thy will on earth
As it is done in heaven—grant me but time!
Nor man nor God will hear my shrieks! All's lost!

LITTLE BENNY.
A Christmas Carol.

I had told him Christmas morning,
    As he sat upon my knee,
Holding fast his little stockings,
    Stuffed as full as full could be,
And attentive, listening to me,
    With a face demure and mild,
That old Santa Claus, who filled them,
    Did not love a naughty child.

"But we'll be dood, won't we, moder?"
    And from off my lap he slid,
Digging deep among the goodies
    In his crimson stockings hid,
While I turned me to my table,
    Where a tempting goblet stood,
Brimming high with dainty custard
    Sent me by a neighbor good.

But the kitten, there before me,
    With his white paw, nothing loth,
Sat, by way of entertainment,
    Slapping off the shining froth;
And, in not the gentlest humor
    At the loss of such a treat,
I confess I rather rudely
    Thrust him out into the street.

Then how Benny's blue eyes kindled!
    Gathering up the precious store
He had busily been pouring
    In his tiny pinafore,
With a generous look that shamed me,
    Sprang he from the carpet bright,
Showing, by his mien indignant,
    All a baby's sense of right.

"Come back, Harney!" called he, loudly,
    As he held his apron white,
"You sall have my candy wabbit!"
    But the door was fastened tight;
So he stood, abashed and silent,
    In the centre of the floor,
With defeated look alternate
    Bent on me and on the door.

Then, as by some sudden impulse,
    Quickly ran he to the fire,
And while eagerly his bright eyes
    Watched the flames grow higher, higher
In a brave, clear key he shouted,
    Like some lordly little elf,
"Santa Kaus, tome down de chimney;
    Make my moder 'have herself!"

"I will be a good girl, Benny,"
    Said I, feeling the reproof;
And straightway recalled poor Harney,
    Mewing on the gallery roof.
Soon the anger was forgotten,
    Laughter chased away the frown,
And they gamboled 'neath the live-oaks
    Till the dusky night came down.

In my dim, fire-lighted chamber
    Harney purred beneath my chair,
And my play-worn boy beside me
    Knelt to say his evening prayer:
"God bess fader, God bess moder,
    God bess sister"—then a pause,
And the sweet young lips devoutly
    Murmured, "God bess Santa Kaus."

He is sleeping; brown and silken
    Lie the lashes, long and meek,
Like caressing, clinging shadows,
    On his plump and peachy cheek;

And I bend above him, weeping
Thankful tears, O Undefiled!
For a woman's crown of glory—
For the blessing of a child.

IVRY.
Thomas Babington Macaulay.

Now glory to the Lord of Hosts, from whom all glories are!
And glory to our sovereign liege, King Henry of Navärre'!
Now let there be the merry sound of music and of dance
Through thy corn-fields green, and sunny vines, oh pleasant land of France!
And thou, Rŏchĕlle', our own Rochelle, proud city of the waters,
Again let rapture light the eyes of all thy murmuring daughters;
As thou wert constant in our ills, be joyous in our joy,
For cold, and stiff, and still are they who wrought thy walls annoy.
Hurrah! hurrah! a single field hath turned the chance of war!
Hurrah! hurrah! for Ivry, and Henry of Navarre.

Oh! how our hearts were beating when, at the dawn of day,
We saw the army of the League drawn out in long array,
With all its priest-led citizens, and all its rebel peers,
And Appenzel's stout infantry, and Egmont's Flemish spears.
There rode the brood of false Lŏrräine', the curses of our land;
And dark Mäyĕnne' was in the midst, a truncheon in his hand;
And, as we looked on them, we thought of Seine's empurpled flood,
And good Coligni's hoary hair all dabbled with his blood;
And we cried unto the living God, who rules the fate of war,
To fight for his own holy name, and Henry of Navarre.

The king is come to marshal us, in all his armor dressed,
And he has bound a snow-white plume upon his gallant crest.
He looked upon his people, and a tear was in his eye;
He looked upon the traitors, and his glance was stern and high.
Right graciously he smiled on us, as rolled from wing to wing,
Down all our line, a deafening shout—"God save our lord the king!"
"And if my standard-bearer fall, as fall full well he may—
For never I saw promise yet of such a bloody fray—
Press where ye see my white plume shine amidst the ranks of war,
And be your oriflamme to-day the helmet of Navarre."

Hurrah! the foes are moving. Hark to the mingled din
Of fife, and steed, and trump, and drum, and roaring culverin.
The fiery duke is pricking fast across Saint Andre's plain,
With all the hireling chivalry of Guĕl'ders and Almäyne'.
Now by the lips of those ye love, fair gentlemen of France,
Charge for the golden lilies—upon them with the lance!
A thousand spurs are striking deep, a thousand spears in rest,
A thousand knights are pressing close behind the snow-white crest;

And in they burst, and on they rushed, while, like a guiding star,
Amidst the thickest carnage blazed the helmet of Navarre.
Now, God be praised, the day is ours: Mayenne hath turned his rein;
D'Aumale hath cried for quarter, the Flemish count is slain;
Their ranks are breaking like thin clouds before a Biscay gale;
The field is heaped with bleeding steeds, and flags, and cloven mail.
And then we thought on vengeance, and all along our van,
"Remember Saint Bartholomew!" was passed from man to man.
But out spake gentle Henry: "No Frenchman is my foe;
Down—down with every foreigner, but let your brethren go."
Oh! was there ever such a knight, in friendship or in war,
As our sovereign lord, King Henry, the soldier of Navarre?
Right well fought all the Frenchmen who fought for France to-day,
And many a lordly banner God gave them for a prey.
But we of the religion have borne us best in fight;
And the good Lord of Rŏs'ny hath ta'en the cornet white—
Our own true Maximilian the cornet white hath ta'en,
The cornet white, with crosses black, the flag of false Lorraine.
Up with it high; unfurl it wide, that all the host may know [woe.
How God hath humbled the proud house which wrought his church such
Then on the ground, while trumpets sound their loudest point of war,
Fling the red shreds, a footcloth meet for Henry of Navarre.

Ho! maidens of Vĭĕn'nä; ho! matrons of Lucerne'—
Weep, weep, and rend your hair for those who never shall return.
Ho! Philip, send, for charity, thy Mexican pistoles,
That Antwerp monks may sing a mass for thy poor spearmen's souls.
Ho! gallant nobles of the League, look that your arms be bright;
Ho! burghers of St. Genevieve, keep watch and ward to-night;
For our God hath crushed the tyrant, our God hath raised the slave,
And mocked the counsel of the wise, and the valor of the brave.
Then glory to his holy name, from whom all glories are,
And glory to our sovereign lord, King Henry of Navarre!

AUCTION EXTRAORDINARY.
LUCRETIA DAVIDSON.

I dreamed a dream in the midst of my slumbers,
And as fast as I dreamed it was coined into numbers;
My thoughts ran along in such beautiful metre,
I'm sure I ne'er saw any poetry sweeter.
It seemed that a law had been recently made
That a tax on old bachelors' pates should be laid;
And, in order to make them all willing to marry,
The tax was as large as a man could well carry.
The bachelors grumbled, and said 'twas no use—
'Twas a horrid injustice and horrid abuse,

And declared that, to save their own heart's-blood from spilling,
Of such a vile tax they would not pay a shilling.
But the rulers determined them still to pursue,
So they set all the bachelors up at vendue;
A crier was sent through the town to and fro,
To rattle his bell and his trumpet to blow,
And to call out to all he might meet in his way,
"Ho! forty old bachelors sold here to-day."
And presently all the old maids of the town,
Each in her very best bonnet and gown,
From thirty to sixty, fair, plain, red, and pale,
Of every description, all flocked to the sale.
The auctioneer then in his labors began,
And called out aloud, as he held up a man,
"How much for a bachelor—who wants to buy?"
In a twink every maiden responded "I—I!"
In short, at a highly extravagant price,
The bachelors all were sold off in a trice;
And forty old maidens, some younger, some older,
Each lugged an old bachelor home on her shoulder.

THE GAIN OF LOSS.

[From "Hymns of Hope and Faith."]

HORATIUS BONAR, D.D.

"*Nay, give me back my blossoms!*"
  Said the palm-tree to the Nile;
But the stream passed on, unheeding,
  With its old familiar smile.

"*Give back my golden ringlets!*"
  Said the palm-tree to the Nile;
But the stream swept on in silence,
  With its dimple and its smile.

With its dimple and its smile it passed—
  With its dimple and its smile,
All heedless of the palm's low wail,
  That sunny, sunny Nile!

By Rodah's island-garden,
  With its ripple and its smile;
By Shûbra's mystic hedgerows
  It swept, that glorious Nile!

By Gizeh's great palm-forest
  It flashed its stately smile—
By Bulak's river-harbor,
  That old, majestic Nile!

By pyramid and palace,
  With its never-ending smile;
By tomb, and mosque, and mazar,
  It flowed, that mighty Nile!

"Come, give me back my blossoms,"
  Sighed the palm-tree to the Nile;
But the river flowed unheeding,
  With its soft and silver smile.

With its soft and silver smile it flowed,
  With its soft and silver smile,
All heedless of the palm-tree's sigh,
  That strange, long-wandering Nile!

It seemed to say, "'Tis better far
  To leave your flowers to me;
I will bear their yellow beauty on
  To the wondering, wondering sea.

"'Tis better they should float away
  Upon my dusky wave,
Than find upon their native stem
  A useless home and grave.

"If your sweet flowers remain with you,
  Fruitless your boughs must be;
'Tis their departure brings the fruit.
  Give your bright flowers to me.

"Nay, ask not back your blossoms,"
  To the palm-tree said the Nile;
"Let me keep them," said the river,
  With its sweet and sunny smile.

And the palm gave up its blossoms
  To its friend so wise and old,
And saw them, all unsighing,
  Float down the river's gold.

The amber tresses vanished,
  And the clear spring-fragrance fled,
But the welcome fruit in clusters
  Came richly up instead.

'Tis thus we gain by losing,
  And win by failure here;
We doff the gleaming tinsel,
  The golden crown to wear.

Our sickness is our healing,
  Our weakness is our might;

Life is but Death's fair offspring,
And Day the child of Night.
'Tis thus we rise by setting—
Through darkness reach our day;
Our own way hourly losing,
To find the eternal way.

'Tis by defeat we conquer—
Grow rich by growing poor;
And from our largest givings
We draw our fullest store.

Then let the blossoms perish,
And let the fragrance go;
All the surer and the larger
Is the harvest we shall know.

All the sweeter and the louder
Our song of harvest-home,
When earth's ripe autumn smileth,
And the reaping-day has come.

THE FIREMAN.
R. T. CONRAD.

The city slumbers. O'er its mighty walls
Night's dusky mantle soft and silent falls;
Sleep o'er the world slow waves its wand of lead,
And ready torpors wrap each sinking head.
Stilled is the stir of labor and of life;
Hushed is the hum, and tranquillized the strife.
Man is at rest, with all his hopes and fears;
The young forget their sports, the old their cares;
The grave are careless; those who joy or weep,
All rest contented on the arm of sleep.

Sweet is the pillowed rest of beauty now,
And slumber smiles upon her tranquil brow;
Her bright dreams lead her to the moonlit tide,
Her heart's own partner wandering by her side.
'Tis a summer's eve: the soft gales scarcely rouse
The low-voiced ripple and the rustling boughs;
And faint and far, some minstrel's melting tone
Breathes to her heart a music like its own.

(*asp.*) When, hark! oh horror! what a crash is there!
What shriek is that which fills the midnight air?
(*ff.*) 'Tis "FIRE! FIRE!" She wakes to dream no more!
The hot blast rushes through the blazing door!

The dim smoke eddies round; and hark! that cry!
(ƒ.) "Help! help! Will no one aid? I die—I die!"
She seeks the casement; shuddering at its height,
She turns again; the fierce flames mock her flight;
Along the crackling stairs they fiercely play,
And roar, exulting, as they seize their prey.
(ƒ.) "Help! help! Will no one come?" She says no more,
But, pale and breathless, sinks upon the floor.

Will no one save thee? Yes, there yet is one
Remains to save, when hope itself is gone;
When all have fled—when all but he would fly,
The *fireman* comes to rescue or to die!
He mounts the stair—it wavers 'neath his tread;
He seeks the room—flames flashing round his head;
He bursts the door, he lifts her prostrate frame,
And turns again to brave the raging flame.
The fire-blast smites him with its stifling breath,
The falling timbers menace him with death,
The sinking floors his hurried steps betray,
And ruin crashes round his desperate way;
Hot smoke obscures—ten thousand cinders rise—
Yet still he staggers forward with his prize.
(ƒ.) He leaps from burning stair to stair. On! on!
Courage! One effort more, and all is won!
The stair is passed—the blazing hall is braved!
(ƒ.) Still on! Yet on! Once more! Thank Heaven, she's saved!

THE PICKET-GUARD.

"All quiet along the Potomac," they say,
 Except now and then a stray picket
Is shot, as he walks on his beat to and fro,
 By a rifleman hid in the thicket.
'Tis nothing: a private or two, now and then,
 Will not count in the news of a battle;
Not an officer lost—only one of the men,
 Moaning out all alone the death-rattle.

All quiet along the Potomac to-night,
 Where the soldiers lie peacefully dreaming;
Their tents in the rays of the clear autumn moon,
 Or the light of the watch-fires are gleaming.
A tremulous sigh as the gentle night-wind
 Through the forest-leaves softly is creeping,
While the stars up above, with their glittering eyes,
 Keep guard, for the army is sleeping.

There's only the sound of the lone sentry's tread
    As he tramps from the rock to the fountain,
And thinks of the two in the low trundle-bed
    Far away in the cot on the mountain.
His musket falls slack; his face, dark and grim,
    Grows gentle with memories tender,
As he mutters a prayer for the children asleep—
    For their mother—may Heaven defend her!

The moon seems to shine just as brightly as then—
    That night when the love, yet unspoken,
Leaped up to his lips—when low, murmured vows
    Were pledged to be ever unbroken.
Then, drawing his sleeve roughly over his face,
    He dashes off tears that are welling,
And gathers his gun closer up to its place,
    As if to keep down the heart-swelling.

He passes the fountain, the blasted pine-tree;
    The footstep is lagging and weary;
Yet onward he goes, through the broad belt of light,
    Toward the shade of the forest so dreary.
Hark! was it the night-wind that rustled the leaves?
    Was it moonlight so wond'rously flashing?
It looked like a rifle: "Ha! Mary, good-by,"
    And the life-blood is ebbing and plashing.

All quiet along the Potomac to-night—
    No sound save the rush of the river,
While soft falls the dew on the face of the dead—
    The picket's off duty forever.

JESUS' SEAT.*

Miss F. Eastwood.

Far, far away o'er the deep blue sea
Lived a man who was kind as kind could be.
He loved little children, and spread every day
A table from which none went empty away.
Poor children came in from the alley and street,
With rags on their backs, and no shoes on their feet;
Girls and boys, large and small, some naughty and rude,
But John Falk loved them all and did them all good.
And while they were eating, he often would tell
Of the Lord Jesus Christ, who on earth did once dwell;
How he loved little children—each one of them there
He was watching from heaven with tenderest care—

    * Published by the American Tract Society.

And how happy and blessed would be the child's part
Who would let that dear Savior come dwell in his heart.
Each day, when the children assembled to eat,
He taught them to offer this grace for their meat:
"Bless, Jesus, the food thou hast given us to-day,
And come and sup with us, dear Jesus, we pray."
But once, when the children had finished this prayer,
One poor little fellow stood still by his chair
For a moment, then ran to the closet where stood
The bright cups of tin and the platters of wood.
"Now what is the matter?" said Falk to the child.
The little one looked in his kind face, and smiled:
"We asked the Lord Jesus just now, in our grace,
To sup with us here, but we've given him no place.
If he should come in, how sad it would be!
But I'll put him a stool close here beside me."
Then the boy, quite contented, sat down to his food;
He was hungry and tired, and his supper was good.
But a few moments after, he heard at the door
A knock low and timid—one knock, and no more.
He started to open it, hoping to meet
The Lord Jesus Christ come to look for his seat;
But when it was open, he no one could see
But a poor little child much poorer than he;
His face blue with hunger; his garments, so old,
Were dripping with rain; and he shivered with cold.
"Come in!" cried the boy, in a tone of delight;
"I suppose the Lord Christ could not come here to-night,
Though we asked him to come and partake of our bread,
So he's just sent you down to us here in his stead.
The supper is good, and we'll each give you some,
And tell the Lord Christ we are glad you have come."
From that time, when the children assembled to eat,
There was always one place called "the Lord Jesus' seat;"
And the best that they had was placed there each day
For one who was poorer and hungrier than they.
And the Lord Jesus Christ, in reply to their grace,
Sent always some person to sit in his place;
And sweet was the food that the Lord did provide
For the stranger he sent them to eat at their side.
Dear friends, who have heard this short story, you know
The words that our Savior once spake when below:
If we wish for his presence to hallow our bread,
We must welcome the stranger he sends in his stead.
When we set out our feasts, this our motto must be,
"As ye do to my poor, ye have done unto me!"

ABOU BEN ADHEM.
LEIGH HUNT.

Abou Ben Adhem (may his tribe increase!)
Awoke one night from a deep dream of peace,
And saw within the moonlight in his room,
Making it rich and like a lily in bloom,
An angel writing in a book of gold:
Exceeding peace had made Ben Adhem bold,
And to the Presence in the room he said,
"What writest thou?" The vision raised its head,
And, with a look made of all sweet accord,
Answered, "The names of those who love the Lord."
"And is mine one?" said Abou. "Nay, not so,"
Replied the angel. Abou spoke more low,
But cheerly still; and said, "I pray thee, then,
Write me as one that loves his fellow-men."
The angel wrote, and vanish'd. The next night
It came again, with a great wakening light,
And showed the names whom love of God had blessed,
And, lo! Ben Adhem's name led all the rest.

DORA.
ALFRED TENNYSON.

With Farmer Allan at the farm abode
William and Dora. William was his son,
And she his niece. He often look'd at them,
And often thought "I'll make them man and wife."
Now Dora felt her uncle's will in all,
And yearn'd towards William; but the youth, because
He had been always with her in the house,
Thought not of Dora.
    Then there came a day
When Allan call'd his son, and said, "My son,
I married late, but I would wish to see
My grandchild on my knees before I die:
And I have set my heart upon a match.
Now therefore look to Dora; she is well
To look to; thrifty too beyond her age.
She is my brother's daughter: he and I
Had once hard words, and parted, and he died
In foreign lands; but for his sake I bred
His daughter Dora; take her for your wife;
For I have wish'd this marriage, night and day,

O

For many years." But William answer'd short:
"I can not marry Dora; by my life,
I will not marry Dora." Then the old man
Was wroth, and doubled up his hands, and said,
"You will not, boy! you dare to answer thus!
But in my time a father's word was law,
And so it shall be now for me. Look to it:
Consider, William: take a month to think,
And let me have an answer to my wish,
Or, by the Lord that made me, you shall pack,
And never more darken my doors again."
But William answered madly; bit his lips,
And broke away. The more he looked at her
The less he liked her; and his ways were harsh;
But Dora bore them meekly. Then before
The month was out he left his father's house,
And hired himself to work within the fields;
And half in love, half spite, he wooed and wed
A laborer's daughter, Mary Morrison.

 Then, when the bells were ringing, Allan call'd
His niece and said, "My girl, I love you well;
But if you speak with him that was my son,
Or change a word with her he calls his wife,
My home is none of yours. My will is law."
And Dora promised, being meek. She thought,
"It can not be: my uncle's mind will change!"

 And days went on, and there was born a boy
To William; then distresses came on him;
And day by day he passed his father's gate,
Heart-broken, and his father helped him not.
But Dora stored what little she could save,
And sent it them by stealth, nor did they know
Who sent it; till at last a fever seized
On William, and in harvest-time he died.

 Then Dora went to Mary. Mary sat
And looked with tears upon her boy, and thought
Hard things of Dora. Dora came and said,
"I have obeyed my uncle until now,
And I have sinned, for it was all through me
This evil came on William at the first.
But, Mary, for the sake of him that's gone,
And for your sake, the woman that he chose,
And for this orphan, I am come to you:
You know there has not been for these five years
So full a harvest: let me take the boy,
And I will set him in my uncle's eye

Among the wheat; that when his heart is glad
Of the full harvest, he may see the boy,
And bless him for the sake of him that's gone."
    And Dora took the child, and went her way
Across the wheat, and sat upon a mound
That was unsown, where many poppies grew.
Far off the farmer came into the field
And spied her not; but none of all his men
Dare tell him Dora waited with the child;
And Dora would have risen and gone to him,
But her heart failed her; and the reapers reaped,
And the sun fell, and all the land was dark.
    But when the morrow came, she rose and took
The child once more, and sat upon the mound;
And made a little wreath of all the flowers
That grew about, and tied it round his hat,
To make him pleasing in her uncle's eye.
Then, when the farmer passed into the field,
He spied her, and he left his men at work,
And came and said, "Where were you yesterday?
Whose child is that? What are you doing here?"
So Dora cast her eyes upon the ground,
And answer'd softly, "This is William's child!"
"And did I not," said Allan, "did I not
Forbid you, Dora?" Dora said again,
"Do with me as you will, but take the child,
And bless him for the sake of him that's gone!"
And Allan said, "I see it is a trick
Got up betwixt you and the woman there.
I must be taught my duty, and by you!
You knew my word was law, and yet you dared
To slight it. Well—for I will take the boy;
But go you hence, and never see me more."
    So saying, he took the boy, that cried aloud
And struggled hard. The wreath of flowers fell
At Dora's feet. She bowed upon her hands,
And the boy's cry came to her from the field,
More and more distant. She bowed down her head,
Remembering the day when first she came,
And all the things that had been. She bowed down
And wept in secret; and the reapers reaped,
And the sun fell, and all the land was dark.
    Then Dora went to Mary's house, and stood
Upon the threshold. Mary saw the boy
Was not with Dora. She broke out in praise
To God, that helped her in her widowhood.

And Dora said, "My uncle took the boy;
But, Mary, let me live and work with you:
He says that he will never see me more."
Then answered Mary, "This shall never be,
That thou shouldst take my trouble on thyself;
And, now I think, he shall not have the boy,
For he will teach him hardness, and to slight
His mother; therefore thou and I will go,
And I will have my boy, and bring him home;
And I will beg of him to take thee back;
But if he will not take thee back again,
Then thou and I will live within one house,
And work for William's child until he grows
Of age to help us."

              So the women kiss'd
Each other, and set out, and reached the farm.
The door was off the latch: they peeped, and saw
The boy set up betwixt his grandsire's knees,
Who thrust him in the hollows of his arm,
And clapped him on the hands and on the cheeks,
Like one that loved him; and the lad stretched out
And babbled for the golden seal that hung
From Allan's watch, and sparkled by the fire.
Then they came in; but when the boy beheld
His mother, he cried out to come to her;
And Allan sat him down, and Mary said,

    "Oh father—if you let me call you so—
I never came a-begging for myself,
Or William, or this child; but now I come
For Dora: take her back; she loves you well.
Oh sir, when William died, he died at peace
With all men; for I asked him, and he said
He could not ever rue his marrying me.
I had been a patient wife; but, sir, he said
That he was wrong to cross his father thus:
'God bless him!' he said, 'and may he never know
The troubles I have gone through!' Then he turned
His face and passed—unhappy that I am!
But now, sir, let me have my boy, for you
Will make him hard, and he will learn to slight
His father's memory; and take Dora back,
And let all this be as it was before."

    So Mary said, and Dora hid her face
By Mary. There was silence in the room;
And all at once the old man burst in sobs:

    "I have been to blame—to blame. I have killed my son.

I have killed him—but I loved him—my dear son!
May God forgive me!—I have been to blame.
Kiss me, my children."
     Then they clung about
The old man's neck, and kissed him many times.
And all the man was broken with remorse;
And all his love came back a hundred fold;
And for three hours he sobbed o'er William's child,
Thinking of William.
    So those four abode
Within one house together; and as years
Went forward, Mary took another mate;
But Dora lived unmarried till her death.

THE BUGLE SONG.
ALFRED TENNYSON.

 The splendor falls on castle walls,
  And snowy summits old in story;
 The long light shakes across the lakes,
  And the wild cataract leaps in glory.
Blow, bugle, blow! set the wild echoes flying;
Blow, bugle; answer, echoes, dying, dying, dying.

 Oh hark! oh hear! how thin and clear,
  And thinner, clearer, farther going;
 Oh sweet and far, from cliff and scar,
  The horns of Elfland faintly blowing.
Blow! let us hear the purple glens replying;
Blow, bugle; answer, echoes, dying, dying, dying.

 Oh love, they die in yon rich sky,
  They faint on hill, on field, on river;
 Our echoes roll from soul to soul,
  And grow forever and forever.
Blow, bugle, blow! set the wild echoes flying;
And answer, echoes, answer, dying, dying, dying.

LITTLE GRETCHEN.
FROM THE GERMAN.

Little Gretchen, little Gretchen wanders up and down the street;
The snow is on her yellow hair, the frost is at her feet.
The rows of long, dark houses without look cold and damp
By the struggling of the moonbeam, by the flicker of the lamp.
The clouds ride fast as horses, the wind is from the north,
But no one cares for Gretchen, and no one looketh forth.

Within those dark, damp houses are merry faces bright,
And happy hearts are watching out the old year's latest night.
With the little box of matches she could not sell all day,
And the thin, thin tattered mantle the wind blows every way,
She clingeth to the railing, she shivers in the gloom—
There are parents sitting snugly by firelight in the room;
And children with grave faces are whispering one another
Of presents for the new year, for father or for mother.
But no one talks to Gretchen, and no one hears her speak,
No breath of little whisperers comes warmly to her cheek.

No little arms are round her: ah me! that there should be,
With so much happiness on earth, so much of misery!
Sure they of many blessings should scatter blessings round,
As laden boughs in autumn fling their ripe fruits to the ground.
And the best love man can offer to the God of love, be sure,
Is kindness to his little ones, and bounty to his poor.
Little Gretchen, little Gretchen goes coldly on her way;
There's no one looketh out at her, there's no one bids her stay.

Her home is cold and desolate; no smile, no food, no fire,
But children clamorous for bread, and an impatient sire.
So she sits down in an angle where two great houses meet,
And she curleth up beneath her, for warmth, her little feet;
And she looketh on the cold wall, and on the colder sky,
And wonders if the little stars are bright fires up on high.
She hears a clock strike slowly, up in a far church tower,
With such a sad and solemn tone, telling the midnight hour.

And she remembered her of tales her mother used to tell,
And of the cradle-songs she sang, when summer's twilight fell;
Of good men and of angels, and of the Holy Child,
Who was cradled in a manger, when winter was most wild;
Who was poor, and cold, and hungry, and desolate and lone;
And she thought the song had told he was ever with his own;
And all the poor, and hungry, and forsaken ones are his—
"How good of Him to look on me in such a place as this!"

Colder it grows and colder, but she does not feel it now,
For the pressure at her heart, and the weight upon her brow;
But she struck one little match on the wall so cold and bare,
That she might look around her, and see if He were there.
The single match has kindled, and by the light it threw,
It seemed to little Gretchen the wall was rent in two;
And she could see folks seated at a table richly spread,
With heaps of goodly viands, red wine and pleasant bread.

She could smell the fragrant savor, she could hear what they did say,
Then all was darkness once again—the match had burned away.

She struck another hastily, and now she seemed to see
Within the same warm chamber a glorious Christmas tree.
The branches were all laden with things that children prize,
Bright gifts for boy and maiden—she saw them with her eyes.
And she almost seemed to touch them, and to join the welcome shout,
When darkness fell around her, for the little match was out.

Another, yet another, she has tried—they will not light;
Till all her little store she took, and struck with all her might:
And the whole miserable place was lighted with the glare,
And she dreamed there stood a little child before her in the air.
There were blood-drops on his forehead, a spear-wound in his side,
And cruel nail-prints in his feet, and in his hands spread wide.
And he looked upon her gently, and she felt that he had known
Pain, hunger, cold, and sorrow—ay, equal to her own.
And he pointed to the laden board and to the Christmas tree,
Then up to the cold sky, and said, "Will Gretchen come with me?"
The poor child felt her pulses fail, she felt her eyeballs swim,
And a ringing sound was in her ears, like her dead mother's hymn:
And she folded both her thin white hands, and turned from that bright board,
And from the golden gifts, and said, "With thee, with thee, O Lord!"
The chilly winter morning breaks up in the dull skies
On the city wrapped in vapor, on the spot where Gretchen lies.

In her scant and tattered garment, with her back against the wall,
She sitteth cold and rigid, she answers to no call.
They have lifted her up fearfully, they shuddered as they said,
"It was a bitter, bitter night! the child is frozen dead."
The angels sang their greeting for one more redeemed from sin;
Men said, "It was a bitter night; would no one let her in?"
And they shivered as they spoke of her, and sighed. They could not see
How much of happiness there was after that misery.

THERE'S BUT ONE PAIR OF STOCKINGS TO MEND TO-NIGHT.

An old wife sat by her bright fireside,
   Swaying thoughtfully to and fro,
In an ancient chair whose creaky craw
   Told a tale of long ago;
While down by her side on the kitchen floor
Stood a basket of worsted balls—a score.

The good man dozed o'er the latest news
   Till the fire of his pipe went out;
And, unheeded, the kitten, with cunning paws,
   Rolled out and tangled the balls about;

Yet still sat the wife in the ancient chair,
  Swaying to and fro in the firelight glare.
But anon a misty tear-drop came
  In her eye of faded blue,
Then trickled down in a furrow deep,
  Like a single drop of dew;
So deep was the channel, so silent the stream,
The good man saw naught but the dimmed eye-beam.

Yet marveled he much that the cheerful light
  Of her eye had weary grown,
And marveled he more at the tangled balls:
  So he said, in a gentle tone,
"I have shared thy joys since our marriage vow,
Conceal not from me thy sorrows now."

Then she spoke of the time when the basket there
  Was filled to the very brim,
And now there remained of the goodly pile
  But a single pair—for him;
Then wonder not at the dimmed eye-light:
There's but one pair of stockings to mend to-night.

I can not but think of the busy feet
  Whose wrappings were wont to lay
In the basket, awaiting the needle's time—
  Now wandered so far away;
How the sprightly steps, to a mother dear,
Unheeded fall on the careless ear.

For each empty nook in the basket old,
  By the hearth there's an empty seat:
And I miss the shadows from off the wall,
  And the patter of many feet:
'Tis for this that a tear gathered over my sight,
At the one pair of stockings to mend to-night.

'Twas said that far through the forest wild,
  And over the mountains bold,
Was a land whose rivers and darkening caves
  Were gemmed with the fairest gold;
Then my first-born turned from the oaken door,
And I knew the shadows were only four.

Another went forth on the foaming wave,
  And diminished the basket's store;
But his feet grew cold—so weary and cold
  They'll never be warm any more;
And this nook, in its emptiness, seemeth to me
To give back no voice but the moan of the sea.

Two others have gone toward the setting sun,
And made them a home in its light,
And fairy fingers have taken their share,
To mend by the fireside bright;
Some other baskets their garments fill—
But mine! oh! mine is emptier still.
Another—the dearest—the fairest—the best—
Was taken by angels away,
And clad in a garment that waxeth not old,
In a land of continual day.
Oh, wonder no more at the dimmed eye-light,
While I mend the one pair of stockings to-night.

THE STARLESS CROWN.*

"They that turn many to righteousness shall shine as the stars forever and ever."—*Dan.* xii., 3.

Wearied and worn with earthly cares, I yielded to repose,
And soon before my raptured sight a glorious vision rose:
I thought, while slumbering on my couch in midnight's solemn gloom,
I heard an angel's silvery voice, and radiance filled my room.
A gentle touch awakened me; a gentle whisper said,
"Arise, oh sleeper; follow me;" and through the air we fled.
We left the earth so far away that like a speck it seemed,
And heavenly glory, calm and pure, across our pathway streamed.
Still on we went; my soul was rapt in silent ecstasy:
I wondered what the end would be, what next should meet mine eye.
I knew not how we journeyed through the pathless field of light,
When suddenly a change was wrought, and I was clothed in white.
We stood before a city's walls most glorious to behold;
We passed through gates of glistening pearl, o'er streets of purest gold;
It needed not the sun by day, the silver moon by night;
The glory of the Lord was there, the Lamb himself its light.
Bright angels paced the shining streets, sweet music filled the air,
And white-robed saints, with glittering crowns, from every clime were there
And some that I had loved on earth stood with them round the throne,
"All worthy is the Lamb," they sang, "the glory his alone."
But fairer far than all besides, I saw my Savior's face;
And as I gazed he smiled on me with wondrous love and grace.
Lowly I bowed before his throne, o'erjoyed that I at last
Had gained the object of my hopes; that earth at length was past.
And then in solemn tones he said, "Where is the diadem
That ought to sparkle on thy brow—adorned with many a gem?
I know thou hast believed on me, and life through me is thine;
But where are all those radiant stars that in thy crown should shine?

* Published by the American Tract Society.

Yonder thou seest a glorious throng, and stars on every brow;
For every soul they led to me they wear a jewel now.
And such *thy* bright reward had been if such had been thy deed,
If thou hadst sought some wandering feet in paths of peace to lead.
Thou wert not called that thou shouldst tread the way of life alone,
But that the clear and shining light which round thy footsteps shone
Should guide some other weary feet to my bright home of rest,
And thus, in blessing those around, thou hadst thyself been blest."

* * * * * * * *

The vision faded from my sight, the voice no longer spake,
A spell seemed brooding o'er my soul which long I feared to break,
And when at last I gazed around in morning's glimmering light,
My spirit felt o'erwhelmed beneath that vision's awful might.
I rose and wept with chastened joy that yet I dwelt below,
That yet another hour was mine my faith by works to show;
That yet some sinner I might tell of Jesus' dying love,
And help to lead some weary soul to seek a home above.
And now, while on the earth I stay, my motto this shall be,
"To live no longer to myself, but Him who died for me."
And graven on my inmost soul this word of truth divine,
"They that turn many to the Lord bright as the stars shall shine."

ONLY WAITING.

[A very aged man, in an alms-house, was asked what he was doing now. He replied, "Only waiting."]

  Only waiting till the shadows
   Are a little longer grown;
  Only waiting till the glimmer
   Of the day's last beam is flown;
  Till the night of earth is faded
   From the heart once full of day;
  Till the stars of heaven are breaking
   Through the twilight soft and gray.

  Only waiting till the reapers
   Have the last sheaf gathered home,
  For the summer-time is faded,
   And the autumn winds have come.
  Quickly, reapers! gather quickly
   The last ripe hours of my heart;
  For the bloom of life is withered,
   And I hasten to depart.

  Only waiting till the angels
   Open wide the mystic gate,
  Where I so long have lingered
   Weary, poor, and desolate.

Even now I hear the footsteps,
And their voices far away;
If they call me, I am waiting—
Only waiting to obey.

Only waiting till the shadows
Are a little longer grown;
Only waiting till the glimmer
Of the day's last beam is flown;
Then from out the gathering darkness
Holy, deathless stars shall rise,
By whose light my soul shall gladly
Tread its pathway to the skies.

"I'M MUSTERED OUT."

Just here, in the shade of this cannon-torn tree,
Here, low on the trampled grass, where I may see
The surge of the combat, and where I may hear
The glad cry of victory, cheer upon cheer,
    Let me lie down.

    Oh, it was grand!
Like the tempest we charged, in the triumph to share;
The tempest—its fury and thunder were there;
On, on, o'er intrenchments, o'er living and dead,
With the foe under foot, and our flag overhead:
    Oh, it was grand!

    Weary and faint,
Prone on the soldier's couch, ah! how can I rest
With this shot-shattered head and sabre-pierced breast?
Comrades, at roll-call, when I shall be sought,
Say I fought till I fell, and fell where I fought—
    Wounded and faint.

    Oh, that last charge!
Right through the dread hell-fire of shrapnel and shell,
Through without faltering—clear through with a yell,
Right in their midst, in the turmoil and gloom,
Like heroes we dashed at the mandate of doom.
    Oh, that last charge!

    It was duty.
Some things are worthless, and some others so good
That nations who buy them pay only in blood;
For Freedom and Union each man owes a part,
And here I pay my share all warm from my heart:
    It is duty.

Dying at last!
My mother, dear mother, with meek, tearful eye,
Farewell; and God bless you, forever and aye!
Oh that I now lay on your pillowing breast,
To breathe my last sigh on the bosom first press'd:
    Dying at last!
        I am no saint;
But, boys, say a prayer. There's one that begins
"Our Father," and then says, "Forgive us our sins:"
Don't forget that part; say that strongly; and then
I'll try to repeat it, and you'll say Amen.
        Ah! I'm no saint.
        Hark! there's a shout!
Raise me up, comrades—we have conquered, I know—
Up, on my feet, with my face to the foe.
Ah! there flies the flag, with its star-spangles bright,
The promise of glory, the symbol of right.
        Well may they shout.
        —I'm mustered out.
O God of our fathers, our freedom prolong,
And tread down Rebellion, Oppression, and Wrong!
O land of earth's hope, on thy blood-reddened sod,
I die for the Nation, the Union, and God!
        I'm mustered out.

WHERE DOES THE WATER SPRING.

Where does the water spring, gladsome and bright?
    Here in the leafy grove,
    Bubbling in life and love,
Born of the sunshine, up-leaping to light,
    Waked in its pebbly bed
    When the still shadows fled,
Gushing, o'erflowing, down-tumbling for flight.
Where does the water flow? Where glides the rill?
    Now 'neath the forest shade,
    Then in the grassy glade,
Dancing as freely as child of the hill;
    Bright cascades leaping,
    Silver brooks creeping,
Wearing the mountains, and turning the mill.
Where does the water dwell powerful and grand?
    Here where the ocean foam
    Breaks in its rocked-ribbed home,
Dashing, land-lashing, upbounding, wrath spanned;

Anon, sweetly sleeping,
Soft dimples o'ercreeping,
Like a babe on its mother's breast, soothed by her hand.
Where smiles the dew-drop the night shadows woo?
Where the young flow'rets dip,
Leaving each perfumed lip
Close in the rose's heart, loving and true;
Poised on an emerald shaft
Where never sunbeam laughed,
Deep in the dingle—the beautiful dew!

THE BRIDES OF ENDERBY; OR, THE HIGH TIDE.

JEAN INGELOW.

  The old mayor climbed the belfry tower,
  The ringers ran by two, by three;
(*f.*) "Pull, if ye never pulled before;
  Good ringers, pull your best," quoth he.
  "Play uppe, play uppe, oh Boston bells!
  Ply all your changes, all your swells,
  Play uppe 'The Brides of Enderby.'"

  Men say it was a stolen tyde—
  The Lord that sent it, He knows all;
  But in myne ears doth still abide
  The message that the bells let fall:
  And there was naught of strange beside
  The flights of mews and peewits pied
  By millions crouched on the old sea wall.

  I sat and spun within the doore;
  My thread brake off, I raised myne eyes;
  The level sun, like ruddy ore,
  Lay sinking in the barren skies;
  And dark against day's golden death
  She moved where Lindis wandereth,
  My sonne's faire wife, Elizabeth.

  "Cusha! Cusha! Cusha!" calling,
  Ere the early dews were falling,
  Farre away I heard her song.
(*p.*) "Cusha! Cusha!" all along;
  Where the reedy Lindis floweth,
   Floweth, floweth,
  From the meads where melick groweth,
  Faintly came her milking song.

(>) "Cusha! Cusha! Cusha!" calling,
  "For the dews will soone be falling;

Leave your meadow-grasses mellow,
    Mellow, mellow;
Quit your cowslips, cowslips yellow;
Come uppe, Whitefoot; come uppe, Lightfoot;
Quit the stalks of parsley hollow,
    Hollow, hollow;
Come uppe, Jetty, rise and follow;
From the clovers lift your head;
Come uppe, Whitefoot; come uppe, Lightfoot;
Come uppe, Jetty; rise and follow,
Jetty, to the milking-shed."

If it be long, aye, long ago,
    When I beginne to think howe long,
Againe I hear the Lindis flow,
    Swift as an arrowe, sharpe and strong;
And all the aire it seemeth mee
Bin full of floating bells (sayth shee),
That ring the tune of Enderby.

Alle fresh the level pasture lay,
    And not a shadowe mote be seene,
Save where full fyve good miles away
    The steeple towered from out the greene;
And lo! the great bell farre and wide
Was heard in all the country side
That Saturday at eventide.

The swannerds where their sedges are
    Moved on in sunset's golden breath,
The shepherd lads I heard afarre,
    And my sonne's wife, Elizabeth;
Till floating o'er the grassy sea
Came downe that kyndly message free,
"The Brides of Mavis Enderby."

Then some looked uppe into the sky,
    And all along where Lindis flows
To where the goodly vessels lie,
    And where the lordly steeple shows.
They sayde, "And why should this thing be?
What danger lowers by land or sea?
They ring the tune of Enderby!

" For evil news from Mablethorpe,
    Of pyrate galleys warping down;
For shippes ashore beyond the scorpe,
    They have not spared to wake the towne;

But while the west bin red to see,
And storms be none, and pyrates flee,
Why ring 'The Brides of Enderby?'"

I looked without, and lo! my sonne
  Came riding downe with might and main:
He raised a shout as he drew on,
  Till all the welkin rang again,
(*ff.*) "Elizabeth! Elizabeth!"
(A sweeter woman ne'er drew breath
Than my sonne's wife, Elizabeth.)

(*ff.*) "The olde sea wall (he cried) is downe,
  The rising tide comes on apace,
And boats adrift in yonder towne
  Go sailing uppe the market-place."
He shook as one that looks on death:
"God save you, mother!" straight he saith;
"Where is my wife, Elizabeth?"

"Good sonne, where Lindis winds away,
  With her two bairns I marked her long;
And ere yon bells beganne to play,
  Afar I heard her milking song."
He looked across the grassy sea,
To right, to left, (*f.*) "Ho Enderby!"
They rang "The Brides of Enderby!"

With that he cried and beat his breast;
  For lo! along the river's bed
A mighty eygre reared his crest,
  And uppe the Lindis raging sped.
It swept with thunderous noises loud;
Shaped like a curling snow-white cloud,
Or like a demon in a shroud.

And rearing Lindis backward pressed,
  Shook all her trembling bankes amaine;
Then madly at the eygre's breast
  Flung uppe her weltering walls again.
Then bankes came downe with ruin and rout—
Then beaten foam flew round about—
Then all the mighty floods were out.

So farre, so fast the eygre drave,
  The heart had hardly time to beat
Before a shallow seething wave
  Sobbed in the grasses at oure feet:

The feet had hardly time to flee
Before it brake against the knee,
And all the world was in the sea.

Upon the roofe we sate that night,
   The noise of bells went sweeping by:
I marked the lofty beacon-light
   Stream from the church-tower red and high—
A lurid mark, and dread to see;
And awsome bells they were to mee,
That in the dark rang "Enderby."

They rang the sailor lads to guide
   From roofe to roofe who fearless rowed;
And I—my sonne was at my side,
   And yet the ruddy beacon glowed:
And yet he moaned beneath his breath,
"O come in life, or come in death!
O lost! my love, Elizabeth."

And didst thou visit him no more?
   Thou didst, thou didst, my daughter deare
The waters laid thee at his doore
   Ere yet the early dawn was clear.
Thy pretty bairns in fast embrace,
The lifted sun shone on thy face,
Downe drifted to thy dwelling-place.

That flow strewed wrecks about the grass,
   That ebbe swept out the flocks to sea;
A fatal ebbe and flow, alas!
   To manye more than myne and me:
But each will mourn his own (she saith).
And sweeter woman ne'er drew breath
Than my sonne's wife, Elizabeth.

      I shall never hear her more
      By the reedy Lindis shore,
(>)   "Cusha, Cusha, Cusha!" calling,
      Ere the early dews be falling;
      I shall never hear her song,
(*f.*)   "Cusha, Cusha!" all along,
      Where the sunny Lindis floweth,
         Goeth, floweth;
      From the meads where melick groweth,
      When the water, winding down,
      Onward floweth to the town.

      I shall never see her more
      Where the reeds and rushes quiver,
         Shiver, quiver;

Stand beside the sobbing river,
Sobbing, throbbing, in its falling,
To the sandy lonesome shore;
I shall never hear her calling,
"Leave your meadow-grasses mellow,
   Mellow, mellow;
Quit your cowslips, cowslips yellow;
Come uppe, Whitefoot; come uppe, Lightfoot;
Quit your pipes of parsley hollow,
   Hollow, hollow;
Come uppe, Lightfoot, rise and follow;
   Lightfoot, Whitefoot,
From your clovers lift the head;
Come uppe, Jetty; follow, follow,
Jetty, to the milking-shed."

THE EVERLASTING MEMORIAL.
[From "Hymns of Hope and Faith."]

HORATIUS BONAR.

Up and away, like the dew of the morning,
  Soaring from earth to its home in the sun;
So let me steal away, gently and lovingly,
  Only remembered by what I have done.

My name, and my place, and my tomb all forgotten,
  The brief race of time well and patiently run,
So let me pass away, peacefully, silently,
  Only remembered by what I have done.

Gladly away from this toil would I hasten,
  Up to the crown that for me has been won;
Unthought of by man in rewards or in praises,
  Only remembered by what I have done.

Up and away, like the odors of sunset,
  That sweeten the twilight as darkness comes on;
So be my life—a thing felt but not noticed,
  And I but remembered by what I have done.

Yes, like the fragrance that wanders in freshness,
  When the flowers that it came from are closed up and gone,
So would I be to this world's weary dwellers,
  Only remembered by what I have done.

Needs there the praise of the love-written record,
  The name and the epitaph graved on the stone?
The things we have lived for—let them be our story,
  We ourselves but remembered by what we have done.

I need not be missed if my life has been bearing
　　(As its summer and autumn moved silently on)
The bloom, and the fruit, and the seed of its season;
　　I shall still be remembered by what I have done.

I need not be missed if another succeed me
　　To reap down those fields which in spring I have sown;
He who plowed and who sowed is not missed by the reaper,
　　He is only remembered by what he has done.

Not myself, but the truth that in life I have spoken—
　　Not myself, but the seed that in life I have sown,
Shall pass on to ages—all about me forgotten,
　　Save the truth I have spoken, the things I have done.

So let my living be, so be my dying;
　　So let my name lie, unblazoned, unknown;
Unpraised and unmissed, I shall still be remembered;
　　Yes—but remembered by what I have done.

THE WORLD WOULD BE THE BETTER FOR IT.

If men cared less for wealth and fame,
　　And less for battle-fields and glory;
If, writ in human hearts, a name
　　Seemed better than in song and story;
If men, instead of nursing pride,
　　Would learn to hate it and abhor it;
If more relied on love to guide,
　　The world would be the better for it.

If men dealt less in stocks and lands,
　　And more in bonds and deeds fraternal;
If Love's work had more willing hands
　　To link this world to the supernal;
If men stored up Love's oil and wine,
　　And on bruised human hearts would pour it;
If "yours" and "mine" would once combine,
　　The world would be the better for it.

If more would act the play of life,
　　And fewer spoil it in rehearsal;
If Bigotry would sheathe its knife
　　Till good becomes more universal;
If custom, gray with ages grown,
　　Had fewer blind men to adore it;
If talents shone in Truth alone,
　　The world would be the better for it.

If men were wise in little things—
Affecting less in all their dealings—
If hearts had fewer rusted strings
To isolate their kindly feelings;
If men, when *Wrong* beats down the Right,
Would strike together and restore it;
If Right made Might in every fight,
The world would be the better for it.

THANK GOD, THERE'S STILL A VANGUARD.

Mrs. H. E. G. ABBY.

Thank God, there's *still a vanguard*
Fighting for the *Right;*
Though the throng flock to rearward,
Lifting (ashen-white)
Flags of truce to Sin and Error,
Clasping hands mute with terror,
Thank God, there's still a vanguard
Fighting for the Right.

Through the wilderness advancing,
Hewers of the way;
Forward far their spears are glancing,
Flashing back the day.
"Back!" the leaders cry who fear them;
"Back!" from all the army near them;
They, their steady tramp advancing,
Cleave their certain way.

Slay them—from each drop that falleth
Springs a hero armed;
Where the martyr's fire appalleth,
Lo! they pass unharmed;
Crushed beneath thy wheel, Oppression,
How their spirits hold possession—
How their dross-purged voice outcalleth,
By the death-throes warmed!

Thank God, there's still a vanguard
Fighting for the right;
Error's legions know their standard
Floating in the light.
When the league of Sin rejoices,
Quick outring the rallying voices,
Thank God, there's still a vanguard
Fighting for the Right.

CREEDS OF THE BELLS.

G. W. BUNGAY.

How sweet the chime of the Sabbath bells!
Each one its creed in music tells,
In tones that float upon the air,
As soft as song, and pure as prayer;
And I will put in simple rhyme
The language of the golden chime.
My happy heart with rapture swells
Responsive to the bells—sweet bells.

(*high.*) "In deeds of love excel—excel,"
Chimed out from ivied towers a bell;
(*pure.*) "This is the church not built on sands,
Emblem of one not built with hands;
Its forms and sacred rites revere,
Come worship here—come worship here;
In rituals and faith excel,"
Chimed out the Episcopalian bell.

(*low.*) "Oh, heed the ancient landmarks well,"
In solemn tones exclaimed a bell;
(*oro.*) "No progress made by mortal man
Can change the just, eternal plan.
With God there can be nothing new;
Ignore the false, embrace the true,
While all is well—is well—is well,"
Pealed out the good old Dutch Church bell.

(*pure.*) "Oh swell, ye purifying waters, swell,"
In mellow tones rang out a bell;
"Though faith alone in Christ can save;
Man must be plunged beneath the wave,
To show the world unfaltering faith
In what the sacred Scripture saith.
Oh swell, ye rising waters, swell,"
Pealed out the clear-toned Baptist bell.

(*p.*) "Not faith alone, but works as well,
Must test the soul," said a soft bell;
"Come here, and cast aside your load,
And work your way along the road,
With faith in God, and faith in man,
And hope in Christ, where hope began:
(*echo.*) Do well—do well—do well—do well,"
Pealed forth the Unitarian bell.

(*oro.*) "Farewell! farewell! base world, farewell,"
In touching tones exclaimed a bell;
"Life is a boon to mortals given,
To fit the soul for bliss in heaven.
Do not invoke the avenging rod;
Come here, and learn the way to God.
Say to the world farewell! farewell!"
Pealed out the Presbyterian bell.

(*p.*) "In after life there is no hell,"
In rapture rang a cheerful bell;
"Look up to Heaven this holy day,
Where angels wait to lead the way.
There are no fires, no fiends to blight
The future life: be just and right.
No hell—no hell—no hell—no hell,"
Rang out the Universalist bell.

(*pure.*) "To all the truth we tell—we tell,"
Shouted, in ecstasies, a bell;
"Come, all ye weary wanderers, see!
Our Lord has made salvation free.
(*fast.*) Repent! believe! have faith! and then
Be saved, and praise the Lord. Amen.
Salvation's free we tell—we tell,"
Shouted the Methodistic bell.

THE BUILDING OF THE SHIP.

LONGFELLOW.

All is finished; and at length
Has come the bridal day
Of beauty and of strength.
To-day the vessel shall be launched!
With fleecy clouds the sky is blanched,
  And o'er the bay,
Slowly, in all his splendors dight,
The great sun rises to behold the sight.

The ocean old—centuries old—
Strong as youth, and as uncontrolled,
  Paces restless to and fro,
Up and down the sands of gold;
His beating heart is not at rest;
  And far and wide,
  With ceaseless flow,
  His beard of snow
Heaves with the heaving of his breast.

He waits impatient for his bride.
   There she stands,
With her foot upon the sands,
Decked with flags and streamers gay
   In honor of her marriage-day;
Her snow-white signals fluttering, blending
Round her like a veil descending,
   Ready to be
The bride of the gray old sea.

* * * * * * * *

   Then the master,
With a gesture of command,
   Waved his hand;
   And at the word,
Loud and sudden there was heard,
All around them and below,
The sound of hammers, blow on blow,
Knocking away the shores and spurs.
   And see! she stirs!
She starts—she moves—she seems to feel
The thrill of life along her keel,
And, spurning with her foot the ground,
With one exulting, joyous bound,
She leaps into the ocean's arms!

And lo! from the assembled crowd
There rose a shout, prolonged and loud,
That to the ocean seemed to say,
"Take her, oh bridegroom old and gray,
Take her to thy protecting arms,
With all her youth and all her charms."

How beautiful she is! how fair
She lies within those arms, that press
Her form with many a soft caress
Of tenderness and watchful care!
Sail forth upon the sea, oh ship!
Through wind and wave right onward steer!
The moistened eye, the trembling lip,
Are not the signs of doubt or fear.

* * * * * * * *

Thou, too, sail on, oh Ship of State!
Sail on, oh Union, strong and great!
Humanity, with all its fears,
With all the hopes of future years,
Is hanging breathless on thy fate.

We know what master laid thy keel,
What workmen wrought thy ribs of steel,
Who made each mast, and sail, and rope,
What anvils rang, what hammers beat,
In what a forge, and what a heat,
Were shaped the anchors of thy hope.

Fear not each sudden sound and shock,
'Tis of the wave, and not the rock;
'Tis but the flapping of the sail,
And not a rent made by the gale.
In spite of rock and tempest roar,
In spite of false lights on the shore,
Sail on! nor fear to breast the sea;
Our hearts, our hopes, are all with thee.
Our hearts, our hopes, our prayers, our tears,
Our faith, triumphant o'er our fears,
Are all with thee—are all with thee.

EVENING AT THE FARM.

Over the hill the farm-boy goes:
His shadow lengthens along the land;
A giant staff in a giant hand;
In the poplar-tree, above the spring,
The katydid begins to sing;
   The early dews are falling:
Into the stone-heap darts the mink;
The swallows skim the river's brink;
And home to the woodland fly the crows,
When over the hill the farm-boy goes,
      Cheerily calling,

(*pure.*)   "Co' boss! co' boss! co'! co'! co'!"
Farther, farther, over the hill,
Faintly calling, calling still,

(*p.*)   "Co' boss! co' boss! co'! co'! co'!"

Into the yard the farmer goes
With grateful heart at the close of day:
Harness and chain are hung away;
In the wagon-shed stands yoke and plow;
The straw's in the stack, the hay in the mow;
   The cooling dews are falling:
The friendly sheep their welcome bleat,
The pigs come grunting at his feet,
And the whinnying mare her master knows
When into the yard the farmer goes,
      His cattle calling,

(*oro.*)   "Co' boss! co' boss! co'! co'! co'!"
While still the cow-boy, far away,
Goes seeking those that have gone astray,
(*pp.*)   "Co' boss! co' boss! co'! co'! co'!"
Now to her task the milkmaid goes:
The cattle come crowding through the gate,
Lowing, pushing, little and great;
About the trough, by the farm-yard pump,
The frolicsome yearlings frisk and jump,
    While the pleasant dews are falling:
The new milch heifer is quick and shy,
But the old cow waits with tranquil eye,
And the white stream into the bright pail flows
When to her task the milkmaid goes,
    Soothingly calling,
(*pure.*)   "So, boss! so, boss! so! so! so!"
The cheerful milkmaid takes her stool,
And sits and milks in the twilight cool,
    Saying "So! so, boss! so! so!"
To supper at last the farmer goes:
The apples are pared, the paper read,
The stories are told, then all to bed.
Without, the cricket's ceaseless song
Makes shrill the silence all night long;
    The heavy dews are falling:
The housewife's hand has turned the lock;
Drowsily ticks the kitchen clock;
The household sinks to deep repose,
But still in sleep the farm-boy goes,
    Singing, calling,
(*sleepy.*)   "Co' boss! co' boss! co'! co'! co'!"
And oft the milkmaid, in her dreams,
Drums in the pail with the flashing stream,
    Murmuring "So, boss! so!"

THE NEWS OF A DAY.

                               Mrs. S. T. Bolton.

(*falsetto.*) "Great battle! Times extra!" the newsboy cried,
But it scarcely rippled the living tide
That ebbed and flowed in the busy street,
With its throbbing hearts and its restless feet.
Again through the hum of the city thrilled—
(*falsetto.*) "Great battle! Times extra! Ten thousand killed!"
And the little carrier hurried away
With the sorrowful news of that winter-day.

To a dreary room in the attic high
Trembled the words of that small, sharp cry,
And a lonely widow bowed down her head
And murmured, "Willie—my Willie is dead!
Oh, I feared it was not an idle dream
That led me, last night, to that deep, dark stream,
Where the ground was wet with a crimson rain,
And strewn all over with ghastly slain!
The stars were dim, for the night was wild,
But I threaded the gloom till I found my child.

"The cold rain fell on his upturned face,
And the swift destroyer had left no trace
Of the sudden blow and the quick, sharp pain,
But a little wound and a purple stain.
I tried to speak, but my voice was gone,
And my soul stood there in the cold gray dawn
Till they rifled his body with ruthless hand,
And covered him up with the reeking sand.

"Willie! oh, Willie! it seems but a day
Since thy baby-head on my bosom lay—
Since I heard thy prattle so soft and sweet,
And guided the steps of thy tottering feet;
And thou wert the fairest and last of three
That the Father in heaven had given to me.
All the life of my heart—love, hope, and joy—
Were treasured in thee, my strong, brave boy;
And the last faint words that thy father said
Were, 'Willie will mind thee when I am dead.'
But they tore the flag from thy death-cold hand,
And covered thee up in the reeking sand."

She read the names of the missing and slain,
But one she read over again and again;
And the sad, low words that her white lips said
Were, "Company C, William Warren—dead."
The world toiled on through the busy street,
With its aching hearts and unresting feet;
The night came down to her cold hearth-stone,
And she still read on in the same low tone;
And still the words that her white lips said
Were, "Company C, William Warren—dead."

The light of the morning chased the gloom
From the emberless hearth of that attic room,
And the city's pulses throbbed again,
But the mother's heart had forgotten its pain,

She had gone through the gates to the better land
With that terrible list in her pale, cold hand—
With her white lips parted, as last she said,
"Company C, William Warren—dead!"

"BORROBOOLA GHA."

A stranger preached last Sunday,
    And crowds of people came
To hear a two-hour sermon
    With a barbarous sounding name.
'Twas all about some heathens
    Thousands of miles afar,
Who lived in a land of darkness,
    Called Borroboola Ghä.

So *well* their wants he pictured,
    That, when the plates were passed,
Each listener felt his pockets,
    And goodly sums were cast;
For all must lend 'a shoulder
    To push a rolling car
That carries light and comfort
    To "Borroboola Ghä."

That night their wants and sorrows
    Lay heavy on my soul,
And deep in meditation
    I took my morning stroll,
Till something caught my mantle
    With eager grasp and wild,
And, looking down with wonder,
    I saw a little child—

A pale and puny creature,
    In rags and dirt forlorn.
What could she want? I questioned,
    Impatient to be gone.
With trembling voice she answered,
    "We live just down the street,
And mammy she's a dyin',
    And we've nothin' left to eat."

Down in a wretched basement,
    With mould upon the walls,
Through whose half-buried windows
    God's sunshine never falls—

Where cold, and want, and hunger
  Crouched near her as she lay,
I found a fellow-creature
  Gasping her life away.

A chair, a broken table,
  A bed of dirty straw,
A hearth all dark and cheerless—
  But these I scarcely saw
For the mournful sight before me—
  The sad and sickening show.
Oh, never had I pictured
  A scene so full of woe.

The famished and the naked,
  The babes that pined for bread,
The squalid group that huddled
  Around the dying bed—
All this distress and sorrow
  Should be in lands afar :
Was I suddenly transplanted
  To "Borroboola Ghä?"

Ah! no; the poor and wretched
  Were close behind the door,
And I had passed them heedless
  A thousand times before.
Alas! for the cold and hungry
  That met me every day,
While all my tears were given
  To the suffering far away.

There's work enough for Christians
  In distant lands, we know ;
Our Lord commands his servants
  Through all the world to go.
Not only for the heathen.
  This was the charge to them :
"Go preach the Word, beginning
  First at Jerusalem."

Oh, Christian, God has promised
  Whoe'er to thee has given
A cup of pure cold water
  Shall find reward in heaven.
Would you secure the blessing,
  You need not seek it far ;
Go find in yonder hovel
  A "Borroboola Ghä."

THE CHRISTIAN MARINER.

MRS. SOUTHEY.

  Launch thy bark, mariner;
   Christian, God speed thee!
  Let loose the rudder-bands;
   Good angels lead thee!
  Set thy sails warily—
   Tempests will come;
  Steer thy course steadily;
   Christian, steer home!

  Look to the weather-bow—
   Breakers are round thee;
  Let fall the plummet now—
   Shallows may ground thee.
  Reef in the foresail, there!
   Hold the helm fast!
  So!—let the vessel wear:
   There swept the blast.

(*calling.*) "What of the night, watchman—
   What of the night?"
(*oro.*)   "Cloudy—all quiet—
   No land yet—all's right."
  Be wakeful—be vigilant;
   Danger may be
  At an hour when all seemeth
   Securest to thee.

(*f.*)   How gains the leak so fast?
   Clean out the hold;
  Hoist up the merchandise,
   Heave out the gold.
  There! let the ingots go;
   Now the ship rights.
(*ff.*)   Hurrah! the harbor's near:
   Lo! the red lights.

  Slacken not sail yet
   At inlet or island;
  Straight for the beacon steer—
   Straight for the highland.
  Crowd all thy canvas on;
   Cut through the foam;
(*slow.*) {Christian, cast anchor now;
   {*Heaven* is thy home!

NO SECT IN HEAVEN.
Mrs. Cleveland.

Talking of sects till late one eve—
Of the various doctrines the saints believe,
That night I stood, in a troubled dream,
By the side of a darkly flowing stream.

And a "Churchman" down to the river came,
When I heard a strange voice call his name.
"Good father, stop; when you cross the tide,
You must leave your robes on the other side."

But the aged father did not mind,
And his long robe floated out behind
As down to the stream his way he took,
His pale hands clasping a gilt-edged book.

"I'm bound for heaven, and, when I'm there,
I shall want my Book of Common Prayer;
And, though I put on a starry crown,
I should feel quite lost without my gown."

Then he fixed his eye on the shining track,
But his gown was heavy, and held him back,
And the poor old father tried in vain
A single step in the flood to gain.

I saw him again on the other side,
But his silk gown floated on the tide;
And no one asked, in that blissful spot,
Whether he belonged to "*the* Church" or not.

Then down to the river a "Quaker" strayed:
His dress of a sober hue was made.
"My coat and hat must be all of gray;
I can not go any other way."

Then he buttoned his coat straight up to his chin,
And steadily, solemnly waded in,
And his broad-brimmed hat he pulled down tight
Over his forehead, so cold and white.

But a strong wind carried away his hat:
A moment he silently sighed over that;
And then, as he gazed to the farther shore,
The coat slipped off, and was seen no more.

As he entered heaven, his suit of gray
Went quietly sailing away—away,
And none of the angels questioned him
About the width of his beaver's brim.

Next came Dr. Watts, with a bundle of psalms
Tied nicely up in his aged arms,
And hymns as many—a very wise thing—
That the people of heaven "all round" might sing.

But I thought he heaved an anxious sigh
As he saw that the river ran broad and high;
And he looked rather surprised as, one by one,
The psalms and hymns in the wave went down.

And after him, with his MSS.,
Came Wesley, the pattern of godliness;
But he cried, "Dear me, what shall I do?
The water has soaked them through and through."

And there on the river, far and wide,
Away they went down the swollen tide,
And the saint, astonished, passed through alone,
Without his manuscripts, up to the throne.

Then, gravely walking, two saints by name
Down to the stream together came;
But, as they stopped at the river brink,
I saw one saint from the other shrink.

"Sprinkled or plunged—may I ask you, friend,
How you attained to life's great end?"
"*Thus*, with a few drops on my brow."
"But *I* have been dipped, as you'll see me now;

And I really think it will hardly do,
As I'm close communion, to cross with you.
You're bound, I know, to the realms of bliss;
But you must go that way, and I'll go this."

Then straightway plunging, with all his might,
Away to the left—his friend to the right,
Apart they went from this world of pain,
But at last together they entered in.

And now, when the river was rolling on,
A Presbyterian Church went down;
Of women there seemed an innumerable throng,
But the men I could count as they passed along.

And concerning the road they could never agree;
The old or the new way—which it should be;
Nor ever a moment paused to think
That both would lead to the river's brink.

And a sound of murmuring, long and loud,
Came ever up from the moving crowd:

"You're in the old way, I'm in the new;
That is the false, and this is the true;"
Or, "I'm in the old way, and you're in the new;
That is the false, and *this* is the true."
I watched them long in my curious dream
Till they stood by the borders of the stream;
Then, just as I thought, the two ways met;
But all the brethren were talking yet,
And would talk on till the heaving tide
Carried them over, side by side—
Side by side, for the way was one.
The toilsome journey of life was done,
And priest, and Quaker, and all who died,
Came out alike on the other side.
No forms, no crosses, or books had they—
No gowns of silk, or suits of gray—
No creeds to guide them, or MSS.,
For all had put on Christ's righteousness.

JOHN BURNS, OF GETTYSBURG.

BRET HARTE.

Have you heard the story that gossips tell
Of Burns of Gettysburg? No? Ah! well:
Brief is the glory that hero earns,
Briefer the story of poor John Burns:
He was the fellow who won renown—
The only man who didn't back down
When the rebels rode through his native town;
But held his own in the fight next day,
When all his townsfolk ran away.
That was in July, sixty-three,
The very day that General Lee,
Flower of Southern chivalry,
Baffled and beaten, backward reeled
From a stubborn Meade and a barren field.

I might tell how, but the day before,
John Burns stood at his cottage door,
Looking down the village street,
Where, in the shade of his peaceful vine,
He heard the low of his gathered kine,
And felt their breath with incense sweet;
Or I might say, when the sunset burned
The old farm gable, he thought it turned
The milk that fell, in a babbling flood

Into the milk-pail, red as blood!
Or how he fancied the hum of bees
Were bullets buzzing among the trees.
But all such fanciful thoughts as these
Were strange to a practical man like Burns,
Who minded only his own concerns,
Troubled no more by fancies fine
Than one of his calm-eyed, long-tailed kine—
Quite old-fashioned and matter-of-fact,
Slow to argue, but quick to act.
That was the reason, as some folks say,
He fought so well on that terrible day.

And it was terrible. On the right
Raged for hours the heavy fight,
Thundered the battery's double bass—
Difficult music for men to face;
While on the left—where now the graves
Undulate like the living waves
That all that day unceasing swept
Up to the pits the rebels kept—
Round shot plowed the upland glades:
Sown with bullets, reaped with blades;
Shattered fences here and there
Tossed their splinters in the air;
The very trees were stripped and bare;
The barns that once held yellow grain
Were heaped with harvests of the slain;
The cattle bellowed on the plain,
The turkeys screamed with might and main,
And brooding barn-fowl left their rest
With strange shells bursting in each nest.

Just where the tide of battle turns,
Erect and lonely stood old John Burns.
How do you think the man was dressed?
He wore an ancient long buff vest,
Yellow as saffron—but his best;
And buttoned over his manly breast
Was a bright blue coat, with a rolling collar,
And large gilt buttons—size of a dollar—
With tails that the country-folk called "swaller."
He wore a broad-brimmed, bell-crowned hat,
White as the locks on which it sat.
Never had such a sight been seen
For forty years on the village green,
Since old John Burns was a country beau,
And went to the " quiltings" long ago.

Close at his elbows all that day,
Veterans of the Peninsula,
Sunburnt and bearded, charged away:
And striplings, downy of lip and chin—
Clerks that the Home Guard mustered in—
Glanced, as they passed, at the hat he wore,
Then at the rifle his right hand bore,
And hailed him, from out their youthful lore,
With scraps of a slangy *répertoire:*
" How are you, White Hat!" " Put her through!"
" Your head's level," and " Bully for you!"
Called him " Daddy"—begged he'd disclose
The name of the tailor who made his clothes,
And what was the value he set on those;
While Burns, unmindful of jeer and scoff,
Stood there picking the rebels off—
With his long brown rifle, and bell-crown hat,
And the swallow-tails they were laughing at.

'Twas but a moment, for that respect
Which clothes all courage their voices checked;
And something the wildest could understand
Spake in the old man's strong right hand;
And his corded throat, and the lurking frown
Of his eyebrows under his old bell-crown;
Until, as they gazed, there crept an awe
Through the ranks in whispers, and some men saw,
In the antique vestments and long white hair,
The Past of the Nation in battle there;
And some of the soldiers since declare
That the gleam of his old white hat afar,
Like the crested plume of the brave Navarre,
That day was their oriflamme of war.

So raged the battle. You know the rest:
How the rebels, beaten and backward pressed,
Broke at the final charge, and ran,
At which John Burns—a practical man—
Shouldered his rifle, unbent his brows,
And then went back to his bees and cows.

That is the story of old John Burns;
This is the moral the reader learns:
In fighting the battle, the question's whether
You'll show a hat that's white or a feather!

ANNIE AND WILLIE'S PRAYER.

Mrs. Sophia P. Snow.

'Twas the eve before Christmas; "Good-night" had been said,
And Annie and Willie had crept into bed;
There were tears on their pillows, and tears in their eyes,
And each little bosom was heaving with sighs,
For to-night their stern father's command had been given
That they should retire precisely at seven
Instead of at eight; for they troubled him more
With questions unheard of than ever before:
He had told them he thought this delusion a sin—
No such being as "Santa Claus" ever had been—
And he hoped after this he should nevermore hear
How he scrambled down chimneys with presents each year.

And this was the reason that two little heads
So restlessly tossed on their soft, downy beds.
Eight, nine, and the clock on the steeple tolled ten;
Not a word had been spoken by either till then,
When Willie's sad face from the blanket did peep,
And whispered, "Dear Annie, is you fast asleep?"
"Why no, Brother Willie," a sweet voice replies,
"I've tried in vain, but I can't shut my eyes,
For somehow it makes me sorry because
Dear papa has said there is no 'Santa Claus.'
Now we know there is, and it can't be denied,
For he came every year before mamma died:
But then, I've been thinking that she used to pray,
And God would hear every thing mamma would say;
And perhaps she asked him to send Santa Claus here,
With the sack full of presents he brought every year"
"Well, why tan't we pay dest as mamma did then,
And ask Dod to send him with presents aden?"
"I've been thinking so too," and, without a word more,
Four little bare feet bounded out on the floor,
And four little knees the soft carpet pressed,
And two tiny hands were clasped close to each breast.
"Now, Willie, you know, we must firmly believe
That the presents we ask for we're sure to receive;
You must wait just as still till I say the 'Amen,'
And by that you will know that your turn has come then.
'Dear Jesus, look down on my brother and me,
And grant us the favor we are asking of thee.
I want a wax dolly, a tea-set and ring,
And an ebony work-box that shuts with a spring.
Bless papa, dear Jesus, and cause him to see

That Santa Claus loves us far better than he;
Don't let him get fretful and angry again
At dear brother Willie and Annie. Amen.'"
"Please, Desus, et Santa Taus turn down to-night,
And bing us some pesents before it is ight;
I want he should div me a nice ittle sed,
With bright shinin unners and all painted ed;
A box full of tandy, a book, and a toy—
Amen—and den, Desus, I'll be a dood boy."
Their prayers being ended, they raised up their heads,
And, with hearts light and cheerful, again sought their beds;
They were soon lost in slumber both peaceful and deep,
And with fairies in Dreamland were roaming in sleep.

Eight, nine, and the little French clock had struck ten,
Ere the father had thought of his children again;
He seems now to hear Annie's half-suppressed sighs,
And to see the big tears stand in Willie's blue eyes;
"I was harsh with my darlings," he mentally said,
"And should not have sent them so early to bed;
But then I was troubled, my feelings found vent,
For bank stock to-day has come down ten per cent.
But of course they've forgotten their troubles ere this,
And that I denied them the thrice asked for kiss;
But, just to make sure, I'll steal up to their door,
For I never spoke harsh to my darlings before."
So saying, he softly ascended the stairs,
And arrived at the door to hear both of their prayers;
His Annie's "bless papa" draws forth the big tears,
And Willie's grave promise falls sweet on his ears.
"Strange, strange, I'd forgotten," said he, with a sigh,
"How I longed when a child to have Christmas draw nigh.
I'll atone for my harshness," he inwardly said,
"By answering their prayers ere I sleep in my bed."

Then he turned to the stairs, and softly went down,
Threw off velvet slippers and silk dressing-gown,
Donned hat, coat, and boots, and was out in the street,
A millionaire facing the cold, driving sleet,
Nor stopped he until he had bought every thing,
From the box full of candy to the tiny gold ring;
Indeed he kept adding so much to his store
That the various presents outnumbered a score;
Then homeward he turned with his holiday load,
And, with Aunt Mary's help, in the nursery 'twas stowed.
Miss Dolly was seated beneath a pine-tree,
By the side of a table spread out for her tea;

A work-box well filled in the centre was laid,
And on it the ring for which Annie had prayed.
A soldier in uniform stood by a sled,
"With bright shining runners and painted all red."
There were balls, dogs, and horses, books pleasing to see,
And birds of all colors were perched in the tree,
While Santa Claus, laughing, stood up in the top,
As if getting ready more presents to drop;
And, as the fond father the picture surveyed,
He thought for his trouble he had amply been paid,
And he said to himself, as he brushed off a tear,
"I'm happier to-night than I've been for a year;
I've enjoyed more true pleasure than ever before—
What care I if bank stock falls ten per cent. more.
Hereafter I'll make it a rule, I believe,
To have Santa Claus visit us each Christmas Eve."
So thinking, he gently extinguished the light,
And tripped down the stairs to retire for the night.

As soon as the beams of the bright morning sun
Put the darkness to flight, and the stars one by one,
Four little blue eyes out of sleep opened wide,
And at the same moment the presents espied.
Then out of their beds they sprang with a bound,
And the very gifts prayed for were all of them found;
They laughed and they cried in their innocent glee,
And shouted for "papa" to come quick and see
What presents old Santa Claus brought in the night
(Just the things that they wanted), and left before light;
"And now," added Annie, in voice soft and low,
"You'll believe there's a 'Santa Claus,' papa, I know."
While dear little Willie climbed up on his knee,
Determined no secret between them should be,
And told in soft whispers how Annie had said
That their dear, blessed mamma, so long ago dead,
Used to kneel down and pray by the side of her chair,
And that God, up in heaven, had answered her prayer.
"Then we dot up and prayed dest as well as we tould,
And Dod answered our prayers—now wasn't he dood?"
" I should say that he was, if he sent you all these,
And know just what presents my children would please.
(Well, well, let him think so, the dear little elf,
'Twould be cruel to tell him I did it myself.)"
Blind father! who caused your stern heart to relent,
And the hasty words spoken so soon to repent?
'Twas the Being who made you steal softly up stairs,
And made you His agent to answer their prayers.

THE SOUL-DIRGE.

A. CLEVELAND COXE.

The organ played sweet music
    The while, on Easter-day,
All heartless from the altar
    The heedless went away;.
And, down the broad aisle crowding,
    They seemed a funeral train,
That were burying their spirits
    To the music of that strain.

As I listened to the organ,
    And saw them crowd along,
I thought I heard two voices
    Speaking strangely, but not strong.
And one it whispered sadly,
    "Will ye also go away?"
But the other spoke, exulting,
    "Ha! the soul-dirge—hear it play!"

Hear the soul-dirge! hear the soul-dirge
    And see the feast divine!
Ha! the jewels of salvation,
    And the trampling feet of swine!
Hear the soul-dirge! hear the soul-dirge!
    Little think they, as they go,
What priceless pearls they tread on,
    Who spurn their Savior so.

Hear the soul-dirge! hear the soul-dirge!
    It was dread to hear it play,
While the *Famishing* were crowding
    From the Bread of Life away.
They were bidden, they were bidden
    To their Father's festal board,
But they all with gleeful faces
    Turned their back upon the Lord.

You had thought the church a prison
    Had you seen how they did pour,
With giddy, giddy faces,
    From the consecrated door.
There was angels' food all ready,
    But the bidden, where are they?
O'er the highways and the hedges
    Ere the soul-dirge ceased to play.

Oh! the soul-dirge, how it echoed
    The emptied aisles along!

As the open street grew crowded
  With the full outpouring throng.
And then—again the voices—
  "Ha! the soul-dirge! hear it play!"
And the pensive, pensive whisper,
  "*Will ye also go away?*"

Few, few were they that lingered
  To sup with Jesus there,
And yet for all that spurned Him
  There was plenty and to spare.
And now the food of angels
  Uncovered to my sight,
All glorious was the altar,
  And the chălice glittered bright.

Then came the hymn Trisăgion,
  And rapt me up on high,
With angels and archangels
  To laud and magnify.
I seemed to feast in heaven,
  And downward wafted then,
With angels chanting round me,
  Good will and peace to men.

I may not tell the rapture
  Of a banquet so divine.
Ho! every one that thirsteth,
  Let him taste the bread and wine.
Hear the Bride and Spirit saying,
  "*Will ye also go away?*"
Or, "Go, poor soul, forever!"
  Ah! the soul-dirge—hear it play!

THE TRIAD.
Alfred B. Street.

Through the air low sounds are stealing,
Softly, sadly, deep with feeling;
Across the ear they slowly draw along,
Wailing like winds in their wild autumn song;
It is Music in its sorrow, and causing by a chain
Of sympathy each bosom to yield an answering strain.

But now the changing sounds leap out!
Merrily, merrily, swift they dance about,
As the glad bluebird on a day in spring,
  When south winds are blowing,
  And bright streams are flowing,

And blossoms are rising and smiling around,
And incense floats up from the altar-like ground.
    Hither and yon,
    In shadow and sun,
Wanders and skims with delight in its wing;
Or like the voice of a frolicsome boy
Chasing the butterfly over the flowers,
When sunshine is painting the summer hours,
His heart in his lips, and his lips shouting free
In the strain that is born and is moulded of glee:
    'Tis music in its joy.
    Hark! once again
  Peals up—peals up the strain!
    Swift, swift on high,
  On lightning wings it seems to fly,
  Lark-like in floods of harmony,
    Until methinks we see
Banners, and swords, and plumes, and hear the sound
Of the keen trumpets, while our bosoms bound:
  'Tis music breathing loud,
Triumph, victorious triumph, glad and proud.

Now swells the strain in one grand solemn roll,
In march majestic sounding through the soul.
  It seems to bid the knee to sink, the eye
  In deepest awe, yet trust, to seek the sky.
It seems to breathe of God, and deeply say,
Man, creature of his love, bow down and pray!
  Full is the sound of most divine emotion—
    'Tis music in devotion.

    Then with mild fire
    His trembling lyre
Strikes Poesy, and Nature gleams
With all her sunshine, flowers, and streams;
Bright Fancy's haunted realm is spread,
And airy, flitting beings tread
From its rich beauty, brightening to the mind;
The lover wanders in the moonlight sweet;
The warrior mounts his battle-steed, to bind
His bow with wreaths, and youths and maidens greet
  Spring's laughing hours with dancing feet;
  Thus all the shapes the heart
  Can dream, arise and act in Poesy's high art.

    Last Eloquence,
With feeling burning and intense,
Loosens its tongue; in honeyed accents now

It bends each will, it makes each bosom bow,
  Witching the sense away;
Then, like a warrior rising from the fray,
Crying "To arms! to arms!" it swells and soars
In flight triumphant—like a stream that pours
Down in a torrent—all our wills are borne
On in one course, urged by this magic power
That lifts its radiant head, the crowned king of the hour.

  Thus the three
Weave the strong spells of their harmony
Over the burning hearts made subject to their sway.
   Coals are they from the loftiest shrine
   Of intellect; their birthplace is divine.
Sparks are they, brightly born of heaven's own ray.
'Their *errand* should be lofty : to refine
The soul, to purify the heart, to bend
Our every feeling to a holy end;
From stains of earth to make our spirits free,
And thus to *consecrate our lives*, oh Heaven, to thee!

THE BOBOLINK.—*From Our Young Folks.*

G. H. BARNES.

Merry meadow bobolink!
White as snow and black as ink—
White the ruffle round your throat,
Black your glossy velvet coat;
White your crest, and black your bill,
And your bosom blacker still;
Little piebald, babbling elf,
Caring only for yourself,
Ever-joyous, ever singing,
Ever through the lilies winging,
Flitting here and flashing there,
Never quiet any where—
Do you ever stop to think,
Merry meadow bobolink?
What a funny song you sing
While you flutter on the wing!
Rest, then, birdie, on that stake;
Keep your black eyes wide awake;
Don't you laugh, and don't you wink,
While I tell you, bobolink,
In a half a dozen rounds,
How your rattling nonsense sounds,
When your crooked carol crazes
School-boys, birds, and bees, and daisies.

"'*Bobolink, link-a-tink!*' Ho, pretty lass!
Up in the sunny sky, down in the grass.
Good morning, Miss Jenny Wren; sweetly you look,
With feathers so bright from a wash in the brook.
'*Tweet-a-lee, tweet-a-lee, link-a-ti-ting!*'
Come, Jenny, with me, on the daisies, and swing;
And out of their cups, my darling, we'll drink
Dew-drops and honey-drops, '*tweet bobolink!*'"

"'Twittering lady-bird, dressed in blue,
Swallow of summer, good morning to you;
'*Pe-le-weet, pe-le-weet!*' your flight is so fleet,
Your shadow goes dancing over the wheat,
And over the mower, who leans on his scythe
To list to my song, so merry and blithe;
'*Tink-a-lum, tink-a-lum!*' sprite of the air,
Bobolink wishes your love to share."

"Hallo! Kitty Catbird, what is the matter?
'*Click, plash, twang, clatter-ti-clatter!*'
Come here on the lilies, and swing and swing,
Bobolink ballads together we'll sing."

"'*Tweet, tweet!*' Goldfinch, out in the grove,
Filling the shade with a chirrup of love,
Trilling your song in one little note,
Just hear a tune from a bobolink's throat."

"'*Tu-ra-lee, tu-ra-lee!*' cherries and clover;
Johnny's come home from the war that is over!
Bessie is down in the grass on her nest,
Brooding young bobolinks under her breast;
Lilies bend over the water, I think,
To look at their beauty—never to drink;
So here on the fence *I* sit and sing,
Proud as a popinjay, '*link-a-ti-ling!*'
'*Ho, ho, cleet! cleet!*' Some other fine day,
My gay little finch, I'll finish my lay.
Good-by for the present. I'd pipe a refrain,
But here comes a school-boy down through the lane.
I know by his step, I know by his wink,
He's a stone in his hand for poor Bobolink.
Good-by, little birds; '*tril-i-link!*' good-by;
I've opened my wings, and away I must fly."

  So the black-eyed bobolink,
  With a mighty knowing wink,
  Gives his snowy cap a shake,
  Flutters from the leaning stake,

And across the clover-bed,
Turning now and then his head,
Clears the meadow in his track
Ere he folds his wings of black:
And we hear him, as he passes
Gayly o'er the nodding grasses,
Singing "*Ting-a-ling-a-link!*
I'm a merry bobolink."

THE RIDE FROM GHENT TO AIX.

ROBERT BROWNING.

I sprang to the stirrup, and Joris, and he;
I galloped, Dirk galloped, we galloped all three:
"Good speed!" cried the watch as the gate-bolts undrew,
"Speed!" echoed the wall to us galloping through.
Behind shut the postern, the lights sank to rest,
And into the midnight we galloped abreast.

Not a word to each other; we kept the great pace—
Neck by neck, stride by stride, never changing our place;
I turned to my saddle and made its girths tight,
Then shortened each stirrup and set the pique right,
Rebuckled the check-strap, chained slacker the bit,
Nor galloped less steadily Rŏ'land a whit.

'Twas a moonset at starting; but while we drew near
Lŏ'keren, the cocks crew and twilight dawned clear;
At Bōom a great yellow star came out to seè;
At Düffeld 'twas morning as plain as could be;
And from Měch'eln (měk'lin) church-steeple we heard the half-chime,
So Joris broke silence with "Yet there is time!"

At Aerschot up leaped of a sudden the sun,
And against him the cattle stood black every one,
To stare through the mist at us galloping past;
And I saw my stout galloper Rŏ'land at last,
With resolute shoulders, each butting away
The haze as some bluff river headland its spray;

And his low head and crest, just one sharp ear bent back
For my voice, and the other pricked out on his track;
And one eye's black intelligence—ever that glance
O'er its white edge at me, his own master, askance;
And the thick, heavy spume-flakes, which aye and anon
His fierce lips shook upward in galloping on.

By Hüs'selt Dirck groaned; and cried Joris, "Stay spur!
Your Roos galloped bravely, the fault's not in her;

We'll remember at Aix" (āks)—for one heard the quick wheeze
Of her chest, saw the stretched neck, and staggering knees,
And sunk tail, and horrible heave of the flank,
As down on her haunches she shuddered and sank.

So we were left galloping, Joris and I,
Past Looz and past Tongres, no cloud in the sky;
The broad sun above laughed a pitiless laugh;
'Neath our feet broke the brittle, bright stubble like chaff;
Till over by Däl'hem a dome-spire sprang white,
And "Gallop," gasped Joris, "for Aix is in sight!"

"How they'll greet us!"—and all in a moment his roan
Rolled neck and croup over, lay dead as a stone;
And there was my Rō'land to bear the whole weight
Of the news which alone could save Aix from her fate,
With his nostrils like pits full of blood to the brim,
And with circles of red for his eye-sockets' rim.

Then I cast loose my buff-coat, each holster let fall,
Shook off both my jack-boots, let go belt and all,
Stood up in the stirrup, leaned, patted his ear,
Called my Roland his pet-name, my horse without peer—
Clapped my hands, laughed and sung, any noise, bad or good,
Till at length into Aix Roland galloped and stood.

And all I remember is friends flocking round,
As I sat with his head 'twixt my knees on the ground;
And no voice but was praising this Roland of mine,
As I poured down his throat our last measure of wine,
Which (the burgesses voted by common consent)
Was no more than his due, who brought good news from Ghent (gĕnt).

THE PASSIONS.
WILLIAM COLLINS.

When Music, heavenly maid, was young,
While yet in early Greece she sung,
The Passions oft, to hear her shell,
Thronged around her magic cell—
Exulting, trembling, raging, fainting—
Possessed beyond the Muse's painting;
By turns they felt the glowing mind
Disturbed, delighted, raised, refined;
Till once, 'tis said, when all were fired,
Filled with fury, rapt, inspired,
From the supporting myrtles round
They snatched her instruments of sound;

And, as they oft had heard apart
Sweet lessons of her forceful art,
Each (for Madness ruled the hour)
Would prove his own expressive power.

First Fear his hand, its skill to try,
  Amid the chords bewildered laid,
And back recoiled, he knew not why,
  E'en at the sound himself had made.

Next Anger rushed; his eyes, on fire,
  In lightnings owned his secret stings:
In one rude clash he struck the lyre,
  And swept with hurried hand the strings.

With woful measures wan Despair,
  Low, sullen sounds his grief beguiled—
A solemn, strange, and mingled air;
  'Twas sad by fits, by starts 'twas wild.

But thou, O Hope, with eyes so fair—
  What was thy delightful measure?
  Still it whispered promised pleasure,
  And bade the lovely scenes at distance hail!
Still would her touch the strain prolong;
  And from the rocks, the woods, the vale,
She called on Echo still, through all the song;
  And, where her sweetest theme she chose,
  A soft responsive voice was heard at every close;
And Hope, enchanted, smiled, and waved her golden hair.

And longer had she sung—but, with a frown,
    Revenge impatient rose;
He threw his blood-stained sword in thunder down,
    And, with a withering look,
    The war-denouncing trumpet took,
And blew a blast so loud and dread,
Were ne'er prophetic sounds so full of woe!
    And, ever and anon, he beat
    The doubling drum, with furious heat;
And though sometimes, each dreary pause between,
    Dejected Pity, at his side,
    Her soul-subduing voice applied,
Yet still he kept his wild, unaltered mein,
While each strained ball of sight seemed bursting from his head.
    Thy numbers, Jealousy, to naught were fixed—
      Sad proof of thy distressful state;
    Of differing themes the veering song was mixed;
      And now it courted Love—now, raving, called on Hate.

With eyes upraised, as one inspired,
Pale Melancholy sat retired;
And, from her wild, sequestered seat,
In notes by distance made more sweet,
Poured through the mellow horn her pensive soul;
  And, dashing soft from rocks around,
  Bubbling runnels joined the sound;
Through glades and glooms the mingled measure stole;
  Or, o'er some haunted stream, with fond delay,
    Round a holy calm diffusing,
    Love of Peace, and lonely musing,
  In hollow murmurs died away.

But oh! how altered was its sprightlier tone
When Cheerfulness, a nymph of healthiest hue,
  Her bow across her shoulder flung,
  Her buskins gemmed with morning dew,
Blew an inspiring air, that dale and thicket rung—
  The hunter's call, to Faun and Dryad known!
The oak-crowned Sisters, and their chaste-eyed queen,
  Satyrs and sylvan boys, were seen
  Peeping from forth their alleys green;
  Brown Exercise rejoiced to hear;
And Sport leaped up, and seized his beechen spear.
Last came Joy's ecstatic trial:
He, with viny crown advancing,
  First to the lively pipe his hand addressed;
But soon he saw the brisk awakening viol,
  Whose sweet, entrancing voice he loved the best;
They would have thought, who heard the strain,
  They saw, in Tempe's vale, her native maids,
  Amidst the festal-sounding shades,
To some unwearied minstrel dancing,
While, as his flying fingers kissed the strings,
Love framed with Mirth a gay fantastic round:
Loose were her tresses seen, her zone unbound;
  And he, amidst his frolic play,
  As if he would the charming air repay,
Shook thousand odors from his dewy wings.

  O Music! sphere-descending maid,
  Friend of Pleasure, Wisdom's aid!
  Why, goddess! why, to us denied,
  Lay'st thou thy ancient lyre aside?
  As, in that loved Athenian bower,
  You learned an all-commanding power,
  Thy mimic soul, O nymph endeared,

Can well recall what then it heard;
Where is thy native simple heart,
Devote to Virtue, Fancy, Art?
Arise, as in that elder time,
Warm, energetic, chaste, sublime;
Thy wonders, in that godlike age,
Fill thy recording sister's page;
'Tis said—and I believe the tale—
Thy humblest reed could more prevail,
Had more of strength, diviner rage,
Than all which charms this laggard age—
E'en all at once together found—
Cecilia's mingled world of sound.
Oh, bid our vain endeavors cease,
Revive the just designs of Greece;
Return in all thy simple state—
Confirm the tales her sons relate.

THE CHILD AND THE SUNSHINE.—*In Memoriam.*

Through the doorway flowed the sunshine
  In a flood of molten gold;
Like a cataract of glory,
  Down the rifted clouds it rolled.

While a child upon the carpet
  Laughing ran to where it lay,
With its little hands outreaching,
  Like a dream it fled away.

For a cloud had wandered o'er us,
  And the blue of heaven had gone,
And the dark wings of the tempest
  Beat the sullen air alone.

Still the child, his hands extended,
  Gazed upon the vacant floor,
Waiting, watching for the sunshine
  Which would come that day no more.

Happy childhood! watching, waiting,
  In your sweet and rosy glow,
You will follow hopes as fleeting
  In the path your feet must go.

And your longing heart will linger
  Where the joy-rays dimly burn,
For the warm and pleasant sunshine
  That will never more return.

TOLERATION.—*An Apologue.*
JEREMY TAYLOR.*

When Abraham sat at his tent door, according to his custom, waiting to entertain strangers, he espied an old man stooping and leaning on his staff, weary with age and travel, coming towards him, who was a hundred years of age.

He received him kindly, washed his feet, provided supper, and caused him to sit down; but, observing that the old man ate and prayed not, nor begged for a blessing on his meat, asked him why he did not worship the God of Heaven. The old man told him that he worshiped the fire only, and acknowledged no other God; at which answer Abraham grew so zealously angry that he thrust the old man out of his tent, and exposed him to all the evils of the night and an unguarded condition.

When the old man was gone, God called to Abraham, and asked him where the stranger was. He replied, "I thrust him away because he did not worship Thee:" God answered him, "I have suffered him these hundred years, although he dishonored me, and couldst thou not endure him one night, when he gave thee no trouble?" Upon this, saith the story, Abraham fetched him back again, and gave him hospitable entertainment and wise instruction. *Go thou and do likewise,* and thy charity will be rewarded by the God of Abraham.

FROM THE DODGE CLUB, OR ITALY IN MDCCCLIX.
JAMES DE MILLE.

La Cica did not speak the best English in the world, yet that could not account for all the singular remarks which she made, still less could it account for the tender interest of her manner. She had remarkably bright eyes. Why wandered those eyes so often to his, and why did they beam with such devotion—beaming for a moment only to fall in sweet innocent confusion? *La Cica* had the most fascina-

* Jeremy Taylor, one of the most eminent of English divines, and often styled the Shakspeare of theological literature, was born in Cambridge, England, in or about the year 1602. He died in 1667.

ting manners, yet they were often perplexing to the senator's soul.

"The countess," he thought, "is a most remarkably fine woman; but she does use her eyes uncommon, and I do wish she wouldn't be quite so demonstrative."

At last the senator came to this conclusion: *La Cica* was desperately in love with him.

She appeared to be a widow. Now if the poor *Cica* was hopelessly in love, it must be stopped at once. For he was a married man, and his good lady still lived, with a very large family, most of the members of which had grown up.

La Cica ought to know this. She ought indeed. But let the knowledge be given delicately, not abruptly.

On the following evening they walked on the balcony of *La Cica's* noble residence. She was sentimental, devoted, charming.

The conversation of a fascinating woman does not look so well when reported as it is when uttered. Her power is in her tone, her glance, her manner. Who can catch the evanescent beauty of her expression or the deep tenderness of her well-modulated voice? Who indeed?

"Does ze scene please you, my senator?"

"Very much indeed."

"Youar countrymen haf tol me zey would like to stay here alloway."

"It is a beautiful place."

"Did you aiver see any thin moaire loafely?" And the countess looked full in his face.

"Never," said the senator, earnestly. The next instant he blushed. He had been betrayed into a compliment.

The countess sighed.

"Helas! my senator, that it is not pairmitted to moartals to sociate as zey would laike."

"'Your senator,'" thought the gentleman thus addressed; "how fond, how tender—poor thing! poor thing!"

"I wish that Italy was nearer to the States," said he.

"How I adamiar youar style of mind, so differente from ze Italiana. You are so stong — so nobile. Yet would I laike to see moar of ze poetic in you."

"I always loved poetry, marm," said the senator, desperately.

"Ah!—good—nais—eccelente. I am plees at zat," cried the countess, with much animation. "You would loafe it moar eef you knew Italiano. Your langua ces not sufficiente musicale for poatry."

"It is not so soft a language as the *I*-talian."

"Ah! no—not so soft. Very well. And what theenka you of ze Italiano?"

"The sweetest language I ever heard in all my born days."

"Ah! now—you hev not heard much of ze Italiano, my senator."

"I have heard you speak often," said the senator, naïvely.

"Ah! you compliment! I sot you was aboove flattera."

And the countess playfully tapped his arm with her little fan.

"What Ingelis poet do you loafe best?"

"Poet? English poet?" said the senator, with some surprise. "Oh—why, marm, I think Watts is about the best of the lot."

"Watt? Was he a poet? I did not know zat. He who invented ze stim-injaine? And yet, if he was a poet, it is naturale zat you loafe him best."

"Steam-engine? Oh no! This one was a minister."

"A meeneestaire? Ah! an abbé? I know him not. Yet I haf read mos of all youar poets."

"He made up hymns, marm, and psalms—for instance: 'Watts's Divine Hymns and Spiritual Songs.'"

"Songs? Spirituelle? Ah! I mus at once procuaire ze works of Watt, which was favorit poet of my senator."

"A lady of such intelligence as you would like the poet Watts," said the senator, firmly. "He is the best known by far of all our poets."

"What! better zan Shakspeare, Milton, Bairon? You much surprass me."

"Better known and better loved than the whole lot. Why, his poetry is known by heart through all England and America."

"Merciful heaven! what you tell me! ees cet possibl!

Q

An yet he is not known here efen by name. It would please me mooch, my senator, to haire you make one quotatione. Know you Watt? Tell me some words of his which I may remembaire."

"I have a shocking bad memory."

"Bad memora! Oh, but you remember somethin, zis most beautiful charm nait—you haf a nobile soul—you must be affecta by beauty—by ze ideal. Make for me one quotatione."

And she rested her little hand on the senator's arm, and looked up imploringly in his face.

The senator looked foolish. He felt even more so. Here was a beautiful woman, by act and look showing a tender interest in him. Perplexing—but very flattering after all. So he replied:

"You will not let me refuse you any thing."

"Aha! you are vera willin to refuse. It is difficulty for me to excitare youar regards. You are fill with the grands ideas. But come—will you spik for me som from your favorit Watt?"

"Well, if you wish it so much," said the senator, kindly, and he hesitated.

"Ah! I do wish it so much!"

"Ehem!"

"Begin," said the countess. "Behold me. I listen. I hear everysin, and will remember it forava."

The only thing that the senator could think of was the verse which had been running in his head for the last few days, its measured rhythm keeping time with every occupation:

"'My willing soul would stay—'"

"Stop one moment," said the countess. "I weesh to learn it from you;" and she looked fondly and tenderly up, but instantly dropped her eyes.

"'Ma willina sol wooda sta—'"

"'In such a frame as this,'" prompted the senator.

"'Een socha framas zees.' Wait—'Ma willina sol wooda sta in socha framas zees.' Ah! appropriat; but could I hope zat you were true to zose lines, my senator? Well?"

"'And sit and sing herself away,'" said the senator, in a faltering voice, and breaking out into a cold perspiration for fear of committing himself by such uncommonly strong language.

"'Ansit ansin hassaf awai,'" repeated the countess, her face lighting up with a sweetly conscious expression.

The senator paused.

"I—ehem! I forget."

"Forget? Impossible!"

"I do really."

"Ah now! Forget? I see by your face—you desave. Say on."

The countess again gently touched his arm with both her little hands, and held it as though she would clasp it.

"Have you fear? Ah! cruel."

The senator turned pale, but finding refusal impossible, boldly finished:

"'To everlasting bliss'—there!"

"'To affarlastin blees thar.' Stop. I repeat it all: 'Ma willina sol wooda sta een socha framas zees, ansit ansin hassaf awai to affarlastin blees thar.' Am I right?"

"Yes," said the senator, meekly.

"I knew you were a poetic sola," said the countess, confidingly. "You air honesto—true—you can not desave. When you spik I can beliv you., Ah! my senator; an you can spik zis poetry!—at soch a toime! I nefare knew befoare zat you so impassione!—an you air so artaful! You breeng ze confersazione to beauty—to poetry—to ze poet Watt—so you may spik verses mos impassione! Ah! what do you mean? Santissima madre! how I wish you spik Italiano."

The countess drew nearer to him, but her approach only deepened his perplexity.

"How that poor thing does love me!" sighed the senator. "Law bless it! she can't help it—can't help it nohow. She is a goner; and what can I do? I'll have to leave Florence."

The countess was standing close beside him in a tender mood waiting for him to break the silence. How could he? He had been uttering words which sounded to her like love; and she—"a widow! a widow! wretched man that I am!"

There was a pause. The longer it lasted the more awkward the senator felt. What upon earth was he to do or say? What business had he to go and quote poetry to widows? What an old fool he must be! But the countess was very far from feeling awkward. Assuming an elegant attitude, she looked up, her face expressing the tenderest solicitude.

"What ails my senator?"

"Why, the fact is, marm—I feel sad—at leaving Florence. I must go shortly. My wife has written summoning me home. The children are down with the measles."

Oh, base fabrication! Oh, false senator! There wasn't a word of truth in that last remark. You spoke so because you wished *La Cica* to know that you had a wife and family. Yet it was very badly done.

La Cica changed neither her attitude nor her expression. Evidently the existence of his wife, and the melancholy situation of his unfortunate children, awakened no sympathy.

"But my senator—did you not say you wooda seeng yousellef away to affarlastin blees?"

"Oh, marm, it was a quotation—only a quotation."

But at this critical juncture the conversation was broken up by the arrival of a number of ladies and gentlemen.

But could the senator have known!

Could he have known how and where those words would confront him again!

SAM WELLER'S VALENTINE.
CHARLES DICKENS.

Mr. Weller having obtained leave of absence from Mr. Pickwick, who, in his then state of excitement and worry, was by no means displeased at being left alone, set forth long before the appointed hour; and, having plenty of time at his disposal, sauntered down as far as the Mansion House, where he paused and contemplated, with a face of great calmness and philosophy, the numerous cads and drivers of short stages who assemble near that famous place of resort, to the great terror and confusion of the old-lady population of these realms. Having loitered here for half an hour or so, Mr. Weller turned, and began wending his way towards Leadenhall Market, through a variety of by-streets and courts.

As he was sauntering away his spare time, and stopped to look at almost every object that met his gaze, it is by no means surprising that Mr. Weller should have paused before a small stationer's and print-seller's window; but, without further explanation, it does appear surprising that his eyes should have no sooner rested on certain pictures which were exposed for sale therein, than he gave a sudden start, smote his right leg with great vehemence, and exclaimed with energy, "If it hadn't been for this, I should ha' forgot all about it till it was too late!"

The particular picture on which Sam Weller's eyes were fixed, as he said this, was a highly-colored representation of a pair of human hearts skewered together with an arrow, cooking before a cheerful fire, while a male and a female cannibal in modern attire—the gentleman being clad in a blue coat and white trowsers, and the lady in a deep red pelisse with a parasol of the same—were approaching the meal with hungry eyes, up a serpentine gravel path leading thereunto.

A decidedly indelicate young gentleman, in a pair of wings and nothing else, was depicted as superintending the cooking; a representation of the spire of the church in Langhorn Place appeared in the distance; and the whole formed a "valentine," of which, as a written inscription in the window testified, there was a large assortment within, which the shopkeeper pledged himself to dispose of to his countrymen generally at the reduced rate of one and sixpence each.

"I should ha' forgot it—I should certainly have forgot it!" said Sam; and, so saying, he at once stepped into the stationer's shop, and requested to be served with a sheet of the best gilt-edged letter-paper, and a hard-nibbed pen which could be warranted not to splutter. These articles having been promptly supplied, he walked on direct towards Leadenhall Market at a good round pace, very different from his recent lingering one. Looking round him, he there beheld a sign-board on which the painter's art had delineated something remotely resembling a cerulean elephant with an aquiline nose in lieu of a trunk. Rightly conjecturing that this was the Blue Boar himself, he stepped into the house, and inquired concerning his parent.

"He won't be here this three quarters of an hour or more," said the young lady who superintended the domestic arrangements of the Blue Boar.

"Wery good, my dear," replied Sam. "Let me have nine penn'orth o' brandy and water luke, and the inkstand, will you, miss?"

The brandy and water luke and the inkstand having been carried into the little parlor, and the young lady having carefully flattened down the coals to prevent their blazing, and carried away the poker to preclude the possibility of the fire being stirred without the full privity and concurrence of the Blue Boar being first had and obtained, Sam Weller sat himself down in a box near the stove, and pulled out the sheet of gilt-edged letter-paper, and the hard-nibbed pen. Then, looking carefully at the pen to see that there were no hairs in it, and dusting down the table so that there might be no crumbs of bread under the paper, Sam tucked up the cuffs of his coat, squared his elbows, and composed himself to write.

To ladies and gentlemen who are not in the habit of devoting themselves practically to the science of penmanship, writing a letter is no very easy task, it being always considered necessary in such cases for the writer to incline his head on his left arm, so as to place his eyes as nearly as possible on a level with the paper, and, while glancing sideways at the letters he is constructing, to form with his tongue imaginary characters to correspond. These motions, although unquestionably of the greatest assistance to original composition, retard in some degree the progress of the writer, and Sam had unconsciously been a full hour and a half writing words in small text, smearing out wrong letters with his little finger, and putting in new ones which required going over very often to render them visible through the old blots, when he was roused by the opening of the door and the entrance of his parent.

"Vell, Sammy," said the father.

"Vell, my Prooshan Blue," responded the son, laying down his pen, "what's the last bulletin about mother-in-law?"

"Mrs. Veller passed a wery good night, but is uncommon perwerse and unpleasant this mornin'—signed upon oath—Tony Veller, Esquire. That's the last vun as was issued, Sammy," replied Mr. Weller, untying his shawl.

"No better yet?" inquired Sam.

"All the symptoms aggerawated," replied Mr. Weller, shaking his head. "But wot's that you're doin' of—pursuit of knowledge under difficulties—eh, Sammy?"

"I've done now," said Sam, with slight embarrassment; "I've been a writin'."

"So I see," replied Mr. Weller. "Not to any young 'ooman, I hope, Sammy."

"Why, it's no use a sayin' it ain't," replied Sam. "It's a walentine."

"A what!" exclaimed Mr. Weller, apparently horror-stricken by the word.

"A walentine," replied Sam.

"Samivel, Samivel," said Mr. Weller, in reproachful accents, "I didn't think you'd ha' done it. Arter the warnin' you've had o' your father's wicious propensities; arter all I've said to you upon this here wery subject; arter actiwally seein' and bein' in the company o' your own mother-in-law, vich I should ha' thought wos a moral lesson as no man could ever ha' forgotten to his dyin' day! I didn't think you'd ha' done it, Sammy—I didn't think you'd ha' done it." These reflections were too much for the good old man. He raised Sam's tumbler to his lips and drank off its contents.

"Wot's the matter now?" said Sam.

"Nev'r mind, Sammy," replied Mr. Weller, "it'll be a wery agonizin' trial to me at my time o' life, but I'm pretty tough, that's vun consolation, as the wery old turkey remarked when the farmer said he was afeerd he should be obliged to kill him for the London market."

"Wot'll be a trial?" inquired Sam.

"To see you married, Sammy—to see you a dilluded wictim, and thinkin' in your innocence that it's all wery capital," replied Mr. Weller. "It's a dreadful trial to a father's feelin's, that 'ere, Sammy."

"Nonsense," said Sam; "I ain't a goin' to get married; don't you fret yourself about that; I know you're a judge of these things. Order in your pipe, and I'll read you the letter—there."

THE SAME SUBJECT CONTINUED.

We can not distinctly say whether it was the prospect of the pipe, or the consolatory reflection that a fatal disposition to get married ran in the family and couldn't be helped, which calmed Mr. Weller's feelings, and caused his grief to subside. We should be rather disposed to say that the result was attained by combining the two sources of consolation, for he repeated the second in a low tone very frequently, ringing the bell meanwhile to order in the first. He then divested himself of his upper coat, and lighting the pipe, and placing himself in front of the fire, with his back towards it, so that he could feel its full heat and recline against the mantel-piece at the same time, turned towards Sam, and, with a countenance greatly mollified by the softening influence of tobacco, requested him to "fire away."

Sam dipped his pen into the ink, to be ready for any corrections, and began with a very theatrical air:

"'Lovely—'"

"Stop," said Mr. Weller, ringing the bell. "A double glass o' the invariable, my dear."

"Very well, sir," replied the girl, who with great quickness appeared, vanished, returned, and disappeared.

"They seem to know your ways here," observed Sam.

"Yes," replied his father, "I've been here before in my time. Go on, Sammy."

"'Lovely creetur'," repeated Sam.

"'Tain't in poetry, is it?" interposed the father.

"No, no," replied Sam.

"Wery glad to hear it," said Mr. Weller. "Poetry's unnat'ral; no man ever talked in poetry 'cept a beadle on boxin'-day, or Warren's blackin', or Rowland's oil, or some o' them low fellers; never let yourself down to talk poetry, my boy. Begin again, Sammy."

Mr. Weller resumed his pipe with critical solemnity, and Sam once more commenced, and read as follows:

"'Lovely creetur', I feel myself a charmed—'"

"That ain't proper," said Mr. Weller, taking his pipe from his mouth.

"No, it ain't charmed," observed Sam, holding the letter up to the light; "it's 'shamed; there's a blot there—'I feel myself ashamed.'"

"Wery good," said Mr. Weller. "Go on."

"'Feel myself ashamed and completely cir—' I forget wot this here word is," said Sam, scratching his head with the pen, in vain attempts to remember.

"Why don't you look at it, then?" inquired Mr. Weller.

"So I *am* a lookin' at it," replied Sam, "but there's another blot; here's a 'c,' and a 'i,' and a 'd.'"

"Circumwented, p'r'aps," suggested Mr. Weller.

"No, it ain't that," said Sam; "circumscribed—that's it."

"That ain't as good a word as circumwented, Sammy," said Mr. Weller, gravely.

"Think not?" said Sam.

"Nothin' like it," replied his father.

"But don't you think it means more?" inquired Sam.

"Vell, p'r'aps it is a more tenderer word," said Mr. Weller, after a few moments' reflection. "Go on, Sammy."

"'Feel myself ashamed and completely circumscribed in a dressin' of you, for you *are* a nice gal, and nothin' but it.'"

"That's a wery pretty sentiment," said the elder Mr. Weller, removing his pipe to make way for the remark.

"Yes, I think it is rayther good," observed Sam, highly flattered.

"Wot I like in that 'ere style of writing," said the elder Mr. Weller, "is, that there ain't no callin' names in it—no Wenuses, nor nothin' o' that kind: wot's the good o' callin' a young 'ooman a Wenus or an angel, Sammy?"

"Ah! what, indeed?" replied Sam.

"You might jist as vell call her a griffin, or a unicorn, or a king's arms at once, vich is wery vell known to be a collection o' fabulous animals," added Mr. Weller.

"Just as well," replied Sam.

"Drive on, Sammy," said Mr. Weller.

Sam complied with the request, and proceeded as follows; his father continuing to smoke with a mixed expression of wisdom and complacency which was particularly edifying.

"'Afore I see you I thought all women was alike.'"

"So they are," observed the elder Mr. Weller, parenthetically.

"'But now,'" continued Sam, "'now I find what a reg-'lar soft-headed, ink-red'lous turnip I must ha' been, for there ain't nobody like you, though *I* like you better than nothin' at all.' I thought it best to make that rayther strong," said Sam, looking up.

Mr. Weller nodded approvingly, and Sam resumed:

"'So I take the privilidge of the day, Mary, my dear—as the gen'lem'n in difficulties did ven he valked out of a Sunday—to tell you that the first and only time I see you, your likeness was took on my heart in much quicker time and brighter colors than ever a likeness was took by the profeel macheen (which, p'r'aps, you may have heerd on, Mary, my dear), altho' it *does* finish a portrait, and puts the frame and glass on complete, with a hook at the end to hang it up by, and all in two minutes and a quarter.'"

"I am afeered that werges on the poetical, Sammy," said Mr. Weller, dubiously.

"No, it don't," replied Sam, reading on very quickly, to avoid contesting the point.

"'Except of me, Mary, my dear, as your walentine, and think over what I've said. My dear Mary, I will now conclude.' That's all," said Sam.

"That's rayther a sudden pull up, ain't it, Sammy?" inquired Mr. Weller.

"Not a bit on it," said Sam; "she'll vish there vos more, and that's the great art o' letter-writin'."

"Well," said Mr. Weller, "there's somethin' in that; and I wish your mother-in-law'd only conduct her conwersation on the same gen-teel principle. Ain't you a goin' to sign it?"

"That's the difficulty," said Sam; "I don't know what *to* sign it."

"Sign it—Veller," said the oldest surviving proprietor of that name.

"Won't do," said Sam. "Never sign a walentine with your own name."

"Sign it—Pickwick, then," said Mr. Weller; "it's a wery good name, and a easy one to spell."

"The wery thing," said Sam. "I *could* end with a werse; what do you think?"

"I don't like it, Sam," rejoined Mr. Weller. "I never know'd a respectable coachman as wrote poetry, 'cept one as made an affectin' copy o' werses the night afore he was hung for highway robbery, and *he* was only a Cambervell man, so even that's no rule."

But Sam was not to be dissuaded from the poetical idea that had occurred to him, so he signed the letter

"Your love-sick   PICKWICK,"

and having folded it in a very intricate manner, he squeezed a down-hill direction in one corner—"To Mary, Housemaid, at Mr. Nupkins's, Mayor's, Ipswich, Suffolk"—and put it into his pocket, wafered, and ready for the General Post.

PUTTING UP STOVES.

One who has had considerable experience in the work of putting up stoves says the first step to be taken is to put on a very old and ragged coat, under the impression that when he gets his mouth full of plaster it will keep his shirt-bosom clean. Next he gets his hands inside the place where the pipe ought to go, and blacks his fingers, and then he carefully makes a black mark down one side of his nose. It is impossible to make any headway, in doing this work, until this mark is made down the side of the nose. Having got his face properly marked, the victim is ready to begin the ceremony. The head of the family—who is the big goose of the sacrifice—grasps one side of the bottom of the stove, and his wife and the hired girl take hold of the other side. In this way the load is started from the wood-shed towards the parlor. Going through the door, the head of the family will carefully swing his side of the stove around, and jamb his thumb-nail against the door-post. This part of the ceremony is never omitted. Having got the stove comfortably in place, the next thing is to find the legs. Two of these are left inside the stove since the spring before; the other two must be hunted after for twenty-five minutes. They are usually found under the coal. Then the head of the family holds up one side of the stove while his wife puts two of the legs in place, and next he holds up the other side while the other two are fixed, and one of the first two falls out. By the time the stove is on its legs he gets reckless, and takes off his coat, regardless of his linen. Then he goes off for the pipe, and gets a cinder in his eye. It don't make any difference how well the pipe was put up last year, it will be found a little too short or a little too long. The head of the family jams his hat over his eyes, and, taking a pipe under each arm, goes to the tin-shop to have it fixed. When he gets back he steps upon one of the best parlor chairs to see if the pipe fits, and his wife makes him get down for fear he will scratch the varnish off from the chair with the nails in his boot-heel. In getting down he will surely step on the cat, and may thank his stars if it is not the baby. Then he gets an old chair, and climbs up to the chimney again, to find that in cutting the pipe off the end has been left too big for the hole in the chimney. So he goes to the wood-shed, and splits one side of the end of the pipe with an old axe, and squeezes it in his hands to make it smaller. Finally he gets the pipe in shape, and finds that the stove does not stand true. Then himself and wife and the hired girl move the stove to the left, and the legs fall out again. Next it is to move to the right. More difficulty with the legs. Moved to the front a little. Elbow not even with the hole in the chimney, and he goes to the wood-shed after some little blocks. While putting the blocks under the legs the pipe comes out of the chimney. That remedied, the elbow keeps tipping over, to the great alarm of the wife. Head of the family gets the dinner-table out, puts the old chair on it, gets his wife to hold the chair, and balances himself on it, to drive some nails into the ceiling. Drops the hammer on to wife's head. At last gets the nails driven, makes a wire-swing to hold the pipe, hammers a little here, pulls a little there, takes a long breath, and announces the ceremony completed.

Job never put up any stoves. It would have ruined his reputation if he had.

THE POWER OF HABIT.
JOHN B. GOUGH.

I remember once riding from Buffalo to the Niagara Falls. I said to a gentleman, " What river is that, sir?"

" That," said he, " is Niagara River."

" Well, it is a beautiful stream," said I; " bright, and fair, and glassy. How far off are the rapids?"

" Only a mile or two," was the reply.

" Is it *possible* that only a mile from us we shall find the water in the turbulence which it must show near the Falls?"

" You will find it so, sir." And so I found it; and the first sight of Niagara I shall never forget.

Now, launch your bark on that Niagara River; it is bright, smooth, beautiful, and glassy. There is a ripple at the bow; the silver wake you leave behind adds to your enjoyment. Down the stream you glide, oars, sails, and helm in proper trim, and you set out on your pleasure excursion. Suddenly some one cries out from the bank, " *Young men, ahoy !*"

" What is it?"

" *The rapids are below you !*"

" Ha! ha! we have heard of the rapids, but we are not such fools as to get there. If we go too fast, then we shall up with the helm and steer to the shore; we will set the mast in the socket, hoist the sail, and speed to the land. Then on, boys! don't be alarmed; there is no danger."

" *Young men, ahoy there !*"

" What is it?"

" *The rapids are below you !*"

" Ha! ha! we will laugh and quaff; all things delight us

What care we for the future! No man ever saw it. Sufficient for the day is the evil thereof. We will enjoy life while we may—will catch pleasure as it flies. This is enjoyment; time enough to steer out of danger when we are sailing swiftly with the current."

"YOUNG MEN, AHOY!"

"What is it?"

"BEWARE! BEWARE! THE RAPIDS ARE BELOW YOU!"

"Now you see the water foaming all around. See how fast you pass that point! Up with the helm! Now turn! Pull hard! Quick! quick! quick! pull for your lives! pull till the blood starts from your nostrils, and the veins stand like whip-cords upon your brow! Set the mast in the socket! Hoist the sail! Ah! ah! it is too late! Shrieking, howling, blaspheming, over they go."

Thousands go over the rapids of intemperance every year, through *the power of habit*, crying all the while, "*When I find out that it is injuring me, I will give it up!*"

CHRYSOSTOM'S ELOQUENCE.

The following burst of eloquence from Chrysostom, when he was sentenced to banishment, is a good specimen of the style of this "silver-tongued" preacher:

"What can I fear? Will it be death? But you know that Christ is my life, and that I shall gain by death. Will it be exile? But the earth and all its fullness is the Lord's. Will it be the loss of wealth? But we brought nothing into the world, and can carry nothing out. Thus all the terrors of the world are contemptible in my eyes, and I smile at all its good things. Poverty I do not fear. Riches I do not sigh for. Death I do not shrink from, and life I do not desire, save only for the progress of your souls. But you know, my friends, the true cause of my fall. It is that I have not lined my house with rich tapestry. It is that I have not clothed me in robes of silk. It is that I have not flattered the effeminacy and sensuality of certain men, nor laid gold and silver at their feet. But why need I say more? **Jezebel** is raising her persecution, and Elijah must fly. Herodias is taking her pleasure, and John must be bound in chains. The Egyptian wife tells her lie, and Joseph must be thrust into prison. And so, if they banish me, I shall be like Elias; if they throw me into the mire, like Jeremiah; if they plunge me into the sea, like the prophet Jonah; if into the pit, like Daniel; if they stone me, it is Stephen that I shall resemble; John, the forerunner, if they cut off my head; Paul, if they beat me with stripes; Isaiah, if they saw me asunder."

PSALM XXIV.—*A Psalm of David.*

The earth is the Lord's, and the fullness thereof; the world, and they that dwell therein.

For he hath founded it upon the seas, and established it upon the floods.

Who shall ascend into the hill of the Lord? or who shall stand in his holy place?

He that hath clean hands and a pure heart; who hath not lifted up his soul unto vanity, nor sworn deceitfully.

He shall receive the blessing from the Lord, and righteousness from the God of his salvation.

This is the generation of them that seek him—that seek thy face, O Jacob. Selah.

Lift up your heads, O ye gates, and be ye lifted up, ye everlasting doors, and the King of glory shall come in.

Who *is* this King of glory? The Lord strong and mighty, the Lord mighty in battle.

Lift up your heads, O ye gates—even lift them up, ye everlasting doors, and the King of glory shall come in.

Who is this King of glory? The Lord of hosts, he is the King of glory. Selah.

DANTE AND MILTON.

MACAULAY.

Milton was, like Dante, a statesman and a lover, and, like Dante, he had been unfortunate in ambition and in love. He had survived his health and his sight, and the comforts of his home and the prosperity of his party. Of the great men by whom he had been distinguished on his entrance into life, some had been taken away from the evil to come, some had carried into foreign climates their unconquerable hatred to oppression, some were pining in dungeons, and some had poured forth their blood on scaffolds. That hateful proscription facetiously termed the Act of Indemnity and Oblivion had set a mark on the poor, blind, deserted poet, and held him up by name to the hatred of a profligate court and an inconstant people. Venal and licentious scribblers, with just sufficient talent to clothe the thoughts of a pander in the style of a bellman, were now the favorite writers of the sovereign and the public. It was a loathsome herd, which could be compared to nothing so fitly as to the rabble of Comus—grotesque monsters, half bestial, half human, dropping with wine, bloated with gluttony, and reeling in obscene dances. Amid these his muse was placed, like the chaste lady of the mask, lofty, spotless, and serene, to be chatted at, and pointed at, and grinned at by the whole tribe of satyrs and goblins.

If ever despondency could be excused in any man, it might have been excused in Milton. But the strength of his mind overcame every calamity. Neither blindness, nor gout, nor penury, nor age, nor domestic afflictions, nor political disappointments, nor abuse, nor proscription, nor neglect had power to disturb his sedate and majestic patience. His spirits do not seem to have been high, but they were singularly equable. His temper was serious, perhaps stern, but it was a temper which no suffering could render sullen or fretful. Such as it was when, on the eve of great events, he returned from his travels, in the prime of health and manly beauty, such it continued to be when, after having experienced every calamity which is incident to our nature —old, poor, sightless, and disgraced—he retired to his hovel to die!

GABRIEL GRUB.
Charles Dickens.

In an old abbey-town down in this part of the country, a long, long while ago, there officiated as sexton and gravedigger one Gabriel Grub.

A little before twilight one Christmas eve, Gabriel shouldered his spade, lighted his lantern, and betook himself towards the old church-yard, for he had got a grave to finish by next morning, and, feeling very low, he thought it might raise his spirits, perhaps, if he went on with his work at once. As he wended his way up the ancient street, he saw the cheerful light of the blazing fires gleam through the old casements, and heard the loud laugh and the cheerful shouts of those who were assembled around them; he marked the bustling preparations for next day's good cheer, and smelt the numerous savory odors consequent thereupon, as they steamed up from the kitchen windows in clouds. All this was gall and wormwood to the heart of Gabriel Grub; and as groups of children bounded out of the houses, tripped across the road, and were met, before they could knock at the opposite door, by half a dozen curly-headed little rascals, who crowded round them as they flocked up stairs to spend the evening in their Christmas games, Gabriel smiled grimly, and clutched the handle of his spade with a firmer grasp as he thought of measles, scarlet fever, thrush, whooping-cough, and a good many other sources of consolation beside.

In this happy frame of mind Gabriel strode along, returning a short, sullen growl to the good-humored greetings of such of his neighbors as now and then passed him, until he turned into the dark lane which led to the church-yard. Now he had been looking forward to reaching the dark lane, because it was, generally speaking, a nice, gloomy, mournful place, and he was not a little indignant to hear a young urchin roaring out some jolly song about a merry Christmas in this very sanctuary. So Gabriel waited till the boy came up, and then dodged him into a corner, and rapped him over the head with his lantern five or six times, just to teach him to modulate his voice. And as the boy hurried away with his hand to his head, singing quite a different sort of tune, Gabriel Grub chuckled very heartily to himself, and entered the church-yard, locking the door behind him.

He took off his coat, set down his lantern, and, getting into the unfinished grave, worked at it for an hour or so with right good will. But the earth was hardened with the frost, and it was no very easy matter to break it up and shovel it out; and, although there was a moon, it was a very young one, and shed little light upon the grave, which was in the shadow of the church. At any other time these obstacles would have made Gabriel Grub very moody and miserable; but he was so well pleased with having stopped the small boy's singing that he took little heed of the scanty progress he had made, and looked down into the grave, when he had finished work for the night, with grim satisfaction, murmuring, as he gathered up his things,

"Brave lodgings for one, brave lodgings for one,
A few feet of cold earth when life is done."

"Ho! ho!" laughed Gabriel Grub, as he sat himself down on a flat tomb-stone, which was a favorite resting-place of his, and drew forth his wicker bottle; "a coffin at Christmas—a Christmas-box. Ho! ho! ho!"

"Ho! ho! ho!" repeated a voice, which sounded close behind him.

Gabriel paused in some alarm, in the act of raising the wicker bottle to his lips, and looked round. The bottom of the oldest grave about him was not more still and quiet than the church-yard in the pale moonlight. The frost glistened on the tomb-stones, and sparkled like rows of gems among the stone carvings of the old church. Not the faintest rustle broke the profound tranquillity of the solemn scene. Sound itself appeared to be frozen up—all was so cold and still.

"It was the echoes," said Gabriel Grub, raising the bottle to his lips again.

"It was *not*," said a deep voice.

Gabriel started up, and stood rooted to the spot with astonishment and terror, for his eyes rested on a form which made his blood run cold.

Seated on an upright tomb-stone, close to him, was a strange, unearthly figure, whom Gabriel felt at once was no being of this world. His long, fantastic legs, which might have reached the ground, were cocked up, and crossed after a quaint, fantastic fashion; his sinewy arms were bare, and his hands rested on his knees. On his short, round body he wore a close covering, ornamented with small slashes, and a short cloak dangled on his back; the collar was cut into curious peaks, which served the goblin in lieu of ruff or neckerchief; and his shoes curled up at the toes into long points. On his head he wore a broad-brimmed sugar-loaf hat, garnished with a single feather. The hat was covered with the white frost, and the goblin looked as if he had sat on the same tomb-stone very comfortably for two or three hundred years. He was sitting perfectly still; his tongue was out out, as if in derision; and he was grinning at Gabriel Grub with such a grin as only a goblin could call up.

"It was *not* the echoes," said the goblin.

Gabriel Grub was paralyzed, and could make no reply.

"What do you do here on Christmas eve?" said the goblin, sternly.

"I came to dig a grave, sir," stammered Gabriel Grub.

"What man wanders among graves and church-yards on such a night as this?" said the goblin.

"Gabriel Grub! Gabriel Grub!" screamed a wild chorus of voices that seemed to fill the church-yard. Gabriel looked fearfully round—nothing was to be seen.

"What have you got in that bottle?" said the goblin.

"Hollands, sir," replied the sexton, trembling more than ever; for he had bought it of the smugglers, and he thought that perhaps his questioner might be in the excise department of the goblins.

"Who drinks Hollands in a church-yard on such a night as this?" said the goblin.

"Gabriel Grub! Gabriel Grub!" exclaimed the wild voices again.

The goblin leered maliciously at the terrified sexton, and then, raising his voice, exclaimed,

"And who, then, is our fair and lawful prize?"

To this inquiry the invisible chorus replied, in a strain that sounded like the voices of many choristers singing to the mighty swell of the old church organ—a strain that seemed borne to the sexton's ears upon a gentle wind, and to die away as its soft breath passed onward; but the burden of the reply was still the same—"Gabriel Grub! Gabriel Grub!"

The goblin grinned a broader grin than before as he said, "Well, Gabriel, what do you say to this?"

The sexton gasped for breath.

"It's — it's — very curious, sir, very curious, and very pretty; but I think I'll go back and finish my work, sir, if you please."

"Work!" said the goblin; "what work?"

"The grave, sir—making the grave," stammered the sexton.

"Oh, the grave, eh?" said the goblin; "who makes graves at a time when all other men are merry, and takes a pleasure in it?"

Again the mysterious voices replied, "Gabriel Grub! Gabriel Grub!"

"I'm afraid my friends want you, Gabriel—I'm afraid my friends want you."

"Under favor, sir, I don't think they can, sir; they don't know me, sir; I don't think the gentlemen have ever seen me, sir."

"Oh, yes they have." "We know the man with the sulky face and the grim scowl, that came down the street to-night, throwing his evil looks at the children, and grasping his burying-spade the tighter. We know the man that struck the boy, in the envious malice of his heart, because the boy could be merry and he could not. We know him—we know him."

"I—I—am afraid I must leave you, sir."

"Leave us! Gabriel Grub going to leave us! Ho! ho! ho!"

As the goblin laughed, the sexton observed for one instant a brilliant illumination within the windows of the church, as if the whole building were lighted up; it disappeared, the organ pealed forth a lively air, and whole troops of goblins, the very counterpart of the first one, poured into the church-yard, and began playing at leap-frog with the tomb-stones, never stopping for an instant to take breath, but overing the highest among them, one after the other, with the most marvelous dexterity. The first goblin was a most astonishing leaper, and none of the others could come near him. Even in the extremity of his terror, the sexton could not help observing that, while his friends were content to leap over the common-sized grave-stones, the first one took the family vaults, iron railings and all, with as much ease as if they had been so many street-posts.

At last the game reached to a most exciting pitch; the organ played quicker and quicker, and the goblins leaped faster and faster, coiling themselves up, rolling head over heels upon the ground, and bounding over the tomb-stones like foot-balls. The sexton's brain whirled round with the rapidity of the motion he beheld, and his legs reeled beneath him as the spirits flew before his eyes, when the goblin-king suddenly darted towards him, laid his hand upon his collar, and sank with him through the earth.

When Gabriel Grub had had time to fetch his breath, which the rapidity of his descent had for the moment taken away, he found himself in what appeared to be a large cavern, surrounded on all sides by crowds of goblins, ugly and grim. In the centre of the room, on an elevated seat, was stationed his friend of the church-yard, and close beside him stood Gabriel Grub himself, without the power of motion.

"Cold to-night," said the king of the goblins—"very cold. A glass of something warm, here."

At this command, half a dozen officious goblins, with a perpetual smile upon their faces, whom Gabriel Grub imagined to be courtiers on that account, hastily disappeared, and presently returned with a goblet of liquid fire, which they presented to the king.

"Ah!" said the goblin, whose cheeks and throat were quite transparent as he tossed down the flame, "this warms one indeed; bring a bumper of the same for Mr. Grub."

It was in vain for the unfortunate sexton to protest that he was not in the habit of taking any thing warm at night; for one of the goblins held him, while another poured the blazing liquid down his throat; and the whole assembly screeched with laughter as he coughed, and choked, and wiped away the tears which gushed plentifully from his eyes after swallowing the burning draught.

"And now," said the king, fantastically poking the taper corner of his sugar-loaf hat into the sexton's eye, and thereby occasioning him the most exquisite pain—"and now show the man of misery and gloom a few of the pictures from our own great store-house."

As the goblin said this, a thick cloud, which obscured the farther end of the cavern, rolled gradually away, and disclosed, apparently at a great distance, a small and scantily-furnished, but neat and clean apartment. A crowd of little children were gathered round a bright fire, clinging to their mother's gown, and gamboling round her chair. The mother occasionally rose, and drew aside the window-curtain, as if to look for some expected object. A frugal meal was ready spread upon the table, and an elbow-chair was placed near the fire. A knock was heard at the door; the mother opened it, and the children crowded round her, and clapped their hands for joy as their father entered. He was wet and weary, and shook the snow from his garments as the children crowded round him, and, seizing his cloak, hat, stick, and gloves with busy zeal, ran with them from the room. Then, as he sat down to his meal before the fire, the children climbed about his knee, and the mother sat by his side, and all seemed happiness and comfort.

But a change came upon the view almost imperceptibly. The scene was altered to a small bedroom, where the fairest and youngest child lay dying; the roses had fled from his cheek, and the light from his eye; and, even as the sexton looked upon him, with an interest he had never felt or known before, he died. His young brothers and sisters crowded round his little bed, and seized his tiny hand, so cold and heavy; but they shrank back from its touch, and looked with awe on his infant face; for, calm and tranquil as it was, and sleeping in rest and peace, as the beautiful child seemed to be, they saw that he was dead, and they knew that he was an angel looking down upon them and blessing them from a bright and happy heaven.

Again the light cloud passed across the picture, and again the subject changed. The father and mother were old and helpless now, and the number of those about them was diminished more than half; but content and cheerfulness sat on every face, and beamed in every eye, as they crowded round the fireside, and told and listened to old stories of earlier and by-gone days. Slowly and peacefully the father sank into the grave, and, soon after, the sharer of all his cares and troubles followed him to a place of rest and peace. The few who yet survived them knelt by their tomb, and watered the green turf which covered it with their tears; then rose, and turned away sadly and mournfully, but not with bitter cries or despairing lamentations, for they knew that they should one day meet again; and once more they mixed with the busy world, and their content and cheerfulness were restored. The cloud settled upon the picture, and concealed it from the sexton's view.

"What do you think of *that?*" said the goblin, turning his large face toward Gabriel Grub.

Gabriel murmured out something about its being very pretty, and looked somewhat ashamed as the goblin bent his fiery eyes upon him.

"*You* a miserable man!" said the goblin, in a tone of excessive contempt. "*You!*" He appeared disposed to add more, but indignation choked his utterance; so he lifted up one of his very pliable legs, and, flourishing it above his head a little, to insure his aim, administered a good sound kick to Gabriel Grub; immediately after which, all the goblins-in-waiting crowded round the wretched sexton, and kicked him without mercy, according to the established and invariable custom of courtiers upon earth, who kick whom royalty kicks, and hug whom royalty hugs.

"Show him some more," said the king of the goblins.

At these words the cloud was again dispelled, and a rich and beautiful landscape was disclosed to view. The sun shone from out the clear blue sky, the water sparkled beneath his rays, and the trees looked greener, and the flowers more gay, beneath his cheerful influence. The water rippled on with a pleasant sound, the trees rustled in the light wind that murmured among their leaves, the birds sang upon the boughs, and the lark caroled on high her welcome to the morning. Yes, it was morning, the bright, balmy morning of summer; the minutest leaf, the smallest blade of grass, was instinct with life. Man walked forth, elated with the scene, and all was brightness and splendor.

"*You* a miserable man!" said the king of the goblins, in a more contemptuous tone than before. And again the king of the goblins gave his leg a flourish; again it descended on the shoulders of the sexton; and again the attendant goblins imitated the example of their chief.

Many a time the cloud went and came, and many a lesson it taught to Gabriel Grub, who, although his shoulders smarted with pain from the frequent applications of the goblins' feet thereunto, looked on with an interest which nothing could diminish. He saw that men who worked hard, and earned their scanty bread with lives of labor, were cheerful and happy, and that to the most ignorant the sweet face of nature was a never-failing source of cheerfulness and joy. Above all, he saw that men like himself, who snarled at the mirth and cheerfulness of others, were the foulest weeds on the fair surface of the earth; and, setting all the good of the world against the evil, he came to the conclusion that it was a very decent and respectable sort of a world after all. No sooner had he formed it than the cloud which had closed over the last picture seemed to settle on his senses, and lull him to repose. One by one the goblins faded from his sight, and as the last one disappeared he sank to sleep.

The day had broken when Gabriel Grub awoke, and found himself lying at full length on the flat grave-stone in the church-yard, with the wicker bottle lying empty by his side, and his coat, spade, and lantern, well whitened by the last night's frost, scattered on the ground. The stone on which he had first seen the goblin seated stood bolt upright before him, and the grave at which he had worked the night before was not far off. At first he began to doubt the reality of his adventures; but the acute pain in his shoulders, when he attempted to rise, assured him that the kicking of the goblins was certainly not ideal. He was staggered again by observing no traces of footsteps in the snow on which the goblins had played at leap-frog with the grave-stones;

but he speedily accounted for this circumstance when he remembered that, being spirits, they would leave no visible impression behind them. So Gabriel Grub got on his feet as well as he could for the pain in his back, and, brushing the frost off his coat, put it on, and turned his face toward the town.

But he was an altered man, and he could not bear the thought of returning to a place where his repentance would be scoffed at, and his reformation disbelieved. He hesitated for a few moments, and then turned away to wander where he might, and seek his bread elsewhere.

The lantern, the spade, and the wicker bottle were found that day in the church-yard. There were a great many speculations about the sexton's fate at first, but it was speedily determined that he had been carried away by the goblins; and there were not wanting some very credible witnesses who had distinctly seen him whisked through the air on the back of a chestnut horse blind of one eye, with the hind quarters of a lion, and the tail of a bear. At length all this was devoutly believed; and the new sexton used to exhibit to the curious, for a trifling emolument, a good-sized piece of the church weathercock which had been accidentally kicked off by the aforesaid horse in his aerial flight, and picked up by himself in the church-yard a year or two afterward.

Unfortunately, these stories were somewhat disturbed by the unlooked-for reappearance of Gabriel Grub himself some ten years afterward, a ragged, contented, rheumatic old man. He told his story to the clergyman, and also to the mayor, and in course of time it began to be received as a matter of history, in which form it has continued down to this very day. The believers in the weathercock tale, having misplaced their confidence once, were not easily prevailed upon to part with it again, so they looked as wise as they could, shrugged their shoulders, touched their foreheads, and murmured something about Gabriel Grub's having drunk all the Hollands, and then fallen asleep on the flat tomb-stone; and they affected to explain what he supposed he had witnessed in the goblins' cavern by saying he had seen the world and grown wiser. But this opinion, which was by no means a popular one at any time, gradually died off; and, be the matter how it may, as Gabriel Grub was afflicted with rheumatism to the end of his days, this story has at least one moral, if it teach no better one—and that is, that if a man turns sulky and drinks at Christmas time, he may make up his mind to be not a bit the better for it, let the spirits be ever so good, or let them be even as many degrees beyond proof as those which Gabriel Grub saw in the goblins' cavern.

PATRICK O'ROURKE AND THE FROGS.—*A Cold-water Story.*
GEORGE W. BUNGAY.

Saint Patrick did a vast deal of good in his day: he not only drove the snakes out of Ireland, but he also drove away the frogs; at least I judge so from the fact that Patrick O'Rourke was unfamiliar with the voices of these noisy hydropaths. Pat had been visiting at the house of a friend, and he had, unfortunately, imbibed more whisky than ordinary mortals can absorb with safety to their persons. On his home return the road was too narrow, and he performed wonderful feats in his endeavors to maintain the centre of gravity. Now he seemed to exert his best efforts to walk on both sides of the road at the same time; then he would fall, and feel upward for the ground; then he would slowly pick himself up, and the ground would rise and hit him square in the face. By the time he reached the meadowlands, located about half way between his home and the shanty of his friend, he was somewhat sobered by the ups and downs he had experienced on the way.

Hearing strange voices, he stopped suddenly to ascertain, if possible, the purport of their language. Judge his astonishment when he heard his own name distinctly called—
"Patrick O'Rourke—Patrick O'Rourke."

"Faith, that's my name, sure."

"Patrick O'Rourke — Patrick — O'Rourke — Rourke — Rourke."

"What do ye want o' the likes o' me?" he inquired.

"When did ye come over—come over—come—over?"

"It is jist tree months ago to the minute; and a bad time we had, sure, for we were all say-sick, and the passage lasted six long wakes."

"What will ye do—do—do? What will ye do—do—do?"

"I have nothing to do at all at all, but then I can do any thing; I can dig, I can tind mason, and I can hould office if I can git it."

"You are drunk—you are drunk—drunk—drunk—drunk—drunk."

"By my sowl, that's a lie."

"You are drunk—dead drunk—drunk—drunk."

"Repate that same, if ye dare, and I will take me shillaly to ye."

"You are drunk—dead drunk—drunk—drunk."

"Jist come out here, now, and stip on the tail o' me coat, like a man," exclaimed Pat, in high dudgeon, pulling off his coat and trailing it upon the ground.

"Strike him—strike him—strike—strike—strike."

"Come on wid ye! I'm a broth of a boy; come on."

"Knock him down—down—down."

"I will take any one in the crowd; and, if Mike Mulligan was here, we wud take all of yees at onct."

"Kill him—kill him—kill him."

"Och, murther! sure ye wud not be after murtherin' me; I was not oncivil to ye. Go back to Pate Dogan's wid me now, and I will trate ivery one o' yees."

"We don't drink rum—rum—rum."

"And are ye all Father Mathew men?"

"We are all cold-water men—water men."

"Take me advice, now, and put a little whasky in the wather, darlings; it will kape the cowld out whin yees git wet, and so it will."

"Moderation—moderation—moderation."

"Yis, that's the talk. But ye are a set o' fut-pads and highwaymen, hidin' behind the rocks and the traas. Whin I onct git to Watertown I will sind Father Fairbanks after ye, and he will chuck ye into the pond, as he did that thafe who stole the public money, and he will howld ye there until ye confess, or he will take yees to the perleese."

"Come on, boys—chase him—chase him."

"Faith and I won't run, but I will jist walk right along; for if any o' me frinds should find me here in sich company, at this hour o' the night, they wud think I was thryin' for to stale somethin'. Take me advice, boys, and go home, for it's goin' for to rain, and ye will git wet to the skin if ye kape sich late hours."

"Catch him—catch him—catch him."

"Sure ye'd betther not, for I haven't got a cint wid me, or I'd lave it in yer jackets. What's the use o' stalin' all a man has whin he has jist nothin' at all at all. Bad luck to ye for botherin' me so."

About this time the frog-concert was in full tune, and the hoarse chorus so alarmed Pat that he took to his heels, for he was now sober enough to run.

A CAMP-MEETING IN TEXAS.

In September, 1836, the following notice might have been seen upon the doors of every public house and grocery, attached to the largest trees near the cross-roads and principal trails, and even in the remote dells of the mountains of Texas, miles away from a human habitation:

"*Barbecue Camp-meeting.*

"There will be a camp-meeting, to commence the last Monday of this month, at the Double-spring Grove, near Peter Brinton's, in the county of Shelby.

"The exercises will open with a splendid barbecue.

"The preparations are being made to suit all tastes: there will be a good barbecue, better liquor, and the best of Gospel. (Signed) PAUL DENTON, Missionary, M. E. C."

The day came, and, as he had anticipated, the meat and drink brought a crowd—a motley crowd of hunters and herdsmen, gamblers and refugees, forgers, thieves, robbers, and murderers—the very ears he wished to reach. A social pandemonium, unprincipled, without courts, or prisons, or churches, or school-houses, or even the shadow of civil authority or subordination.

Hence all prudent evangelists soon learned to shun the

left bank of the Sabine as if it had been infested by a cohort of demons.

The tumult was deafening—a tornado of babbling tongues talking, shouting, quarreling, betting, and cursing for amusement. Suddenly a cry arose: "*Colonel Watt. Foeman—hurrah for Colonel Watt. Foeman!*" and the crowd parted right and left to let the lion lyncher pass. The loadstar advanced with a satanic countenance, ferocious—murderous. He was a tall, athletic, powerful man; his train, a dozen armed desperadoes. He ordered the dinner served, and it was spread before him. When prepared to commence the sumptuous repast, a voice pealed from the pulpit loud as the blast of a trumpet in battle, "*Stay, gentlemen and ladies, till the giver of the barbecue asks God's blessing!*"

Every ear started, every eye was directed to the speaker, and a whisperless silence ensued, for all alike were struck by his remarkable appearance. He was a giant in stature, though scarcely twenty years of age; his hair, dark as the raven's wing, flowed down his immense shoulders in masses of natural ringlets more beautiful than any ever wreathed around the jeweled brow of a queen by the labored achievements of human art; his eyes, black as midnight, beamed like stars over a face as pale as Parian marble—calm, passionless, spiritual. The heterogeneous mass gazed in mute astonishment. The missionary prayed, but it sounded like no other prayer ever addressed to the throne of the Almighty. It contained no encomiums on the splendors of the divine attributes—no petitions in the tones of command—no orisons for distant places, times, or objects; it related exclusively to the present people and the present hour: it was the cry of the naked soul, and that soul a beggar for the bread and water of eternal life. "*Now*, my friends," he said, "partake of God's gifts at the table, and then come and sit down, and listen to his Gospel."

One heart, however humbled the rest, was maddened by the preacher's wonderful powers. Colonel Watt. Foeman exclaimed, in a sneering voice, "Mr. Paul Denton, your reverence has lied. You promised us not only a good barbecue, but better liquor; where is your liquor?"

"THERE!" answered the missionary, in tones of thunder, and pointing his motionless finger at the double spring gushing up in two strong columns, with a sound like a shout of joy, from the bosom of the earth. "*There!*" he repeated, with a look terrible as lightning, while his enemy actually trembled at his feet; "there is the liquor which God, the Eternal, brews for all his children! Not in the simmering still, over smoking fires, choked with poisonous gases, and surrounded with the stench of sickening odors and rank corruption, doth your Father in heaven prepare the precious essence of life, pure cold water. But in the green glade and grassy dell, where the red deer wanders and the child loves to play, there God himself brews it; and down, low down in the deepest valleys, where the fountains murmur and the rills sing—and high upon the mountain-tops, where the naked granite glitters like gold in the sun, where the storm-cloud broods and the thunder-storms crash—and away, far away out on the wide, wide sea, where the hurricane howls music, and big waves roar the chorus, 'sweeping the march of God'—*there* he brews it, that beverage of life, health-giving water!

"And every where it is a thing of beauty. Gleaming in the dew-drop, singing in the summer rain, shining in the ice-gem till the trees seem turned to living jewels, spreading a golden veil over the setting sun, or a white gauze around the midnight moon; sporting in the cataract, sleeping in the glacier, dancing in the hail-shower, folding bright snow-curtains softly above the wintry world, and weaving the many-colored iris, that seraph's zone of the sky, whose warp is the rain of earth, whose woof is the sunbeam of heaven, all checkered over with celestial flowers by the mystic hand of rarefaction—still always it is beautiful, that blessed cold water! No poison bubbles on its brink—its foam brings not madness and murder—no blood stains its liquid glass—pale widows and starving orphans weep not burning tears in its clear depths—no drunkard's shrieking ghost from the grave curses it in words of despair! Speak out, my friends; would you exchange it for the demon's drink—alcohol?"

A shout like the roar of the tempest answered "No! NO!"

AN IRISH LETTER.

Tullymucclescrag, Parish of Ballyraggett, near }
Ballyslughgathey, Sunday (God bless us), 1864. }

MY DEAR NEPHEW,—I haven't sent ye a letther since the last time I wrote to ye, bekase we have moved from our former place of livin', and I didn't know where a letther would find ye; but I now with pleasure take up me pin to inform ye of the death of yer own livin' uncle, Ned Fitzpatrick, who died very suddenly last week afther a lingerin' illness of six months. The poor fellow was in violent convulsions the whole time of his sickness, lyin' perfectly quiet, speechless, all the while talkin' incoherently, and cryin' for wather. I had no opportunity of informin' ye of his death sooner, except I wrote to ye by the last post, which same went off two days before he died; and then ye would have postage to pay. I'm at a loss to tell what his death was occasioned by, but I fear it was by his last sickness, for he was niver well ten days togither durin' the whole of his confinement, and I believe his death was brought about by his aitin' too much of rabbit stuffed with pais and gravy, or pais and gravy stuffed with rabbit; but, be that as it may, when he brathed his last, the docther gave up all hope of his recovery. I needn't tell ye any thing about his age, for ye well know that in March next he would have been just seventy-five years old lackin' ten months, and, had he lived till that time, would have been just six months dead. His property now devolves to his next of kin, which all died some time ago, so that I expect it will be divided between us; and ye know his property, which was very large, was sold to pay his debts, and the remainder he lost at a horse-race; but it was the opinion of ivery body at the time that he would have won the race if the baste he run aginst hadn't been too fast for him.

I niver saw a man in all my life, and the docthers all said so, that observed directions or took medicine betther than he did. He said he would as leve dhrink bitter as sweet if it had only the same taste, and ipecakana as whisky-punch if it would only put him in the same humor for fightin'.

But, poor sowl! he will niver ate or dhrink any more, and ye haven't a livin' relation in the world except meself and yer two cousins who were kilt in the last war. I can not dwell on the mournful subject any longer, and shall sale me letther with black salin'-wax, and put in it yer uncle's coat-of-arms. So I beg ye not to brake the sale when ye open the letther, and don't open it until two or three days afther ye resave this, and by that time ye will be well prepared for the sorrowful tidings. Yer old sweetheart sinds her love unknownst to ye. When Jary McGhee arrives in America, ax him for this letther, and if he don't brung it from amongst the rest, tell him it's the one that spakes about yer uncle's death, and saled in black.

I remain yer affectionate ould grandmother,
BRIDGET O'HOOLEGOIN.

P.S.—Don't write till ye resave this.

N.B.—When yez come to this place, stop, and don't rade any more until my next.

Direct to Larry O'Hoolegoin, late of the Town of Tullymucclescrag, Parish of Ballyraggett, near Ballyslughgathey, County of Kilkenny, Ireland.

SCENE FROM RICHARD III.*

SHAKSPEARE.

KING RICHARD, *starting out of his dream.*

(*h.*) (*ff.*) *Rich.* Give me another horse—bind up my wounds—
Have mercy, Jesu! (*p.*) Soft; I did but dream.
(*tr.*) Oh coward conscience, how dost thou afflict me!
The lights burn blue. It is now dead midnight.
Cold, fearful drops stand on my trembling flesh.
What do I *fear?* Myself? There's none else by:
Richard loves *Richard;* that is, *I* am *I.*
Is there a murderer here? No—yes; *I* am.
Then fly. What, from myself? Great reason! Why?
Lest I revenge. *What?* Myself on myself?

---

* Richard III. was born in 1452. By successive murders he reached the throne. In this extract he appears just after waking from a fearful dream, wherein the ghosts of his victims appear to him.

I love myself. Wherefore? For any *good*
That I myself have done unto myself?
Oh no; alas! I rather *hate* myself
For hateful deeds committed by myself.
I am a villain; yet I *lie*—I am not.
Fool, of thyself speak well—fool, do not flatter.
My conscience hath a thousand several tongues,
(<) And every tongue brings in a several tale,
(<) And every *tale* condemns me for a *villain*.
(*ff.*) PERJURY, PERJURY in the high'st degree,
Murder, stern murder, in the dir'st degree,
All several sins, all used in each degree,
Throng to the bar, crying all, (*h.*) (*ff.*) GUILTY! GUILTY!
(*l.*) I shall despair. There is no creature *loves* me;
And, if I die, no soul will *pity* me:
Nay, wherefore should they? since that I myself
Find in myself no pity to myself.
Methought the souls of all that I had murdered
Came to my tent; and every one did threat
To-morrow's vengeance on the head of Richard.

SCENE FROM THE SIEGE OF VALENCIA.
MRS. HEMANS.

[ALVAR GONZALEZ is the Governor of Valencia; ELMINA, his wife. Their two sons, ALPHONSO and CARLOS, are held by ABDALLAH, the chief of the besieging army, as hostages of war, the price of whose ransom is treason—the yielding of the city of Valencia. GONZALEZ enters, having on his trappings of war. ELMINA addresses him as he enters.]

Elmina. My noble lord,
Welcome from this day's toil! It is the hour
Whose shadows, as they deepen, bring repose
Unto all weary men; and wilt not thou
Free thy mailed bosom from the corslet's weight,
To rest at fall of eve?
Gonzalez. There may be rest
For the tired peasant, when the vesper bell
Doth send him to his cabin, there to sit
Watching his children's sports; but unto me,
Who speaks of rest?

R 2

Elm. Oh why is this? How my heart sinks.

Gonz. It must not fail thee *yet*,
Daughter of heroes! Thine inheritance
Is strength to meet all conflicts. Thou canst number
In thy long line of glorious ancestry
Those whom the earth call martyrs;
While heaven but claimed their blood, their lives, and not
The things which grew as tendrils round their hearts—
No, not their *children!*

Elm. Mean'st thou? Know'st thou aught?
I can not utter it—my sons! my sons!
Is it of them? Oh, would'st thou speak of them?

Gonz. A mother's heart divineth but too well.

Elm. Speak, I conjure thee! I can bear it all.
Where are my children?

Gonz. In the *Moorish camp!*

Elm. Say they live!

Gonz. They live, but there is asked a ransom far too high.

Elm. What! have we wealth
Which might redeem a monarch, and our sons
The while wear fetters? Take thou all for them.
Thou knowest not how serenely I could take
The *peasant's* lot upon me, so my heart
Amidst its deep affections undisturbed
May dwell in silence.

Gonz. Canst thou bear *disgrace?*

Elm. We were not born for this.

Gonz. No, thou say'st well.
Hold to that lofty faith. But he for whom
Freedom and life may but be won with shame,
Hath naught to do save fearlessly to fix
His steadfast look on the majestic heavens,
And proudly die.

Elm. Gonzalez, *who* must die?

Gonz. They on whose lives a fearful price is set,
But to be paid by treason.
Our sons must die unless I yield the city.

Elm. Is there no hope? Tell me there is some hope.

Gonz. Hope but in *Him*

Who bade the patriarch lay his fair young son
Bound on the shrine of sacrifice, and when
The bright steel quivered in the father's hand,
Just raised to strike, sent forth His awful voice
Commanding to withhold! Earth has no hope;
It rests with Him.
  Elm.   *Thou* canst not tell me this—
Thou, father of my sons, within whose hands
Doth lie my children's fate!
  Gonz.   Hast thou cause,
Wife of my youth, to deem it lies within
The bounds of possible things, that I should link
My name with that word—*traitor?* They that sleep
On their proud battle-fields, thy sires and mine,
Died not for this.
  Elm.   Then their doom is sealed.
Thou wilt not save thy children?
  Gonz. Think'st thou *I* feel no pangs?
He that hath given me sons doth know the heart
Whose treasure he recalls. Of this no more;
'Tis vain I tell thee that the inviolate Cross
Still from our ancient temples must look up
Through the blue heavens of Spain, though at its foot
I perish, with my *race.*
  Elm.   Scorn me not
In mine extreme of misery. Thou art strong;
Thy heart is not as mine. My brain grows wild—
I know not what I ask. And yet 'twere but
Anticipating fate, since it must fall—
That Cross must fall. There is no power,
No hope within this city of the grave,
To keep its place on high.
  Gonz. We have but to bow the head in silence
When heaven's voice calls back things we love.
  Elm. Love! love! there is none
In all this cold and hollow world—no fount
Of deep, strong, deathless love, save that within
The mother's heart. It is but pride wherewith
To his fair son the father's eye doth turn,

Watching his growth. Ay, on the boy he looks,
The bright, glad creature springing in his path,
But as the heir of his great name, the young
And stately tree whose rising strength ere long
Shall bear his trophies well. And this is love!
This is *man's* love! What marvel? *You* ne'er made
Your breast the pillow of his infancy;
You ne'er kept watch
Beside him till the last pale star had set,
And morn all dazzling, as in triumph, broke
On your dim, weary eye. Not yours the face
Which, early faded through fond care for him,
Hung o'er his sleep, and, duly as heaven's light,
Was there to greet his wakening. *You* ne'er smoothed
His couch, ne'er sang him to his rosy rest,
Caught his least whisper, when his voice from yours
Had learned soft utterance, pressed your lip to his
When fever parched it, hushed his wayward cries
With patient, vigilant, never-wearied love!
No; these are *woman's* tasks. In these her youth,
And bloom of cheek, and buoyancy of heart
Steal from her all unmarked. My boys! my boys!
Hath vain affection borne with all for this?

  Gonz.   Is there strength in man
Thus to endure? That thou couldst read, through all
Its depth of silent agony, the heart
Thy voice of woe doth rend!

  Elm. *Thy* heart! *thy* heart! Away! it feels not *now;*
But an hour comes to tame the mighty man
Unto the infant's weakness; nor shall Heaven
Spare you that bitter chastening. May you live
To be alone when loneliness doth seem
Most heavy to sustain! For me, my voice
Of prayer and fruitless weeping shall be soon
With all forgotten sounds; my quiet place
Low with my lovely ones; and we shall sleep—
Though kings lead armies o'er us, we shall sleep,
Wrapped in earth's covering mantle. You the while
Shall sit within your vast forsaken halls,

And hear the wild and melancholy winds
Moan through their drooping banners, nevermore
To wave above your race. Ay, then call up
Shadows, dim phantoms from ancestral tombs,
To people that cold void. And when the strength
From your right arm hath melted, when the blast
Of the shrill clarion gives your heart no more
A fiery wakening, if at last you pine
For the glad voices and the bounding steps
Once through your home re-echoing, and the clasp
Of twining arms, and all the joyous light
Of eyes that laughed with youth, and made your board
A place of sunshine—when those days are come,
Then, in your utter desolation, turn
To the cold world—the smiling, faithless world,
Which hath swept past you long—and bid it quench
Your soul's deep thirst with *fame*—immortal *fame*.
Fame to the sick of heart! A gorgeous robe—
A crown of victory unto him that dies
I' the burning waste for water!

Gonz. This from thee!
Now the last drop of bitterness is poured.
Elmina, I forgive thee.
     Aid me, Heaven,
From whom alone is power. Oh, thou hast set
Duties so stern of aspect in my path
They almost to my startled gaze assume
The hue of things less hallowed. Men have sunk
Unblamed beneath such trials. Doth not He
Who made us know the limits of our strength?
My wife! my sons! Away! I must not pause
To give my heart one moment's mastery thus!

SCENE FROM THE MERCHANT OF VENICE.
Belmont. A Room in Portia's House.

Portia. By my troth, Nerissa, my little body is aweary of this great world.

Nerissa. You would be, sweet madam, if your miseries

were in the same abundance as your good fortunes are; and yet, for aught I see, they are as sick that surfeit with too much as they that starve with nothing. It is no mean happiness, therefore, to be seated in the mean; superfluity comes sooner by white hairs, but competency lives longer.

Por. Good sentences and well pronounced.

Ner. They would be better if well followed.

Por. If to do were as easy as to know what were good to do, chapels had been churches, and poor men's cottages princes' palaces. It is a good divine that follows his own instructions. I can easier teach twenty what were good to be done, than be one of the twenty to follow mine own teaching. The brain may devise laws for the blood, but a hot temper leaps over a cold decree; such a hare is madness, the youth, to skip o'er the meshes of good counsel, the cripple. But this reasoning is not in the fashion to choose me a husband. Oh me! the word choose! I may neither choose whom I would, nor refuse whom I dislike; so is the will of a living daughter curbed by the will of a dead father. Is it not hard, Nerissa, that I can not choose one, nor refuse none?

Ner. Your father was ever virtuous, and holy men at their death have good inspirations; therefore the lottery that he hath devised in these three chests of gold, silver, and lead (whereof who chooses his meaning, chooses you), will, no doubt, never be chosen by any rightly, but one whom you shall rightly love. But what warmth is there in your affection toward any of these princely suitors that are already come?

Por. I pray thee overname them; and, as thou namest them, I will describe them; and, according to my description, level at my affection.

Ner. First, there is the Neapolitan prince.

Por. Ay, that's a colt, indeed, for he doth nothing but talk of his horse; and he makes it a great appropriation to his own good parts that he can shoe him himself.

Ner. Then there is the County Palatine.

Por. He doth nothing but frown, as who should say, "And you will not have me choose;" he hears merry tales and smiles not; I fear he will prove the weeping philosopher when he grows old, being so full of unmannerly sadness in his youth. I had rather be married to a death's-head with a bone in his mouth than to either of these. God defend me from these two!

Ner. How say you by the French lord, Monsieur Le Bon?

Por. God made him, and therefore let him pass for a man. In truth, I know it is a sin to be a mocker; but he! why, he hath a horse better than the Neapolitan's; a better bad habit of frowning than the Count Palatine. He is every man in no man; if a throstle sing he falls straight a capering; he will fence with his own shadow. If I should marry him I should marry twenty husbands. If he would despise me, I would forgive him; for if he love me to madness, I should never requite him.

Ner. What say you, then, to Faulconbridge, the young baron of England?

Por. You know I say nothing to him, for he understands not me, nor I him; he hath neither Latin, French, nor Italian; and you will come into the court and swear that I have a poor pennyworth in the English. He is a proper man's picture; but, alas! who can converse with a dumb show? How oddly he is suited; I think he bought his doublet in Italy, his round-hose in France, his bonnet in Germany, and his behavior every where.

Ner. What think you of the Scottish lord, his neighbor?

Por. That he hath neighborly charity in him, for he borrowed a box of the ear of the Englishman, and swore he would pay him again when he was able. I think the Frenchman became his surety, and sealed under for another.

Ner. How like you the young German, the Duke of Saxony's nephew.

Por. Very vilely in the morning, when he is sober; and most vilely in the afternoon, when he is drunk; when he is best, he is a little worse than a man, and when he is worst, he is little better than a beast; and the worst fall that ever fell, I hope I shall make shift to go without him.

Ner. If he should make offer to choose, and choose the right casket, you would refuse to perform your father's will if you should refuse to accept him.

Por. Therefore, for fear of the worst, I pray thee set a deep glass of Rhenish wine on the contrary casket; for, if the devil be within, and that temptation without, I know he will choose it. I will do any thing, Nerissa, ere I will be married to a sponge.

Ner. You need not fear, lady, the having any of these lords; they have acquainted me with their determinations, which is, indeed, to return to their home, and to trouble you with no more suit, unless you may be won by some other sort than your father's imposition, depending on the caskets.

Por. If I live to be as old as Sibylla, I will die as chaste as Diana, unless I be obtained by the manner of my father's will. I am glad this parcel of wooers are so reasonable, for there is not one among them but I dote on his very absence, and I pray God grant them a fair departure.

Ner. Do you not remember, lady, in your father's time, a Venetian, a scholar and a soldier, that came hither in company of the Marquis of Montferrat?

Por. Yes, yes; it was Bassanio; as I think, so he was called.

Ner. True, madam; he, of all the men that ever my foolish eyes looked upon, was the best deserving a fair lady.

Por. I remember him well, and I remember him worthy of thy praise.

Enter a Servant.

How now! what news?

Serv. The four strangers seek for you, madam, to take their leave; and there is a forerunner come from a fifth, the Prince of Morocco, who brings word the prince, his master, will be here to-night.

Por. If I could bid the fifth welcome with so good heart as I can bid the other four farewell, I should be glad of his approach; if he have the condition of a saint, and the complexion of a devil, I had rather he should shrive me than wive me.

Come, Nerissa. Sirrah, go before.

While we shut the door upon one wooer, another knocks at the door. [*Exeunt.*

SCENE FROM THE RIVALS.

RICHARD BRINSLEY SHERIDAN.*

ACT II. Scene 1.

Enter Sir Anthony.

Sir, I am delighted to see you here, and looking so well; your sudden arrival at Bath made me apprehensive for your health.

Sir Anthony. Very apprehensive, I dare say, Jack. What! you are recruiting here, hey?

Capt. Absolute. Yes, sir, I am on duty.

Sir A. Well, Jack, I am glad to see you, though I did not expect it; for I was going to write to you on a little matter of business. Jack, I have been considering that I grow old and infirm, and shall probably not trouble you long.

Capt. A. Pardon me, sir, I never saw you look more strong and hearty, and I pray fervently that you may continue so.

Sir A. I hope your prayers may be heard, with all my heart. Well, then, Jack, I have been considering that I am so strong and hearty, I may continue to plague you a long time. Now, Jack, I am sensible that the income of your commission, and what I have hitherto allowed you, is but a small pittance for a lad of your spirit.

Capt. A. Sir, you are very good.

Sir A. And it is my wish, while yet I live, to have my boy make some figure in the world. I have resolved, therefore, to fix you at once in a noble independence.

Capt. A. Sir, your kindness overpowers me. Yet, sir, I presume you would not wish me to quit the army?

Sir A. Oh! that shall be as your wife chooses.

Capt. A. My wife, sir!

Sir A. Ay, ay, settle that between you—settle that between you.

* The scene of the comedy is laid in Bath. Sir Anthony is a high-spirited, kind-hearted old gentleman, and Captain Absolute is his nephew, whom he pets and scolds. The lady that Sir Anthony proposes for his nephew is really the lady that the captain loves, but he, in ignorance of that fact, rejects the proposition with determination.

Capt. A. A wife, sir, did you say?

Sir A. Ay, a wife—why, did not I mention her before?

Capt. A. Not a word of her, sir.

Sir A. Odds so! I mustn't forget her, though. Yes, Jack, the independence I was talking of is by a marriage—the fortune is saddled with a wife; but I suppose that makes no difference.

Capt. A. Sir! sir! you amaze me!

Sir A. Why, what the deuce is the matter with the fool? Just now you were all gratitude and duty.

Capt. A. I was, sir; you talked to me of independence and a fortune, but not a word of a wife.

Sir A. Why—what difference does that make? Odds life, sir, if you have the estate, you must take it with the live-stock on it, as it stands.

Capt. A. Pray, sir, who is the lady?

Sir A. What's that to you, sir? Come, give me your promise to love and marry her directly.

Capt. A. Sure, sir, this is not very reasonable, to summon my affections for a lady I know nothing of.

Sir A. I am sure, sir, 'tis more unreasonable in you to object to a lady you know nothing of.

Capt. A. You must excuse me, sir, if I tell you, once for all, that in this point I can not obey you.

Sir A. Hark ye, Jack! I have heard you for some time with patience; I have been cool—quite cool; but take care; you know I am compliance itself—when I am not thwarted; no one more easily led—when I have my own way; but don't put me in a frenzy.

Capt. A. Sir, I must repeat it; in this I can not obey you.

Sir A. Now, hang me if ever I call you Jack again while I live!

Capt. A. Nay, sir, but hear me.

Sir A. Sir, I won't hear a word—not a word—not one word; so give me your promise by a nod. And I'll tell you what, Jack—I mean you dog—if you don't, by—

Capt. A. What, sir, promise to link myself to some mass of ugliness?

Sir A. Zounds! sirrah, the lady shall be as ugly as I

choose: she shall have a hump on each shoulder; she shall be as crooked as the Crescent; she shall have a skin like a mummy, and the beard of a Jew—she shall be all this, sirrah! yet I'll make you ogle her all day, and sit up all night to write sonnets on her beauty.

Capt. A. This is reason and moderation indeed!

Sir A. None of your sneering, puppy! no grinning, jackanapes!

Capt. A. Indeed, sir, I never was in a worse humor for mirth in my life.

Sir A. 'Tis false, sir; I know you are laughing in your sleeve; I know you'll grin when I am gone, sirrah!

Capt. A. Sir, I hope I know my duty better.

Sir A. None of your passion, sir—none of your violence, if you please. It won't do with me, I promise you.

Capt. A. Indeed, sir, I never was cooler in my life.

Sir A. 'Tis a confounded lie! I know you are in a passion in your heart; I know you are, you hypocritical young dog; but it won't do.

Capt. A. Nay, sir, upon my word—

Sir A. So, you will fly out! Can't you be cool, like me? What good can passion do? Passion is of no service, you impudent, insolent, overbearing reprobate! There, you sneer again! Don't provoke me! But you rely upon the mildness of my temper—you do, you dog! you play upon the meekness of my disposition! Yet take care; the patience of a saint may be overcome at last. But, mark! I give you six hours and a half to consider of this: if you then agree, without any condition, to do every thing on earth that I choose, why—confound you, I may in time for give you; if not, zounds! don't enter the same hemisphere with me; don't dare to breathe the same air, or use the same light with me, but get an atmosphere and a sun of your own. I'll strip you of your commission; I'll lodge a five-and-threepence in the hands of trustees, and you shall live on the interest. I'll disown you, I'll disinherit you, and hang me if ever I call you Jack again. [*Exit.*

Capt. A. Mild, gentle, considerate father, I kiss your hands.

QUARREL SCENE BETWEEN BRUTUS AND CASSIUS.
SHAKSPEARE.

Cassius. That you have wronged me doth appear in this:
You have condemned and noted Lucius Pella
For taking bribes here of the Sardians;
Wherein my letters, praying on his side,
Because I knew the man, were slighted off.
  Brutus. You wronged yourself to write in such a case.
  Cas. In such a time as this, it is not meet
That every nice offense should bear his comment.
  Bru. Let me tell you, Cassius, you yourself
Are much condemned to have an itching palm;
To sell and mart your offices for gold
To undeservers.
  Cas.   I an itching palm?
You know that you are Brutus that speak this,
Or, by the gods, this speech were else your last.
  Bru. The name of Cassius honors this corruption,
And chastisement doth therefore hide his head.
  Cas. Chastisement!
  Bru. Remember March, the ides of March remember.
Did not great Julius bleed for justice' sake?
What villain touched his body, that did stab,
And not for justice? What, shall one of us,
That struck the foremost man of all this world
But for supporting robbers—shall we now
Contaminate our fingers with base bribes,
And sell the mighty space of our large honors
For so much trash as may be grasped thus?
I had rather be a dog, and bay the moon,
Than such a Roman.
  Cas.   Brutus, bay not me;
I'll not endure it: you forget yourself
To hedge me in; I am a soldier—I,
Older in practice, abler than yourself
To make conditions.
  Bru.   Go to; you're not, Cassius.
  Cas. I am.

Bru.   I say you are not.
Cas. Urge me no more; I shall forget myself;
Have mind upon your health; tempt me no further.
Bru. Away, slight man!
Cas.   Is't possible?
Bru. Hear me, for I will speak.
Must I give way and room to your rash choler?
Shall I be frighted when a madman stares?
   Cas. Oh ye gods! ye gods! must I endure all this?
   Bru. All this? ay, more: Fret till your proud heart breaks;
Go show your slaves how choleric you are,
And make your bondmen tremble. Must I budge?
Must I observe you? Must I stand and crouch
Under your testy humor? By the gods,
You shall digest the venom of your spleen,
Though it do split you; for, from this day forth,
I'll use you for my mirth, yea, for my laughter,
When you are waspish.
   Cas.   Is it come to this?
   Bru. You say you are a better soldier:
Let it appear so; make your vaunting true,
And it shall please me well: for mine own part,
I shall be glad to learn of noble men.
   Cas. You wrong me every way; you wrong me, Brutus;
I said an elder soldier, not a better:
Did I say better?
   Bru.   If you did, I care not.
   Cas. When Cæsar lived, he durst not thus have moved me.
   Bru. Peace, peace; you durst not so have tempted him.
   Cas. I durst not?
   Bru.   No.
   Cas. What? durst not tempt him?
   Bru.   For your life you durst not.
   Cas. Do not presume too much upon my love;
I may do that I shall be sorry for.
   Bru. You *have* done that you should be sorry for.
There is no terror, Cassius, in your threats;

For I am armed so strong in honesty,
That they pass by me as the idle wind,
Which I respect not. I did send to you
For certain sums of gold, which you denied me—
For I can raise no money by vile means:
By Heaven, I had rather coin my heart,
And drop my blood for drachmas, than to wring
From the hard hands of peasants their vile trash
By any indirection. I did send
To you for gold to pay my legions,
Which you denied me: was that done like Cassius?
Should I have answered Caius Cassius so?
When Marcus Brutus grows so covetous,
To lock such rascal counters from his friends,
Be ready, gods, with all your thunderbolts—
Dash him to pieces!

    Cas.   ·I denied you not.
    Bru. You did.
    Cas.   I did not: he was but a fool
That brought my answer back. Brutus hath rived my heart;
A friend should bear his friend's infirmities;
But Brutus makes mine greater than they are.
    Bru. I do not, till you practice them on me.
    Cas. You love me not.
    Bru.   I do not like your faults.
    Cas. A friendly eye could never see such faults.
    Bru. A flatterer's would not, though they do appear
As huge as high Olympus.
    Cas. Come, Antony, and young Octavius, come,
Revenge yourselves alone on Cassius;
For Cassius is aweary of the world:
Hated by one he loves; braved by his brother;
Checked like a bondman; all his faults observed,
Set in a note-book, learned and conned by rote,
To cast into my teeth. Oh, I could weep
My spirit from mine eyes! There is my dagger,
And here my naked breast; within, a heart
Dearer than Plutus' mine, richer than gold:

If that thou be'st a Roman, take it forth;
I, that denied thee gold, will give my heart:
Strike, as thou didst at Cæsar; for I know,
When thou didst hate him worst, thou lovedst him better
Than ever thou lovedst Cassius.
 Bru.   Sheathe your dagger:
Be angry when you will, it shall have scope;
Do what you will, dishonor shall be humor.
Oh Cassius, you are yoked with a lamb
That carries anger as the flint bears fire;
Who, much enforced, shows a hasty spark,
And straight is cold again!
 Cas.   Hath Cassius lived
To be but mirth and laughter to his Brutus,
When grief, and blood ill-tempered vexeth him?
 Bru. When I spoke that, I was ill-tempered too.
 Cas. Do you confess so much? Give me your hand.
 Bru. And my heart too.
 Cas.   Oh Brutus!
 Bru.   What's the matter?
 Cas. Have you not love enough to bear with me
When that rash humor, which my mother gave me,
Makes me forgetful?
 Bru.   Yes, Cassius; and, henceforth,
When you are over-earnest with your Brutus,
He'll think your mother chides, and leave you so.

FROM "SCHOOL FOR SCANDAL."
RICHARD BRINSLEY SHERIDAN.
ACT I. SCENE 2. *Sir Peter's House.*

Enter Sir Peter.

Sir P. When an old bachelor marries a young wife, what is he to expect? 'Tis now six months since Lady Teazle made me the happiest of men, and I have been the most miserable dog ever since! We tiffed a little going to church, and came to a quarrel before the bells had done ringing. I was more than once nearly choked with gall during the honeymoon, and had lost all comfort in life before my friends had done wishing me joy. Yet I chose with caution—a girl bred wholly in the country, who never knew luxury beyond one silk gown, nor dissipation above the annual gala of a race-ball. Yet now she plays her part in all the extravagant fopperies of the fashion and the town with as ready a grace as if she had never seen a bush or a grass-plot out of Grosvenor Square! I am sneered at by all my acquaintance, and paragraphed in the newspapers. She dissipates my fortune, and contradicts all my humors; yet the worst of it is, I doubt I love her, or I should never bear all this. However, I'll never be weak enough to own it.

Enter Lady Teazle.

Sir P. Lady Teazle, Lady Teazle, I'll not bear it.

Lady T. Sir Peter, Sir Peter, you may bear it or not, as you please; but I ought to have my own way in every thing, and, what's more, I will too. What! though I was educated in the country, I know very well that women of fashion in London are accountable to nobody after they are married.

Sir P. Very well, ma'am, very well; so a husband is to have no influence—no authority?

Lady T. Authority! No, to be sure. If you wanted authority over me you should have adopted me, and not married me: I am sure you were old enough.

Sir P. Old enough! ay—there it is. Well, well, Lady Teazle, though my life may be made unhappy by your temper, I'll not be ruined by your extravagance.

Lady T. My extravagance! I am sure I am not more extravagant than a woman ought to be.

Sir P. No, no, madam, you shall throw away no more sums upon such unmeaning luxury. 'Slife! to spend as much to furnish your dressing-room with flowers in winter as would suffice to turn the Pantheon into a green-house, and give a *fête champêtre* at Christmas.

Lady T. Sir Peter, am I to blame because flowers are dear in cold weather? You should find fault with the climate, and not with me. For my part, I'm sure, I wish it were spring all the year round, and that roses grew under our feet.

Sir P. Zounds! madam, if you had been born to this, I should not wonder at your talking thus; but you forget what your situation was when I married you.

Lady T. No, no, I don't; 'twas a very disagreeable one, or I should never have married you.

Sir P. Yes, yes, madam; you were then in a somewhat humbler style — the daughter of a plain country squire. Recollect, Lady Teazle, when I saw you first sitting at your tambour, in a pretty-figured linen gown, with a bunch of keys at your side—your hair combed smooth over a roll, and your apartment hung round with fruits in worsted of your own working.

Lady T. Oh yes, I remember it very well; and a curious life I led. My daily occupation, to inspect the dairy, superintend the poultry, make extracts from the family recipe-book, and comb my Aunt Deborah's lap-dog.

Sir P. Yes, yes, ma'am, 'twas so indeed.

Lady T. And then, you know, my evening amusements— to draw patterns for ruffles which I had not materials to make up, to play Pope Joan with the curate, to read a novel to my aunt, or to be stuck down to an old spinet to strum my father to sleep after a fox-chase.

Sir P. I am glad you have so good a memory. Yes, madam, these were the recreations I took you from; but now you must have your coach—*vis-à-vis*—and three powdered footmen before your chair, and, in the summer, a pair of white cats to draw you to Kensington Gardens. No recollection, I suppose, when you were content to ride double, behind the butler, on a docked coach-horse!

Lady T. No, I swear I never did that; I deny the butler and the coach-horse.

Sir P. This, madam, was your situation, and what have I done for you? I have made you a woman of fashion, of fortune, of rank; in short, I have made you my wife.

Lady T. Well, then—and there is but one thing more you can make me add to the obligation, and that is—"

Sir P. My widow, I suppose?

Lady T. Hem! hem!

Sir P. I thank you, madam; but don't flatter yourself;

for, though your ill-conduct may disturb my peace of mind, it shall never break my heart, I promise you. However, I am equally obliged to you for the hint.

Lady T. Then why will you endeavor to make yourself so disagreeable to me, and thwart me in every little elegant expense?

Sir P. 'Slife! madam, I say, had you any of these little elegant expenses when you married me?

Lady T. Lud! Sir Peter, would you have me be out of the fashion?

Sir P. The fashion, indeed! What had you to do with the fashion before you married me?

Lady T. For my part, I should think you would like to have your wife thought a woman of taste.

Sir P. Ay—there again—taste! Zounds! madam, you had no taste when you married me!

Lady T. That's very true, indeed, Sir Peter; and, after having married you, I should never pretend to taste again, I allow. [*Laughs.*] But now, Sir Peter, since we have finished our daily jangle, I presume I may go to my engagement at Lady Sneerwell's.

Sir P. Ay, there's another precious circumstance—a charming set of acquaintance you have made there.

Lady T. Nay, Sir Peter, they are all people of rank and fortune, and remarkably tenacious of reputation.

Sir P. Yes, egad, they are tenacious of reputation with a vengeance, for they don't choose any body should have a character but themselves. Such a crew! Ah! many a wretch has rid on a hurdle who has done less mischief than these utterers of forged tales, coiners of scandal, and clippers of reputation.

Lady T. What! would you restrain the freedom of speech?

Sir P. Ah! they have made you just as bad as any one of the society.

Lady T. Why, I believe I do bear a part with a tolerable grace.

Sir P. Grace, indeed!

Lady T. But I vow I bear no malice against the people I abuse. When I say an ill-natured thing, 'tis out of pure good humor, and I take it for granted they deal exactly in the same manner with me. But, Sir Peter, you know you promised to come to Lady Sneerwell's too.

Sir P. Well, well, I'll call in just to look after my own character.

Lady T. Then, indeed, you must make haste after me, or you'll be too late. So good-by to ye. [*Exit.*

Sir P. So—I have gained much by my intended expostulation; yet with what a charming air she contradicts every thing I say, and how pleasingly she shows her contempt for my authority! Well, though I can't make her love me, there is great satisfaction in quarreling with her; and I think she never appears to such advantage as when she is doing every thing in her power to plague me. [*Exit.*

ACT II. SCENE 1.

Enter Lady Teazle.

Sir P. I mean shortly to surprise you; but shall we always live thus, hey?

Lady T. If you please. I'm sure I don't care how soon we leave off quarreling, provided you'll own you're tired first.

Sir P. Well, then, let our future contest be who shall be most obliging.

Lady T. I assure you, Sir Peter, good nature becomes you. You look now as you did before we were married, when you used to walk with me under the elms, and tell me stories of what a gallant you were in your youth, and chuck me under the chin, you would, and ask me if I thought I could love an old fellow who would deny me nothing; didn't you?

Sir P. Yes, yes; and you were kind and attentive—

Lady T. Ay, so I was, and would always take your part when my acquaintances would abuse you and turn you into ridicule.

Sir P. Indeed!

Lady T. Ay; and when my cousin Sophy has called you a stiff, peevish old bachelor, and laughed at me for thinking of marrying one who might be my father, I have always defended you, and said I didn't think you ugly by any means.

Sir P. Thank you.

Lady T. And I dared say you would make a very good sort of husband.

Sir P. And you prophesied right; and we shall now be the happiest couple—

Lady T. And never differ again?

Sir P. No, never—though at the same time, indeed, my dear Lady Teazle, you must watch your temper very seriously, for in all our little quarrels, my dear, if you recollect, my love, you always begin first.

Lady T. I beg your pardon, my dear Sir Peter; indeed you always gave the provocation.

Sir P. Now see, my angel, take care; contradicting isn't the way to keep friends.

Lady T. Then don't you begin it, my love.

Sir P. There, now! you—you—are going on. You don't perceive, my life, that you are just doing the very thing which, you know, always makes me angry.

Lady T. Nay, you know, if you will be angry without any reason, my dear—

Sir P. There, now, you want to quarrel again.

Lady T. No, I'm sure I don't; but if you will be so peevish—

Sir P. There, now; who begins first?

Lady T. Why, you, to be sure. I said nothing. But there's no bearing your temper.

Sir P. No, no, madam, the fault's in your own temper.

Lady T. You are just what my cousin Sophy said you would be.

Sir P. Your cousin Sophy is a forward, impertinent gipsy.

Lady T. You are a great bear, I'm sure, to abuse my relations.

Sir P. Now may all the plagues of marriage be doubled on me if ever I make friends with you any more!

Lady T. So much the better.

Sir P. No, no, madam; 'tis evident you never cared a fig for me, and I was a madman to marry you—a pert rural coquette, that had refused half the honest squires in the neighborhood.

Lady T. And I was a fool to marry you, an old dangling bachelor, who was single at fifty only because no one would have him.

Sir P. Ay, ay, madam, but you were pleased enough to listen to me. You never had such an offer before.

Lady T. No! didn't I refuse Sir Tivy Terrier, who every body said would have been a better match? for his estate is just as good as yours, and he has broke his neck since we were married.

Sir P. I have done with you, madam! You are an unfeeling, ungrateful—but there's an end of every thing. I believe you capable of every thing that is bad.

Lady T. Take care, Sir Peter, you had better not insinuate!

Sir P. Very well, madam, very well! A separate maintenance as soon as you please. Yes, madam, or a divorce! I'll make an example of myself for the benefit of all old bachelors.

Lady T. Agreed! agreed! And now, my dear Sir Peter, we are of a mind once more, we may be the happiest couple —and never differ again, you know—ha! ha! ha! Well, you are going to be in a passion, I see, and I shall only interrupt you, so by-by. [*Exit.*

Sir P. Plagues and tortures! Can't I make her angry either? Oh, I am the most miserable fellow! But I'll not bear her presuming to keep her temper; no! she may break my heart, but she sha'n't keep her temper.

COURTSHIP UNDER DIFFICULTIES.

SNOBBLETON *solus.*

Snobbleton. Yes, there is that fellow Jones again. I declare, the man is ubiquitous. Wherever I go with my cousin Prudence we stumble across him, or he follows her like her shadow. Do we take a boating? So does Jones. Do we wander on the beach? So does Jones. Go where we will, that fellow follows or moves before. Now that was a cruel practical joke which Jones once played upon me at college. I have never forgiven him. But I would gladly

make a pretense of doing so if I could have my revenge.
Let me see. Can't I manage it? He is head over ears in
love with Prudence, but too bashful to speak. I half believe she is not indifferent to him, though altogether unacquainted. It may prove a match if I can not spoil it. Let
me think. Ha! I have it. A brilliant idea! Jones, beware! But here he comes.

Enter Jones.

Jones. (*Not seeing Snobbleton, and delightedly contemplating a flower which he holds in his hand.*) Oh, rapture!
what a prize! It was in her hair; I saw it fall from her
queenly head. (*Kisses it every now and then.*) How warm
are its tender leaves from having touched her neck! How
doubly sweet is its perfume—fresh from the fragrance of
her glorious locks! How beautiful! how— Bless me, here
is Snobbleton, and we are enemies!

Snob. Good morning, Jones — that is, if you will shake
hands.

Jones. What! you—you forgive! You really—

Snob. Yes, yes, old fellow! All is forgotten. You played me a rough trick; but let bygones be bygones. Will
you not bury the hatchet?

Jones. With all my heart, my dear fellow!

Snob. What is the matter with you, Jones? You look
quite grumpy—not by any means the same cheerful, dashing, rollicking fellow you were.

Jones. Bless me, you don't say so! (*Aside.*) Confound
the man! Here have I been endeavoring to appear romantic for the last month—and now to be called grumpy—it is
unbearable!

Snob. But never mind. Cheer up, old fellow! I see it
all. I know what it is to be in—

Jones. Ah! you can then sympathize with me. You know
what it is to be in—

Snob. Of *course* I do! Heaven preserve me from the toils!
And then the letters—the interminable letters!

Jones. Oh yes, the letters! the *billet-doux!*

Snob. And the bills—the endless bills!

Jones. The bills!

Snob. Yes; and the bailiffs, the lawyers, the judge, and the jury.

Jones. Why, man, what are you talking about? I thought you said you knew what it was to be in—

Snob. In debt. *To be sure* I did.

Jones. Bless me! I'm not in debt—never borrowed a dollar in my life. Ah me! it's worse than *that.*

Snob. Worse than that! Come, now, Jones, there is only one thing worse. You're surely not in love?

Jones. Yes I am. Oh, Snobby, help me, help me! Let me confide in you.

Snob. Confide in me! Certainly, my dear fellow. See! I do not shrink—I stand firm.

Jones. Snobby, I—I love her.

Snob. Whom?

Jones. Your cousin Prudence.

Snob. Ha! Prudence Angelina Winter?

Jones. Now don't be angry, Snobby; I don't mean any harm, you know. I—I—you know how it is.

Snob. Harm! my dear fellow. Not a bit of it. Angry! Not at all. You have my consent, old fellow. Take her. She is yours. Heaven bless you both.

Jones. You are very kind, Snobby, but I haven't got her consent yet.

Snob. Well, that is something, to be sure. But leave it all to me. She may be a little coy, you know; but, considering your generous overlooking of her unfortunate defect—

Jones. Defect! You surprise me.

Snob. What! and you did not know of it?

Jones. Not at all. I am astonished! Nothing serious, I hope.

Snob. Oh no; only a little— (*He taps his ear with his finger knowingly.*) I see you understand it.

Jones. Merciful heaven! can it be? But, really, is it serious?

Snob. I should think it was.

Jones. What! But is she ever dangerous?

Snob. Dangerous! Why should she be?

Jones. Oh, I perceive. A mere airiness of brain—a gentle aberration—scorning the dull world—a mild—
Snob. Zounds! man, she's not crazy!
Jones. My dear Snobby, you relieve me. What then?
Snob. Slightly deaf—that's all.
Jones. Deaf!
Snob. As a lamp-post. That is, you must elevate your voice to a considerable pitch in speaking to her.
Jones. Is it possible? However, I think I can manage. As, for instance, if it was my intention to make her a floral offering, and I should say (*elevating his voice considerably*), "Miss, will you make me happy by accepting these flowers?" I suppose she could hear me, eh? How would that do?
Snob. Pshaw! Do you call that elevated?
Jones. Well, how would this do? (*Speaks very loudly.*) "Miss, will you make me happy—"
Snob. Louder, shriller, man!
Jones. "Miss, will you—"
Snob. Louder, louder, or she will only see your lips move.
Jones. (*Almost screaming*). "Miss, will you oblige me by accepting these flowers?"
Snob. There, that may do. Still, you want practice. I perceive the lady herself is approaching. Suppose you retire for a short time, and I will prepare her for the introduction.
Jones. Very good. Meantime I will go down to the beach, and endeavor to acquire the proper pitch. Let me see: "Miss, will you oblige me—" [*Exit* Jones.

Enter Prudence.

Prudence. Good morning, cousin. Who was that speaking so loudly?
Snob. Only Jones. Poor fellow, he is so deaf that I suppose he fancies his own voice to be a mere whisper.
Pru. Why, I was not aware of this. Is he very deaf?
Snob. Deaf as a stone fence. To be sure, he does not use an ear-trumpet any more, but one must speak excessively high. Unfortunate, too, for I believe he's in love.

Pru. In love! with whom?
Snob. Can't you guess?
Pru. Oh no; I haven't the slightest idea.
Snob. With yourself! He has been begging me to obtain him an introduction.
Pru. Well, I have always thought him a nice-looking young man. I suppose he would hear me if I should say (*speaks loudly*) "Good morning, Mr. Jones?"
Snob. Do you think he would hear *that?*
Pru. Well, then, how would (*speaks very loudly*) "Good morning, Mr. Jones?" How would that do?
Snob. Tush! he would think you were speaking under your breath.
Pru. (*Almost screaming.*) "Good morning!"
Snob. A mere whisper, my dear cousin. But here he comes. Now do try and make yourself audible.

Enter Jones.

Snob. (*Speaking in a high voice.*) Mr. Jones, cousin. Miss Winter, Jones. You will please excuse me for a short time. (*He retires, but remains where he can view the speakers.*)
Jones. (*Speaking in a loud orotund voice.*) Miss, will you accept these flowers? I plucked them from their slumber on the hill.
Pru. (*In a high falsetto voice.*) Really, sir, I—I—
Jones. (*Aside.*) She hesitates. It must be that she does not hear me. (*Increasing his tone.*) Miss, will you accept these flowers—FLOWERS? I plucked them sleeping on the hill—HILL.
Pru. (*Also increasing her tone.*) Certainly, Mr. Jones. They are beautiful—BEAU-U-TIFUL.
Jones. (*Aside.*) How she screams in my ear. (*Aloud.*) Yes, I plucked them from their slumber—SLUMBER, on the hill—HILL.
Pru. (*Aside.*) Poor man, what an effort it seems for him to speak. (*Aloud.*) I perceive you are poetical. Are you fond of poetry? (*Aside.*) He hesitates. I must speak louder. (*In a scream.*) Poetry—POETRY—POETRY!

Jones. (*Aside.*) Bless me, the woman would wake the dead! (*Aloud.*) Yes, miss, I ad-o-r-e it.

Snob. Glorious! glorious! I wonder how loud they *can* scream. Oh, vengeance, thou art sweet!

Pru. Can you repeat some poetry—POETRY?

Jones. I only know one poem. It is this:

> You'd scarce expect one of my age—AGE,
> To speak in public on the stage—STAGE.

Pru. Bravo! bravo!

Jones. Thank you! THANK—

Pru. Mercy on us! Do you think I'm DEAF, sir?

Jones. And do you fancy *me* deaf, miss? (*Natural tone.*)

Pru. Are you not, sir? You surprise me!

Jones. No, miss. I was led to believe that you were deaf. Snobbleton told me so.

Pru. Snobbleton! Why, he told me that you were deaf.

Jones. Confound the fellow! he has been making game of us.

RAGE.

FEAR.

LAUGHTER.

MELANCHOLY.

Supine.   Prone.   Vertical.

Clasped.   Applied.   Folded.

Crossed.   Enumerating.   Touching.

www.ingramcontent.com/pod-product-compliance
Lightning Source LLC
Chambersburg PA
CBHW051733300426
44115CB00007B/545